Introduction to Aging

Judith A. Sugar, PhD, a nationally recognized teacher and scholar in gerontology, has served in leadership roles in prominent professional gerontological organizations, including the Association for Gerontology in Higher Education (AGHE), the Gerontological Society of America (GSA), and the American Psychological Association's Division of Adult Development and Aging. She received her PhD in psychology from York University in Toronto. She has chaired the gerontology program at Colorado State University, and served as associate director of the Borun Center for Gerontological Research at UCLA and director of the Graham and Jean Sanford Center for Aging at the University of Nevada, Reno, where she continues to develop innovative approaches to teaching gerontology and recruiting students into the discipline. Her national and regional reputation in the field of aging led Governor Miller to appoint her to the Nevada State Commission on Aging, and she was later appointed as a facilitator for the 1995 White House Conference on Aging. Valued both by students and faculty, she has been honored with numerous awards as a teacher and scholar, including Fellow of the AGHE, Woman of Achievement by the University of Nevada, Reno, and the inaugural award for Distinguished Faculty Scholar by the Sanford Center for Aging.

Robert J. Riekse, EdD, is the founder of the Older Learner Center (OLC) at Grand Rapids Community College (GRCC) and the Calvin College–GRCC Consortium on Aging. Currently, he is the principal researcher of the GRCC Older Learner Center. He received his EdD from Michigan State University as a Fellow in the Kellogg Community Leadership Training Program after receiving his MA from the University of Michigan. A pioneer in aging education, he has developed a wide range of gerontology programs for college students, service providers in the aging network, and older persons and their family members. He was awarded a fellowship in the American Council on Education's Academic Leadership Program, and is a recipient of the Everett J. Soop Distinguished Adult Education Award, presented by the Michigan Society of Gerontology. He has authored, coauthored, and directed numerous research grants from local/regional foundations, state government, and the U.S. Administration on Aging. He is a past president of the board of directors of Senior Neighbors, Inc., a regional direct service provider. He is a frequent presenter and committee member for the AGHE and a member of numerous regional organizations promoting aging education. He is currently a developer of gerontology-based television productions across Michigan and award-winning videos distributed to colleges and universities across the nation. He coauthored the textbook *Growing Older in America* and a trade book, *The Christian Guide to Parent Care*, and was co-general editor of *The Complete Guide to Caring for Aging Loved Ones*.

Henry Holstege, PhD, is Emeritus Professor of Sociology/Gerontology at Calvin College in Grand Rapids, Michigan. He currently is community educator/researcher for the GRCC Older Learner Center. He received his PhD in sociology from Michigan State University, where he was elected to Alpha Kappa Delta, the national sociological honor society. He is the recipient of the Everett J. Soop Distinguished Adult Educator Award, presented by the Michigan Society of Gerontology. He is the coauthor of several books on various topics in gerontology and the author or coauthor of numerous monographs on aging. He has received federal and state grants for research on the aging process and has been a keynote speaker at conferences throughout the nation on various aspects of aging. He has been the host and coproducer of over 20 videos on aging that have been shown on television throughout the United States, several of which have received the Telly Award for video excellence.

Michael A. Faber, MA, is a licensed social worker and holds a BS in gerontology and an undergraduate mental health and aging certificate from Madonna University. He earned an MA in sociology, specializing in aging and the life course, from Marquette University. He has worked with older adults, their families, and caregivers for the last 22 years in a wide variety of roles including case coordinator for frail homebound elderly, long-term care advocate, and dementia specialist. His current role is educational gerontologist and program administrator at GRCC. In his current position, he is responsible for fund development, programming, strategic direction, and the daily operations of the Older Learner Center, which serves older adults, their caregiving families, and aging service professionals. He teaches and coordinates the Gerontology Certificate Program. He has authored and coauthored numerous research grants in aging education/outreach and made many presentations at local, state, and national levels. He is a member of the team that produced the national award-winning *Successful Aging* television/video series, and has cofounded and coleads the nationally recognized Caregiver Resource Network (www. caregiverresource.net). He has served on a variety of boards and committees at the local, state, and national levels including the Membership Committee of the AGHE, as chair of the AGHE Community College Task Force, and as former chairperson of the Michigan Partnership for Community Caring Board of Directors. He is also Associate Editor of the *AGHE Exchange*—the national newsletter of the AGHE. In 2010, he was elected a Fellow of the Association for Gerontology in Higher Education, and awarded the Anthony DeVito II Memorial Award from the University of Michigan Geriatric Center.

Introduction to Aging
A Positive, Interdisciplinary Approach

Judith A. Sugar, PhD, Robert J. Riekse, EdD,
Henry Holstege, PhD, and Michael A. Faber, MA

SPRINGER PUBLISHING COMPANY
NEW YORK

Springer Publishing Company, LLC
11 West 42nd Street
New York, NY 10036
www.springerpub.com

Acquisitions Editor: Sheri W. Sussman
Production Editor: Joseph Stubenrauch
Composition: Newgen Imaging

ISBN: 978-0-8261-0880-7
e-book ISBN: 978-0-8261-0881-4

Instructors Materials: Qualified instructors may request supplements by emailing textbook@springerpub.com:
Instructors Manual: 978-0-8261-1921-6
Instructors PowerPoints: 978-0-8261-1918-6

13 14 15 / 5 4 3 2 1

The author and the publisher of this Work have made every effort to use sources believed to be reliable to provide information that is accurate and compatible with the standards generally accepted at the time of publication. The author and publisher shall not be liable for any special, consequential, or exemplary damages resulting, in whole or in part, from the readers' use of, or reliance on, the information contained in this book. The publisher has no responsibility for the persistence or accuracy of URLs for external or third-party Internet websites referred to in this publication and does not guarantee that any content on such websites is, or will remain, accurate or appropriate.

Library of Congress Cataloging-in-Publication Data

Sugar, Judith.
 Introduction to aging: a positive, interdisciplinary approach / Judith A. Sugar, Ph.D., Robert J. Riekse, Ed.D., Henry Holstege, Ph.D., Michael A. Faber, M.A.
    pages cm
 Includes index.
 ISBN 978-0-8261-0880-7
 1. Gerontology. 2. Aging. 3. Older people. I. Title.
 HQ1061.S848 2014
 305.26—dc23

2013032728

Printed in the United States of America by Bradford and Bigelow.

Contents

Preface

Our nation is experiencing an aging revolution. Its population is growing older at a rather remarkable rate. For the first time in its history, America is beginning to move away from a youth-based culture. However, there has been a lack of recognition of, and even a reluctance to recognize, the realities of an aging population on the part of many movers and shakers in the worlds of business, government, entertainment, religion, and advertising. But the realities must be faced.

In a newspaper article entitled, "A Nation in Denial About Its Age," a CEO of a large nonprofit in Texas stated, "People don't want to grow old—I just don't think it's a big issue for a lot of people" (Hull, 2008, p. 1A). The article went on to point out that "the graying of the population carries complex economic, political, cultural, and social implications for America" (p. 12A). The late Robert Butler, MD, a legendary gerontologist and geriatrician, stated that "the biggest challenge of all is actually denial" for a nation whose elderly population will almost double by 2030 (Hull, 2008, p. 1A). It is interesting to note that all of the persons who will make up this large number of older people in 2030 have already been born.

Some years ago the term *gerontology* was coined to describe the study of aging. Like many terms used to describe a subject area taught in college, *gerontology* is the joining of two Greek words; it literally means the scientific study of the old. What an appropriate area of study this is, given the realities of an aging America as well as an aging world. The study of aging is essential to understand the opportunities and challenges of the fastest-growing sector of our population.

The field of gerontology remains somewhat hard to define, despite the high level of professionalism of both the pioneers in the field and its current academic leaders. This is due in part to the fact that—as the late Professor David Peterson, a pioneer in gerontology at the University of Southern California, pointed out—gerontology is both an academic discipline and a profession. It has the characteristics and functions of both.

As a profession, "it is a field of practice in which professionals and paraprofessionals plan, provide, administer, and evaluate a variety of programs and services aimed at meeting the needs of older persons and their families" (Peterson, 1993, p. 1). As Professor Peterson pointed out, the "real purpose of professionals is to apply knowledge in order to solve problems rather than to create knowledge for its own sake" (p. 2).

There is a range of jobs that use the knowledge and skills of professional gerontologists (Peterson, Wendt, & Douglass, 1991). What typically comes to mind are the jobs in the "aging networks" across the nation, in the wide array of agencies and organizations that focus all or part of their activities on meeting the needs of older people—for example, senior centers, area agencies on aging, respite care centers, adult day care facilities, senior meal programs, and many others. But some businesses are beginning to recognize the explosive growth of the older portions of the population, to appreciate older people as contributors to our society and consumers of products and services, and to acknowledge the need to have staff members who are knowledgeable about aging. Opportunities for professional gerontologists should grow rapidly in the years ahead.

As a discipline, gerontology is multifaceted and interdisciplinary. By necessity, it encompasses a broad range of subject areas that address the issues and conditions older people, their families, and persons who work with them experience. They include, but are not limited to:

- Psychology, because of the psychological changes and challenges older people and those around them experience as a result of the aging process, including personal adjustment to losses, interaction with family members and peers, and adjustment to some forms of dependency;
- Sociology, because older people live in social settings that affect their lives and experience social forces such as racism, sexism, and ageism, as well as social stratification and deviancy;
- Humanities, because older people and society can benefit from reminiscing about lifetime experiences as well as the enrichments derived from the arts and religion/spirituality;
- Political Science, because societal decision making—who makes decisions and how they are made—directly relates to the political power of older people and governmental programs that relate to our older population;
- Public Policy, because assessing the needs of various groups in society and devising strategies to balance and address these needs—particularly in the face of competing demands for limited resources—require public policy expertise;
- Medicine, because maintaining health into the later years and managing chronic health conditions, which generally increase as people grow older, should be top priorities of our health care professionals;
- Public Health, because health promotion, disease prevention, nutritional needs/awareness/safeguards, and coping with disability among the old present challenges to public health policies and strategies;
- Economics, because some older people are concerned with investment strategies and estate management while others are challenged by basic economic survival;
- Biology, because the biological process of aging is integral to the human condition and directly affects the lives of older people;
- Public Safety, because older people are the special target of confidence scams, schemes, and particular forms of abuse;
- Communications, because communication strategies can help older persons in their interpersonal relationships, and communication training will improve the ability of health care professionals to be more effective in promoting health and

diagnosing and treating their patients, and the ability of service providers to be more effective in designing, delivering, and advocating for social services;

- Architecture, because the physical living environments of older people in their homes, apartments, retirement homes, and long-term care facilities greatly affect the quality of their lives;

- Vocational Skills, because home repairs and adapting everyday items to the physical needs of older people are vital to safe and secure living;

- Education, because through educational programs older people can train/retrain for appropriate jobs, acquire coping skills for changing life circumstances, and gain enjoyment through avocational recreational activities; and

- Law, because millions of older persons face legal issues in trying to qualify for benefit programs, in attempting to comply with tax and governmental regulations, and in coping with estate planning.

Indeed, gerontology encompasses every academic discipline that in some way relates to the lives of older people and their families in contemporary America.

As gerontology is both a profession and a multifaceted academic discipline, what type of book is appropriate for an introductory gerontology course? Having taught gerontology courses for many years in community college and university settings, we have felt the need for a text specifically designed for the range of students who typically populate the introductory courses. Although many fine gerontology texts have been developed over the years, for some time we have looked for a text that covers the range of issues that persons interested in aging or persons working with or preparing to work with older people face on a practical level. This book is designed to systemically address the conditions, issues, opportunities, and problems people face as they grow older. It is designed to acquaint the reader with the realities of the aging process and with what it means to grow older in the 21st century; to describe theories about aging; and to explain the social and economic realities of aging in our society.

The methodology of the book is direct. Each chapter addresses the issues at hand, using extensive research in a simplified, applied manner. The application of important historic and current research to the issues older people face is the primary goal of this text. Current demographic and research data are used whenever possible. Some older research findings are included where they are appropriate or where more current data are not available. Extensive instructor's resources are available by contacting textbook@ springerpub.com.

This new book is developed for gerontology courses as well as other courses that have gerontology components—a trend we have seen develop in many colleges and universities. It is designed to be academically sound but easily readable by a range of students in our colleges and universities. The thrust of the book addresses the reality that we are facing a new paradigm in aging. By this we mean that the roles of older people (including the near-old, the young-old, the aged, and the oldest-old) in the family, in the workplace, and in the broader society continue to evolve. We explore this evolution as older people become more diverse, more capable in identifiable aspects, more numerous, and hopefully more productive and integrated into society.

Judith A. Sugar, PhD
Robert J. Riekse, EdD
Henry Holstege, PhD
Michael A. Faber, MA

REFERENCES

Hull, V. (2008). A nation in denial about its age. *Manatee Herald—Tribune*, pp. 1A, 12A.

Peterson, D. A. (1993). *The professional field of gerontology*. Los Angeles, CA: University of Southern California.

Peterson, D. A., Wendt, P. F., & Douglass, E. B. (1991). *Determining the impact of gerontology preparation of personnel in the aging network: A national survey*. Los Angeles and Washington, DC: University of Southern California and Association for Gerontology in Higher Education.

Acknowledgments

We deeply appreciate the help and support that we have received from so many people and institutions throughout the development of this textbook. First and foremost, we thank our editor, Sheri W. Sussman, whose insights, encouragement, prodding, and much appreciated patience brought the book to fruition.

The Nevada-based author (JAS) also thanks the University of Nevada, Reno, for granting her a sabbatical, which was especially helpful in the early stages of this project, and she thanks administrators and colleagues in her department and college for their support, especially Arnold Greenhouse, MD, and the late Dr. A. Lois Harry. National and international colleagues and friends in academia and in aging services, too numerous to name, have contributed much to the subject matter of the book through our many conversations, discussions, and debates about gerontology over the years. Undergraduate students in the introductory aging course at the University of Nevada, Reno, have provided feedback on many of the book's topics, and they always inspire passion to work hard to engage them in the aging enterprise. Invaluable in preparing the book were the skillful technical and editorial advice and support of Richard Tracy, the help in tracking down reference materials and websites by graduate students Emily Wozniak and Penny Jernberg, and, the proficient typing of Maxine Fifer.

I am also indebted to my family for their patience, their encouragement, and for those far away, their toleration of many curtailed visits.

Judith A. Sugar, PhD

For the Michigan-based authors (RJR, HH, and, MAF), this book would not be possible without the very valuable editorial assistance and computer skills of Linda Hayes; the inspirational encouragement of Michael Faber, director of the Grand Rapids Community College (GRCC) Older Learner Center; the invaluable assistance of Hannah Faber, with APA reference formatting; and skilled typists, Christina Davis, Erika Freire, Mary Faber, and Cherie Smith. The GRCC Older Learner Center (OLC) has a long history of pioneering a wide range of academic courses, programs, and services in aging education that have received state and national acclaim. Linked to the OLC's successes is the administrative support for aging education at GRCC that dates back to the early 1970s under former president Richard Calkins, and former Executive Vice President Cornelius Evingaard, which continues under the creative leadership of President Steven Ender and Eric Williams, executive director for equity, community, and legislative affairs.

We also wish to express our appreciation to our partners in the aging network, especially Thomas Czerwinski, executive director of Region VIII's Area Agency on Aging of Western Michigan, Inc., one of the most effective Area Agency on Aging directors in the nation.

We also wish to recognize the contributions of our academic colleagues in gerontology across the state and nation, particularly Dr. Cullen Hayashida of the Kupuna Education Center, Kapi`olani Community College; and, Dr. Jan Abushakrah, Gerontology Faculty Department Chair, Portland Community College—Sylvania Campus.

And, of course, we send our love and appreciation to our families who have provided support, indulgence, and a myriad of illustrations from everyday living.

Robert J. Riekse, EdD
Henry Holstege, PhD
Michael A. Faber, MA

PART I

GROWING OLDER IN THE 21ST CENTURY

CHAPTER 1

We Are Growing Older

The learning objectives of this chapter include understanding

- How the United States and the world are experiencing an aging evolution—we are growing older.
- How this population paradigm shift calls us to be joyful for extended years of life but realistic about the personal and societal outcomes of longer life.
- The importance of mobilizing all sectors of society to address the realities of an aging society.
- The categories of older people—the young-old, the aged, and the oldest-old—each having different characteristics that uniquely impact society.
- How Baby Boomers will continue to impact the future of aging.

THE NEW AMERICAN REVOLUTION

America is going through a revolution. No, we are not being overthrown by some sinister internal plot or another nation. And no, we are not referring to the technological revolution that swept business, industry, and education beginning in earnest in the 1990s that continues into the 21st century. We are referring to a revolution that some key leaders are beginning to recognize—the aging of America. It is a paradigm shift in the overall composition of not only the U.S. population, but also the world's population. As a whole, Americans are becoming older, and there are many more older people among us than ever before in our history (U.S. Census Bureau, 2011).

Upon first hearing this news, it may not sound too exciting or even interesting. We now have the opportunity to see what the aging of America really means to the life of each of us as individuals; persons in relationships; family members; students; workers; or potential workers, retirees, and citizens. We can begin to understand how this social revolution is changing America. This revolution is not over—it is not even slowing down. In fact, with the aging of the 76 million Baby Boomers (who began turning age 65 in 2011) this revolution is gaining momentum. If we think that the United States is experiencing many issues dealing with all of the needs of an aging population currently, to paraphrase old-time comedians, "You ain't seen nothing yet." But in a new paradigm of aging, this does not mean that an aging population with all its associated needs is something to be feared or looked at as a burden to society. It simply means that as a society, we have to be joyful for our extended years, realistic about the outcomes of longer life, and creative in mobilizing and utilizing our vast national resources for all sectors of our growing population.

AGE CATEGORIES OF OLDER AMERICANS

To better understand what an aging America means, it is important to look at whom we are referring to when we use terms such as *older Americans, the elderly, senior citizens, mature persons, people of the third age, old people,* and so forth. According to the U.S. Census Bureau, the overall older population is defined as people aged 65 and older. However, there are subcategories that are significant when studying aging. We will need to use these subcategories of the older age population to adequately address the characteristics, issues, and needs of each age group. For convenience and simplicity, the U.S. Census Bureau (2011) provides three subcategories of the elderly population:

1. The young-old (65 through 74 years);
2. The aged (75 through 84 years); and
3. The oldest-old (85 years and older).

In addition to these major subcategories of older people, two other distinctions are important: the frail elderly and the centenarians. The frail elderly refers to persons aged 65 and older with significant physical and mental health problems. Centenarians are persons aged 100 years or more. They represent a small but relatively fast-growing sector of the older population.

The reason these subcategories are important is because the characteristics, desires, strengths, and needs of people at different stages of life can be very different. There can be great differences between the vigor and good health of so many of those classified as young-old to the multiple chronic conditions and frailties of so many of the oldest-old. This obviously does not mean that all persons who are in the young-old category are vigorous and healthy, but there is a greater likelihood of this being the case. Nor does it mean that most of the oldest-old persons are frail and living in a nursing home, but there is a greater likelihood of having some form of dependency as a person moves into the oldest years of life.

It is important to know that the fastest-growing sector of the American population is made up of persons 85 years and older. This is not the largest sector of our population—far from it. This group of the older population is important to focus on because the oldest-old consistently need the most assistance with their daily activities and the most support from their families, community agencies, and long-term care facilities to survive (U.S. Census Bureau, 2011).

THE EMERGING OLD

It is no longer adequate to consider just the categories of those persons aged 65 and older when studying the field of gerontology. Another cohort of our population that is not technically defined as old or elderly has great impact on the study of gerontology. This is the cohort called *Baby Boomers*, those persons born between 1946 and 1964 numbering between 76 and 77 million persons, depending on how immigrants are counted. The first of the Baby Boomers began turning age 62 in 2008 (the first year they could begin collecting old age Social Security benefits) and age 65 in 2011 (U.S. Census Bureau, 2011).

THE YOUNG-OLD

In contrast to the oldest-old sector of the population that is more likely to have characteristics that make them vulnerable and dependent, today's young-old (aged 65 through 74 years) are more likely to be entering their later years with relatively good health, higher educational attainment, more vigor and vitality, more mobility, and financial security. Of course, this is a generalization. The people in this young-old group are more likely to have these characteristics, just as we have seen that the members of the oldest-old category are more likely to have other characteristics. Obviously all cohorts (age group categories) of the population—youth, young adults, middle-aged, young-old, oldest-old—are heterogeneous. They are all made up of different people with a wide range of needs and resources. Nonetheless, the young-old can be described as a pioneering generation in health, affluence, and vitality.

Who Are the Young-Old?

The young-old are the youngest category of the population generally referred to as elderly. They are persons aged 65 through 74, by far the largest segment of the elderly population. Of the 40.3 million older people in the United States, over half (21.7 million) are in the young-old category compared to 13.06 million aged 75 through 84, and 5.4 million aged 85 and older (U.S. Census Bureau, 2011).

Among the young-old, the number of men compared to women is much closer than in the two other elderly categories. The excess of women is most pronounced at older ages. This is termed the *sex ratio*, which is defined as the number of men per 100 women. A sex ratio of 100 would show an equal number of men and women. A sex ratio under 100 would show more women than men. At birth, the sex ratio in the United States is about 105, meaning more boys are born than girls. Because death at every age is mostly higher for men, the sex ratio declines as people age. This sex ratio progresses through ages 85 and older, which results in more and more women compared to men as the population ages. As a result, for the three categories of older people, the sex ratio decreases as people progress from the young-old, the aged, and the oldest-old. However, between 2000 and 2010, the sex ratios increased somewhat for the three older-age categories due to increased longevity for men at the older ages (U.S. Census Bureau, 2011).

Health and Vigor of the Young-Old

When some people think about the elderly as a whole, they picture frail, weak, dependent persons, some in nursing homes and many confined to their homes. This is certainly not a picture of the young-old. Some 78% of the young-old consider their health to be good to excellent compared to 66% for persons aged 85 and older (*Older Americans 2010*). The rest consider their health to be good, or excellent.

The following chart (Figure 1.1) demonstrates the differences the various age categories have in relation to selected chronic health conditions that cause limitations of activity.

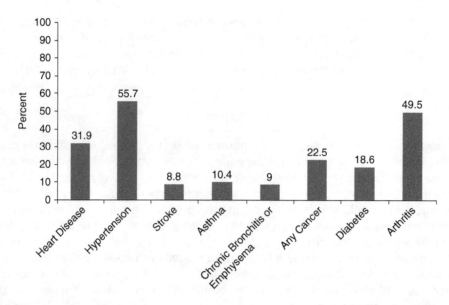

FIGURE 1.1 Percentage of People Age 65 and Over Who Reported Having Selected Chronic Health Conditions, 2007–2008.

Reference population: These data refer to the civilian noninstitutionalized population.

Source: Adapted from *Older Americans 2010*, Table 16a.

The Young-Old Helping Parents

Even though the health and vitality of the young-old person is likely to be good, it is this group and the middle-aged sector of the population that bears most of the responsibility for caring for aging parents and other elderly relatives. It has long been established that family members provide 80% to 90% of the care needed by the dependent old (Brody, 1990). Never before has there been so many middle-aged and young-old caregivers providing so much care to so many oldest-old dependent relatives. A MetLife Mature Market Institute report in June 2011 indicated that the number of adults aged 50 and older caring for parents has tripled since 1994. And an AARP study in 2009 showed that as many as 61.6 million family members were providing care for an older adult during that year (Abrahms, 2011).

Financial Status of the Young-Old

As might be expected, the young-old tend to be better off financially than persons in the aged and oldest-old categories. The young-old are likely to have higher incomes (*65+ in the United States*, 2005).

In looking at income and poverty rates for the young-old compared to the aged and the oldest-old, it is easy to understand why the young-old are better off. Even though there had been a trend toward early retirement, many more of the young-old are working compared to persons in the other elderly categories. And many in this category have had better paying jobs with pensions. Higher incomes also impact the amounts of Social Security benefits workers receive in retirement.

Mobility and Location of the Young-Old

It is the young-old who are likely to move, especially to put some fun into their lives. Research indicates that it is the healthier, financially secure, and younger old that typically travel to better climates or more ideal living environments in retirement. The frail-old, according to research over the years, particularly the oldest-old, are less likely to move unless they need to be placed in a nursing home or move to an area where they have relatives and friends when they need assistance with daily living (Rosenwaike, 1985).

Widowhood and Living Alone

Widowhood is much more common for elderly American women than for older men (*Older Americans 2010*). Women aged 65 and older are three times as likely as men to be widowed. Among the young-old, only 7% of the men are widowed compared to 25% of women. And among women 85 and older, 76% are widowed.

Closely related to widowhood is the probability of living alone. As women grow older, the likelihood increases that they will live alone, regardless of their ethnicity. This is because of the shorter life expectancies of men and the tendency of men to marry younger women. But living alone for young-old women does not necessarily mean they are isolated or experiencing a poor quality of life. If their health and economic status are reasonably good, research going back many years has shown that women living alone can live satisfying lives (Chappell & Badger 1989; Riley, 1983). Women are better at developing and maintaining social contacts. They typically have more and better friends. Many enjoy not being dependent on others.

Implications of a Vigorous Young-Old Population

The emergence of a pioneering generation experiencing better health, greater affluence, and more vitality is having, and will increasingly have, significant impacts on the people in this age category, and on businesses, governments, and society as a whole.

THE OLDEST-OLD: A PIONEERING GENERATION IN LONGEVITY

The oldest-old sector of the elderly population—persons 85 years of age and older—has been defined previously. Having people in this age category among us is not new in America. Benjamin Franklin was in his 80s when he participated in the Constitutional Convention in 1787, but he was an exception. Most of the men who developed the U.S. Constitution were young. America has been a "young" nation, young in years, young in its people, and young in spirit; but the dramatic aging of its population is bringing about a social revolution.

The Growth of the Oldest-Old Population

Nowhere is the aging of America more evident than among its oldest-old population. Never before have we had so many people in this age category. As we have not had significant numbers of persons in this age group, not much attention had been paid to their characteristics and needs. Indeed, it was some years ago (1984) that the term *oldest-old* was coined by the American Association for the Advancement of Science (Suzman, Manton, & Willis, 1992). In that same year, the U.S. Senate Appropriations Committee recognized the importance of the rapidly growing oldest-old sector of the population and set up funds for the National Institutes of Health to carry out research concerning persons in this age group. Since that time, research and interest in this sector of the population have grown rapidly.

The oldest-old population could grow from 5.7 million in 2008 to 19 million by 2050 (U.S. Census Bureau, 2010). Some researchers predict that death rates at older ages will fall more rapidly than is characterized in the U.S. Census Bureau's projections, which could lead to faster growth of this aged population (*Older Americans 2010*). This is because Baby Boomers will move into the oldest-old category.

Characteristics of the Oldest-Old

The following are characteristics that tend to define the oldest-old population:

Female Predominance

At all ages, the death rates for men are higher than those for women. As a result, as people grow older, there are fewer and fewer men compared to women. This has been identified earlier as the *sex ratio*. The 2000 Census indicated that the age of 85 years was the point at which there were twice as many women as men. That age point has increased by 4 years to the age point of 89 years, according to the 2010 Census. This later age point is further evidence of the narrowing gap in mortality between men and women at the older ages (U.S. Census Bureau, 2011).

Although the sex ratio of the oldest-old has indicated increased numbers of men between 2000 and 2010 and is expected to decrease in the future, it is still projected to show about 5 million more women than men in this oldest-old age category.

Higher Levels of Disability

As people get progressively older, their chances of having multiple chronic health conditions increase. Similarly, with advancing age, the need for assistance with the basic activities of daily living (ADLs) increases. ADLs include such functions as bathing, dressing, getting out of bed, going to the bathroom, and feeding oneself. The following chart (Figure 1.2) demonstrates the increase in assistance needed as people age.

Less Likely to Be Married

Only 15% of women aged 85 and older are still married compared to 55% for men the same age (*Older Americans 2010*). This has major social and economic implications for the lives of older women.

More Likely to Live in a Nursing Home

The likelihood of living in a long-term care facility increases with advancing age. Only 2% of people aged 65 to 74 live in a long-term care facility or community housing with services, compared to 15% of those aged 85 and older living in a long-term care facility, and 7% living in community housing with services (*Older Americans 2010*). And almost three fourths of older nursing home residents are women according to studies over the years (Centers for Disease Control and Prevention, 2004).

Implications of a Booming Oldest-Old Population

The main reason the study of the oldest-old has become so important is not simply because there are so many oldest-old people, nor is it because this group makes up the fastest-growing sector of our population—and will continue to do so for years to come. The primary reason these people are so important is because they are having and will continue to have major impacts on themselves, their families, other groups in society, and governments.

Impact of the Oldest-Old as Individuals

When the authors surveyed members of the oldest-old group on how they prepared or looked forward to becoming 85, 89, 91, or 94 years of age, most laughed and said they had no idea or no expectation that they would ever live so long. Being so old and knowing there are many like them were not part of their expectations while they were young

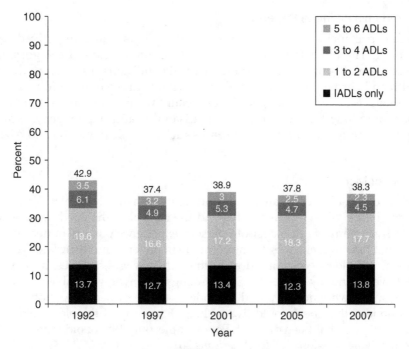

FIGURE 1.2 Percentage of Medicare Enrollees Age 65 and Over Who Have Limitations in Activities of Daily Living (ADLS) or Instrumental Activities of Daily Living (IADLS), Selected Years 1992 to 2007.

Note: ADL limitations refer to difficulty performing (or inability to perform for a health reason) one or more of the following tasks: bathing, dressing, eating, getting in/out of chairs, walking, or using the toilet. IADL limitations refer to difficulty performing (or inability to perform for a health reason) one or more of the following tasks: using the telephone, light housework, heavy housework, meal preparation, shopping, or managing money. Rates are age adjusted using the 2000 standard population. Data for 1992, 2001, and 2007 do not sum to the totals because of rounding.

Reference population: These data refer to Medicare enrollees.

Source: Adapted from *Older Americans 2010,* Table 20a.

or middle-aged. To be sure, there were oldest-old people in the past, but not so many that reaching oldest age was a common expectation. Hence, a large proportion of our current oldest-old people did not prepare for these very elderly years. It could be argued that even if many had expected to live to 85 years and beyond, the social and economic conditions through which they lived offered limited opportunities to plan and prepare for these years. Having been born in the late 19th or in the early 20th century, these people lived through two world wars and the Great Depression plus other foreign and domestic crises.

Compared to today, there was little emphasis on health and wellness in the maturing years of our oldest-old. Cigarette smoking was considered a norm, especially for men. Physical fitness and nutrition counseling were almost unknown. Essentially, physicians had no training in nutrition until relatively recent times. And trying to survive through the economic crises of the 20th and 21st centuries has left many of the oldest-old incapable of coping with today's prices and expenditures for everyday living.

Women Live Longer—Implications

We have already noted that the death rates for men are higher than those for women at all ages. Women simply live longer than men do—currently, by about five years. The longevity advantage of women has great implications for the oldest-old. As noted, the proportion of widowed persons is higher at the older ages. Older women are more likely than older men to live in poverty. And poverty tends to increase with age (*Older Americans 2010*).

Women Predominate in the Dependency Years

Longer life expectancies, with women the clear winners, can bring mixed results for the oldest-old. The older the person, especially in the oldest-old category, the more likely he or she will suffer from chronic medical conditions that lead to dependency. Poor health and chronic conditions are not inevitable in the oldest-old years, but they are more likely. More and more people, especially women, are living long enough to experience more long-term chronic illness, disability, and dependency. More people are living long enough to suffer from diseases such as senile dementia and Alzheimer's disease.

Running Out of Money

Reaching the oldest-old years can mean running into financial troubles. This may result from a combination of factors, many beyond the control of the aged persons and their families. Indeed, many of our oldest-old persons experience poverty or near-poverty status for the first time in their lives. Some continue in poverty into their later years.

Most of the oldest-old worked at a time when wages, salaries, and prices were generally lower than they are today. Even among those who were able to save for their retirements, many were not prepared for today's prices or needs. As noted previously, many had no idea that they would live so long. For many of the oldest-old, saving for their retirement years has been difficult. For example, only 19% of older persons' incomes comes from private pensions (*Older Americans 2010*).

Even though Social Security benefits have had a tremendous impact on the economic lives of the elderly in America, receiving Social Security as the primary or sole income in old age does not protect against poverty. In 2008, Social Security accounted for 83% of the total income of the poor elderly (*Older Americans 2010*).

Perhaps the biggest economic threat most of the oldest-old face is the possibility of being placed in a long-term care facility. It is important to note that persons in the oldest-old category have the greatest probability of needing the services of a nursing home. With the high costs of nursing homes, a majority of older Americans are required to "spend down" into poverty to qualify for Medicaid assistance, currently the only major government assistance program available to pay for long-term care.

In addition, with the demise of defined-benefit pension plans and the shift to defined-contribution retirement plans, where the employee is forced to save and invest in his or her retirement (typically in the equity markets), there is no guarantee that there will be retirement payments for life. There is a finite amount of retirement money, which can run out before death.

Impact of the Oldest-Old on Families

Never before in history has America had so many oldest-old people. This has great implications for American families. We have already seen that as people reach their oldest-old years, they are much more likely to develop a variety of chronic and disabling conditions that limit their ability to perform the range of activities necessary for daily living. The likelihood of needing assistance increases with advancing age.

A good way to look at the roles families play in the lives of the oldest-old is to be aware that families provide most of the support the people in this age category need, and to consider the number of oldest-old people relative to the number of people aged 50 to 64, the age of the likely family-member caregivers. This is called the *family* or *parent support ratio*. In 1960, the parent support ratio—the number of persons aged 85 and older per 100 people aged 50 to 64—was 3.4. In 2000, it was 10.1. By 2050, it will be 30.4 (*65+ in the United States*, 2005).

THE BABY BOOMERS

So far, we have focused on the categories of older people as defined by the United States. According to the U.S. Bureau of the Census, these categories are the young old (aged 56–74), the aged (75–84), and the oldest old (85 years and older). The numbers and percentages of these groups have increased dramatically changing the nature of the American population. To fully understand the scope of this paradigm shift, however, it is important to turn to another group in the American population, the *emerging old*. For planning purposes, preparations need to begin now to accommodate the largest group of persons ever born in one period of American history—Baby Boomers. The aging of Baby Boomers will solidify the shift America is experiencing with the aging of its population.

Born between 1946, the year following the end of World War II when millions of service personnel returned from overseas duty, and 1964, Baby Boomers number about 76 million. The huge number of births in this period was 70% greater than the number of babies born in the previous two decades (U.S. Census Bureau, 1993).

When Baby Boomers were babies, there were not enough of the things they needed. For example, when they began to go to school, there were not enough schools. Such has been the way with this generation. Their numbers have always given them visibility and power in American society. It was no accident that the TV program *Thirty Something* aired when it did—many of the Boomers were moving through their 30s. To date, the United States has had three presidents classified as Baby Boomers: Bill Clinton, George W. Bush, and Barack Obama, although Obama is classified by some as a post–Baby Boomer because he was born near the end of that period and because the culture of the youngest Boomers is often different from the oldest Boomers.

Baby Boomer Growth

According to the U.S. Census Bureau projections, a substantial increase in the number of older people occurred when the Baby Boom generation began to turn 65 years old in 2011. In fact, the older population is projected to grow by leaps and bounds over the next four decades—from 13% of the U.S. population in 2010 to over 20% by 2050. And, the percentage of those age 85 years and over is projected to more than double during this time (*Older Americans 2010*). The following chart (Figure 1.3) illustrates this projected increase.

Again, these rates are important because the oldest-old are the most likely to have daily needs for economic and physical assistance. The pressing needs of the oldest-old who require the assistance of their families, especially their adult children, are most likely to come at the very time when their adult children are planning for, or have reached, their own retirement years. Some of these caregiving adult children of the frailest oldest-old have health problems of their own or are caring for a spouse with such problems.

U.S. POPULATION GROWTH COMPARED TO OTHER DEVELOPED COUNTRIES

Despite the growth of the older population, the United States is still relatively young compared to other developed countries. For example, in 2010, 13% of the U.S. population was 65 and older, while in many developed countries, that proportion ranged between 16% and 18%. Some of the reasons for this difference are that the United States has had higher levels of fertility and immigration in recent decades than other countries have had (*65+ in the United States*, 2005; U.S. Census Bureau, 2011).

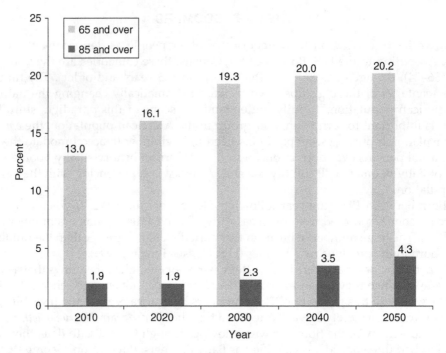

FIGURE 1.3 Percentage of the Population Age 65 and Over and 85 and Over, Selected Years 2010 to 2050.
Reference population: These data refer to the resident population.
Source: Adapted from *Older Americans 2010*, Table 1b.

GROWING DIVERSITY OF THE OLDER POPULATION

As the older population grows larger, it will also grow more diverse, which reflects the changes in the overall U.S. population. By 2050, programs and services for the elderly will need to be more flexible to meet the needs of a more diverse population (*Older Americans 2010*). For example, in 2008, non-Hispanic Whites accounted for 80% of the U.S. older population. Black Americans made up 9%, Hispanics 7%, and Asians 3% of this population. By 2050, it is projected that the composition of the older population will be 59% non-Hispanic, 20% Hispanic, 12% Black American, and 9% Asian (*Older Americans 2010*).

Even though the older population among all racial and ethnic groups will grow, the Hispanic population is projected to grow the fastest, from just under 3 million in 2008 to 17.5 million by 2050. During this same period, the Asian older population is projected to grow from just over 1 million to 7.5 million. That is why when studying gerontology, it is important to consider age, sex, race, education, and health status.

DEFINING RACIAL GROUPS

In discussing issues of race and older persons in the United States, it is important to be aware of the terms the U.S. Census Bureau uses to identify the different racial groups in the nation. The following descriptions used for the census are taken from the federal standards the Census Bureau uses, as established by the Office of Management and Budget (OMB) in 1997:

1. The term *White* refers to people having origins in any of the original peoples of Europe, the Middle East, or North Africa. It includes people who indicate their

race or one of their races as *White*, or write entries in the Census such as Irish, German, Italian, Lebanese, Near Easterner, Arab, or Polish.

2. *Black* or *African American* refers to people having origins in any of the Black racial groups of Africa. It includes people who indicate their race or one of their races as *Black*, *African American*, or *Negro* or write in entries in the Census such as African American, Afro American, Nigerian, or Haitian.

3. *American Indian* and *Alaska Native* refers to people having origins in any of the original peoples of North and South America (including Central America), and who maintain tribal affiliation or community attachment. It includes people who indicate in the Census their race by marking this category or writing in their principal or enrolled tribe, such as Rosebud Sioux, Chippewa, or Navajo.

4. *Asian* refers to people having origins in any of the original peoples of the Far East, Southeast Asia, or the Indian Subcontinent. It includes people who indicate in the Census their race or one of their races as Asian Indian, Chinese, Filipino, Korean, Japanese, Vietnamese, or Other Asian, or write in entries such as Burmese, Hmong, Pakistani, or Thai.

5. *Native Hawaiian* and *Other Pacific Islander* refers to people having origins in any of the original peoples of Hawaii, Guam, Samoa, or other Pacific Islands (U.S. Census Bureau, 2007).

CENTENARIANS

Reduced mortality rates at older ages in recent decades has also increased the number of people living to very old ages, such as 100 years or more, who are called *centenarians*. Centenarians make up a small percentage of the total U.S. population. But researchers want to learn from their experiences. What helped them live so long? In 1990, there were 37,000 centenarians. By 2010, there were 53,364. Nine out of 10 centenarians are between 100 and 104 years of age (U.S. Census Bureau, 2011).

MEDIAN AGE

As the number of people aged 65 and older increases, the U.S. population as a whole becomes older. One measure of population aging is its median age—the age that divides a population into two groups—half younger and half older.

In 1900, the median age in the United States was 22.9 years, which represented a young population—similar to moderately high-fertility populations found in the developing world today. Due primarily to a decline in fertility, the U.S. population became progressively older, so that by 1950, the median age was 31.1 years. The Baby Boom era—a period of high-fertility rates—caused the U.S. median age to decline in the 1950s and 1960s. But since the 1970s, the population has been aging as the fertility rate dropped following the Baby Boomers. By 2010, the median age increased to 37.2 years and is projected to increase to 39 years in 2030 before leveling off once again (*65+ in the United States*, 2005; U.S. Census Bureau, 2011).

OLDER WOMEN AND OLDER MEN

As in most countries of the world, older women outnumber older men in the United States, and women's share of the older population increases with age. The reason for the preponderance of women at older ages is due to the sex differentials in death rates.

Even though male births outnumber female births by about 5%, males generally have higher mortality rates at every age. These higher mortality rates translate into women outnumbering men starting at about age 35. The outnumbering of women over men is most pronounced at the older ages.

As men are generally older than their spouses and women have a longer life expectancy, high proportions of women, especially the oldest-old women (aged 85 and older), are widows, many of whom end up living alone. This situation influences the tendency for these women to be institutionalized, have reduced incomes, and live in poverty. All of these factors, combined with the large number of older and especially oldest-old women, raise the issue of what types of support systems—from families and the larger society including government supports—are needed and how they can be provided.

OUR AGING WORLD

To better understand aging in the United States, it is helpful to look at aging trends in the rest of the world. As fertility (birth) and mortality (death) rates have declined in most countries of the world, populations are aging in virtually all countries—although at different rates. Developed countries have relatively high proportions of people 65 and older. But the most rapid increases in the proportions of older populations are in the developing countries. For example, even in countries where the percentage of 65 and older people remains small, the actual numbers of these people are increasing rapidly.

In 2000, 420 million people in the world were 65 and older, which was about 7% of the world's population. By 2030, the number is expected to double to 974 million, which will be 12% of the world's population. Also, in 2000, the majority of the world's older population—59%—lived in developing countries. That proportion is expected to rise to over 70% by 2030 and to nearly 80% by 2050 (*65+ in the United States*, 2005).

LIFE EXPECTANCY (LONGEVITY)

Life expectancy represents the average number of years of life remaining to a person at a given age if death rates remain constant. Improvements in health with lower death rates have led to increases in life expectancy—more people living to older ages. Americans are living longer than ever before. Life expectancies of persons both 65 and 85 years of age have increased. Under current mortality conditions, people who survive to age 65 can expect to live an average of 18.5 years, about 4 years longer than people age 65 in 1960. The life expectancy of people who live to age 85 is 6.8 years for women and 5.7 years for men (*Older Americans 2010*).

At the beginning of the 20th century (1900), 88% of infants survived to their first birthday, and 41% of adults lived to age 65. Over the course of the 20th century, the percentage of people who lived to 75 years of age increased from 6% to 35% (*65+ in the United States*, 2005).

The Gender Gap in Life Expectancy

Historically, female life expectancy has been higher than male life expectancy at most all ages, and both Black American and White women live longer than their male counterparts. The sex difference in life expectancy is due to differences in attitudes, behaviors, social roles, and biological risks between men and women. In 1900, life expectancy at birth was 47.9 years for men and 50.7 years for women. By 1940, the year before the beginning of World War II, life expectancy had increased to 61.6 years for men and to 65.9 years for women, about a 4-year difference. By 1990, the life expectancy difference between men and women had increased to 7 years (Centers for Disease Control and Prevention, 2010).

It should be noted that the gender gap in life expectancy has declined in recent years. This is due largely to male heart disease and lung cancer—both of which are related to widespread cigarette smoking among men. The gender gap in life expectancy has narrowed due to proportionately larger increases in lung cancer among women than men and a proportionately greater decline in heart disease among men than women (*65+ in the United States*, 2005).

Racial Gaps in Life Expectancy

While improvements in life expectancy have occurred across racial groups, racial differences in life expectancy and survivorship remain. In 1900, an estimate of life expectancy at birth for Black Americans was 33 years, while life expectancy for Whites was 47.6 years. That nearly 15-year gap had narrowed to 5.7 years by 1982 but increased to 7.1 years in 1993 before renewing a declining trend after 1993. By 2006, the racial gap for life expectancy was still five years (Centers for Disease Control and Prevention, 2010).

International Life Expectancy

Life expectancy at age 65 in the United States is lower than that of many other industrialized countries. For example, in Japan, women age 65 can expect to live 3.7 years longer than women in the United States. For men, the difference is 1.3 years (Centers for Disease Control and Prevention, 2010).

Limits to Longevity

Considerable progress has been made in increasing life expectancy over the past century. Although most of the advances early in the 20th century came from improvements in socioeconomic factors, living conditions, and a decrease in infectious disease deaths, gains during the later part of the century and into the 21st century have come from breakthroughs in public health and medical research that have led to new treatments for, and a later onset of, chronic diseases.

Two basic views on human longevity are currently under debate. The first contends that the practical limits have already been reached. The second view is that old-age mortality will decline at a more accelerated rate in the future. Some researchers believe that the maximum average life expectancy is about 85 years. They argue that the incremental improvements needed to achieve much higher levels of life expectancy are unlikely. Others believe that recent declines in mortality rates will continue, given the steady progress against the diseases of old age, that life expectancy could reach much higher levels in the 21st century, and that medical developments will extend life expectancy to 100 years or more.

Among the steps toward progress in life expectancy are advances in the prevention and treatment of heart disease; improved knowledge of the genetic links to cancer; and adoption of healthy lifestyles, such as engaging in physical activity, eating a balanced diet, and maintaining a stable, lean body weight.

Although women can expect to live longer than men, the gap is narrowing as death rates by sex have started to come closer together over the last couple of decades. Some

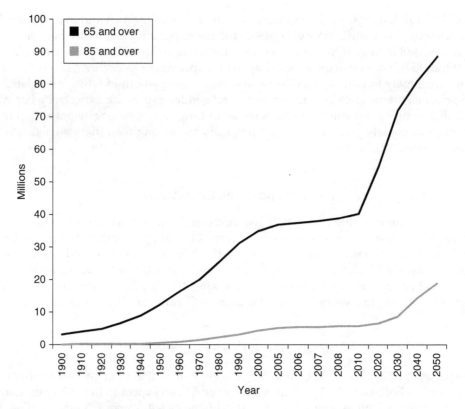

FIGURE 1.4 Population Age 65 and Over and Age 85 and Over, Selected Years 1900 to 2008, and Projected 2010 to 2050.

Reference population: These data refer to the resident population.

Source: Older Americans 2010, Table 1a.

researchers suggest that this narrowing of death rates is due to changes in women's behavior, including increased cigarette smoking and stresses related to multiple roles such as housework, occupational activities, and caregiving (including childcare and elder care; U.S. Census Bureau, 2005).

A Snapshot of Older Persons

Figure 1.4 demonstrates the projected growth of the older population age 65 and over and age 85 years and over.

A CHANGING AMERICA

In colonial America, half the population was under the age of 16. Most people never made it to old age. At age 83, Benjamin Franklin was a rarity among the framers of the U.S. Constitution. Two factors kept America a youthful nation in terms of population: high-mortality (death) rates and high-fertility (birth) rates. But now fertility rates have dropped dramatically, from an average of seven births per woman to two. Death rates have also declined (U.S. Census Bureau, 2005).

Population aging is one of the most important demographic dynamics affecting families and societies throughout the world. The growth of the population aged 65 and older is challenging lawmakers, families, businesses, and health care providers to meet the needs of aging persons. How people experience aging depends on a variety of factors including social and economic characteristics as well as health status. This text will detail the range of factors that impact aging in America in the 21st century as well as how an aging America is changing the social paradigm of our nation.

SUGGESTED RESOURCES

65+ in the United States: 2005: http://www.census.gov/prod/2006pubs/p23–209.pdf
MetLife Mature Market Institute: http://www.metlife.com/mmi/index.html
> The MetLife Mature Market Institute is MetLife's center of expertise in aging, longevity, and the generations and is a recognized thought leader by business, the media, opinion leaders, and the public.

National Centenarian Awareness Project: http://www.adlercentenarians.org
> This nonprofit organization celebrates active centenarians as role models for the future of aging.

U.S. Census Bureau: http://www.census.gov

CHAPTER 2

The Evolution of Aging

The learning objectives of this chapter include understanding

- The different perceptions of aging in American society.
- The historical perspectives on aging that enhance our knowledge of aging in America.
- The factors that impact the rules and status of older people in society.
- The social theories of aging that have been developed over the years to attempt to describe variation in the aging process.
- The major implications in recognizing the paradigm shift of an aging population.

Section A: Aging in a New Century

PERCEPTIONS OF GROWING OLDER

What is it like to grow older in America in the 21st century? What is "old" anyway? It is important to keep in mind that there are distinct stages or periods of old age. The young-old, persons aged 65 through 74, are very different in many ways from the oldest-old, persons 85 years and older. And the aged, people 75 through 84 years, are unique from the other two categories. In addition, it is essential to recognize persons in their 50s and early 60s (the older Baby Boomers) as these people already experience some of the consequences of being older, especially in employment. The large number of people in their 50s and early 60s who will become elderly in the years ahead requires us to alter our concepts of what it means to grow older.

As the nation moves further into the new century, we are in a state of transition regarding our view of older people and their place in society. Since America has changed in many ways, and is continuing to change, the status and role of older people have changed and will continue to change.

Changing Perceptions of Old Age

As we will see in the following sections of this chapter, over the years there have been many views of older people, of growing older, and of old age. These views change as a result of changing circumstances in any society; America is no exception. We will look at specific factors that affect the role and status of the elderly in a society and how these factors came into play as America became an industrialized nation. We will then examine the changes that occurred as we moved into a postindustrial era, which should affect our views of older people.

Perceptions of Older People in the 21st Century

According to a massive survey by the National Council on Aging, the American public has various views of aging (Cutler, Whitelaw, & Beattie, 2002). Some of these views differ according to the age of the respondents. For example:

- In identifying the chronological age at which "the average man" and the "average woman" become middle-aged, old, and very old, respondents aged 65 and older defined middle age beginning at 50 to 53, old age as starting at 70 to 75, and very old coming at age 80 to 85. To show an "age gap" in the perceptions of aging, persons aged 18 to 34 (both men and women) saw old age as beginning about age 50, while persons aged 65 and older saw old age as beginning about age 70 or later.
- On specific issues concerning health and finance, more than a quarter of older respondents incorrectly believed that Medicare pays for about 100% of doctor's bills for people over age 65, and more than half incorrectly believed that employers who provide pension plans are also required to provide health insurance to their retirees.
- Many older adults (80%) thought there would be dramatic cures or treatments that will improve their chances of living past 75 (or another 10 years for those already 75 and older). But nearly half were worried that they would not be able to afford these new treatments.
- In thinking ahead to their older years, ages 75 and beyond, the biggest worries for most older adults were health-related issues. When asked about specific worries, 61% said that they were worried about losing their memory; 49% were worried about uncontrollable pain; and 45% were worried about spending all their money on long-term care.
- A majority of all age groups agreed that 75-year-olds can be sexy.

A NEW PARADIGM OF AGING

But these perceptions by and of older people are not the real concerns facing society in regard to an aging America. It is the contention of the authors that the nation is facing the reality of a new paradigm of aging in the 21st century—a new view of what it means to be older. In previous generations, older people were often viewed as unique or a separate group from the population as a whole. One reason for this is that there were not too many of them. Another reason is that they were not too visible as they were part of extended families that generally looked out for them. Another reason they were not too visible is that in many instances they were somewhat frail and dependent; at least they were generally thought to be.

But all this changed with the coming of the industrial revolution, nuclear families, increased longevity, *senior power* (where older people demanded their rights and support systems, such as entitlements), and the coming of Baby Boomers into their later years—a population shift that many experts believe will dramatically change the way we grow older in America.

The late Dr. Robert N. Butler, a leading expert in gerontology and geriatric medicine and a Pulitzer Prize–winning author and founder of the International Longevity Center—USA, outlined the challenges and changes of an aging society in his book, *The Longevity Revolution*, and in journal articles. He pointed out that writers, economists, politicians, and policymakers have been—and continue to be—afraid that the United States is unable to cope with the rapidly increasing number of older people as outlined in Chapter 1 (Butler, 2008). They are concerned about the cost of having so many elderly people in the country. They believe that a large percentage of older people in society will lead to intergenerational conflicts—the young and some middle-agers against the old, especially in regard to social supports from government sources. Many go on to predict that the aging of America will lead to the stagnation of productivity (Butler, 2008).

But Dr. Butler believed that society will adapt to the great achievements in longevity—so many people living much longer. To Dr. Butler, the greatest challenges of the new longevity include facing head on the fallacies and outright myths about old age and its costs that are so prevalent in society, especially in the media and among many politicians. These fallacies include: (a) the idea that Social Security and Medicare are too broken to be rejuvenated and that they will bankrupt the nation (this is addressed in Chapter 10); (b) that the older generation is the main factor causing the rise in America's health care costs; (c) that at the end of life people are given expensive, heroic, high-tech treatments; (d) that ageism (prejudice against older people) has been eliminated by existing laws; (e) that older workers are not as productive as younger workers (see Myths About Older Workers in Chapter 10); and (f) that older persons are provided more public and private support than children or adolescents.

Dr. Butler believed strongly that it is important to confront and dispel these fallacies and myths that permeate so much of our current culture in the United States—to promote an "active, engaged, and productive older population that once and for all buries the myths of selfish and useless old age" (Butler, 2008, p. 34). Butler goes on to say that this is possible by calling for new responsibilities, new goals, and new achievements. He points out that developing new roles and new attitudes toward work and civic engagement will enhance the human condition in ways that society is just beginning to explore.

The authors contend that all of this will be possible only if the majority of society—politicians, pundits, civic leaders, and citizens in general, including older persons themselves—develop a new paradigm of growing older in America. This paradigm consists of looking at aging and all the components of the older population—the near-old (aged 55–64), the young-old (aged 65–74), the aged (aged 75–84), and the oldest-old (aged 85 and over)—as an integral part of the whole society. Of course, some components in the older population—the oldest-old, the frail, the sick, and so forth—will continue to need special and unique support systems such as caregivers, disability income, and so forth. But a new paradigm of aging in America envisions older people playing vital roles as normal participants in everyday living—play, worship, personal relationships, family life, civic engagement, and overall citizenship. This theme—a new paradigm in aging—is the only way Dr. Butler's goals for an integrated society can be realized. For additional information on ageism and how to overcome societal stereotypes and myths of aging consult the Practical Application at the end of Part I of this textbook.

HISTORICAL PERSPECTIVES ON BEING OLD IN AMERICA

After having looked at some of the perceptions of becoming older, as well as the need to develop a new paradigm of aging as we move further into the 21st century, it is helpful to examine the major factors that have influenced how the views of aging and the elderly developed throughout American history.

The Colonial Period

An examination of social perceptions of what it means to grow old indicates that perceptions of aging varied over time. In Colonial America, the aged had a place of honor, especially if they owned land or had other sources of wealth, prestige, or power. Fischer (1977) argued that in Colonial times sons had reason to give deference to their fathers because the fathers controlled the farm, owned the land, and had power in the community. Frequently at public gatherings special seating arrangements were made for older people. A study of the use of language at that time indicates that words of honor, prestige, and power were used to describe older persons. There was also a religious emphasis on honoring older persons; religious leaders stressed, "Thou shalt honor thy father and thy mother."

While not rejecting Fischer's contention that honored terms and special places were reserved for some older persons, other studies have pointed out that impoverished widows and landless transients were often treated poorly (Haber, 1983). Poor widows often had to beg for food and lodging. Some had to wander from village to village trying to find basic food and shelter. It is from this context that a perception of the *old crone*, an ugly withered old woman, began to surface in American culture. It is also from this era that a belief in old witches began to be part of the folklore of rural life.

In Colonial times, there seems to have been a mixed perception and treatment of older persons. Those who owned land were given respect; others, the poor, the widowed, and the landless, were not respected at all. At this time, though, the pervasive use of terms disrespectful of the elderly had not developed. Of the scholars studied, none argued that Colonial times were a golden era for older Americans where they were basking in respect from the family and society. Most people in Colonial times did not live into old age, and it is doubtful that overworked family members were eager to care for a deranged, frail, or incontinent older relative. Neither were there community resources comparable to today to give assistance to families struggling to care for older relatives. Older people of this era, however, were honored more than they were in the period that followed, a period that produced the industrial revolution and a massive migration from the farm to the city.

The Industrial Era

When Americans began to leave the farms to move to the cities and work in the factories, older people began to lose honor and respect because they had neither the knowledge of industry by which they could instruct their children, nor the knowledge of city life, which would enable them to be tutors to their children and grandchildren. In addition, older people began to be a serious financial burden. Furthermore, they had no power by which they could help their children obtain positions in the new world of work. Increasingly, in the 19th century, very negative terms began to be used to describe older persons. These included terms such as *old crock, old goat, old-fashioned, over-the-hill, fuddy-duddy, geezers, old codger, washed-up, out to pasture, hag, gummer* (a person with no teeth), *crone, old duffer, old fogy, old maid, dried-up old prune, old galoot,* and even less flattering terms referring to sexual incompetence. There is no comparable list of antonyms. Just try listing the exact opposite of each of these terms, words that have been used in American society to refer to older persons. It cannot be done.

America was beginning to change with a marked shift from a rural to an industrial society. Farming, which had been the focus of employment, began to decrease in importance. American young people began to leave the farms and move to the cities. Increasingly, employment opportunities were being created in the cities, employment opportunities that involved fewer hours of work and higher pay than workers received on the farm. Between 1880 and 1930, the hours worked in city-based jobs decreased from 60 to fewer than 45 a week. America became increasingly urbanized. Between 1800 and 1890, cities grew by 87-fold, while population increased only 12-fold. During this time, a national youth culture began to develop. Young people created fads that were featured in the national media and exploded into a national mania in the post–World War II years.

Older Americans were among the last to be affected by these changes. It was mostly the young who moved to the cities. Young people became a more dominant group in the population. Older persons mostly stayed on the farm and continued to work as long as their health permitted; there were no governmental pensions such as Social Security or Supplemental Security Income. Very few farmers had any type of private security in old age other than their children to help them farm, the value of their property, and their savings. Social Security did not begin in the United States until 1935. There is no evidence that prior to the 20th century there was any widespread and significant change in the lifestyle of older Americans.

Achenbaum (1983) stated that there were several factors that had an impact on older Americans. They slowly began to make up a larger percentage of the population. Prior to the Civil War, less than 5% of Americans were aged 65 or older. Since that time there has been a steady increase in the percentage of the elderly population. At the present time, about 13% of all Americans are 65 or older.

The Old as a Problem

Increasingly, Achenbaum (1983) pointed out, Americans began to perceive older people as a problem. More and more articles appeared describing the older person in terms of "pathological deterioration, eccentric behavior, and painful irrelevance" (p. 15). The rapid changes that occurred in American life emphasized the adaptability of youth and the irrelevance of the "wisdom" of the "old farmer," who increasingly was the brunt of jokes about "country hicks."

Social workers, policy makers, politicians, and writers increasingly portrayed the elderly as impoverished and maudlin stories began to appear concerning the tragic plight of America's aged. Out of this type of environment, as well as the changes taking place in Europe in regard to the acceptance of various forms of social welfare, a movement began in the United States to help the elderly, which culminated in the Social Security Act of 1935. This movement and emphasis resulted in a political orientation that old age was a legitimate social welfare category. That emphasis, though, is being challenged by a contemporary view that does not see old age as a legitimate social welfare category and contends that social welfare policy should be based on need, not on age. The emphasis by some today is that Social Security in the 1930s fulfilled widespread financial and social needs of older citizens, but that today with private pensions, private savings, and a lifetime of earnings, many older people should not be getting benefits on the basis of their age alone. This changing emphasis is tied to cultural changes that increasingly perceive older people, at least the young-old, as affluent, vigorous, and consumer oriented. There is an element of truth in this perception, but it is an overgeneralization that ignores the oldest-old, minorities, and those suffering from chronic and catastrophic illnesses who are struggling to survive. Achenbaum (1983) stated:

> Because the society in which we live is constantly changing, the normative foundations and socio-cultural political economy that sustain the realm of ideas and social policy are continually shifting. Thus, if we truly hope to address people's real needs and help them satisfy their desires, we must forever be sensitive to the tension between tradition and novelty. We must be prepared to alter our conceptions and policies to confirm more accurately to current circumstances. (p. 176)

Historical Myths of Old Age

Every society has a conception of what it means to be old. In contemporary, rapidly changing societies, these concepts are also in a process of change, and yet the myths and conceptions of the past persist. Are the modern conceptions of aging and the elderly based on reality, or are they just new myths developed within a specific cultural context? What does old mean? What should it mean? When is one old? How does one determine when a person is old? Is aging affected by cultural definitions or is it primarily a genetically driven biological process? Are old people wiser than young people? What is wisdom? Do we learn from experience and from wisdom acquired over the decades? Does the media accurately portray aging and the aging process?

Social Perceptions of Aging

Again, looking at history, Fischer (1977) argued that there are two main periods in American history that relate to social perceptions of the aging person. He referred to the years between 1600 and 1800 as a period of *gerontophilia* when old age was honored and in general, older persons were respected. He did not disagree with those who pointed out that there were older persons during this period who had characteristics that resulted in their being mocked and discriminated against. He contended that this began to change in the 1970s when there was some indication that the fear and loathing of the aging process was decreasing. But many myths about aging and the aging process persist (Riekse & Holstege, 1996). These include the following factors.

All Are Poor, Lonely, and Isolated

A Louis Harris poll back in 1981 showed that many Americans believed that older Americans are poor, lonely, isolated, in poor health, and decrepit. The reality is that most Americans 65 and over are not living in poverty, are not lonely, are not in poor health, are not isolated, are certainly not abandoned by their families, and are not in living institutions (*Older Americans 2010*).

Most Live in Long-Term Care Facilities

Only a small minority (about 4%) of Americans 65 and older are in institutions (Centers for Medicare and Medicaid Services, 2010). The majority (64%) of those not in institutions have no limitations that prevent them from independently taking care of themselves in their everyday lives (Centers for Medicare and Medicaid Services, 2010).

Most Are in Poor Health

Poor health is not a common feature of life for the elderly, especially among the young-old. Some 75% of people aged 65 to 74 consider their health to be good, very good, or excellent (*Older Americans 2010*). The vast majority (74%) of persons aged 75 and older who are not in institutions also consider their health to be good, very good, or excellent (Centers for Disease Control and Prevention, 2006).

Most Have No Interest in Sex

Certainly many Americans in the past, and many younger persons today, perceive older people as being asexual. Even today, many birthday or anniversary cards for the elderly feature jokes about sexual impotence. Some older people internalize these myths and think that there is something wrong with them if they continue to have sexual desires into old and even oldest-old age. In reality, many older people enjoy active sex lives that they indicate are better than what they experienced in earlier years, as outlined in Chapter 6.

Aging Means Mental Decline

Some people think that with aging comes an inevitable mental decline, an inability to learn new procedures, and a significant loss of memory. If one tests older persons who are not suffering from some chronic debilitating disease, the differences between old and young begin to disappear. It is true, whatever the reason, that older persons need a longer time to take tests. Reaction time does seem to decline somewhat with the aging process. However, research going back many years has shown that older persons can learn, be creative, and remember quite well as Chapter 5 describes.

Families Forget Them

Older Americans are visited regularly by their children and are part of holiday festivities and family celebrations such as birthdays, anniversaries, and graduations. Research going back many years has consistently shown that older people generally are not being abandoned by their children, which is discussed later in Chapter 12.

Most Older People Have About the Same Amount of Money

The stereotype of financial need or financial greed on the part of older people points to complex questions, which are discussed in greater detail in Chapter 10. It should be stated, though, that most older Americans are not living in poverty. Until the advent of the cost of living adjustment (COLA) to Social Security, there were many more older Americans living in poverty than at the present time. There are categories of older people, primarily single women, minorities, and the oldest-old, who have many of their members living in poverty.

Older People Are Poor Workers

As long ago as 1977, Palmore found that a third of college students believed that older workers were not as effective as younger workers. Contemporary research evidence has indicated just the opposite. Older persons work as well as, or better than, younger persons. They have less absenteeism, work harder, have fewer acute illnesses, and have fewer accidents (Krauss, 1987). In addition, older workers pay more attention to satisfying customers and are more willing to work overtime (Commonwealth Fund, 1991; Krauss, 1987).

A YOUTH-ORIENTED CULTURE

We have had a youth-oriented culture in the United States for some time. The Baby Boom (1946–1964) brought about a tremendous bulge in our population. Because their numbers represented a huge market for sales, Baby Boomers got tremendous attention from the media and from retailers. In addition, the media began to emphasize youth as crime began to increase.

Who Is Considered Old?

Crews (1993) stated that, "chronological age alone is a poor proxy for the study of measure of aging and senescence" (p. 30). We are almost entering a new period in American society where age by itself will mean less and less in our view of people, including ourselves.

In the United States, the age of 65 has been emphasized for retirement because of an event in history. Count Otto von Bismarck of Prussia, in the late 1880s, was under pressure from political forces to provide assistance to the elderly poor. He instructed his legislators to enact legislation for some type of help. They agreed to enact a law to support the elderly, but were uncertain as to what age recipients should be able to collect benefits. After his advisors told the Count that the average Prussian lived to be about 65, benefits were granted to Prussians when they reached 65. France, Britain, and the United States followed in passing such Social Security–type legislation. The debate in the United States over this legislation was ferocious. Those advocating Social Security were frequently referred to as communists, Marxists, socialists, or leftists. There was, however, little debate over the concept that one was old at 65 and should retire or be retired from employment at that age. The fact is that from birth to death, the age 65 does not take on any physical or psychological significance. In American society, we have taken that age, 65, and reified it (constructed a reality about it that is not true, but which we believe is true). As a result, we treat people who are 65 and older as "old people." That concept is being questioned. Who is old? How does one determine who is old? Is old primarily a question of chronological age or of functional ability? If determining what is old is based on functional ability, then what significance should age play in political, economic, and educational decisions? Should age by itself give a person certain advantages or disadvantages in governmental programs and policies? What do you think of when you use the word *old*?

CHANGING ROLES FOR OLDER PEOPLE IN THE 21ST CENTURY

Given the reality that we have moved into a postindustrial society, it is important to assess what the roles and status of older people are and will be in this new era.

A postindustrial era means a shift away from the ongoing expansion in manufacturing and industry, even though they are important. Many believe that the postindustrial age can bring reduced working hours, a 4-day workweek, and a diminished emphasis on the old Protestant work ethic, which historically placed total emphasis on the role of work in a person's life with recreation and leisure not being very important (Cox, 1994).

The postindustrial society puts more emphasis on the expansion of the service sector of the economy, along with entertainment, athletics, recreation, and leisure activities. All of this can open new nonwork roles for older people, which could give them a higher status in a postindustrial environment than the status they experienced in an industrial environment. Indeed, older people in this new era could have a range of options to choose from. In a society that puts less emphasis on the importance of productivity and more emphasis on the quality of life, older people can choose roles that are more socially supported than they were for much of the 20th century. They may choose to focus on family roles, recreation and leisure roles, volunteer roles, political roles, or second careers (Cox, 1994).

A Normal Phase of Life

In an era of competition for governmental resources in the form of assistance programs, and given the realities of contemporary aging as outlined previously, we are going to need a perception of aging that fosters individual creativity and productivity regardless of age if we are to avoid worsening the intergenerational tensions that have already surfaced. As far back as 1993, Theodore Koff and Richard Park stated in their book, *Aging Public Policy*, "It appears likely that older people will feel better about themselves when being old is accepted as being of no real consequence" (p. 274). What this can do to age-based assistance programs is discussed in detail in the chapter on public policy and politics (Chapter 18). These programs can be intergenerational in nature. One could point out that even a program such as Social Security, typically identified with older people, has provisions to help workers of all ages when they become disabled, as well as their family members of all ages if they lose the support of a covered worker through death.

Overcoming Ageism

Motivating people of all ages to perceive older people in a more favorable light, including older people themselves, is no easy task. Prejudice against the elderly—ageism—is real. It is real in the way much of society, including the elderly themselves, perceive what are believed to be the inevitable declines of aging. Georgia O'Keefe, Benjamin Franklin, Frank Lloyd Wright, and a long list of other creative individuals did some of their best work in their later years. Examples of people excelling in old age have been around for years; still, there is a general disregard of the abilities of the elderly, as if these examples were exceptions.

Liberating the Talents of All

What do these broadened perceptions of old age mean? In a complex society with all of the needs that are evident every day, the nation cannot afford to discard or ignore the ongoing contributions people can make, even in their oldest years, given reasonably good physical and mental health. Recognizing the diversity of the elderly population, within and between the specific elderly age groups, a new perception of aging needs to be developed that avoids stereotypes that have molded society's perception of older people as well as the perception older people have of themselves. Too often in American society, people have acted "old" because they thought this was expected of them. By acting "old," they begin to demonstrate the negative characteristics of what they thought was old. For example, how many older people upon misplacing an item such as car keys say, "I must be getting older," as if younger people never misplace or lose anything.

What does it mean to grow older in the 21st century—when society begins to realize the social revolution it is undergoing, at a time when more and more people are reaching the oldest-old years (85 and older), and the ranks of the youngest-old are beginning to be populated with millions of Baby Boomers who are reaching their mid-60s and soon their 70s with more vigor, vitality, and better health than any previous generation? Growing older increasingly will need to be viewed simply as another phase of life without intrinsic negative characteristics. People need to be encouraged to continue to work if they need to or want to. Job training and retraining should be open to all, regardless of age, to secure or retain employment. This does not mean that entitlement programs for the elderly should be abandoned; they are vital. It does mean that our society needs to stop closing doors to people simply because of advancing years. The technologies of the new age, including the information superhighway, should open opportunities for older people to play a vital role in determining their own destinies and have an impact on their families and their communities in the 21st century.

Section B: Historical Social Theories of Aging

In addition to looking at the perceptions of older people, their place in history since the beginning of our nation, myths and realities concerning them, and the need for a new paradigm of aging, over the years social scientists have tried to construct social as well as biological theories of aging. The main social theories have been outlined as follows:

Disengagement Theory

One of the earliest theories of aging was the Disengagement Theory by Elaine Cumming and William Henry in 1961. It was an attempt to explain the role and status of older people in the 1960s. This theory proposes that old age is a time when older people and society mutually separate. For example, older people leave work—retire—as this is the natural thing to do. According to this theory, it reflects the basic biological rhythms of life. This theory grew out of a 10-year study of the transition from middle age to old age (known as the *Kansas City Studies of Adult Life*, Williams & Wirths, 1965).

This theory has been criticized by many scholars because older people may disengage from work activities but then become engaged in a range of other activities associated with volunteering, family activities, and leisure pursuits. As Harry Moody (1998) pointed out, "Total withdrawal from society is quite uncommon" (p. 74). In addition, many older people do not accept a concept that leads to mandatory retirement because of age. Indeed, the resentment of a mandatory age for retirement led Congress to end such practices for most workers in 1986 (Moody, 1998).

But the Kansas City Studies did reveal that there is a trend toward more *interiority*—increased focus on an inner psychological world. Older people do seem to become more detached and more focused on an inner attitude toward life (Peak, 1968).

Activity Theory

Opposite from the Disengagement Theory of aging is the Activity Theory of aging. This theory contends that the more active older people are, the more likely they will be happy in older ages. According to this theory, self-perception in old age is largely based on the roles people have in society and the activities in which they participate.

Much research seems to support parts of the Activity Theory according to Harry Moody. Exercise, being involved socially, and productive roles tend to enhance mental health and satisfaction with being older (Moody, 1998).

Continuity Theory

A theory of aging closely related to the Activity Theory is called the Continuity Theory. This theory contends that as people grow older, they are inclined to retain, as much as they can, their same or similar personalities, habits, and lifestyles that they had in the previous years (Costa & McCrae, 1980). Both the Activity Theory and the Continuity Theory contend that any decrease in activities in the later years is due to poor health or disability (Havighurst, Neugarten, & Tobin, 1968).

The Activity Theory goes on to contend that older people will develop substitutes for roles and activities they may be forced to give up due to retirement or age limitations (Atchley, 1985). But Moody (1988) points out that this theory may be better suited to the young-old rather than the oldest-old.

Modernization Theory

Closely related to all these theories is the role of older people. The Modernization Theory postulates that the role of the old declines in a modern society. Looking back through history, Moody (1998) pointed out that depending on the needs of the society at specific times, the roles and status of older people varied. In hunting and gathering societies, the status of older people was rather low because they were not as valuable as younger people in doing these types of activities. In agricultural societies, where the control of land was important, older people were more valuable because they tended to own the land. In industrialized societies, older people were not very valuable and their status was not too high. The Modernization Theory of aging suggests that technology reduces the status of the aged because wisdom and life experiences are not really important (Cowgill & Holmes, 1972). Moody (1998) stated that, "the history of old age includes variations according to race, gender, special class, and culture" (p. 72).

Moody (1998) contended that there is a problem with trying to construct an overall social/psychological theory of aging. He went on to point out that "there is no clear agreement that a single social theory of aging is best" (p. 73). Indeed, all of the postulated social theories of aging, along with the historical views of aging, need to face the realities embedded in an aging society and be open to looking at a new paradigm of aging as suggested previously in this chapter. As we embark on new journeys in the 21st century, we do so with a rapidly changing population in terms of age structure. From a nation absorbed with the culture of youth, we move to a society that is made up of people who are generally older and who continue to grow older. See the Practical Application at the end of Part I of this textbook for information on why it is important to examine the social theories of aging.

A NEW VIEW OF AGING

As indicated previously, the fastest growing sector of the population is made up of persons aged 85 and older. And as has been noted, these are the people who are most likely to need various forms of support from their families, their communities, and governmental programs. It is clear from looking at the general characteristics of the young-old, the aged, and the oldest-old that it is inadequate to use one term, one theory, or one view to describe them.

All of this calls for a new view of aging—a view that does not automatically classify persons as "over the hill" once they reach ages 62, 65, or 70; a view that takes into account the diversity and potential productivity of persons in each age sector. Some people are "burned out" at ages 50 or 55. Others are in their prime at ages 68 or 70. Some are vulnerable in their late middle years due to chronic health conditions. Others find work the most important part of their lives in their late 60s and 70s. Some have experienced discrimination all their lives because their sex, race, or ethnic background has limited their educational opportunities and negatively impacted their earning power and financial status. This is particularly true for elderly minority women who have faced double discrimination when they were younger and then triple discrimination in their later years.

With the booming growth of the oldest-old, and the young-old entering their later years as a pioneering generation in better health, affluence, and vitality than previous generations experienced, we need a new and broader view of what growing older in America means. All who study aging must realistically understand the aging process; be aware of the major and rapid population changes that are occurring; examine what growing older currently means to older people themselves and their families; be aware of the resources and supports that are available; realize the impacts of an aging society on business, government, and family structures; and participate in the discussions and debates that surround the issues affecting the elderly and their families. This book is designed to help the reader in these endeavors.

SUGGESTED RESOURCES

International Longevity Center-USA: www.mailman.columbia.edu/academic-departments/centers/international-longevity-center/

Founded in 1990 by world-renowned gerontologist Robert N. Butler, the center was created to educate individuals on how to live longer and better, and advise society on how to maximize the benefits of today's longer life spans.

National Council on Aging (NCOA): www.ncoa.org

NCOA is a nonprofit service and advocacy organization. Bringing together nonprofit organizations, businesses, and government, it champions issues and creates innovative programs that focus on making life better for older adults, especially those who are vulnerable and disadvantaged.

Professor Palmore's Amazing *Facts on Aging* Quiz: www.timegoesby.net/weblog/2004/09/dr_erdmans_amaz.html

Website includes some background information on the quiz and the actual quiz.

Practical Application   I

Growing Older in the 21st Century

Michael A. Faber

INTRODUCTION

Each of the six parts of this book will be followed by a practical application section. This section will include practical information that compliments content included in the chapters that precede it. You might ask, *why include information on practical application in a gerontology textbook?* Simply put, this book includes research-based facts, figures, data, and theoretical information related to aging and the realities of an aging society; yet to know these things is often not enough to work effectively with an older adult population. Therefore, the practical application sections of this book will share practice-based practical information learned through years of real life experience in working with older persons, their families, caregivers, and the professionals who serve them.

Ageism: Overcoming Societal Stereotypes and Myths of Aging

The first two chapters of this textbook outline key aging demographics, perceptions of growing older and old age, historical perspectives on aging, common myths and stereotypes of aging, and the main social theories of aging. Yet, the section on "overcoming ageism" found in Chapter 2 may have the greatest relevance to the actual day-to-day practice of gerontology.

There is a tendency when writing about and/or teaching gerontology to generalize certain characteristics and attributes of aging to all older people. If taken out of context, this practice can lead to the perpetuation of many of the myths and stereotypes of aging that gerontology educators are working to dispel. Careful effort has been taken by the authors of this text to accurately report the facts, issues, trends, and concerns of aging and an aging society, and at the same time present a new and more positive paradigm of aging in the 21st century.

Contrary to the stereotypes of aging, most older persons live happy, active, and productive lives. The stereotypic view of aging as a time of decline, poor health, and poverty is just not true for the majority of older persons. Yes, these conditions do exist for many older people, especially in the oldest-old age category; however, they are not commonplace with all older persons.

Those who choose gerontology as a profession should not inadvertently perpetuate the myths and stereotypes of aging. Whether one is a student considering entry into the field, or a seasoned professional, one should always ask: *Is anything I am doing or saying helping to perpetuate a negative stereotype of aging?* Damage might be caused by the jokes or the way one speaks of or to an elder. Education is the key to eliminating these negative biases. The myths and negative stereotypes of aging will not be dispelled until the roles that we all play in perpetuating these fallacies are recognized and altered.

For example, a person may feel free of biases toward older people until she or he is slowed by an older driver on a narrow, winding road. Does an old bias against older drivers suddenly return? At that point, it may be helpful to recognize that many older drivers are offered lower insurance rates for being good drivers with excellent safety records.

Unfortunately, middle- and younger-aged people are not alone in perpetuating the myths and stereotypes of aging. Often older persons themselves are their own worst culprits. This may not be intentional on their part, but rather the result of their buying into the myths and stereotypes of aging already so commonplace in our society. A frequent refrain in working with some older persons is "I'm too old to ____." An example of this is an 89-year-old relative who has Parkinson's disease and poor hearing. When she is asked if she is exercising, or invited to go somewhere away from the home, her usual response is, "I'm too old to do that." In reality, she does have some very real physical challenges due to her condition, but she is able to do so much more than she allows herself to do. This response is not completely due to her view of aging. It is also the result of her fear of falling and not being able to communicate effectively with others due to her hearing loss. Her quality of life could be so much better than it is today if she just had a more positive view of aging and greater confidence in her abilities. This is one of the greatest challenges we face in working with older persons, allowing them to have autonomy in making their own decisions (whether we agree or not) and still encouraging them.

A Personal Account by a Professional in the Aging Network

One of the earliest lessons that I learned in working with older persons came in my first job after graduate school, when at age 25 I had just been hired to do case coordination and support for frail homebound older persons. Armed with plenty of information, lots of energy, and a genuine zeal for meeting the needs of those I hoped to serve, I was shocked when the initial reaction of many of my homebound clients was less than favorable. I didn't understand why my reception was so poor, where in some cases clients even refused to let me enter their homes. I guess I didn't take into account the fact that I was young and how vulnerable some of these individuals felt in the situation. For some reason, I thought that I should simply be accepted because I was a professional in a helping role. In reality, what I quickly learned was that respect is not simply given, it has to be earned, and first and foremost, to earn respect one must give respect. This starts with the way that one addresses elders. It is important to address an older person in a way that he or she desires. Does she or he prefer to be addressed as Mrs. or Ms. or Mr. or by a professional title such as Dr. or to be addressed by her/his first name?

The language that we choose to use in addressing older persons is important. An October 6, 2008, article in the *New York Times* by John Leland speaks of what professionals call *elderspeak*. Elderspeak is the use of such sweetly belittling terms as "sweetie" and "dear" by those caring for older persons. In this article Dr. Becca Levy, associate professor of epidemiology and psychology at Yale University, is quoted as saying that research supports the fact that "little insults [like these] lead to more negative images of aging, and those who have more negative images of aging have worse functional health over time, including lower rates of survival." It is important to be careful about what one says and how one says it, because contrary to the old adage, words can hurt you.

Social Theories of Aging

Why is it important to examine the social theories of aging, and how can these theories help us to better understand and address the needs and issues of aging individuals? Social theories of aging help us to better understand the actions and reactions of aging individuals, as well as provide insight into how and why older people spend their time the way that they do later in life. Can each of these theories apply to all older persons? Of course not. As with any age group, everyone is unique and no two individuals are exactly alike. However, knowledge of these social theories does give us valuable insight into the actions and behaviors of those we attempt to serve within the aging community.

PART II

THE REALITIES OF GROWING OLDER

CHAPTER 3

Physical Changes and the Aging Process

The learning objectives of this chapter include understanding

- The three basic theories of aging: rate-of-living, aging as an adaptive program, and evolutionary senescence.
- The distinction between normal physical changes that accompany aging and the diseases and conditions that are more common with age.
- The normal physical changes that accompany aging.
- The adaptations that older people can make to accommodate normal physical changes.
- That attention to normal physical changes can prevent serious consequences for older people.

EVERYBODY IS A LITTLE DIFFERENT—EVEN THE OLD

Sam is 73 and works out several times a week. He lifts weights at least three times a week and jogs almost every day. He also runs in several marathons a year. He skis, swims, plays softball in a league for people age 70 and older, and is proud of the fact that he can do more pushups than his 19-year-old grandson. He walks with vigor and has a strong, firm voice and an even stronger handshake. He says he might reduce his vigorous schedule on his 90th birthday, or by then he might decide to take up skydiving!

Josephine is 77. She thinks that exercising is for young people and that older people who engage in physical activity are risking a heart attack. She says that by the time you get into your late 70s, you just don't do much, and she doesn't. Most days, Josephine just stays in her home and putters around.

BIOLOGICAL THEORIES OF AGING

Biologists will tell you that aging is a part of the circle of life. We all begin aging from the day we are born, with the process of aging proceeding at different rates for different body parts, functions, and abilities. From a biological point of view, aging has been defined as the gradual decline in physiological functions as a consequence of increasing chronological age. Beginning in the late 1800s, ideas about the causes of aging have proliferated to the point where as many as 300 such ideas have been put forward to date. Most of these ideas can be organized into three basic theories of aging: rate-of-living, aging as an adaptive program, and evolutionary senescence. To date, only the evolutionary senescence theory has sufficient evidence to support it, although it requires further development (Austad, 2009).

Rate-of-Living Theory

The basic idea of the rate-of-living theory is that biological aging is a consequence of accumulating tissue and organ damage, an inherent result of the body's use of energy to support cellular and molecular processes (Austad, 2009). The ideas that oxygen-free radicals or oxidative stress cause aging are among those related to this mechanistic theory. Much evidence refutes this theory, however. For example, the theory predicts that a faster metabolism should result in faster aging. But this is not the case for all species. In fact, based on the amount of energy expended daily per unit of body mass, some smaller animals who expend much more energy, nevertheless live significantly longer than larger animals who expend much less energy (Speakman, van Acker, & Harper, 2003).

Aging as an Adaptive Program

The basic idea that aging could be adaptive for the human species is that it is best to minimize competition for resources in a species by eliminating "old and decrepit" individuals for the benefit of the young (Weismann, 1882). The problem with this evolutionary point of view, however, is that if individuals did not age, they would not become decrepit. In addition to the circular thinking in the adaptive program argument, there are other problems with this theory. For this theory to be correct, group selection would have to be a prevalent phenomenon in all species, which is definitely not the case (Rose, 1991). The theory in its current state of development also cannot explain differences in aging rates between species, or why it is that large species generally live longer than do small species (Austad, 2009). So this theory, and ideas related to it, do not seem to be promising avenues for explaining the causes of aging.

Evolutionary Senescence Theory

Evolutionarily speaking, genes are selected for or selected against only if they affect the number and survival of offspring. The basic idea of the evolutionary senescence theory, a term coined by Austad (2009), is that actions of our genes over our lifetime cause aging. Two mechanisms for such gene actions have been proposed: mutation accumulation (Medawar, 1952) and antagonistic pleiotropy (Williams, 1957).

The mutation accumulation hypothesis proposes that genes with negative effects on survival in late life accumulate in the genome, causing the decline and damage that we associate with aging. Genes, whose negative effects on survival appear only later in life, will continue to exist in the genome and thus be passed from generation to generation because they do not affect offspring production. A good example of this principle can be found in Huntington's disease, an almost entirely inherited disease. Most people who are carriers of Huntington's have already had their children, and hence passed on the disease to the next generation, by the time they are diagnosed. Though Huntington's is a rare disease, its prevalence could be significantly reduced, if genetic testing became widely used.

The basic idea of the antagonistic pleiotropy hypothesis is that some genes that confer positive benefits early in life, and are therefore selected for, can also confer negative effects later in life. *Pleiotropy* means that one gene influences more than one observable characteristic of an organism. In antagonistic pleiotropy, one of these effects is beneficial and another is detrimental. One example comes from considering the possibility that one allele could have a positive effect on bone growth during an individual's early stages of development, but a negative effect of depositing excess calcium within arterial walls later in life (Williams, 1957), which could lead to high blood pressure and blood clots, increasing the risk of strokes and heart attacks. The preponderance of evidence currently supports antagonistic pleiotropy as the best explanation for evolutionary senescence.

Rate of Aging: Caloric Restriction, Human Growth Hormone, and Exercise

Whatever the cause of aging, there is much interest in discovering ways to decrease the rate at which aging takes place. There are very large differences among individuals in the aging process. Among the possible ways of changing the rate of aging, caloric restriction, the use of human growth hormone (hGH), and physical activity have all been suggested. Caloric restriction refers to the idea that perhaps aging can be slowed by decreasing the number of calories consumed each day. In fact, caloric restriction has been demonstrated to delay the aging process, prevent the onset of aging-related diseases, and increase the life span of several invertebrate organisms, as well as laboratory rats, although the reasons for these outcomes are not yet known (Xiang & He, 2011). Nevertheless, the extent to which reducing daily food consumption might increase humans' life span has yet to be determined. Furthermore, it is not at all clear that many people would look favorably on reducing their caloric intake to a level that might be necessary to slow the aging process. In the case of human growth hormone, its many dangerous side effects also do not bode well for it having a role in slowing individuals' aging processes. Physical activity, however, has much promise in keeping people healthy throughout their life span. The importance of physical activity for older adults is discussed in the chapter on Health, Wellness, and Normal Aging.

NORMAL PHYSICAL CHANGES THAT ACCOMPANY AGING AND ADAPTATIONS TO THEM

Most researchers who focus on the aging processes have pointed out that normal aging can be differentiated from the diseases and conditions that are more common as we age, for example, arthritis and heart disease. Furthermore, there is no specified common timetable for human aging; instead, there are enormous individual differences in the aging process, and all older people do not experience all the documented possible changes.

Nevertheless, as people grow older, changes tend to occur throughout the physical systems of the body that may be hardly noticeable at first. Among the physical changes that can be expected to occur as we age, some, such as gray hair and wrinkling skin, are more visible, while others, such as hearing loss and hypothermia, may be less visible.

Hair

One of the most noticeable physical changes that occur with aging is hair color turning gray or white. No one knows why specific hairs turn gray or white and others do not. Within each hair follicle (tubelike organs in the skin) are cells that add color to the hair shaft. Each specific hair grows for about three years, then rests for several months before it starts growing again. As one ages, the color-producing cells cease functioning, and the hair grows out gray or white. At the present time, there is no known process to help those cells continue producing their original color. It is known that there is a genetic component to the action of those cells, and as a result, persons whose ancestors' hair turned gray early in life have a higher probability of developing gray hair (Saxon, Etten, & Perkins, 2010). Many older adults adapt to this change by coloring or dyeing their hair.

Skin

As people grow older, their skin begins to wrinkle. For most people that process begins in their 20s. The process is accelerated by smoking and frequent exposure to the sun. The wrinkling process also relates to a person's genetic heritage. The skin of blonde, pale-skinned people tends to wrinkle sooner than it does for those with darker skin. In addition, as a person ages their skin becomes drier and more susceptible to cracking. That process is accelerated by dry air and exposure to the sun (Saxon et al., 2010).

Adaptations for age-related changes to our skin abound. One is to minimize the effects of the sun by avoiding prolonged direct exposure and using a sunscreen lotion that offers good protection from ultraviolet A and B solar radiation. Tanning parlors are also something to be avoided. Rooms should be kept moist so that dry skin will not crack. If a humidifier is unaffordable, pans of water placed on a heat register can be used to put moisture into the air. In addition, liberal use of creams and ointments softens dry skin thereby prevent cracking. Massages and facials are excellent choices for hydrating the skin. Manicures and pedicures can also be helpful because they involve massaging creams into the hands and feet.

Temperature Control

Elderly people do not adjust to temperature changes as well as young people , and they are more likely to take prescription medications or have a chronic medical condition that changes their body's ability to regulate its temperature. For these reasons, older people are more prone to negative effects of cold temperatures, which can result in hypothermia, and also to hot temperatures, which can result in heat stress. Both hypothermia and severe heat stress can be fatal, so they require immediate medical attention.

Hypothermia

With age comes a loss of subcutaneous fat, and a diminished flow of blood to the skin and extremities, so there is an increased danger of hypothermia for older persons. Hypothermia is a reduction in body temperature, with a danger that the body temperature will get so low that a person's life may become endangered. Research seems to indicate that the danger of hypothermia among older persons is much greater than previously believed. Hypothermia can even result in death, although it is often overlooked as a cause of death. Thus, it is important to know the symptoms of hypothermia. One should be alert for the *umbles*—stumbles, mumbles, fumbles, and grumbles. Check for confusion or sleepiness; slow, slurred speech or shallow breathing; weak pulse; irregular heartbeat; a lot of shivering or no shivering; stiffness in the arms or legs; poor control over body movements; or slow reactions. Whenever an older person has any of these symptoms and their temperature drops to 96°F or below, immediate medical attention should be sought (National Institute on Aging, 2010).

Prevention of hypothermia among older adults, especially those aged 75 or older, is quite simple: Room temperatures should be maintained at no less than 68°F, and warm outdoor clothing appropriate for the temperature should be worn when temperatures fall. It should be noted that a room temperature that is comfortable for older people may seem too hot for those who are younger. There is a special problem in nursing facilities where a comfortable room temperature for the residents is usually too warm for the younger, active staff (Aging in Michigan, 1992). Older adults also need to be sure to wear adequate clothing in cold temperatures.

Heat Stress

Heat stroke is the most serious heat-related illness. It occurs when the body becomes unable to control its temperature. Warning signs vary but may include an extremely high body temperature (above 103°F); red, hot, and dry skin, with no sweating; a rapid, strong pulse; a throbbing headache; dizziness; and nausea. Heat exhaustion is a milder form of heat-related illness that can develop after several days of exposure to high temperatures and inadequate or unbalanced replacement of fluids. Warning signs may include heavy sweating, paleness, muscle cramps, tiredness, weakness, dizziness, headache, nausea or vomiting, fainting, cool and moist skin, a fast and weak pulse, and fast and shallow breathing. Prevention of heat stress includes drinking cool, non-alcoholic beverages; resting; taking a cool shower or bath; wearing lightweight clothing; not engaging in strenuous activities; and, if possible, seeking an air-conditioned environment or remaining indoors in the heat of the day. For any signs of severe heat stress, medical attention should be sought immediately (Centers for Disease Control and Prevention, 2009).

Vision

Only 18% of older adults report any trouble seeing (*Older Americans 2010*). Even so, several changes occur in our eyes as we age, including presbyopia (farsightedness), dry eyes, and cataracts, all of which can be dealt with relatively simply nowadays. These changes usually occur after the age of 40, but younger people can also experience them. There are numerous ways to adapt to aging eyes so that a good quality of life can be maintained throughout the life span. (More serious eye conditions, including glaucoma and macular degeneration, are discussed in Chapter 14.)

Presbyopia/Farsightedness

Presbyopia, or farsightedness, usually begins to develop when a person is about 40 years of age. Presbyopia is a normal condition, not a disease, and should not disrupt the daily lives of most people. As we age, our eyes begin to lose the ability to adjust for different distances, and eventually most people will need bifocals or trifocals to maintain good vision. Presbyopia also means that as a person grows older, it is more difficult to adjust to darkness and to glare, and it takes more time to adapt to changes in light and darkness. These changes in vision make nighttime driving more hazardous for older people.

Cataracts

Cataracts are very common in older adults, though they can occur in children too. Research has shown that the risk of cataracts is related to frequent sun exposure, which has its greatest effects on younger people (Neale, Purdie, Hirst, & Green, 2003). Protecting our eyes from intense sunlight throughout our life span will decrease susceptibility to cataracts. Eventually, though, most people will develop cataracts if they live long enough. Cataracts result in increasingly blurred or misty vision as the eye's lens becomes milky. Some cataracts grow larger or denser over time, causing severe vision changes. These cataracts can cause loss of independence for older adults because decreased vision may affect driving, working, reading, or hobbies. In the United States, cataract surgery, which replaces the clouded lens with a synthetic one, is the most commonly performed surgery in adults over age 65. Its success rate is very high. Cataract growth can be slowed by protecting our eyes from the sun and from sunlamps, eating healthy foods, limiting alcoholic drinks, and avoiding smoking (Kline & Wenchen, 2005).

Dry Eyes

Some people develop dry eyes as they grow older. This dryness can also cause redness in the eye. Mild cases can usually be treated with over-the-counter artificial tear solutions. Optometrists can diagnosis and recommend other treatments for more serious cases of dry eye (American Optometric Association, n.d.).

Some age-related changes in vision can be dealt with by wearing bifocals or trifocals for presbyopia, by surgery for cataracts, and by using artificial tears for dry eyes. Most other changes are best dealt with by changes to our environment. Our built environment has been constructed using parameters that work best for young people. Thus, the amount of light, the existence of stairs and escalators, and the typical size of print, for example, have all been determined for the society we used to be—a society of mostly young people. With our changing demographics, and our desire to make our environment more accessible to people with disabilities, it is time for us to make changes to our existing environment, and rethink parameters for future built environments, to accommodate people of all ages and ability levels.

As we age, we require more light to see as well as we did when we were younger (as much as a threefold increase). Thus, simply increasing the amount of light assists older eyes to see better. Depth perception is also affected, so constructing environments that clearly differentiate changes in levels, for example on stairways, is a good way to increase visibility of those changes, and thus help decrease falls in older people. Varying textures, materials, and colors is often helpful in signaling level changes, too. And, ramps are preferable, especially to escalators, for moving from one level to another because they are much safer for everyone.

A few serious conditions can develop more readily in older people, and thus require periodic eye examinations by qualified professionals (e.g., opthalmologists). These serious vision conditions—macular degeneration, glaucoma, and retinopathy—are discussed in the Medical Care chapter. In general, a complete eye examination is recommended for those older than age 45, and then follow-up examinations every 2 to 4 years thereafter.

Hearing

As we age, limitations in our hearing become much more common than limitations in our vision. In 2008, 28% of people age 65 to 74 years reported trouble hearing, and that percentage rose to 60 for people age 85 and over. Older men are almost 50% more likely to have hearing problems than are older women (*Older Americans 2010*). As people grow older, a condition known as presbycusis occurs. This refers to a loss in hearing brought about by various, not well-understood, age-related changes. Most people lose the ability to hear high-pitched sounds first, which leads to poor hearing when there is background noise, and major difficulty hearing women's and children's voices, and distinguishing different words because consonants, such as Bs and Ps, and Cs and Ks, tend to be higher pitched than are vowels. Presbycusis can occur because of changes in the inner ear, auditory nerve, middle ear, or outer ear. Some of its causes are aging, loud noise, heredity, head injury, infection, illness, certain prescription drugs, and circulation problems such as high blood pressure.

An important factor in hearing loss is the increasing isolation of the person with impaired hearing. For most people, hearing loss is gradual. At the beginning of the loss of hearing, it is not unusual for people to be irritable, to seem to be distracted from conversation, and to be unsociable. Often a person may be unaware of the hearing loss and frequently give inappropriate answers to questions that he or she did not hear adequately. As a result, relationships may become strained as others believe him or her to be a bit confused. As this process continues, the person may begin to feel rejection conveyed in the nonverbal communication of others, and there is a real danger that depression may set in (Gopinath et al., 2009), leading to a cyclical process in which he or she becomes even more isolated and more depressed.

Hearing is an essential component of well-being, especially for people who have enjoyed normal hearing for most of their lives. Losing the ability to hear adequately in the routine activities of daily life can be very detrimental. Older adults with moderate to severe hearing loss report more difficulty with tasks such as preparing meals, shopping, and using the telephone than do those with no hearing loss (Gopinath et al., 2012). Once daily activities such as these become compromised, independence and quality of life can be reduced.

Adaptations to age-related changes in hearing involve those communicating with older people as well as the older people themselves. In communicating with people who have hearing problems, it is helpful to speak slowly and enunciate clearly. Shouting should be avoided. It is beneficial to speak face-to-face so the person can see lip movements. Because much communication is nonverbal, one can attempt to communicate emotions, moods, and acceptance by body language and facial expressions. It is always helpful to eliminate background noise, including noise created by fans, air conditioners, and other appliances. It is important that the acoustics in an auditorium be very good for a presentation to older persons. In addition, it is wise to use good sound equipment, because most people experience some hearing loss as they grow older.

Older persons who believe they are suffering hearing loss can benefit from having a hearing checkup with an audiologist or with an ear, nose, and throat specialist. If there is significant organic reason for hearing loss, many aids are available today that can help. It is important for a person to be diagnosed by a certified specialist, such an audiologist, and not by a person who only sells hearing aids. Unfortunately, most people who could benefit from some type of hearing aid do not have one. In the first national study that included audiometric testing of a large, representative sample, Chien and Lin (2012) analyzed data from the *National Health and Nutritional Examination Surveys* (NHANES) on hearing loss and hearing aid use. Of the 27 million Americans 50 years of age or older with a hearing loss, they found that only 3.8 million (14%) used hearing aids. A variety of reasons have been suggested for the relatively low-level use of hearing aids. Some people feel that they cannot afford them—hearing aids are expensive and are not covered by Medicare. Others are concerned about the stigma associated with wearing a hearing aid. There are also those who think their hearing loss is relatively minor, and they would rather not bother with hearing aids, which do not restore the entire range of lost frequencies and still do not eliminate distracting background sounds in a noisy environment. At first, a hearing aid may seem unnatural and strange because it amplifies sounds other than speech. It usually takes some time to adjust to a hearing aid, and families and friends, as well as the user of the aid, will need patience during the adjustment process. Modern hearing aids are marvels of technological advancement. Many types are available, including ones that fit in the ear canal (completely or partly), in the ear, or behind the ear. Most have been miniaturized so that they are comfortable to wear and are cosmetically acceptable. Hearing aids can be indistinguishable in their appearance from earpieces for electronic devices, so the stigma of wearing a hearing aid may disappear in the near future!

Smell and Taste

Research suggests that our sense of smell becomes impaired with age, and to a lesser extent, taste sensitivity is also affected (Murphy, 2008). About 25% of persons aged 65 to 80 lose some ability to smell. After the age of 80, this increases to 50%. Usually people do not begin to lose their sense of smell until they are in their 50s. Apparently, what happens is that the sense receptors for odor in the upper nose begin to lose their ability to function because of disease or injury. In addition, odor-related brain activation is significantly reduced in normally aging persons (Cerf-Ducastel & Murphy, 2003).

When it comes to taste, in comparison to smell, much less is known about changes that may take place as we age or their causes, in part because distinguishing the effects of aging from the effects of a disease or medications can be very difficult. Some studies have found a decline in the number of taste buds while others have not, but in general, taste seems to remain a relatively intact sense as we age (Seiberling & Conley, 2004). Our sense of taste is important for the pleasures we derive from consuming good food as well as for helping us to avoid consuming harmful substances. It is important to note, too, that our smell and taste senses interact. For example, a person might prefer saltier food because increased saltiness can make up for a reduced ability to smell flavor components.

Potentially serious problems can arise as a result of changes in our sense of smell and taste. A reduction in these sensory abilities can result in changes in food intake and selection, and, consequently nutritional status. Changes in salt perception can negatively impact the likelihood that hypertensive patients will maintain a low-salt diet, and changes in sweet perception can negatively impact the likelihood that diabetics will limit their sugar intake. Some older persons have difficulty smelling gas leaks, smoke, and spoiled food. At the same time, they lose the pleasure of smelling flowers, perfumes, and well-cooked and seasoned foods, which can lead to a diminished quality of life (Seiberling & Conley, 2004).

Adaptations for older adults with a decreased sense of smell include ensuring that smoke detectors are in place and working, and paying attention to food safety guidelines as well as expiration dates on food products. Friends, neighbors, and family members can be helpful in detecting problematic smells or tastes, too. When taste seems to be affected, the enjoyment of food can be enhanced by adding spices and incorporating a diversity of food flavors, textures, and temperatures during meal preparation. "Eye appeal" can also positively affect enjoyment, so garnishes, variety in food colors, and placement of food on a plate should not be overlooked.

For additional information on tips for adapting to common aging-related changes in vision, hearing, touch, taste, and smell, consult the Practical Application at the end of Part II of this textbook.

Feet

By the time we reach old age, our feet have had years of wear and tear, so good foot care becomes especially important. Checking regularly for cuts, blisters, and ingrown toenails is a good practice; people with diabetes should check their feet every day. Raising feet when sitting helps keep blood moving to the feet. Stretching, walking, and gentle foot massages can serve a similar function. Warm footbaths are helpful, too. Wearing comfortable shoes that fit well can prevent many foot problems. Sometimes, foot problems are the first sign of more serious medical conditions such as arthritis, diabetes, and nerve or circulatory disorders. In addition, foot pain contributes to falls in older adults (Mickle, Munro, Lord, Menz, & Steele, 2010). If there seems to be a foot problem, a podiatrist (foot specialist) can be consulted.

The Urinary Tract

Although some age-related changes occur in our kidneys, in the absence of disease, they usually continue to function quite well throughout the later years of life. "Exercise; proper diet, including adequate fluid intake; limited use of medications; and quitting smoking help the urinary system maintain adequate functioning" (Saxon et al., 2010, p. 218). Bladder capacity does decline by 30% to 40%, but this is not a symptom of disease, it is simply a result of the aging process (Saxon et al., 2010). Most elderly persons need to get up in the night to empty their bladder. Older persons should know that having to arise in the night to go to the bathroom is not in itself an indication of any serious disease. If they have to arise more frequently than twice a night, however, they ought to see a health care professional.

The *micturition reflex* changes as one ages. Micturition is the signal a person receives when he or she has to urinate. For a young person, that signal is usually sent when the bladder is about half full. As a result, young people have some time left before they must absolutely get to a bathroom. Not so for the elderly. The signal to urinate is given when the bladder is nearly full. Obviously that means when they receive the signal, there is not much time for delay. The reduced capacity of the bladder, coupled with a delayed signal to urinate, can lead to problems of frequent urination and the need to urinate immediately (Saxon et al., 2010).

Some older persons also have a problem with dribbling urine or urinary incontinence (UI). This can be viewed as both physiologically and psychologically damaging. There is a higher probability that women will have incontinence than will men, likely the result of childbirth and the associated weakening of the bladder outlet and pelvic musculofascial attachments. Although UI is more common in older adults, people of any age can experience it. The most common type is stress incontinence, which is brought about by a laugh, a cough, a sneeze, or lifting. In addition to stress incontinence, some older persons suffer from urge incontinence, the sudden urge to go to the bathroom without time to get there. Others suffer from overflow incontinence, a condition in which the bladder becomes too full and urine leaks out (Saxon et al., 2010).

There is an increased chance of urinary tract infections as a person grows older. Symptoms of a bladder infection include cloudy or bloody urine, a low-grade fever, pain, or a burning sensation during urination, and a strong need to urinate often, even right after the bladder has been emptied. If the infection spreads to the kidneys, symptoms may include chills and shaking or night sweats; fatigue, fever above 100°F; mental changes or confusion; nausea and vomiting; and side, back, or groin pain. In either case, a health care professional should be consulted for diagnosis and treatment. A course of antibiotics usually clears up infections fairly quickly.

Older people, especially older men, are at higher risk of developing kidney stones than are younger people. Kidney stones are hard masses that form in the kidney out of substances in the urine. They may be as small as a grain of sand or as large as a pearl. Some stones are even as big as golf balls! Most kidney stones pass out of the body with urine. But sometimes a stone will not pass by itself and then medical attention is necessary. The larger the stone, the more likely it is to cause severe pain, in the back or side, that will not go away. Other symptoms include fever and chills, vomiting, urine that smells bad or looks cloudy, a burning sensation during urination, or blood in the urine. The most common treatment is extracorporeal shockwave lithotripsy (ESWL), in which a machine sends shock waves to the stone and breaks it into smaller pieces, which can then be passed out of the body in urine. The best way to prevent kidney stones is to drink lots of water, which helps to flush away the substances that form kidney stones (National Kidney & Urologic Diseases Information Clearinghouse, 2011). Producing at least a liter (slightly more than a quart) of urine per day is indicative of drinking adequate fluids.

Awareness of age-related changes in the urinary tract, including its reduced capacity, can also be helpful because then older people can plan to regularly visit lavatory facilities, and avoid foods and drinks that may cause them to urinate more often, thereby avoiding the incontinence that might ensue. Another adaptation older people can make to changes in their urinary tracts is to learn to do kegel exercises to strengthen pelvic muscles, which can even prevent urinary incontinence.

The Musculoskeletal System: Bones and Muscles

Bones play many roles in the body. They provide structure, protect organs, anchor muscles, and store calcium. Beginning early in life, engaging in regular weight-bearing physical activity and eating foods that are rich in calcium and vitamin D (which helps the body to absorb calcium) build strong bones, optimize bone mass, and may reduce the risk of osteoporosis later in life. Bone thinning, or loss of bone mineral density, begins at about age 35 when the body begins to reabsorb bone cells faster than it makes new bone. Bone thinning, though, does not have to result in osteoporosis, a disease that weakens bones, making them more likely to break. It is important for young people, and especially young women who are more susceptible to osteoporosis than are young men, to reach their peak bone mass (genetic potential for bone density) in order to maintain bone health throughout life. A person with high bone mass as a young adult will be more likely to have a higher bone mass later in life. Inadequate calcium consumption and physical activity early on could result in a failure to achieve peak bone mass in adulthood, resulting in an increased risk for osteoporosis. Chapter 4 has more information on preventing osteoporosis.

Skeletal muscles help our body to move, keep our body upright and standing tall, and give us the power to lift things. Some even say that "the speed at which we age is down to how fast we allow our skeletal muscle to erode based on the physical and dietary decisions we make each day" (http://sarcopenia.com). Unfortunately, muscle mass begins to decrease in middle adulthood. Arts, Pillen, Overeem, Schelhaas, and Zwarts (2007) measured quadricep and bicep muscles in a sample of healthy men and women between the ages of 2 months and 90 years. Between 40 and 90 years of age, quadricep muscle thickness decreased by 50% in men and 30% in women; bicep muscles fared not much better, their thickness decreased by 30% in men and 20% in women.

Such declines in muscle mass, and the resulting declines in strength are associated with sarcopenia (from the Greek word for loss of flesh). Although a full understanding of the causes of sarcopenia does not yet exist, it is known that the likelihood of acquiring the condition increases with age and is related to the cumulative loss of musculoskeletal mass and strength due to insufficient exercise. Preventing saropenia, not surprisingly, requires muscle training of some kind. Resistance training, using free weights, resistance machines, or isometrics, has been the exercise method of choice for improving muscle strength. Although older adults seem to require more training than do younger adults, with the right exercise program, they are nevertheless able to increase muscle and maintain it as well as, or better than, their younger counterparts who do not train (Bickel, Cross, & Bamman, 2011). Research is also showing that power training may be even more effective in improving functional independence because it enhances older adults' ability to carry out *activities of daily living* (ADLs; Hazell, Kenno, & Jakobi, 2007). Of course, older people should consult their health care provider prior to beginning a new exercise program. Finally, mounting evidence suggests that a moderate increase in dietary protein to 1.0 to 1.2g/kg of weight per day for older adults (0.8 g/kg per day is currently recommended for adults aged 19 and older), distributed across the day's meals, has beneficial effects on both bone and muscle health (Gaffney-Stomberg, Insogna, Rodriguez, & Kerstetter, 2009; "New findings on frailty and diet," n.d.).

Menopause

Menopause, the cessation of menstruation, is a normal part of every woman's life. Symptoms can begin several years earlier than the last period occurs. They include changes in menstruation (e.g., increasing variation in length of the cycle, lighter or heavier bleeding), hot flashes (sudden feelings of heat, usually in the upper part of the body, lasting between 30 seconds and 20 minutes), vaginal drying, trouble sleeping, and mood changes. Some symptoms of menopause can last for months or years after. Changing levels of estrogen and progesterone are related to these symptoms. The average age for menopause is 51, but for some women it happens in their 40s, and some have it in their late 50s.

The majority of women experience some symptoms, though not all women find them bothersome. Hot flashes and night sweats can be alleviated by sleeping in a cool room, drinking cold water or juice when a hot flash is coming on, dressing in layers, and using sheets and clothing that let the skin "breathe." Exercise and slow, deep breathing may also help reduce hot flashes. Low-dose birth control pills will make menstrual cycles and flow more regular and also help with hot flashes. A water-based lubricant (but not petroleum jelly) may relieve vaginal discomfort, enabling a normal sex life. Sleep problems may be relieved by adopting good sleep hygiene practices, such as adhering to a bedtime routine and creating a comfortable sleeping environment (see more suggestions in Chapter 4).

Some women require medication. Menopausal hormone therapy (MHT; or estrogen replacement therapy [ERT] or hormone replacement therapy [HRT]) was a widely recommended treatment for menopausal symptoms until it was learned that side effects may include an increased risk of breast cancer and heart disease. The current recommendation for those women who can benefit most from MHT is for them, in consultation with their physician, to take the lowest dose of a combined estrogen–progesterone formula for the shortest time that is consistent with the reason for the therapy (National Institute on Aging, 2009). Like all prescription medications, MHT should be re-evaluated regularly.

Sleep

Older adults need about the same amount of sleep as do young adults—7 to 9 hours each night. On the other hand, sleep patterns change with age. Seniors often need more time to fall asleep as they grow older. The amount of time spent in REM (rapid eye movement) sleep and non-REM sleep (the deepest and most restful sleep) shifts as we get older, with a decrease of time in deep sleep. Compared to younger people, seniors tend to sleep more lightly and awaken more quickly in response to noises. Once awake, they often find it harder to get back to sleep.

It is not clear how many of the changes in sleep result from the normal aging process or from factors such as medications, lack of exercise, napping during the daytime, or disease. Seniors tend to take more medications than do younger people, and medications and their side effects can impair sleep or even stimulate wakefulness. A sedentary lifestyle can lead to sleepiness all the time, or a lack of sleepiness. Sleep may be disturbed more frequently in old age by an increased probability of needing to urinate during the night, by rhythmic leg movements, or by sleep-disordered breathing such as snoring or sleep apnea. Older persons may suffer from pain due to arthritic or other medical problems. In addition, psychological stress brought about by significant life changes, such as the death of a loved one or moving, can inhibit sleep.

It is not a part of normal aging, however, for older persons to be sleepy and to feel the need to sleep during the day. Among the adaptations to age-related sleep changes is to maintain daytime activities with some exposure to fresh air, if possible. In addition, for people of all ages good sleep hygiene, which is discussed in Chapter 4, can go a long way towards regularly obtaining a good night's sleep.

SUGGESTED RESOURCES

Center of Design for an Aging Society: http://www.centerofdesign.org
> The Center's website provides guidance on designing homes, and modifying existing homes, to maximize older adults' health, wellness, and independence.

Hearing Loss Association of America (HLAA): http://www.shhh.org
> HLAA provides assistance and resources for people with hearing loss and their families to learn how to adjust to living with hearing loss. HLAA is working to eradicate the stigma associated with hearing loss and to raise public awareness about the need for prevention, treatment, and regular hearing screenings throughout life.

National Association for Continence: http://www.nafc.org
> This nonprofit association's goal is to de-stigmatize, promote prevention, and educate the community about incontinence. It provides a national database for individuals seeking support and diagnosis of incontinence and incontinence-related disorders.

National Eye Institute: http://www.nei.nih.gov
> Established by Congress in 1968 to protect and prolong the vision of the American people, NEI's research leads to sight-saving treatments, reduces visual impairment and blindness, and improves the quality of life for people of all ages.

National Heart, Lung, and Blood Institute (NHLBI): http://ww.nhlbi.nih.gov
> The NHLBI's website has information on research, training, and education programs to promote the prevention and treatment of heart, lung, and blood diseases and enhance the health of all individuals so that they can live longer and more fulfilling lives.

CHAPTER 4

Health, Wellness, and Normal Aging

The learning objectives of this chapter include understanding

- The value of proper nutrition, physical activity, and good sleep hygiene in the health of older adults.
- Nutrition guidelines for older adults, as contained in *MyPlate for Older Adults*, and how they differ from those for younger adults.
- The four vaccines that all older adults should have.
- Basic screening tests for diseases and conditions that are preventable or for which there is good prognosis if detected early.
- Key negative health behaviors to avoid to decrease the risks for chronic diseases.

SENIORS AGING HEALTHFULLY

When she turned 60, Pearl decided she wanted to stay healthy and active as long as possible. She was careful about what she ate. She became more physically active. Now she takes a long, brisk walk three or four times a week. In bad weather, she joins the mall walkers at the local shopping mall. When it's nice outside, Pearl works in her garden. When she was younger, Pearl stopped smoking and started using a seatbelt. Now she's using the Internet to find healthy recipes. Last month, at the age of 84, she danced at her granddaughter's wedding!

ENHANCING AND MAINTAINING HEALTH IN THE LATER YEARS

Life expectancy has risen dramatically in many countries around the world, including the United States. Simply being alive for more years, though, is not a particularly worthy achievement. When it comes to aging, everyone's goal is to age in the best possible health.

No one wants to live a long life in poor health, or in increasingly poorer health. Of course, to a large extent genetic make-up influences risks for different health conditions, and individuals have little or no control over many these risks. Common health problems, however, are strongly influenced by health behaviors, including those related to nutrition and physical activity, and health literacy. In addition, health behaviors affect the rate at which aging occurs and the quality of life that accompanies aging.

The majority (75%) of people 65 years of age and over who are not institutionalized rate their own health as good, very good, or excellent. Even among elders who are 85 years of age and over, more than 66% report good to excellent health (*Older Americans 2010*). Poor health is indeed experienced by many older adults, but clearly they are in the minority. Despite this fact, ageism and other factors result in many people assuming that aging is always accompanied by poor health.

Maintaining, and even enhancing, health and wellness is an active, lifelong process that requires awareness of one's state of health and wellness, and continually learning and making changes to maximize it. Keep in mind, of course, that in order to engage in this lifelong process, opportunities for healthy choices and healthy living must be readily available. In addition, there are motivational factors that influence health and wellness behaviors, which are discussed in the Practical Applications at the end of Part II of this textbook. Positive health behaviors are things to do to improve or maintain health, and negative health behaviors are things to avoid, or stop doing to improve or maintain health. Among positive health behaviors are eating nutritious foods, regularly engaging in physical exercise, and following a regular schedule for immunizations and screening tests. Among negative health behaviors are smoking, drinking excessive amounts of alcohol, and tanning.

HEALTH PROMOTION

Health promotion and measures to prevent illnesses and health care problems are important at all ages of life. But younger people can get away with paying much less attention to positive health behaviors than can older people. As people age, neglecting their health begins to take its toll on them.

Nutrition

Good nutrition is important for everyone, but it is particularly important to older people. It directly relates to their health and wellness. Properly nourished older adults enjoy a higher quality of life, live longer, and have decreased disability, fewer infections, wounds that heal faster, fewer secondary medical complications, and shorter hospital stays than older adults who are undernourished (Challa, Sharkey, Chen, & Phillips, 2007). As researchers learn more about nutrition as well as the aging process, more information is becoming available about the unique nutritional needs of people as they age.

MyPlate for Older Adults

The first food guide designed specifically for older adults was published by researchers at Tufts University in 1999 (Russell, Rasmussen, & Lichtenstein, 1999). The current guide, which has been updated to be consistent with *MyPlate*, the newest U.S. Department of Agriculture (USDA) food guide, is depicted in Figure 4.1 ("Scientists unveil MyPlate for Older Adults," 2011). The guidelines for older adults differ from those aimed at the general adult population. For example, they include different forms of food that can have

FIGURE 4.1 MyPlate for Older Adults.

Used with permission. Copyright 2011 Tufts University.

advantages for older adults, such as frozen and canned fruits and vegetables, which can be easier to prepare and last longer than do fresh fruits and vegetables.

The guidelines for older adults also contain seven major recommendations for maximizing the value of nutritional intake to maintain or improve health (Lichtenstein, Rasmussen, Yu, Epstein, & Russell, 2008). The first two recommendations are related: One is to reduce food consumption, thereby reducing calories, and the second is to eat nutrient-rich foods. As metabolism slows and energy needs decrease with age, the need for calories decreases. Women with relatively low physical activity may need only 1,600 calories per day, but women who are fairly active may need up to 2,200 calories per day. Comparable numbers of calories for men range from 2,000 to 2,800 calories per day. However, even though less food is needed, requirements for nutrients remain the same (except for iron in postmenopausal women). This means eating more foods that are high in a variety of nutrients and eating less fat, sugar, and refined foods. The third recommendation is to eat foods that are lower in fat and saturated fat.

The fourth recommendation is to eat foods high in fiber. Fiber is found in foods from plants, so some ways to add fiber to diets are eating cooked dry beans, peas, and lentils often; choosing whole fruit over fruit juice; eating whole-grain breads and cereals; and, leaving skins on fruits and vegetables, if possible. Eating more fiber may prevent stomach or intestine problems, such as constipation, and it may also help lower cholesterol as well as blood sugar. It is better to get fiber from food than dietary supplements. Increasing the amount of fiber slowly helps to avoid unwanted gas.

The fifth recommendation is to be aware of the potential need for supplements, in particular, calcium and vitamins D and B12. Both calcium and vitamin D are needed to keep bones fracture free. Postmenopausal women need as much as 1,200 milligrams of calcium per day, and older men need 1,000 milligrams per day. No more than 500 milligrams of calcium should be taken at one time because that is all the body can digest at once. Much research suggests that vitamin D is also very helpful in conjunction with calcium. Dowd and Stafford (2008), authors of the book, *The Vitamin D Cure*, contend that new research demonstrates that vitamin D helps the body protect against osteoporosis, high blood pressure, and cancer. Vitamin D deficiency can lead to a variety of immuno-related diseases, fatigue, Seasonal Affective Disorder (SAD), and headaches. Also, aging skin does not make vitamin D as readily as younger skin does, so a vitamin D supplement may be in order. An adequate amount of vitamin D can be obtained by adults of all ages with a balance of sun exposure and supplements, while avoiding too much exposure. Ten to 15 minutes of exposure to the sun, several times a week, is probably adequate for most persons. Because of decreased gastric juices, it is recommended that those over 50 years of age take a vitamin B12 supplement to avoid the anemia and nerve damage that result from deficiencies of this vitamin. Total vegetarians especially must supplement with B12 throughout their lives.

The sixth recommendation is to drink plenty of fluids. With age, some of the sense of thirst is lost, so older adults should not wait until they feel thirsty. It is important for them to drink plenty of liquids such as water (several large glasses per day), juice, milk, and soup. Urine should be pale yellow. If it is a bright or dark yellow, more liquids need to be consumed. Seniors often stop drinking liquids in order to control their urine; however, health care professionals can give them much better ways to alleviate any problems of bladder control. Drinking plenty of liquids also helps fiber move through the intestines. The seventh recommendation included with *MyPlate for Older Adults* is to be physically active.

In addition to these seven recommendations, there are two additional matters to pay attention to when it comes to seniors' nutrition: One is protein and the other is antioxidants. Individuals need a bit more protein as they get older, 1.0 g/kg of weight rather than the 0.8 g/kg that they needed as younger adults. For example, an older person weighing 154 pounds (154/2.2 = 70 kg) should consume 70 g of protein per day. Four ounces of chicken, sirloin steak, ground beef, or canned tuna provide between 31 g and 35 g of protein; one cup of cooked lentils, lima beans, or kidney beans provides 16 g of protein; and one cup of 2% cottage cheese provides 32 g of protein. Antioxidants are natural substances found in food that may help protect against some diseases. Antioxidants and common sources of them include beta carotene (dark orange and dark green fruits and vegetables), selenium (seafood, liver, meat, and grains), vitamin C (citrus fruits, peppers, tomatoes, and berries), and vitamin E (wheat germ; nuts; sesame seeds; and canola, olive, and peanut oils).

Specific quantities of nutrients for active 75-year-old men and women are listed in Table 4.1. Table 4.2 focuses on nutrients, listing recommended daily allowances (RDA), sources, and functions of nutrients.

Eating Well on a Tight Budget

For many seniors with limited budgets, it might take some thought and planning to be able to pay for the foods they should eat. Here are some suggestions. First, seniors can buy only the foods they need, planning meals and checking the supply of staples such as flour and cereal prior to shopping. In case cooking or going out are not good options, having some canned or frozen food available is an alternative. Powdered, canned, or ultra-pasteurized milk in a shelf carton can be stored easily. Large packages of food can be shared with a friend. Frozen vegetables in bags save money because small amounts can be used and the rest can be kept frozen. If a package of meat or fresh produce is too

TABLE 4.1 Food Pattern Recommendations for Active 75-Year-Old Men and Women

	WOMEN	MEN
Energy	2,000 kcal	2,600 kcal
Grains	6 oz	9 oz
Vegetables	2.5 cups	3.5 cups
Fruits	2 cups	2 cups
Milk	3 cups	3 cups
Lean meat & beans	5.5 oz	6.5 oz
Oils	6 tsp	8 tsp
Discretionary calories	267 kcal	410 kcal

Source: Adapted from Lichtenstein et al. (2008).

large, a store employee may be able to repackage it in a smaller size. Other ways to keep food costs down include using store brands, which often cost less than name brands; planning meals around food that is on sale; and dividing leftovers into small servings, labeling, dating, and freezing them to use within a few months.

Funded through the federal Administration on Aging, in some communities, senior centers serve lunch up to 5 days a week at no cost to those age 60 and over. Low- or no-cost meals are also often available for older people at a community center, church, or school. This is a chance for seniors to eat good food and to be with other people. In some locales, home-delivered meals are available for those who are homebound. The federal Supplemental Nutrition Assistance Program (SNAP, formerly, the Food Stamp Program) helps people with low incomes buy groceries.

Nutrition Services

Adequate nutrition services for elderly people include screening, assessment, counseling, and therapy. All of these are important because even when older adults seem to know a lot about nutrition, their ability to use that information in making dietary choices is limited (Hand, Antrim, & Crabtree, 1990).

Nutrition services can be provided to older adults through parts A and B of the Medicare program, the state Medicaid home- and community-based services waiver program, and the food programs of the federal Administration on Aging. Unfortunately, some individual local carriers for federal government programs may not pay for nutrition services. As a result, the very services that could help older people maintain their health, independence, and quality of life may not be available in some communities.

Physical Activity and Exercise

Regular exercise and physical activity are important to the physical, emotional, and mental health of almost everyone, including older adults. Being physically active can help seniors continue to do the things they enjoy and stay independent as they age. Regular physical activity over long periods of time can produce long-term health benefits. That's why health experts say that older adults should be active every day to maintain their health. In addition, regular exercise and physical activity can reduce the risk of developing some diseases and disabilities as people grow older. In some cases, exercise is an effective treatment for many chronic conditions. For example, studies show that people

TABLE 4.2 Nutrients: RDA, Sources, and Functions

NUTRIENT	RDA (WOMEN—MEN)	SOURCES	FUNCTIONS
Protein	1.0 g/kg	nuts, legumes, fish, meat, eggs, dairy products	builds & repairs body tissues; aids nutrient transport, muscle contractions; energy source
Carbohydrates	130 g	whole-grain breads & cereals, rice, pasta, beans, fruits, starchy vegetables	main source of fuel for heat and energy; keep intestinal tract healthy
Fats	15%–30% of calories	animal & vegetable oils, meat, cheese, butter, nonskim milk	provide energy; absorb some vitamins; insulate & cushion the body; add flavor to food
Fiber	21–30 g	*soluble*: oats, barley, beans, fruit and vegetables *insoluble*: corn, wheat bran, leafy green vegetables	*soluble*: lowers cholesterol; stabilizes blood glucose levels *insoluble*: prevents constipation
Vitamins			
A	700–900 mcg	animal products, orange and yellow fruit & vegetables	maintains vision, skin, tissue health; aids new cell growth
B1 (thiamine)	1.1–1.2 mg	whole and enriched grains, legumes, organ meats, leafy green vegetables	energy metabolism; aids proper function of nervous system; prevents beriberi
B2 (riboflavin)	1.1–1.3 mg	whole and enriched grains, liver, dairy products	energy metabolism; building tissue; maintains good vision
B3 (niacin)	14–16 mg	poultry, fish, meat, eggs dairy products, legumes	aids in proper digestion; skin & nerve functioning
B6 (pyridoxine)	1.5–1.7 mg	whole grains, meat, fish, eggs, carrots	food digestion, metabolism, and absorption; boosts immune system; brain & nerve function
B9 (Folate)	400 mcg (200 mcg folic acid)	dark green leafy vegetables, legumes, liver, yeast	promotes normal digestion; essential for red blood cells; may reduce risk of heart disease
B12 (cobalamin)	2.4 mcg	meat, liver, kidney, yogurt, dairy products, fish	builds proteins, red blood cells; aids nervous tissue function
C (ascorbic acid)	75–90 mg	fresh vegetables & fruits	antioxidant; infection resistance; aids collagen formation
D	10 mcg	cheese, whole eggs, salmon, fortified milk; sun	promotes calcium & phosphate use for healthy bones & teeth
E	15 mg	vegetable oil, wheat germ, leafy green vegetables	protects red blood cells; preserves vitamins A & C
K	90–120 mcg	leafy green vegetables, organ meats, cereals, dairy products	normal blood clotting; protein synthesis in plasma, bone, kidneys
Minerals			
Calcium	1200 mg	dairy products, salmon, sardines, broccoli, cabbage	healthy bones & teeth; normal blood clotting; nervous system
Magnesium	320–420 mg	dairy products, meat, fish poultry, legumes	healthy bones & teeth; nervous system; energy metabolism
Potassium	4.7 g	bananas, fresh & dried fruit, potatoes, broccoli, spinach	proper fluid balance; muscle function

NUTRIENT	RDA (WOMEN—MEN)	SOURCES	FUNCTIONS
Selenium	55 mcg	kidney, liver, shellfish, brazil nuts	boosts immune system; maintains thyroid function
Zinc	8–11 mg	meat, seafood, liver, eggs, milk, whole-grain products	cell reproduction; tissue growth and repair

Note: Lists of food sources are not exhaustive.

B5 (pantothenic acid) is available in many different foods and is also produced by intestinal bacteria, so there are no known major deficiencies of this vitamin. RDA has not been determined. Adequate intake is 5 mcg. B7 (biotin) is found in all foods, and thus deficiencies are rare. RDA has not been determined. Adequate intake is 30 mcg.

g = grams; mg = milligrams; mcg = micrograms; RDA = Recommended daily allowance (Where a range is given, the lower number is for women and the higher number is for men. RDAs are based on minimum requirements.)

Source: Adapted from USDA's Food and Nutrition Information Center website; includes data from National Policy and Resource Center on Nutrition and Aging, Florida International University.

with arthritis, heart disease, or diabetes benefit from regular exercise. Exercise also helps people with high blood pressure, balance problems, or difficulties with walking.

Physical exercise of all kinds is helpful for older adults. Of course, it is critical that all seniors consult a health professional prior to beginning any exercise regime. Most older people do not have health problems that would prevent them from doing moderate activity or the types of exercises that can be beneficial. In fact, there is a way for almost every older adult to exercise safely and get meaningful health benefits. Anyone who has been leading a mostly sedentary lifestyle, or who is not used to energetic activity, should approach exercise in a gradual way, increasing both the amount and the intensity to an optimal level over time.

According to results from the National Health Interview Survey, only 28% of men and 27% of women between the ages of 65 and 74 engage in regular, leisure-time physical activity (Schoenborn & Adams, 2010). The numbers do drop a little for those who are 75 or older, for men to 23%, and for women to 21%. Yet, there are so many ways to be active. For example, activity can be in short spurts throughout the day, or specific times can be set aside on specific days of the week to exercise. Many physical activities, such as brisk walking, raking leaves, or taking the stairs whenever possible, are free or low cost and do not require special equipment. Older adults can also check out an exercise video or DVD from their public library or use a fitness center at their local senior center.

Both physical activity and exercise burn calories. Physical activities are activities that get the body moving, such as gardening, walking the dog, raking leaves, and taking stairs instead of an elevator. Exercise is a form of physical activity that is specifically planned, structured, and repetitive, such as weight training, tai chi, or aerobics. Exercises generally fall into four main categories: endurance, strength, balance, and flexibility. Some activities fit into more than one of these categories. For example, many endurance activities also help build strength, and strength exercises can help improve balance.

Endurance, or aerobic, activities increase breathing and heart rate. These activities help people remain healthy, improve their fitness, and help them to do their daily tasks. Endurance exercises improve the health of the heart, lungs, and cardiovascular system. They also delay or prevent many diseases that are more common in older adults, such as diabetes, colon and breast cancers, heart disease, and others. Physical activities that build endurance include brisk walking, dancing, jogging, swimming, biking, playing tennis, yard work (mowing, raking), and climbing stairs.

Even small increases in muscle strength can make a big difference in older adults' ability to stay independent and accomplish everyday activities such as carrying groceries and climbing stairs. Using weights to improve muscle strength is sometimes called *strength training* or *resistance training*. Strength exercises include lifting weights and using resistance bands to exercise. Balance exercises help prevent falls. Many lower body strength exercises, such as standing on one foot, as well as the popular tai chi, improve balance. Stretching can help one's body to stay flexible and limber, which provides more freedom of movement for regular physical activity as well as for everyday activities. Shoulder and upper-arm stretches, calf stretches, and yoga are all ways to improve flexibility.

Episode 6: Senior Lifestyles

High Bandwidth:
http://raidercast.grcc.edu/flash/2011_2012/grcctv/successful_aging/success_aging_6_large/grcc_player.html
Low Bandwidth:
http://raidercast.grcc.edu/flash/2011_2012/grcctv/successful_aging/success_aging_6_small/grcc_player.html

Physical exercise has also been shown to enhance mental ability and decrease depression. In fact, recent research indicates that physical exercise may be more important for mental abilities and mental health than are mental exercises (Wilcox et al., 2009).

Older adults talk about the advantages of regularly engaging in physical exercise in Video 6.

Mental Activity

The brain is an organ, and like all organs in the body, it needs to be used and exercised regularly. People who remain active by dancing (or any other type of physical activity), playing musical instruments, or engaging in focused games (e.g., scrabble, etc.) can reduce the probability of mental decline. Also, persons who become involved in groups such as civic organizations, church groups, social groups, athletic events, and so forth, seem to have less mental decline than those who are not so engaged. Social relationships are also important and seem to stimulate brain functioning. The old cliché, "use or lose it," seems to be true in regard to the brain. Much more information about the role of mental activity is presented in Chapter 5.

Good Sleep Hygiene

It is important to get a good night's sleep at all ages. Sleep provides the opportunity for the body to repair cell damage, it helps to prevent disease by refreshing the immune system, and it improves concentration and memory function. With age, it is harder to get quality sleep because physiological sleep patterns change, reducing periods of the most restful type of sleep, Rapid Eye Movement (REM) sleep. Nevertheless, daytime sleepiness is not a part of normal aging (Edwards et al., 2010). Therefore, it is especially important for older adults to practice good sleep hygiene.
Good sleep hygiene includes the following elements:

- Engaging in activities to keep energy level up during the day, preparing the body for sleep at night;
- Etablishing a regular daily schedule of going to bed and rising;
- Creating a comforting environment: a good mattress, pillow, and bedding; a quiet, dark room with a suitable temperature and ventilation;

- Reserving the bed for sleeping, and sex, so it will be associated with only those things;
- Developing a relaxing bedtime routine, such as taking a bath or listening to calming music; and,
- For periods of wakefulness during the night, trying to stay relaxed by engaging in a repetitive, nonstimulating activity, such as counting sheep; and, if a wakefulness period extends to 15 minutes, getting out of bed and doing a quiet activity, keeping the lights dim.

Other tips for improving sleep include

- Taking a daily walk, because exercise releases chemicals in the body that promote restful sleep;
- Taking a 15- to 30-minute nap early in the afternoon, which can improve overall restfulness;
- Getting 2 hours or more of sunlight a day because bright sunlight increases melatonin, which regulates sleep–wake cycles;
- Combining sex and sleep because sex and physical intimacy, such as hugging and massage, can lead to restful sleep;
- Limiting caffeine late in the day;
- Eating no more than a light snack 3 hours prior to going to bed;
- Limiting beverages within 90 minutes of bedtime;
- Quiting smoking, or at least avoiding it within 3 hours of bedtime, because nicotine is a stimulant;
- Avoiding alcohol before bedtime—it may seem to aid sleep, but it actually causes waking during the night;
- Blocking out snoring or other noises with earplugs or a white-noise machine;
- Limiting use of sleeping aids and sleeping pills because many of them have unpleasant side effects and thus are not a long-term solution to sleep problems;
- Reducing mental stress by jotting down worries or concerns, checking off tasks completed on a to-do list, and listing goals for the next day, before retiring; and
- Using relaxation techniques, such as progressive relaxation or deep breathing, which can prepare the body for sleep.

PREVENTIVE MEASURES

Preventive health measures include immunizations, screening tests, avoiding negative health behaviors, and health literacy. Medicare Part B covers a number of preventive services, for which there is no cost to Medicare enrollees. The topic of Medicare, including eligibility, what it covers, and what it costs, is discussed in Chapter 14.

Immunizations

Most older adults have heard that they should get a flu shot every year, even if they do not all get one. They may not know that there are three other vaccines they should be sure to get—pneumococcal, shingles, and Tdap/Td (tetanus, diphtheria, and pertussis). Information on vaccinations is updated regularly on the website of the Centers for Disease Control and Prevention (www.cdc.gov).

Influenza (Flu) Vaccine

Seniors are among those risk groups who can benefit significantly from being vaccinated against influenza (flu). Every year, on average, 24,000 Americans die from the flu and most of these deaths are among older adults. Although the proportion of older people being vaccinated has risen significantly over the previous two decades, in 2008 only 67% had received a flu shot within the previous 12 months. The goal of *Healthy People 2020*, which is for 90% of older adults to be vaccinated annually for the flu, is not yet within reach, although annual flu vaccinations are covered by Medicare.

Pneumococcal Vaccine

Pneumonia (pneumococcal disease), which can cause serious infections in the lungs, bloodstream, and the covering of the brain, is one of the leading reasons that seniors go to hospital emergency rooms. It is all too frequently also a cause of death for them. To avoid or minimize the effects of pneumonia, it is recommended that seniors receive a pneumonia vaccine once every 10 years. Until recently, very few seniors were receiving this vaccine. In 2010, compared to 65- to 74-year-olds, a higher proportion of adults age 75 and up had received at least one shot in their lifetime (54% and 66%, respectively). As is the case for flu vaccination rates, racial and ethnic disparities in pneumonia vaccination rates still exist (Ward, Barnes, Freeman, & Schiller, 2011). The fact that pneumonia vaccinations are covered by Medicare increases the potential to achieve *Health People 2020*'s goal of 90% of seniors being vaccinated for the disease.

Shingles Vaccine

Shingles is a painful skin rash caused by the varicella zoster virus (VZV). As this virus is the same one that produces chicken pox, everyone who has had the chicken pox is at risk for getting shingles, because the virus remains in the body and then can become active again in the later years. About half a million Americans age 60 or older come down with shingles every year, and by the time they are 80, one out of two people will have had shingles (National Institute of Neurological Disorders and Stroke, 2011). Consequently, the CDC recommends that adults age 60 years or older receive the shingles vaccine, whether or not they recall having had chicken pox. Although shingles is not contagious, grandparents should be mindful of the fact that a person with active shingles can transmit the virus to a person who has never had chicken pox. Generally, Medicare Part D plans cover this vaccine.

Tdap/Td Vaccine

Tdap/Td is a vaccine that immunizes again tetanus, diphtheria, and pertussis. The vaccine is recommended for older adults because vaccine-induced immunity seems to wane with age, and thinner skin can make them more vulnerable to wounds that would allow the tetanus bacteria into the body. Tetanus ("lockjaw") is an acute bacterium that affects the central nervous system, causing tightening and spasms of muscles, particularly in the jaw, and fever and headaches. It may even result in death by suffocation. Diphtheria is an acute bacterial disease that affects the throat and skin, causing breathing problems, and potentially paralysis and heart failure. Pertussis ("whooping cough") is an acute bacterium that affects the upper respiratory system. Symptoms include intense fits or spells of coughing, and a thick, sticky mucus in the throat, with the potential to cause pneumonia, seizures, and brain damage. Diphtheria and pertussis are highly contagious, and both can result in death. These infections are easily passed on to babies who are too young to be vaccinated. Older adults should receive a Tdap vaccine, if they have not had one, and then a Td booster once every 10 years. The Tdap/Td vaccine is generally a Part D covered drug for Medicare patients.

Screening Tests

Screening tests are best for those diseases or chronic conditions that are accompanied by few or no symptoms but are preventable, or have good success rates from treatments when they are detected early. Recommendations for screening tests are regularly reviewed and can be found on the website of the U.S. Preventive Services Task Force (www.uspreventiveservicestaskforce.org/recommendations.htm).

Blood Pressure

Routine blood pressure measurement is recommended at least every 2 years for those with normal readings, and every year otherwise. Although individual differences abound, target rates are still 120/80 mm/HG, with the first number (systolic pressure) being more important than the second (diastolic pressure) for adults over age 50. There are no symptoms of high blood pressure, but if uncontrolled, it can lead to a stroke, a heart attack, heart failure, or kidney failure.

Cholesterol

Cholesterol should be checked regularly, at least once every 5 years to estimate the risk of developing heart disease. A cholesterol level of 200 mg/dL is considered desirable. High blood cholesterol has been associated with heart disease, an increased risk of death from heart attacks, and hardening of the arteries (*atherosclerosis*).

Cancer Screenings

Research and advances in medical treatments have meant that many cancers that used to go undiagnosed and run their course quickly can now be detected early, leading to much better prognoses for recovery and longer lives despite cancer. An important key to the progress in this area is screening tests. Everyone over age 50 should be screened for colorectal cancer. Several different tests are available, and a health care provider can help determine which one may be best and when it should be given.

Women over age 40 should have a mammogram every 1 to 2 years for early detection of breast cancer. Breast self-examination and regular physical breast exams by a health care provider are also essential parts of regular breast care. For early detection of precancer and cervical cancer, women should have a papanicolaou (Pap) smear every 1 to 3 years. Women who are older than 65 years of age with at least three recent normal Pap test results and no abnormal results in the previous 10 years do not need a Pap smear. Low-cost or free screenings are available to low-income, uninsured, and underinsured women through the National Breast and Cervical Cancer Early Detection Program (NBCCEDP), which is administered by the Centers for Disease Control and Prevention. In addition, Planned Parenthood offers low-cost Pap tests, and state and local health departments can provide information on where affordable screenings are available. Medicare covers one Pap test and pelvic exam every 2 years for women who are at low-risk for cervical cancer.

For men, Medicare provides for an annual prostate-specific antigen (PSA) test. A PSA-based screening has limitations and is still controversial, because it results in the detection of more cases of cancer, but small to no reduction in prostate cancer-specific mortality after 10 years. False-positive results in 12% to 13% of screened men result in unnecessary follow-up procedures and treatments that can be harmful. As a consequence, the U.S. Preventive Services Task Force has recommended that men age 75 and older should not be screened for prostate cancer, and younger men should discuss the benefits and harms of the PSA test with their clinicians before being tested (Lin, Croswell, Koenig, Lam, & Maltz, 2011). Researchers are studying ways to improve the PSA test and to find other ways to detect prostate cancer early.

Blood Sugar

The American Diabetic Association recommends that all adults over age 45 be considered for diabetes screening by their health care provider every 3 years. Risk factors include high blood pressure and obesity.

Bone Density

Baseline bone density should be established prior to menopause, which occurs on average around age 50. Postmenopausal women should be tested regularly to ensure that bone density does not dip into the range of T-scores that indicate osteoporosis. Although on average women lose 20% of bone mass in the first 5 years following menopause, diet and exercise can maintain bone density loss at an acceptable, nonosteoporotic level. Routine screening can reduce the incidence of hip fractures and other effects of bone thinning.

Body Mass Index (BMI)

The best test for obesity is a BMI, a measure of body fat based on height and weight. Monitoring BMI and keeping it in check are important to reduce the sequelae of being overweight and obese, which include increased risks for heart disease and diabetes.

Sexual Health Screenings

Older adults should talk with their health care provider about being tested for sexually transmitted infections. Seniors will find they need to be proactive in this area, because physicians often feel uncomfortable about discussing sexual matters with their older patients, and thus may avoid doing so.

HIV

Those at high risk for HIV should talk to their health care provider about screening. Conditions for high risk include having a blood transfusion between 1978 and 1985, being treated for sexually transmitted diseases, having unprotected sex with multiple partners, and having used injection drugs.

Eye Examinations

A few serious conditions, such as macular degeneration, glaucoma, and retinopathy, which can all result in serious vision loss and even blindness, can develop more readily in older people (see the Medical Care chapter for information about these conditions). More common and more easily treated are presbyopia, dry eyes, and cataracts (which were discussed in the Physical Changes chapter). For the sake of both the serious and the more common eye conditions, a complete eye examination by a qualified professional (e.g., ophthalmologist) is recommended for those older than age 45, and then follow-up examinations every 2 to 4 years thereafter.

Dental Checkups and Teeth Cleaning

Regular visits to the dentist will minimize tooth loss, as well as allow the dentist to check for oral cancers.

Depression

Depression is not a normal part of aging. Depression is associated with distress and suffering and can lead to impairments in physical, mental, and social functioning. The good news is that it is highly treatable. Older adults should talk with their health care provider about being screened for depression if they have felt down, sad, or hopeless over a period of 2 or more weeks, or have felt little interest or pleasure in doing things. Chapter 5 includes information on some treatment programs that have been proven to work well for older adults.

Avoiding Negative Health Behaviors

In addition to engaging in behaviors that enhance and maintain health, some behaviors and habits should be avoided so that health is not compromised. Negative health behaviors that should be avoided or discontinued are smoking, overuse of alcohol, and tanning.

Smoking

The good news is that only 9.5% of older adults aged 65 years and older are current smokers, although many more used to be and, fortunately, have quit smoking. This rate compares favorably to the 20% to 25% of 18- to 64-year-olds who are current smokers (*Older Americans 2010*). In addition to being a primary cause of lung cancer and emphysema, cigarette smoking worsens the prognosis and symptoms of all chronic diseases. Among older people, the death rate for chronic lower respiratory diseases (the fourth leading cause of death among people age 65 and over) increased 50% between 1981 and 2006. This increase reflects, in part, the effects of cigarette smoking. Smokers can do nothing better for their health than to quit smoking. There are many approaches to becoming a nonsmoker, and health professionals can help individuals choose one that can be helpful to them.

Part of the difference in longevity between various social–economic groups in the United States is related to the difference in the smoking rates between persons in these groups. Highly educated Americans have a 5.6% smoking rate. American adults ages 25 years and older with less than a high school education have a 28.5% smoking rate (Centers for Disease Control and Prevention [CDC], 2010). A college education seems to promote healthy living, as there seems to be a clearer understanding of the devastating effects of using tobacco. In addition, there is probably a significant difference in peer pressure, given that smoking is increasingly stigmatized among college students.

Overuse of Alcohol

According to Schoenborn and Adams (2010), 12.5% of adults 65 years of age and older are considered moderate drinkers (3–7 drinks per week for women, 3–14 drinks for men) and 4% of older adults are considered heavier drinkers (more than 7 drinks per week for women, or more than 14 drinks per week for men. Age-related physiological changes increase the risks associated with alcohol. For example, compared to younger people, older adults have higher blood alcohol levels per amount consumed. Furthermore, 90% of older adults use medications, and as many as 100 of these medications may interact adversely with alcohol. Chronic conditions, such as hypertension, gout, diabetes, insomnia, and depression, may be triggered or worsened by alcohol use.

Safe amounts and frequency for drinking are consuming on average of less than 1 drink per day, less than seven drinks per week, and less than three drinks on heavier drinking occasions. Drinking and using drugs that interact with alcohol should be avoided. No alcohol should be consumed if activities are planned that can be impaired by alcohol, for example, driving or caregiving for others. It takes about 1 hour for the body to metabolize one drink. Health professionals can provide counseling about safe drinking practices or advise on interventions for those at risk for alcohol abuse or dependence.

Tanning

Sun exposure at any age can cause skin cancer, as well as premature aging, immune suppression, eye damage, and allergic reactions (U.S. Food and Drug Administration [FDA], 2010). There are no safe ultraviolet (UV) rays and no safe suntans. During midday (10 a.m.–4 p.m.), when the sun is most severe, limiting direct sun exposure is a good. Except for the 10 to 15 minutes of sun that older people should get a few times a week to enhance their intake of vitamin D, it is recommended that skin be covered when in sunlight, or sunscreen lotion be used for protection from UVB solar radiation. The U.S. Food and Drug Administration (2010) also recommends that people should avoid artificial UV sources, such as tanning beds, entirely.

Health Literacy

Health literacy is the ability to locate and understand health-related information and services. It requires skills in the ability to search, comprehend, and use information from prose, and from charts and graphs, and the ability to identify and perform computations using numbers embedded in printed materials. Among the domains of health for which health literacy is important are information and services related to clinical health, prevention, and navigation of the health care system. Unfortunately, health literacy is quite poor at all ages. Among elderly people, health literacy is poorest among the oldest-old, as can be seen in Figure 4.2.

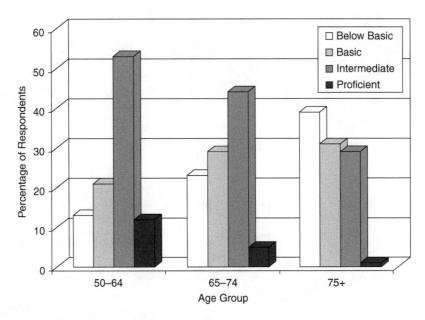

FIGURE 4.2 Health Literacy in Older Adults by Age Group.

Source: Adapted from *Older Americans 2008: Key indicators of well-being.* (2008). Special topic: Literacy table. Federal Interagency Forum on Aging-Related Statistics. Washington, DC: U.S. Government Printing Office.

SUGGESTED RESOURCES

MedlinePlus: http://www.medlineplus.gov
  Health information from the National Library of Medicine and the National Institutes of Health.
NIHSeniorHealth: http://www.nihseniorhealth.gov
  An easy-to-use website that features basic health and wellness information for older adults from the National Institutes of Health.
Tufts University's Human Nutrition Research Center on Aging: http://hnrc.tufts.edu
  The focus of this nutrition research center is on the needs of older adults.
U.S. Food and Drug Administration: http://www.fda.gov/ForConsumers/ConsumerUpdates/default.htm
  Consumer updates on dietary supplements, drugs, food, medical devices, nutrition, vaccines, pet products, and more.

CHAPTER 5

Mental Health and Mental Abilities

The learning objectives of this chapter include understanding

- Positive mental health aspects of aging.
- Treatments for mental health conditions, when they exist, can lead to significant improvements in older adults' quality of life.
- The myth of inevitable decline in intellectual abilities with age.
- The cognitive changes that accompany dementia and how they differ from normal aging.
- The positive contributions that the creative arts can make to older adults', and society's, quality of life.
- Factors that can positively or negatively affect older adults' mental health and abilities.

Alice is 77 and is extremely active in her church. She chairs a committee on education, and she never misses a church function. She drives not only in town but several 100 miles to visit her children. She reads several magazines a week, is always reading a new book, is articulate in speech, and has a good memory. She lives independently and does her own cooking, shopping, and house cleaning. She is sought after by her friends and family for advice.

Harold is 68 and has been severely depressed since his wife died 2 years ago. He has isolated himself. He looks unkempt. He seems to have little interest in the affairs of the world or in anything else. He has insomnia, does not care to eat, has been losing weight, and cannot concentrate long enough to enjoy a book or even read the local newspaper.

Mary is 81 and is taking classes at the local community college. She is enjoying her classes and has a B average. She is articulate and speaks up in class. She relates well to the younger students and has a keen sense of humor. She complains that she is too old to remember all the material in the books and in the class notes, and then does as well or better than the younger students on her tests. She has learned to use computers and is extremely proud of her computer ability.

MENTAL HEALTH AND MENTAL ABILITIES OF OLDER PEOPLE

Older people are the happiest people in America. How can this be? It defies all the ste-reotypes about aging. After all, older people experience significant losses in their lives, including physical changes to their own bodies, deaths of close friends, and the losses that accompany leaving the workforce. This seeming mismatch between the reality of older people's lives and the stereotypes about them comes about because when thinking about aging, people most often focus on the negative things that can accompany it, while not noticing the positive ones. Of course, there are negative things that come along with aging, but negative things are experienced at every life stage.

One goal of this chapter is to present a more balanced view of aging. Some memory losses occur, but unless a person is beset by Alzheimer's, these losses do not have to inter-fere with everyday life. For the previous several decades, we've been slowly uncovering more and more areas of life where older adults thrive and make contributions, not only to their own lives, but also to the lives of others. The creative arts is one of these areas that is discussed in this chapter.

MENTAL HEALTH

Now that we are beginning to look at more positive aspects of aging, we are discovering some facts about the lives of seniors that are surprising to many people. When it comes to discussing mental health and aging, much of the focus in research and in the media has been on mental health problems that are, in fact, not that common among older adults. In this section of Chapter 5, we begin with seniors' overall sense of well-being and hap-piness. Seniors can become depressed, just as anyone can (except not usually young chil-dren), but they are less likely than are younger people to become so. Moving away from the stereotypes, we find that there are specific treatments that work particularly well for older adults.

Psychological Well-Being and Happiness

What is known about adults' general sense of well-being as they get older? Researchers Arthur Stone, Joan Schwartz, Joan Broderick, and Angus Deaton (2010) interviewed 340,847 people between the ages of 18 and 85 years about various aspects of psychologi-cal well-being. They found that global well-being follows a U-shaped pattern, with a high point in the youngest age group (18–21-year-olds), then a decline to the most negative ratings when people are in their early 50s, and an upward trend beginning in the late 50s through the oldest ages. Enjoyment and happiness show a modest increase into old age, again beginning when people are in their late 50s. Stress and anger, on the other hand, decline with age, and worry subsides after age 50.

Older adults' may display more happiness than younger adults do because they ignore, overlook, or downplay negative information and situations (Mather, 2012). Their years of experience allow them to put negative events into perspective, resulting in their being able to take things in stride. In the *2010 National Health Interview Survey*, 27,157 adults in the United States responded to a series of questions about their health, includ-ing questions about their mental health. Consistent with the findings of Stone and his colleagues, the survey showed that, compared to young and middle-aged adults, people aged 65 and over were the least likely to report feeling sad or hopeless all or most of the time (see Figure 5.1; Schiller, Lucas, Ward, & Peregovy, 2012). As they age, adults improve their ability to regulate their emotions and become better at recognizing and focusing on those things that are more meaningful in their life, including close relationships

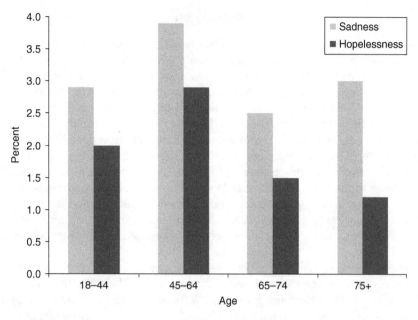

FIGURE 5.1 Percentages of Adults With Feelings of Sadness and Hopelessness All or Most of The Time, United States, 2010.

Note: In separate questions, respondents were asked how often in the past 30 days they felt so sad that nothing could cheer them up, or so hopeless that nothing could cheer them up.

Source: Adapted from Schiller, Lucas, Ward, & Peregovy, 2012, Table 14, pp. 55–56.

(Charles & Carstensen, 2010). This is another reason that seniors are likely to be happier than people who are their juniors.

Effects of Beliefs About Mental Health and Aging

Now well past the age of 60, rock musician Pete Townshend has a positive outlook on what it is like to be an older person. In 1965, though, when he was just 20 years old, he wrote *My Generation*, a song that included the lyrics, "Hope I die before I get old." Using those lyrics in the title of a journal article, Heather Lacey, Dylan Smith, and Peter Ubel (2006) discuss how beliefs about well-being in old age can negatively affect both younger and older adults.

> Beliefs about aging are important—if younger adults mispredict old age as miserable, they may make risky decisions, not worrying about preserving themselves for what they predict will be an unhappy future. Conversely, exaggerating the joys of youth may lead to unwarranted nostalgia in older adults, interfering with their appreciation of current joys. (p. 168)

Clearly, the majority of older adults have positive feelings about their own well-being. Nevertheless, just like anyone else, older people do experience emotional lows and mental health problems, and when they are serious, diagnosis and treatment should be available and encouraged. Perhaps a better understanding of depression can help us see how to avoid ageist stereotypes about mental health.

Depression

Depression is not a normal part of aging, but because of ageist stereotypes, a common myth is that older people are usually depressed. "Who wouldn't be?" is what some people think when they dwell on the changes and losses that can accompany aging. A number of helpful tips on adapting to some of these more common age-related changes are presented in the Practical Applications at the end of Part II of this textbook. Of course, older adults can become depressed, and when they do it is often a result of significant losses in their lives—loss of a job and a decrease in income when they leave the paid workforce, deaths of their partner and friends, and loss of their home when they move to be near their children or grandchildren or to senior living communities. In addition, they may lose one or more of their children. People who in the past were respected because of their jobs, energy, and wisdom, often find themselves disregarded in their later years. Some who have several of these losses amazingly still retain emotional stability and feelings of well-being. Others, however, become overwhelmed by their losses and need professional help.

Although depression is the most prevalent mental health problem among older adults (Centers for Disease Control and Prevention [CDC], 2009), the rate for them is lower than it is for any other age group: 6.1% for adults 55 years and over, compared to 10.2% for 18- to 24-year-olds; 8.3% for 25 to 34 and 35- to 44-year-olds; and 10.2% for 45- to 54-year-olds (Reeves et al., 2011). These rates are based on self-reports so they may underrepresent the problem in all the age groups. Rates are higher for elders in nursing homes and other residential settings.

Whatever its prevalence, depression is a serious mental health problem that is associated with feelings of despair, a denial of self-worth, and somatic symptoms, including loss of appetite, sleeping difficulties, and fatigue. Older adults with depression use more medication, visit health care professionals and hospital emergency rooms more often, and if they enter the hospital, they stay longer (CDC, 2008). The vast majority of cases (as many as 80%) are highly treatable, so there is considerable hope for those who get professional help.

Successful Depression Care Management
for Older Adults

Three community-based programs have proven to be especially helpful for treating depression in older adults: IMPACT, PEARLS, and Healthy IDEAS (CDC, 2009). They all include the use of well-validated measures of depression; ongoing assessment to monitor the effectiveness of treatment and to make appropriate changes when the chosen treatment is found to be ineffective; and a depression care manager, who may be a nurse, social worker, psychologist, or other practitioner. In consultation with the primary care provider and the patient, the care manager delivers or facilitates the treatment plan, educates the patient, and keeps track of the patient's progress. These programs have also been designed to help overcome one of the barriers to treatment for older people—their resistance to seeking and participating in mental health treatments. Many older people have very negative attitudes toward the mental health profession and so they are reluctant to seek help. Mental health stereotypes and stigmas and how to help overcome them are discussed further in the Practical Application at the end of Part II of this textbook.

In addition to these three effective treatment programs, prescription drugs can be part of the treatment process for many depressed persons. Currently, many drugs, if adequately prescribed and used, can help people through difficult psychiatric conditions. For all treatment approaches, it is helpful when friends and family can provide comfort to their loved ones who are depressed. Psychologist Michael Ryan talks about losses and depression in older adults and some strategies and treatments that can be helpful in Video 5.

Episode 5: Aging and Your Health

High Bandwidth:
http://raidercast.grcc.edu/flash/2011_2012/grcctv/successful_
aging/success_aging_5_large/grcc_player.html
Low Bandwidth:
http://raidercast.grcc.edu/flash/2011_2012/grcctv/successful_
aging/success_aging_5_small/grcc_player.html

Suicide

Although persons over age 65 comprise only about 13% of the U.S. population, 15.6% of suicides are among persons in this age group (American Association of Suicidology, 2010). The evidence seems clear that when older persons talk about suicide, they mean it. When they attempt suicide, they usually complete it. Men are much more likely to commit suicide at every age. In 2010, that was almost 6,000 suicides among those 65 years of age and older, 84% of which were male. Any older person talking about suicide should be taken seriously.

Many of the factors associated with depression are also associated with suicide. In fact, depression is often a precursor to suicide, so prevention and treatment for depression is considered to be pivotal in lowering suicide rates among older people. After reviewing the research literature on prevention programs, Sylvie Lapierre and her colleagues (2011) suggested several innovative strategies with the potential to be successful, among them turning patients' focus to positive aging, engaging family members, using the Internet, and improving education on elderly suicide for health care providers. Clearly, much more work needs to be done to reduce the prevalence of suicide in the elderly.

Although our emphasis has been on deterring older people from committing suicide, there are some who believe that terminally ill patients should be able to access resources to end their lives legally. Two states, Oregon and Washington, have established assisted suicide laws for this purpose and you can learn more about them in Chapter 7.

MENTAL ABILITIES

Infants and children all begin to crawl, walk, and talk at about the same age. In fact, if they do not meet these developmental milestones "on time," it is usually a sign of a problem that needs to be addressed. In stark contrast to what happens at these early stages of development, adults become more and more different from one another as they age. This is one of the most common themes in the field of aging, and the three scenarios at the beginning of this chapter exemplify this theme.

Such large individual differences among older people have challenged researchers who seek to understand how mental processes develop into late life. On the one hand, some adults seem to reach their older years with mental abilities that are as good, and sometimes even better, than when they were younger. For others, mental abilities seem to decline as they age, even if they do not acquire a dementia such as Alzheimer's disease.

Good News About Mental Abilities in the Later Years of Life

For years it was just assumed that as we grew older, the brain would deteriorate, leading to a progressive and irreversible decline in mental abilities. Now it is known that, although the generation of new brain cells slows down in old age, it never ceases. Furthermore, physical and mental activity throughout life increase the potential for new cells to develop (Kempermann, 2009).

In general, researchers have found that some mental abilities do seem to decline with age, including speed of information processing—how quickly information is perceived and acted upon—and working memory—how much information can be actively maintained and manipulated in memory at one time. On the other hand, some mental abilities seem to be maintained, or even improve with age, including general knowledge and vocabulary. Timothy Salthouse is a psychologist who has conducted research on cognitive abilities in older adults for decades. Observing what he termed a "dramatic discrepancy" between how well seniors function in their everyday lives and their test scores on cognitive tests in the laboratories of research scientists, Dr. Salthouse (2010) has concluded:

> People seldom need to perform at their maximum levels; effects of age likely vary across tasks or activities; there are large individual differences in the level of cognitive functioning at each age; cognition is not the only important factor associated with success in most activities; increased age is often accompanied by greater amounts of experience, which may minimize negative consequences of declining abilities; and people may accommodate to declining abilities in a manner that could minimize any effects on real-world functioning. (p. 150)

Indeed, we are learning that people who are happy, who feel better about their abilities, and who have good social support usually do much better on challenging mental tasks.

Cross-Sectional and Longitudinal Studies

Most studies of mental abilities use cross-sectional research methods. In cross-sectional studies, two or more groups of people defined by age are tested at a given period in time. For example, in Table 5.1, each of the columns for the year of study (2010, 2020, and 2030) represents possible cross-sectional groups. These groups, consisting of people in different age categories, may have had very different life experiences, so that results of these cross-sectional studies are influenced not only by the age of the people, but also by the cohort, or generation, in which they were born. In longitudinal studies, the same person is tested over a period of time (usually years). For example, in Table 5.1, each of the rows for the year of birth (1950, 1970, and 1990) represents possible longitudinal groups. Longitudinal studies can reveal changes over time in individuals, but they have their own difficulties,

TABLE 5.1 Cross-Sectional and Longitudinal Research Variables

YEAR OF BIRTH	YEAR OF STUDY		
	2010	2020	2030
1950	60-yr-olds	70-yr-olds	80-yr-olds
1970	40-yr-olds	50-yr-olds	60-yr-olds
1990	20-yr-olds	30-yr-olds	40-yr-olds

including the fact that people are tested repeatedly, which also may affect the results. Few longitudinal studies of mental abilities exist, because they are much more difficult to carry out; abilities of interest, as well as how they are measured, change over time; and they are much more costly.

Memory and Aging

One of the most studied mental abilities is memory. Human memory is fallible and people are generally bothered when they forget. Concerns about memory loss increase with age, especially because it is the most well-known symptom of Alzheimer's. Myths about memory and aging abound in our society, and belief in these myths has been shown to affect memory performance in older adults (Levy, Zonderman, Slade, & Ferrucci, 2012).

A common myth about memory is that the best memory is one in which nothing is ever forgotten. However, there are significant pitfalls of having a so-called perfect memory. Luria (1968) described one man who had such an exact memory for people that he could not recognize them if they changed their clothing or had a different haircut. There are also some things that no one wants to remember—all their old phone numbers, for example.

Yet, forgetting important things is not good, and high levels of forgetting are usually a symptom of a problem, ranging from stress to dementia. So, memory strategies are valuable because when effectively applied, they make it possible to remember important things that might otherwise be forgotten. Adopting strategies to remember events indicates a high level of cognitive functioning, and proficient use of memory strategies is a sign of good cognitive management skills.

In research comparing the use of memory strategies by young and older adults, the young adults are almost always in college, where they have ongoing opportunities to learn and practice strategies for remembering. Most of the older adults, who were in school during the 1950s or earlier, learned only one strategy for remembering—rote rehearsal, that is, repeating things over and over. Rote rehearsal by itself is not a good memory technique because it does not help to establish long-term remembering. In fact, it was not until the 1960s that a significant body of experimental evidence began to demonstrate the positive effects of categorizing strategies on recall of verbal materials. These important historical facts about the development of thinking about memory strategies must be recognized as critical factors in affecting the kinds of strategies that many of today's older adults will tend to use when faced with a task requiring memory (Sugar, 2007). Older adults even reject as valuable those strategies, such as categorizing and grouping, that are particularly effective for learning and remembering, and instead often regard them as "cheating." In the absence of being in school, engaging in intellectually challenging activities with a high memory demand, such as chess, may provide opportunities during later adulthood to continue to exercise the mental capacities required to learn and practice memory strategies.

Too often, fears of family members and friends about an older loved one's perceived forgetfulness lead to premature, or unnecessary, institutionalization. Concerns about a steam iron being left on or bills not being paid on time can worry older adults as well as their families and friends. Appropriate instruction in using memory strategies and modern technology, however, can do much to alleviate these fears—for example, using lists and reminder notes to remember to carry out important actions in everyday life and to prevent memory failures that could jeopardize safety. New products and services furnish other means for reducing concerns about older adults' personal vulnerability, such as steam irons that shut off after a short period of not being used and automatic bill paying services. With all the new technology, there are many applications that already exist, and many more that could be designed, to help everyone, regardless of their age, to remember the important things in their lives.

Cognitive Health: The Healthy Brain Initiative

Rather than focusing on abilities that might wane as we get older, researchers and health professionals have begun to look at opportunities to maintain and even improve *cognitive health*. Recognized only recently as an important issue for the public health system, cognitive health

> can be viewed along a continuum—from optimal functioning to mild cognitive impairment to severe dementia...and cognitive health should be respected for its multidimensional nature and embraced for the positive changes that occur as a natural part of the aging process...components of healthy cognitive functioning include: language, thought, memory, executive function (the ability to plan and carry out tasks), judgment, attention, perception, remembered skills such as driving, and the ability to live a purposeful life. (CDC, 2011, p. 7)

In 2007, the Centers for Disease Control launched *The Healthy Brain Initiative: A National Public Health Road Map to Maintaining Cognitive Health*. The initiative has three purposes: to find out what is already known about cognitive health, to investigate gaps in knowledge, and to determine how public health can contribute to cognitive health (CDC, 2011). Sadly, despite its name, most of the effort on this initiative has been invested in studying and assessing cognitive impairment, determining needs and services related to it, and developing state dementia action plans.

Alzheimer's Disease and Other Dementias

Although people at every age regularly forget things, and there may be more forgetting and more to forget as we age, those who develop dementia show progressively more and more forgetting that eventually affects their day-to-day living. Dementia, which means "absence of mind" (from Latin, *de-* "without," and *ment* "mind"), is used to describe more than 70 disorders that with one thing in common—a loss of brain function resulting from progressive, degenerative damage to neurons (nerve cells) in the brain. It affects memory, thinking, language, judgment, and emotional behavior, eventually affecting daily functioning and leading to death.

The most common type of dementia, accounting for approximately 80% of cases, is Alzheimer's disease, which was first described by a German physician, Alois Alzheimer, in 1906. It is the sixth leading cause of death among adult Americans. Other common types of dementia are vascular (poststroke) dementia and Pick's disease (Alzheimer's Association, 2012). Changes that occur in the brain with most types of dementia are not reversible. However, sometimes dementia can be reversed, or at least stopped, if the cause is diagnosed soon enough, and if it is related to low vitamin B12 levels; changes in blood sugar, sodium, or calcium levels; hypothyroidism; chronic drug abuse; a brain tumor; or, the use of certain medications (such as some cholesterol-lowering drugs).

Causes of Alzheimer's

Many avenues of research have been explored to determine what causes Alzheimer's. One hypothesis is gaining support from basic research on the immune system, and on neuroinflammation in particular. According to this hypothesis, Alzheimer's begins with neuronal stress, from sources such as infections, traumatic brain injury, and genetic variations in protein alleles. Neuronal stress increases the production of proinflammatory cytokines, including beta-amyloid precurser proteins, which are thought to bring about the increased density of plaques and tangles in the brains of Alzheimer's patients (Griffin, 2011).

Researchers are concluding that Alzheimer's "should be designated as a *syndrome* rather than a *disease*" because it is "heterogeneous with regard to age of symptoms' onset, pattern and mix of clinical features, neuropathology, expression of markers, comorbid conditions, response to treatment, risk factors, and genetics/family history" (Hampel, Lista, & Khachaturian, 2012, p. 326). Clinically, the progression of Alzheimer's seems to be unique in each person.

> Some individuals decline rapidly in the initial phases, but then reach a plateau for awhile, and even show occasional glimmers of improvement, before they lapse into further deterioration. Others may decline more slowly in the early stages, but then degenerate more quickly toward the end. Every individual does not suffer the same symptoms during the course of the disease or suffer them at the same time or to a similar degree. (Andreae, 1992, p. 61)

Diagnosis and Treatment of Alzheimer's

Memory problems are the most well known indication of Alzheimer's, but there are other signs, too. The Alzheimer's Association (2012) notes 10 signs to be aware of, which are listed in Table 5.2. It can be difficult to distinguish these signs from changes that may occur with normal aging, so Table 5.2 includes brief descriptions of them, too.

TABLE 5.2 Comparing Signs of Alzheimer's With Typical Age-Related Changes

ALZHEIMER'S	TYPICAL AGE-RELATED CHANGE
Memory loss that disrupts daily life.	Sometimes forget names or appointments, but remember them later.
Challenges in planning or solving problems.	Sometimes make errors when balancing a checkbook.
Difficulty completing familiar tasks.	Occasionally needing help to use settings on a microwave or to record a TV show.
Confusion with time or place.	Getting confused about the day of the week but figuring it out later.
Trouble understanding visual images and spatial relationships.	Vision changes related to cataracts.
New problems with words in speaking or writing.	Sometimes having trouble finding the right word.
Misplacing things and losing the ability to retrace steps.	Misplacing things from time to time and retracing steps to find them.
Decreased or poor judgment.	Making a bad decision once in a while.
Withdrawal from work or social activities.	Sometimes feeling weary of work, family, and social obligations.
Changes in mood and personality.	Developing very specific ways of doing things and becoming irritable when a routine is disrupted.

Note: Information in Table 5.2 is from the Alzheimer's Association website (www.alz.org).

A common approach for diagnosing Alzheimer's has been to administer a combination of neuropsychological and neurological tests, the latter often directed at eliminating other conditions, such as strokes, tumors, or other neurological diseases. The Mini-Mental Status Exam (MMSE; Folstein, Folstein, & McHugh, 1975), which primarily measures memory and orientation to place and time, is the most frequently used neuropsychological test. This approach works reasonably well once cognitive and behavioral signs are obvious. However, it is believed that changes in the brain begin long before such signs are readily observed (Alzheimer's Association, 2012).

New approaches for detecting Alzheimer's in its earlier stages are beginning to produce encouraging results. Biomarkers of amyloid-beta protein deposits can be obtained through cerebrospinal fluid and a PET scan, and biomarkers of neurodegeneration can be obtained through cerebrospinal fluid, a PET scan, and an MRI. Once a comprehensive assessment of cognitive function indicates probable Alzheimer's, these biomarkers can lead to a reasonably definitive diagnosis. Even so, confirmation of Alzheimer's is still only achieved through examining the brain after the patient has died because the characteristic neurofibrillary and amyloid pathologies and loss of synapses can be readily observed then.

The U.S. Food and Drug Administration has approved several prescription drugs that can improve symptoms of Alzheimer's, although they do not change the course of the disease (*Alzheimer's Disease Medications*, 2008/2012). For mild to moderate Alzheimer's, three cholinesterase inhibitors have been shown to lead to a temporary improvement in memory function: donepezil (*Aricept*), rivastigmine (*Exelon*), and galantamine (*Razadyne*). These drugs stop the action of acetylcholinesterase, which is overabundant in Alzheimer's patients and which degrades acetylcholine, a neurotransmitter associated with learning. For moderate to severe Alzheimer's, memantine (*Namenda*) may be helpful. This drug protects brain cells from the damage caused by an excess of the chemical, glutamate, which is brought on by Alzheimer's.

Although no cure is yet in sight, actively managing Alzheimer's can significantly improve the quality of life of patients and their caregivers.

> Active management includes: (1) appropriate use of available treatment options, (2) effective management of coexisting conditions, (3) coordination of care among physicians, other health care professionals and lay caregivers, (4) participation in activities and adult day care programs, and (5) taking part in support groups and supportive services such as counseling. (Alzheimer's Association, 2012, p. 136)

The Probability of Getting Alzheimer's

There is disagreement as to how many people have Alzheimer's disease in the general population. The most common current estimate is 5 million Americans. More women than men are affected because they live longer than men do. The rate is very low for people under age 65. However, after age 65, there seems to be a continual increase in the prevalence of Alzheimer's. There is speculation that after age 85 the prevalence may increase substantially, perhaps reaching as high as 50%. However, a comprehensive study of over 1,000 people aged 85 and older in one community, including those in institutional care, found just 12% with moderate or severe cognitive impairment, and an estimated additional 7% with undiagnosed dementia (Collerton et al., 2009). Furthermore, in 2009, of 1.8 million deaths among Americans 65 years of age and older, Alzheimer's was listed as a cause of death just 4.3% of the time (Kochanek, Xu, Murphy, Miniño, & Kung, 2011). Although it is likely that Alzheimer's often goes undiagnosed, and is likely underreported as a cause of death, taken together these data suggest that the prevalence of Alzheimer's, especially after age 85, is much lower than some have speculated.

A small percentage of cases of Alzheimer's (1% to 2%) occur prior to age 65. Accordingly, these cases are termed *early-onset* and, different from most late-onset cases, they appear to have a hereditary component. Mutations in three genes—amyloid precursor protein gene (*APP*), presenilin 1 gene (*PSEN1*), and presenilin 2 gene (*PSEN2*)—seem to be responsible for this type of Alzheimer's (Rogaeva, 2002).

Impact of Alzheimer's on Families

Alzheimer's is often referred to as a family disease, because all members of the family are affected by it—emotionally, socially, and financially. As the disease progresses, families are forced to give more and more time to caring for their loved one because they cannot be left alone. If they wander away, they may not be able to find their way back. They often have strange sleep schedules and disrupt their caregiver's sleep. Eventually, they will need constant care for feeding and toileting.

On average, once diagnosed with Alzheimer's, a person lives approximately 4 to 8 years, but this varies substantially depending on how soon it is diagnosed. Some individuals live 20 years or longer with the disease (Alzheimer's Association, 2012). Support groups can bolster caregivers emotionally, and offer practical suggestions, as well as opportunities to exchange information about community resources. More information about the value of support groups is discussed in Chapter 12. Supporting family caregivers helps them to keep their loved one at home as long as possible, with demonstrated health benefits for patients and caregivers alike, and financial benefits that surpass the cost of support programs (Habermann, Cooper, Katona, & Livingston, 2009). For further information about the effects of Alzheimer's disease on the brain and caring for those with Alzheimer's, watch Video 8.

> ### Episode 8: Aging and Alzheimer's
>
> **High Bandwidth:**
> http://raidercast.grcc.edu/flash/2011_2012/grcctv/successful_
> aging/success_aging_8_large/grcc_player.html
> **Low Bandwidth:**
> http://raidercast.grcc.edu/flash/2011_2012/grcctv/successful_
> aging/success_aging_8_small/grcc_player.html

A National Plan to Address Alzheimer's

In 2007, the Alzheimer's Association and thousands of individual citizens began advocating for a national strategy to combat the disease. Their work culminated in the National Alzheimer's Project Act (NAPA), which was signed into law by President Barack Obama in January 2011 to coordinate research and services; improve diagnosis, treatments, and outcomes; and work with countries around the world to combat Alzheimer's and related dementias. Accordingly, a *National Plan to Address Alzheimer's Disease* has been developed (U.S. Department of Health and Human Services, 2012). The five goals of the plan are:

- To prevent and effectively treat Alzheimer's disease by 2025;
- To enhance care quality and efficiency;
- To expand supports for people with Alzheimer's disease and their families;
- To enhance public awareness and engagement;
- To improve data collection and analysis to track progress on the plan.

Accompanied by additional funding for research, public education, and support for people with Alzheimer's and their families, the National Alzheimer's Project and the National Plan have the potential to change the trajectory of Alzheimer's in the United States and around the world.

Creativity and Aging

When people think about mental abilities and aging, they do not usually think about creativity. Two aspects of creativity are of particular interest when it comes to aging. One is the extent to which creative ability is influenced by age, and the other is the extent to which participation in the creative arts can positively affect older adults', and others', quality of life.

Creativity has often been thought of as a domain of the young. Research over the last two decades, however, indicates otherwise. David Galenson (2010), a pioneer in the economics of creativity, examined the careers of renowned painters, sculptors, poets, novelists, and movie directors, using a variety of measures to characterize an artist's best work. His research led him to categorize important artists into two types—*experimental* innovators, such as Paul Cézanne, who seem to be most creative in their later years, and *conceptual* innovators, such as Pablo Picasso, who seem to be most creative when they are young.

> *Experimental* innovators seek to record their perceptions. They work tentatively, by trial and errors.... They consider making art a process of searching, in which they wish to make discoveries in the course of executing their works. They build their skills gradually, and their innovations appear incrementally in a body of work. In contrast, *conceptual* innovators use their art to express ideas or emotions. Their innovations are conspicuous, transgressive, and often irreverent. These innovations appear suddenly, as a new idea produces a result different not only from other artists' work, but also from the artist's own previous work. (Galenson, 2010, pp. 354–355)

Based on his own research as well as that of others, psychologist Dean Simonton (1990) has concluded that there are many reasons to be optimistic about creative potential in the later years:

- Those who are creative when they are young continue to be so in late life, though the quantity of their work may decrease;
- Older people can, and do, overcome physically disabling conditions to continue their creative work;
- Some people are late bloomers; and
- There can be a resurgence of creativity at the end of life.

There are many ways to express creativity—through performance arts, such as music, theater, and dance, as well as creative writing and the visual arts. Different from the crafts that are often a component of senior center activities, the arts "engage the mind, body, and emotions, sparking curiosity, problem solving, and artistic accomplishment" (Patterson & Perlstein, 2011, p. 28). In other words, engaging in the arts is a complex cognitive activity.

In order to evaluate the potential positive effects of participating in the arts, the late Gene Cohen and his colleagues (Cohen et al., 2006) conducted a study comparing older adults who were recruited to participate in a chorale group (the intervention group) with older adults in a comparison group. A total of 166 people with an average age of 79 years were in the study. Chorale members attended professionally conducted rehearsals once a week for 30 weeks and gave several public performances over the course of a year. At the end of 12 months, relative to the comparison group, the chorale group members reported improvements in their overall health, fewer physician visits, fewer falls, and higher morale. Cohen and his fellow researchers concluded that, "we have witnessed true health promotion and prevention effects...achieved through sustained involvement in a high-quality participatory art program—in this case, in an ongoing chorale directed by a professional conductor" (p. 733).

In 2012, the National Academy of Sciences convened a workshop "to identify research gaps and opportunities to foster greater investment in promising arts-related research that can seed interventions to improve quality of life for older adults" (Kent & Li, 2013, p. 1). Among the outcomes of the workshop were calls for research to evaluate the effects of arts programs across the lifespan; to compare the effects of different art forms, individually, and in combination; to broaden the diversity of people involved in the studies; and to examine the results of changing from a familiar art form to something new. New technologies are making it possible both to conduct and evaluate all kinds of programs, and arts interventions are no exception.

A pioneer in studying creativity and aging, Gene Cohen (2000), stated:

The importance of understanding creativity in relation to aging is profound, because doing so will not only enable older people to have access to their potential in later life, but it will also challenge younger age groups to think about what is possible in their later years in a different way. (pp. 5–6)

POSITIVE AND NEGATIVE INFUENCES ON MENTAL HEALTH AND MENTAL ABILITIES

Our mental health and mental abilities are influenced by many factors: physical, mental, and social activities; medical conditions; medications; and nutrition, among others. Some are very well-known, others less so, and we are learning more about yet others every day. Attention to these factors can help us maintain good cognitive function and indicate when it is time to seek medical attention.

Use It or Lose It: The Role of Physical, Mental, and Social Activities

Physical exercise is as important as, or more important than, mental exercise for retaining intellectual abilities. Physical exercise brings oxygen and increases blood flow to the brain, helping to maintain intellectual abilities, in part by stimulating the growth of new brain cells. Then mental exercise can ensure their survival.

The brain is an organ, and like all organs in the body, it needs to be used and exercised regularly. The old cliché "use it or lose it" seems to be true when it comes to the brain. Remaining mentally active helps people to maintain their mental abilities. Mental activity may include challenging tasks such as playing chess, doing crossword puzzles, and learning to play new pieces of music, and also participating in civic organizations, church activities, and social groups. And, researchers have concluded that educational programs can also improve cognitive functioning among older adults (Zelinski, Dalton, & Hindin, 2011). The gains from educational and training programs, however, can be expected to be lost if those who participate in the programs return to nonstimulating environments or fail to exercise the skills they have learned.

Medical Conditions

Chronic illness can also affect a person's mental health. Congestive heart failure, for example, can cause a loss of oxygen that can lead to abnormal brain functioning. The tremendous fatigue caused by congestive heart failure can lead to depression. Diabetes can lead to impotence in men, resulting in a damaged self-image, depression, and irritability. In addition, severe diabetes in either men or women can result in significant mood swings, depending upon their blood sugar levels. The pain that accompanies arthritis can lead to fatigue and result in irritability and depression. Chronic conditions, including high blood pressure, cardiovascular disease, and diabetes, have also all been linked to lower cognitive functioning among older adults. Even young and middle-aged adults can experience the reduced cognitive abilities associated with these conditions (Schaie, 2011).

Medications

As might be expected, misuse of medications can have deleterious effects on mental health. Instructions for taking medications can be difficult to read and understand, leading patients to take too little or too much medication. When older people take drugs that are helping them, it is not uncommon for them to share even their prescription drugs with a friend who may have similar health problems. Still others, because of limited resources, take only a few of their prescribed drugs, trying to save money.

In most clinic trials, over-the-counter and prescription drugs are tested in isolation so we know relatively little about the effects of taking several different medications simultaneously. Yet, as we learn in Chapter 14, older adults often take five or more prescription drugs per week. One of the authors worked with a senior citizens' center director who had a woman attending her neighborhood center who was lucid, energetic, and a great helper. Over a period of 3 months, the helper became increasingly confused and irritable. The director began to think she might need to be placed in a nursing facility. One day the center director, upon visiting her home, found 21 different prescriptions from five different physicians. The woman had not told each physician that she was also going to others. Among the prescriptions, the director found psychotropic drugs (major mood changers), such as chlorpromazine and diazepam, and a host of other drugs for numerous physical ailments. Because of the medications, the woman had deteriorated mentally to the point where she was not only mixing the drugs in dangerous combinations, but was taking them in quantities that would make most individuals act irrationally. The happy outcome of this story is that the woman was taken off most of the drugs, put under the supervision of one physician, and recovered her mental and emotional health. When one works with older persons and mood or mental changes take place, it is important to inquire about the medications they are taking. Health care professionals need to be informed about others who might be treating a person, just as elderly patients should be apprised about side effects that drugs might have on their moods or mental condition.

Nutrition

Inadequate nutrition can cause changes in mental health. For example, low levels of vitamin B12 can lead to mood changes, depression, and symptoms of dementia, such as memory loss. Often persons living alone do not cook or eat wholesome meals. As a result, they do not get the vitamins, minerals, or protein that their bodies need. Persons working with the elderly need to be aware of the eating habits of their clients. Inadequate nutrition over a period of time can have a negative impact on mental health.

THE MYTH OF INEVITABLE DECLINE

Just as physical abilities change with aging, so do mental abilities. Nevertheless, we know that much of what has been believed about older adults' mental health and mental abilities is overly negative, or just plain wrong. We also know that many factors have an impact, and maintenance, and even improvements, in mental functioning can occur throughout the lifespan. There is much to learn within this area of aging, but one thing we know for certain is that it is never too late to begin a new endeavor, be it physical, mental, or social.

SUGGESTED RESOURCES

American Psychological Association, Office on Aging: http://www.apa.org/pi/aging/
> This website offers information specific to mental health for older adults. It features webinars, book suggestions, research, services, and programs, with recommendations for how to deal with mental health issues.

Dementia Advocacy and Support Network (DASN): http://www.dasninternational.org/
> DASN is an international network of organized by and for those diagnosed with dementia. Educational materials about dementia and resources and strategies for living positively with dementia are provided through the organization's website.

National Center for Creative Aging (NCCA): http://www.creativeaging.org
> Formed in 2001, the Center's mission is to explore the connections between creative expression and healthy aging and to maximize opportunities for people to participate in the creative arts. The website has links to research, publications, programs, events, news, and blogs all focused on creativity and aging.

National Institute on Aging, Alzheimer's Disease Education & Referral Center (ADEAR): http://www.nia.nih.gov/Alzheimers/
> This website provides referrals and information for people interested in Alzheimer's. It features new research, and a scientific understanding of the disease.

SharpBrains: http://www.sharpbrains.com
> SharpBrains is a for-profit business that collects data and provides evaluations for consumers about the growing market in "brain fitness" tools and products.

CHAPTER 6

Sexuality and Aging

The learning objectives of this chapter include understanding

- Sexuality in the context of aging in the 21st century.
- Sexuality and aging in a second sexual revolution.
- Sexuality as a normal and vital part of life at any age—even old age.
- The factors that inhibit sexuality including physical limitations, cultural considerations, menopause, and prescription drugs.
- A new paradigm for sexuality and aging that focuses on relationships, prevention of HIV/AIDS, and practices (some specific) that can enhance sexuality.

JANE AND CARL: EVER ACTIVE

Jane and Carl are both 67 and have a vigorous, active sexual life. Throughout their marriage, they have been sexually active. They see sex not only as a period of intimacy, but also as a fun, creative, and fulfilling process. Neither Jane nor Carl smoke; their drinking is moderate. They exercise regularly, are in great physical condition, and have a zest for life. Jane went through menopause without many physiological or psychological problems. Their three children were out of the home by the time Jane completed the menopausal process. Her gynecologist gave her some strategic information that enhanced her sex life.

DORIS AND BEN: BORED AND TIRED

Doris is 73. Ben is 76. They have rarely had sexual intercourse during the last 10 years. Doris went through menopause at the age of 54, rather late for most women. At the time she was going through menopause, the last of her six children left home. She had been a full-time house-wife and mother, and most of her self-image revolved around her children. She never had a great deal of communication with her husband, who worked at two jobs to support his large family. After menopause Doris went into a period of depression, which her very religious husband found difficult to understand. He became angry at her lack of sexual responsiveness during her periods of depression. After menopause sexual intercourse became increasingly painful. In her earlier years, she always found sex rather perfunctory. There was a repetitive sameness in their sex life that even Ben began to find less than stimulating. As a result, their sexual activities decreased markedly, a decrease that Doris found acceptable. Ben, always a heavy smoker, had difficulty after age 50 obtaining and maintaining an erection. He fantasized about sex and periodically masturbated; increasingly as he got older, he was ready to ignore their sexual life. In their late 60s, they began to sleep in separate bedrooms, and eventually they ceased most sexual activities.

SEXUALITY: AN INTEGRAL PART OF LIFE

Sexuality is best viewed in the context of relationships, attitudes, and values. It involves more than reproductive systems and genitalia; it is more than the hormonal system. Sexuality is an attempt to gain intimacy, to have warmth, and closeness. It is a physical and psychological closeness that is part of human necessity. With that in mind, sexuality is seen as much more than just sexual contact. It includes an embrace, mutual stimulation, a touch, a couple holding hands on their daily walk.

Unfortunately, in the past, older people were thought to have no interest in sexuality. The elderly were seen as prudish, asexual people. It was almost as if eventually everyone was expected to lose sexual desire and any interest in the erotic or the sensual. Added to this was the emphasis within our youth culture of relating things erotic to the young, to the perfect bodies of the late adolescent or young adult. Sexual desire, it has been thought, might last through middle age at a significantly reduced level, but surely would disappear in later life.

Research, however, increasingly indicates that older people are sensual, have real needs for closeness and intimacy, and are involved in continuing sexual activities of various types. Whether by intercourse, masturbation, mutual masturbation, or other means, the vast majority of older people are still sexually active. Among happily married older people, most still find the sexual side of their relationships important. About two thirds of unmarried older persons, even those over the age of 70, are sexually active. Although they may find sex less intense than when they were young, many older people experience tender and satisfying sexual experiences.

A Second Sexual Revolution

No topic lends itself so well to the concept of a new paradigm of aging than sexuality and aging. Once perceived as asexual or sexless, many older people have challenged old stereotypes and myths regarding sexual attitudes and practices. But these liberating attitudes and practices obviously do not apply to all older people. Some old myths and taboos still prevail among some subgroups of the elderly. But with the inclusion of Baby Boomers into the older ages—the generation that pioneered the gender and sexual revolutions—there is a continuing redefining of sexuality and aging.

The story is told of an 18-year-old young woman in 1964—among the first of the Baby Boomers—who visited three gynecologists in her small Midwestern town in which she lived before she found one who would prescribe the newly available birth control pill because she was unmarried (Jacoby, 2005). These pills changed the sex lives of a whole generation, and they led to the sexual revolution of the 1960s and 1970s. "The pill" changed the thinking of Baby Boomers in the 1960s by making young women feel that they had the right to enjoy sex without fear of pregnancy (Jacoby, 2005). And now, over 40 years later with another pill (actually multiple pills that treat erectile dysfunction [ED]), along with changing attitudes and sexual practices, Baby Boomers are creating a second sexual revolution. And, this sexual revolution will change forever the way people think about sex and aging. This is a revolution in spirit and attitude about sexuality in midlife (and beyond), and at its core is the belief that many physical problems should be treated and overcome rather than be thought of as a normal part of growing older (Jacoby, 2005). With this social revolution occurring in America brought about by the increasing size of the older population, it is important to view sexuality as an integral part of the whole life span—into the oldest ages.

A NEW PARADIGM FOR SEXUALITY AND AGING

In spite of some changes to sexual function for older men and women, progressive older people, as well as aging Baby Boomers, feel that sex can still be an integral part of life— now and into their later years. In order to realize this goal, in addition to the newer medical approaches to enhance sexuality, new sexual attitudes and practices are emerging. This is in spite of the reality that "senior sexuality still ruffles some feathers in a society that prefers not to acknowledge its existence" (Golden, 2004, p. 3). Indeed, it is reported that many physicians will not even raise the issue of sexuality with their older patients. Dr. Robert Butler said, "What affection is subject to ridicule seems just wrong, ageist" (Golden, 2004, p. 3). (Dr. Butler originally developed the term *ageism* to describe prejudice against the elderly.)

Medical Interventions to Improve Sexual Functioning

Research has demonstrated that the production of the male sex hormone testosterone—which occurs in both sexes—drops and consequently can result in lowered interest in sexual activities. Some physicians prescribe testosterone as a libido booster for women who are diagnosed "low-T." It is often given in the form of a testosterone patch. However, some experts warn that this treatment could have only a limited effect because female sexual libido is tied to emotions, stresses, and other factors that no one patch or pill can treat (Klein, 2004). When Viagra was developed to treat ED in men, many women wanted something similar to enhance their sexuality. Low sexual desire, inability to become aroused, lack of orgasm, or painful intercourse can occur at any age but become more common with age. Among the many factors that can contribute to these problems are inhibitions, anxiety, insufficient lubrication or stimulation, and previous sexual trauma or abuse, as well as hormonal changes, chronic health conditions, and medications.

Enhancing Female Sexuality in Aging

Some experts have cautioned that biological treatments for women (including testosterone) can sometimes have only limited effects because female sexual response is related to multiple factors. In its report on testosterone treatment for men and women, the *Consumer Reports on Health* pointed out that measuring testosterone is ineffective for women because the tests are really not accurate and normal levels have not been established ("Healthy Sex: His and Hers," 2006). In fact, this report went on to state that women should not use testosterone if they have had uterine or breast cancer, heart disease, or liver disease because of the dangers of exacerbating disease processes.

Hormone-Replacement Therapy

In the past, hormone-replacement therapy (HRT) was widely used to treat the symptoms associated with menopause including sexual dysfunction. In the summer of 2002, however, a major longitudinal study—the Women's Health Initiative—was halted when it became clear that HRT actually increased the risk of breast cancer and heart disease (Noonan, 2003). More recently, estrogen is sometimes being combined with testosterone in a product called Estratest, which is the only testosterone application approved for women in the United States ("Healthy Sex: His and Hers," 2006). Nevertheless, this product can cause the reduction of HDL, the "good" cholesterol. In addition, for women who wish to try estrogen for vaginal dryness and reduced clitoral sensitivity, some creams such as Estrace and Premarin are available along with vaginal inserts such as Estring that allow smaller and safer doses. Short-term use of low-dose estrogen patches or pills are sometimes used for women who are not at high risk for heart disease or breast cancer ("Healthy Sex: His and Hers," 2006).

Viagra and Female Sexuality

Although sildenafil (Viagra) may improve clitoral sensitivity in a small minority of women, many physicians and researchers warn that there is no good reason for women to try these types of drugs that that were developed to treat ED in men ("Healthy Sex: His and Hers," 2006). Instead, simply reducing coronary risk factors may improve clitoral sensitivity, and prolonging foreplay and using nonpetroleum lubricants (such as K-Y Jelly and Replens) can increase vaginal moisture. It is also claimed that remaining sexually active may promote vaginal moisture. Combining these approaches with treating issues that impair the libido may improve a woman's ability to achieve orgasm. In summary, a combination of steps can be used to enhance the sexual functioning of women. These include treating underlying medical disorders, adjusting dosages, or substituting drugs for underlying medical conditions, reducing stress, and/or dealing with problems in relationships with the help of a marriage counselor or a sex therapist who focuses on sexual attitudes and practices.

Enhancing Male Sexuality in Aging

As indicated earlier in this chapter, one of the biggest breakthroughs in promoting sexual functioning in aging males was the development of sildenafil (Viagra), and the related drugs tadalafil (Cialis) and vardonafil (Levitra), all of which can be used to treat ED—insufficient penile erection. ED is typically the result of physical problems, often ones that relate to heart disease, although anxiety can be the cause. These three drugs (Cialis, Levitra, and Viagra) dilate blood vessels in the penis, enabling increased blood flow, which leads to an erection. Tadalafil lasts about 36 hours, while the others last about 4 hours. The 36-hour pill is designed for men who want spontaneity in sexual activities. It is advised that before a man begins treatment with any of these three drugs, he should have his vision and heart examined because of potential negative side effects ("Healthy Sex: His and Hers," 2006).

Other Benefits of Treating Male ED

A major finding of an AARP sexual survey—surprising to many—is the increased plea-sure these treatments for men have given their female partners (Jacoby, 2005). This is directly contrary to the old myth that older women do not enjoy sex. Another myth dis-pelled by this survey is that the main reason men take these new medications is to have sex with younger women. In reality, most of these men want to continue to have sex with their older spouses or partners, and the women in the survey (of all age groups) reported that their own sexual satisfaction was improved by their partners' use of these drugs. Jennifer Berman, MD, a leading sex researcher and counselor, said that the notion that "older women are just happy to be done with sex" is based on cultural stereotypes that equate women's sexual desire—and desirability—with a youthful body (Jacoby, 2005, p. 57). Dr. Berman went on to say that for every older woman who comes to her office complaining that her husband wants too much sex, there is another older woman who complains that she wants sex, but that her husband has no interest. "This woman can be 30 or she can be 70," according to Berman (Jacoby, 2005, p. 57).

Testosterone Replacement

Testosterone replacement therapy (TRT) became the "hot" hormone therapy of choice for hundreds of thousands of men in the early years of the 21st century (Noonan, 2003). This treatment was believed by many middle- and older-aged men to treat sexual dysfunc-tions—such as ED and loss of libido that some have termed *andropause*, the male version of menopause in women. But while a man produces less testosterone as he ages, most men remain within normal limits, unlike the major shutdown of hormone production that women face in menopause, according to Stanley Slater at the National Institute on Aging (NIA; Greider, 2003). Slater stated that many people incorrectly blame lowered tes-tosterone for male sexual problems in middle and later life. In the vast majority of cases, he said, erectile difficulties in men are due to circulatory problems.

TRT has also been credited with improving memory and bones, building vitality, and enhancing sexual desire. But Slater indicated these claims are not necessarily true. Only a small number of men—younger men with damaged pituitary glands or testes—may be helped by this therapy. Slater seriously questioned the value and safety of TRT for healthy older men. He went on to state that "testosterone feeds the growth of tumors in men who have metastatic prostate cancer," noting that most older men have inactive and harmless "nests" of cancer cells (Greider, 2003, p. 16).

Other studies have indicated that supplemental testosterone may trigger excessive red blood cell production, which can thicken the blood and increase the risk of a stroke. In 2002, the NIH (National Institutes of Health) cancelled a major large-scale trial related to testosterone because of questions of the study's design and the opposition of the direc-tor of the National Cancer Institute due to concerns about potentially increasing prostate cancer (Greider, 2003). In addition, the answer to the question of what is "normal" for tes-tosterone levels varies greatly. It is tricky to measure hormone levels in men because the tests can be fickle, the results varying depending on when they are administered—times of day, seasons—and levels of exercise.

Growth Hormone

Another hormone treatment for men that is very controversial is the growth hormone dehydroepiandrosterone (DHEA). In fact, the reservations about using DHEA are dou-ble those for using testosterone because of its safety hazards. In addition, in its dietary supplement formats, DHEA is mostly unregulated. As a result, labeled dosages are questionable and the use of this potent hormone is not likely to be monitored by a physician ("Healthy Sex: His and Hers," 2006). Instead, physicians and researchers of *Consumer Reports on Health* advise avoiding DHEA entirely.

High Blood Pressure and Sexuality

As hypertension (high blood pressure) is fairly widespread among older people—women and men—it is important to treat this condition to prevent strokes, heart disease, kidney failure, and the risk of ED. According to *The Harvard Men's Health Watch*,

> men with hypertension are four times more likely to develop erectile dysfunction than men with normal blood pressures. High blood pressure contributes to erectile dysfunction in the same way it causes to strokes and heart attacks, by damaging blood vessels. Erections depend on a six-fold increase in the amount of blood in the penis, and that requires healthy arteries to let the blood in and healthy veins to keep it there. ("High Blood Pressure," 2003, p. 4)

Therefore, for healthy sexual functioning, it is important to control blood pressure because some medications for hypertension actually contribute to ED. Most often, this is related to the thiazide diuretics category of drugs. As a result, ED caused by some medications can sometimes be treated by switching to other blood pressure drugs ("High Blood Pressure" 2003).

Psychological Factors in Sexuality

Some couples drift into sexual apathy because of unresolved anger. They attempt to "get at" their partner by refusing sexual activity or significantly reducing the amount or type of sexual contact. This can happen to couples at any age. Unfortunately, too many older people assume that their reduced sexual contact is simply the result of growing older. As a result, they do not obtain the type of counseling that would enable them to resolve their feelings of anger and once again become sexually active partners.

Depression can also be a major factor in the loss of sexual desire. Depression can also occur at any age; it is a major factor in sexual dysfunction at all ages. Unfortunately, once again, the older the person, the higher the probability that he or she will assume that sexual dysfunction is the result of physical factors due to aging, and thus will not seek the help that could rejuvenate his or her sexual life. In instances where there is no physical basis for the loss of sexual desire, professional counseling can be helpful. A competent counselor can assist in understanding the factors and processes that lead to a loss of sexual desire. An effective counselor can also be helpful in recovering sexual drive.

Sex and Health

Experts point out that sexual satisfaction is not just for personal pleasure. Dr. Julia Heiman, Director of the Kinsey Institute for Research in Sex, Gender, and Reproduction at Indiana University, pointed out that a satisfying sex life can promote good emotional and physical health. In addition, sex itself may have direct health benefits. Orgasm or any loving touch may result in the body releasing substances that can ease pain, improve immunity, and elevate mood long after the immediate pleasure of sex. It is contended that people who have strong, intimate relationships are more likely to experience fewer chronic diseases and more likely to live longer ("Healthy Sex: His and Hers," 2006). As a result, there are important reasons to look into and address any significant loss of sexual interest and functioning in all ages of life.

RELATIONSHIPS AND SEXUALITY

Personal relationships are integral to understanding sexuality in the older ages, whether they are between partners who are married or cohabiting or single individuals.

Older Couples

Many years ago, Robert Atchley (1991) indicated that couplehood for older people has four basic functions: (a) intimacy, (b) sexual intimacy, (c) interdependence, and (d) belonging. In some ways, all of these relate to sexuality in older adults even though not all of them focus directly on sexual activities. They all contribute to feelings of closeness, being needed, and having someone to turn to in all aspects of life.

As they grow older, couples ideally develop an ability to anticipate each other's sexual needs. With years of experience, they can acquire the ability to fulfill those needs. They may develop a reciprocity of sexual responses that comes only after years of interaction. Many decades ago, Masters and Johnson (1970a, 1970b) indicated that two persons committed to each other in a loving relationship can learn to give sexual pleasure to each other as they communicate their sexual preferences in an atmosphere of trust and acceptance. With the passing years, many learn how to articulate and listen in the interplay of sexual recreation and desire.

Postmenopausal Women

For some postmenopausal heterosexual women, the realization that they will no longer get pregnant liberates them sexually. In addition, many postmenopausal women become liberated from inhibitions that kept them from a free expression of their sexual desires. With no worries about kids opening their bedroom doors while engaged in sexual activities, older couples have fewer reasons to be uptight about sex. In addition, they tend to be better able to please each other, knowing where and how to arouse sexual feelings and pleasures (Golden, 2004). In fact, some sex counselors have seen quite a bit of what anthropologist Margaret Mead termed *PMZ* (postmenopausal zest). "Indeed, some women begin to have orgasms for the first time as they grow older," according to the late Dr. Robert Butler and the late Myrna Lewis, his wife, (he was a leading gerontologist and geriatrician, and she was a psychotherapist) in their book, *The New Love and Sex After 60* (Golden, 2004, p. 1).

Strains in Older Marriages

A survey by AARP of Baby Boomers as well as people in their late 60s, 70s, 80s, and older, found that a majority of those questioned said that a satisfying sex life was important to a person's quality of life. But for most, it was not the number one priority. Rather, good spirits, good health, close ties with friends and family, financial security, spiritual well-being, and good relationships with a partner were all rated higher than good sex (Jacoby, 2005).

Indeed, men put a higher priority on sex than women did in the survey. Some 66% of men compared to 48% of women stated that good sex was important to their quality of life. By age 60, the gender gap on the value of good sex widens with 62% of the men versus 27% of the women putting a high priority on satisfying sex. But some experts find these statistics misleading because so many older women no longer have partners. The AARP survey found that nearly one third of the older women and men with partners described their sex life somewhere between "yawn" and "bloody awful." Yet 63% of the men and women with partners described themselves as either "extremely satisfied" or "somewhat satisfied" with their sex lives (Jacoby, 2005, p. 58).

The late Helen Gurley Brown, founding editor of *Cosmopolitan* magazine, stated, "When people say they can't have sex because of a bad back or arthritis or things that can affect our bodies, I think they're really looking for an excuse not to have sex" (Jacoby, 2005, p. 82). What is needed is the ability to negotiate sexual issues and problems that are related to age in order to develop or maintain strong relationships.

Marriage and Frequency of Sex

Researchers in Britain surveyed people in 59 countries for a report in the medical journal, *The Lancet*, and found that married people in every country engaged in more sexual activities than did single persons with the ratio between married and singles as high as 9 to 1 (Moore, 2006). The differences in sexual activity were evident in both the industrialized nations as well as those in the developing world.

The question can be raised as to where do all the stereotypes of sexless marriages come from? A Canadian researcher and therapist stated that many people in the Western world have vague ideas as to how much sex is appropriate. He went on to point out that there is a great myth that the single life is the most active, with sexual encounters almost every day (Moore, 2006). But in regard to the four industrialized countries studied—Australia, Britain, France, and the United States—more than 80% of married people reported that they recently had sex compared to only 50% to 60% of singles.

Romantic/Passionate/Companionate Love

An analysis of 25 studies involving over 6,000 people in short- and long-term relationships focused on finding different levels of satisfaction (Acevedo & Aron, 2009). This analysis, reported by researchers at Stony Brook University, differentiated between three kinds of love: *romantic love*—being able to retain "intensity, engagement, and sexual interest" for both short-term and long-term relationships (p. 59); *passionate love*—romantic love with "high obsession, uncertainty, and anxiety" (p. 63); and *companionate love*—"a warm, less intense love, devoid of attraction and sexual desire" (p. 59). The researchers concluded that "contrary to what has been widely believed, long-term romantic love…appears to be a real phenomenon that may be enhancing to individuals' lives—positively associated with marital satisfaction, mental health, and overall well-being" (p. 64).

Single Older Women

Single older women cannot be stereotyped. Words such as *lonely, shy,* or *insecure* no longer apply. Nearly half of the single women in the AARP survey reported that, as singles, they were happier than they had ever been in their lives. But given the opportunity, many of the single women said they would be open to a committed relationship (Mahoney, 2006). This survey, entitled, "Lifestyles, Dating and Romance: A Study of Midlife Singles," found that 31% of single women aged 40 through 69 were already in an exclusive relationship, and another 32% were dating nonexclusively. But about 10% had no desire to date at all, with another 14% willing to date if the right man came along, but they were not really trying very hard to find such a person. The remaining 13% in this survey said they were actively looking for a mate (Mahoney, 2006).

Gail Sheehy, a contributing editor at *Vanity Fair* magazine and author of the bestselling book, *Passages,* as well as a more recent book, *Sex and the Seasoned Woman*, points out that 75% of divorced older women have a serious relationship after divorce (Longcore, 2006). To obtain the data for her book on older women and sex, Sheehy posted a questionnaire on her website about sex and romance and followed that up by meeting with groups of women across America. Her findings dispel two myths: (a) that women are not interested in sex after menopause, and (b) that there are no good men out there for these women. Among women aged late 40s to their mid-80s, some 20%, a group Sheehy terms *seekers*, "are hungry for sex" and have not given up on finding a new relationship (Longcore, 2006, p. E1). And one third of the single women in her surveyed groups were dating younger men. Sheehy points out, as have others, that older women will likely spend more time unmarried than married, yet they have been largely ignored in many sex studies. The drive to love is one of the most powerful human drives, yet, Sheehy says, there is a persistent gap between cultural beliefs about sex and private sexual behavior.

Dating Younger Men

Sheehy found that the reason single older women date younger men is because men their own age are typically looking for traditional wives with the same roles that these women played in their child-rearing years. The women surveyed in Sheehy's groups said they played these roles for 25 years. Now they want to be an equal life partner, not a caretaker, and they want time for themselves. Today's older single women, Sheehy says, are interesting, accomplished, and independent. Older men tend to be intimidated by all these attributes, whereas younger men are not. In the new sexual paradigm, older women no longer have to wait to be contacted by men; they can take the initiative to contact men. Primarily this has been brought about by online dating services, and online connections such as chat rooms, Facebook, and so forth. The Internet has brought about a whole new era in developing relationships of all kinds. There are even online dating services geared specifically for older adults, *OurTime.com* and *SeniorPeopleMeet.com* being two of them. Sheehy summed up her research by stating that, "continuing interest and pleasure in sexuality is very much a part of the senior years" (Longcore, 2006, p. E2).

THE PREDOMINANCE OF BEING SINGLE

Surveys indicate that over half (57%) of adult Americans live single lives ("Single life in vogue for 51% of women," 2007). And, married couples have become a minority of all households for the first time in modern American history. In 1950, only 35% of American women were living without a spouse.

The reasons for these two new realities fall on both ends of the age spectrum. At younger ages, women are marrying later or they are living with unmarried partners in greater numbers for longer periods of time. In older ages, women are living longer as widows, and after divorces, women are more likely than men to delay remarriage.

As a result, it is estimated that American women are likely to spend more years of their lives as single persons than as part of a couple with a partner, according to Bella De Paulo, professor at the University of California, Santa Barbara, and author of a book on single people. She says that "the reality is relationships are now what happens between longer periods of singleness" (Mahoney, 2006, p. 50).

In addition, there are ethnic and racial differences in marriage rates. About 30% of Black American women live with a spouse compared to 49% for Hispanic women, 55% for non-Hispanic White women, and more than 60% of Asian women, according to the Census Bureau ("Single Life in Vogue For 51% of Women," 2007). It is estimated that the only times in American history that single living was so widespread were during major wars, such as World War II, and when Black American couples were separated by slavery.

Sex and Personal Values

Even though physical intimacy in sexual relationships is vital to many older people, it can be in direct conflict with the value systems they have lived with all their lives. This can result in mixed feelings on the part of some older people as well as attempts to hide their behavior from friends and families. Still, not too many unmarried couples want to marry their dating partners. Some are not willing to give up their independence. Others say they do not have the same reasons for marriage that younger people do, such as starting a new life and beginning a new family. Others are fearful of deteriorating health; they do not want to become caregivers for sick spouses. Many older couples do not marry because of financial considerations, including possible loss of pensions or Social Security incomes, complex estate provisions, and inheritances for children.

OLDER LESBIAN, GAY, BISEXUAL, AND TRANSGENDER PEOPLE

Not much is known about the physical or mental health and social service needs of older self-identified lesbians, gay men, bisexuals, and transgender individuals even in the first decade of the 21st century.

Historical Context

In order to begin to understand the lives of older homosexuals, it is important to briefly look at the history through which they lived. For much of the 20th century, homosexuality was linked to mental illness and criminality. In some ways, this is ironic because up until the early 1900s, for example, lesbianism was looked at as rather harmless. Indeed, some homosexual activity actually was thought to prepare young women for "real sex," meaning sex with men (Clunis, Fredrikson-Goldsen, Freeman, & Nystrom, 2005). The term *Boston marriage* was used to define the long-term relationships women developed and maintained with other women leading into their older ages. These lesbian relationships were often given respectability because the women were generally well educated and financially secure, and thus not considered social or economic burdens to their families (Clunis et al., 2005).

On the other hand, after 1910, societal views toward lesbianism changed dramatically because of the medicalization of this form of sexuality and the negative publicity it received. Increased newspaper coverage of the dangers of lesbianism, along with police raids on bars and clubs catering to gays and lesbians, became common in bringing attention to America's supposed homosexual threat as perceived at that time. Indeed, homosexuality was classified as a disease by the American Psychiatric Association until 1973, which is why the term *medicalization of homosexuality* is used.

Attitudes and actions toward gays and lesbians varied throughout the 20th century, but for the most part, focused on the notions that these folks were perverse and predatory. As a result, laws were passed and enforced that criminalized homosexuals and ultimately drove them underground (Clunis et al., 2005). It was believed that the "illness" of homosexuality could be "cured" by psychiatrists or mental health workers. Freudian and other forms of analysis, which could go on for years, and insulin shock therapy were often used to combat lesbianism in female adolescents. Electroconvulsive shock therapy (ECT) was also employed when other approaches did not work. In some cases, lobotomy, a surgical procedure performed on the brain, was also used (Clunis et al., 2005).

To avoid being caught up in the criminal laws and mental health codes targeting them, many homosexuals simply married members of the opposite sex. Estimates vary, but it is thought that about 40% of lesbians have been married to men at some time in their lives, with some 25% to 33% having children (Barker, 2003). The reasons cited for getting married included (a) not recognizing their lesbianism, (b) doing what was expected of them, (c) suppressing lesbian desires, and (d) marrying because of being pregnant or wanting to have children (Clunis et al., 2005). In addition, many homosexuals were pressured into heterosexual marriage by their psychiatrists or their churches.

Changing Times

Finally, beginning with the sexual revolutions of the 1960s, the visibility and plight of the nation's sexual minorities—lesbians, gays, bisexuals, and transgender people—began to change. Some of the milestones in the advance of sexual minority visibility over the last few decades include the Stonewall riots (rioting over homosexual rights), the civil rights movement, the feminist movement, the coming of gay and lesbian "pride" parades and celebrations in cities across America, unisex clothing fashions, the HIV/AIDS epidemic, and more recently, legalized same-sex marriage in some parts of the country.

The ages at which homosexuals recognize and/or declare their homosexuality varies. Older lesbians discover, or disclose, their sexual orientation at various ages including adolescence, early adulthood, and middle and older ages. They may also "come out" after a heterosexual marriage or in retirement (Barker, 2003).

Although long-term romantic partner relationships vary among lesbians, this type of relationship tends to be the most sought after by middle- and older-age lesbians (Weinstock, 2003). Indeed, it is estimated that many, if not most, adult lesbians want to grow old with a partner. Lesbians typically move through courtship with the object of establishing permanent relationships. And increasingly, these relationships involve children (Weinstock, 2003).

Older gay men have also experienced coming out at various ages. Some older gay men marry women when they are young adults but discover their homosexuality later in their lives. Others acquire male partners earlier in life and live in marriage-like unions with them most of their lives. Still others stay single and have short-term relationships with multiple male partners or brief sexual encounters with many men (Kristiansen, 2003).

In 1996, Congress passed the Defense of Marriage Act (DOMA, Pub.L. 104–199), which defined marriage as between a man and a woman. On June 6, 2013, the U.S. Supreme Court in a 5 to 4 decision declared part of the Defense of Marriage Act unconstitutional which defined marriage solely as a legal union between a man and a woman.

On the same day the U.S. Supreme Court declined to address the constitutionality of California's Proposition 8 ballot initiative banning same-sex marriage which kept intact a U.S. 9th Circuit Court of Appeals decision which declared Proposition 8 unconstitutional.

As of October 2013, 14 states plus the District of Columbia issued same-sex marriage licenses. Five states came by court decisions, six by state legislatures, and three by popular votes. In addition, New Mexico had no law banning or legalizing same-sex marriages. As a result, marriage licenses for same-sex couples were issued in various counties (www.gaymarriage.procon.org/view.resource.php?reso).

HIV/AIDS AND OLDER PEOPLE

Older people are not usually thought of as a high-risk group to be exposed to the HIV virus. This is due in large part to the old misconceptions about the sexual activities of people in their later years. In addition, even professionals within the health care system are not immune to ageist thinking because many are hesitant to discuss sexual issues with their older patients. And many older persons are not comfortable confiding in anyone about their sexual activities.

The reality is that of all HIV/AIDS cases, persons aged 55 and over account for 10.5% of new HIV/AIDS diagnoses, and 31.2% of deaths. There are more than a quarter of a million persons aged 55 and over who are currently living with HIV/AIDS, and the Centers for Disease Control & Prevention (CDC) estimates that by 2015 half of the Americans with HIV will be age 50 or older (Centers for Disease Control & Prevention [CDC], 2012).

HIV Risk Factors for Older Adults

Some factors associated with growing older tend to make older adults more vulnerable to the transmission of HIV. These include (a) the normal postmenopausal changes in women, (b) the declining effectiveness of the immune system, (c) the decreased use of condoms and other safe sex practices, and (d) the reduced likelihood that older adults have ever been tested for HIV.

Results from the West Central Florida Research Project, a survey of older persons in Florida who contracted HIV, found that 68% of those with the disease got it through unprotected sex (Nichols, 2004). The same study found that 62% of those with HIV had little or no knowledge of the disease or the risky sexual behaviors that can lead to its spread. The rise in divorce rates among the old, and the widespread reality of widowhood among women and to a lesser extent among men, increases the likelihood that more older persons will have multiple sex partners during their life span. In addition, medications to improve sexual functioning, such as Viagra, extend active sexual activities of people into their later years. All of this demonstrates the need for health and disease prevention education aimed at older adults.

PRACTICES TO ENHANCE SEXUALITY IN AGING

To spice up their sex lives, Baby Boomers (and many elderly persons) have been experimenting with sex practices and activities that in an earlier time would have seemed forbidden or racy.

Masturbation/Mutual Masturbation

An increasing number of older people say they have masturbated at least once in the last 6 months. Almost 50% of women aged 45 to 49 report masturbating, while 20% of those aged 70 and older report doing so. A majority of all women—even those aged 70 and over—say that self-stimulation is an important part of sexual pleasure at any age. The rate of masturbation among men has not changed much in the last few years (Jacoby, 2005).

When one hears someone talk about *having sex*, being *sexually active* or *sexually involved*, being *in a sexual relationship* or *intimate* with someone, it is usually assumed these phrases refer to sexual intercourse. This has been a part of the American culture. In an article proposing a new and more realistic approach to sexuality, Dr. Sylvia Hacker (1990, p. 93), of the University of Michigan, advocates new sexual norms for society. She indicates that sexual intercourse is only one part of a wide range of sexual activities that can bring pleasure and satisfaction to people. She points out that sexual pleasure can be achieved outside of sexual intercourse. For example, men get pleasure from ejaculation, which can be achieved by masturbation; but the greatest pleasure is achieved when both sexual partners have orgasms, which are not achieved by many women through intercourse. This is particularly true for older, postmenopausal women who lose vaginal lubrication. Many women do not achieve orgasm through sexual intercourse because of a lack of adequate stimulation, and intercourse can be painful without supplemental lubrication.

Dr. Hacker focused on developing "great lover" techniques, which include slowing down and getting in touch with each person's sensuality. This means achieving very pleasurable orgasms by focusing on bringing pleasure to each partner through touching, caressing, massaging, hugging, fondling, and bringing to orgasm each partner by manipulation. For older persons who have been socialized in an old cultural norm of sexuality, mutual masturbation/pleasuring can be a liberating experience.

Other Forms of Sexual Stimulation

Media spokespeople have emerged to promote a sexual liberation theme for older people as well as the emerging old (Baby Boomers). Perhaps two of the most well known have been Dr. Ruth Westheimer, who makes media appearances as Dr. Ruth speaking honestly and forthrightly on a wide variety of sex-related topics, and Sue Johanson, a leading sex educator in Canada for more than 30 years.

Good sex after midlife is an important theme of Johanson's. "Who says you shouldn't have exciting sex after 70?" she asked (Matthews, 2004, p. 25.). Johanson points out that arousal in both sexes takes longer in the later years, and the need for orgasm diminishes greatly. But she contends that the need for a sex life is ongoing, even if the grown children disapprove or say, "Mother! At your age!" She contends that sex in nursing homes and assisted-living facilities is becoming more common.

She dispels myths and reassures people who call in to her radio or TV programs about specific sexual practices and even fetishes—but always from a safe sex approach. For example, in response to a woman caller who was upset by her husband wearing women's silk panties while masturbating, Johanson assured her that this kind of role-playing is nothing to worry about. She advised her to let him enjoy it and enjoy it with him. Experimentation is encouraged if mutually agreed upon, and if it meets safe sex standards.

Johanson believes that aging Baby Boomers will permanently redefine post-50 sex. "Women in their 70s and 80s have begun asserting their ongoing interest in a sex life," she said. "So why accept arbitrary age parameters? The basic rules of sex apply at every life stage"—an example of a new paradigm of aging (Matthews, 2004, p. 25).

SUGGESTED RESOURCES

American Geriatric Society's Foundation for Health in Aging, Safe Sex for Seniors: http://www. healthinaging.org/files/documents/tipsheets/*safe_sex_for_seniors*.pdf

This document is about safe sex and made for the senior population by health care providers. It provides information on having safe sex, tips for dating and why it is important to have safe sex at an older age. It also addresses age specifi c sexual health concerns, such as ED.

Mayo Clinic, *Sexual Health and Aging: Keep the Passion Alive*: http://www.mayoclinic.com/health/ sexual-health/HA00035

This Internet resource discusses ways to be sexually active in a healthy way. The website provides tips on sexual health, aging, and communication in regards to sexual lifestyle. It integrates feelings and sexuality among an older population.

NIA, *Sexuality in Later Life:* http://www.nia.nih.gov/health/publication/sexuality-later-life

The National Institute on Aging provides information on common health problems associated with aging and how they affect sexuality later in life.

The Kinsey Institute: http://www.kinseyinstitute.org/

The goal of the Institute, located at Indiana University, is to have the most accurate and upto date information on sexual health, gender, and sexual behavior. Articles, publications, and other research materials are available on the website.

CHAPTER 7

Death, Dying, and Bereavement

The learning objectives for this chapter include understanding

- Perspectives on active and passive euthanasia.
- The stages of dying.
- The origin of hospice and its purposes.
- Organ donations and the process by which they can occur.
- The various aspects of grief and bereavement.

PERPLEXING CASES

James has been in a nursing home for 3 years. After three major strokes, he cannot talk or take care of any of his bodily needs. In his last attempts at communication, he said he wanted to die. He has pneumonia and the staff wants to send him to an acute care hospital for intensive treatment. Should they?

Grace is being kept alive by a feeding tube. She has no lucidity. If the tube is removed, she will die. What should the family do?

Alice is 89. She is lucid but suffering from severe diabetes, which has led to the amputation of her legs and to blindness. She refuses to eat. She says that she wants to die. Should the staff "force feed" her?

Two years ago, Ralph lost his wife after 62 years of marriage. He is still in deep depression because of her death. He mostly talks about how much he misses her. He does not care to continue living and frequently says that he wishes he would die. He has not responded well to psychiatric treatment. He has a severe heart condition and refuses to take his medications. If he has a heart attack he might die, and yet he has thrown away his latest prescription. What should the family do?

David, after 46 years of marriage, is struggling with what type of funeral he should have for his wife. In his grief and lack of knowledge about funerals, he is totally dependent on the funeral director. His bill for the funeral will be $6,750. Excessive? Moderate?

Martha has been attending Widowed Persons meetings for the last 15 months. It has helped her though the grieving process. She is now beginning to have interesting conversations with some of the men at the meetings. She is 69 and is beginning to think of "dating." Most of the men are in their 70s. Should her children be worried about the relationships that their mother might be developing?

Peter is 63 and quite rich. He has been a widower for 2 years. He is retired and in excellent health. If he wanted to, he could spend his time traveling around the world. He is dating a 46-year-old divorcee with two dependent children. Peter's three children are worried that their father is going to spend the rest of his life supporting and being devoted to another family. They think he is being set up. Should his children be concerned?

DEATH: A NORMAL PART OF HUMAN EXISTENCE

In spite of the marvelous advances that have been made in medical technology, the increased availability of medical services, and a better standard of living for many people in the United States that has resulted in a considerable longer life expectancy in this century, death is still part of all human existence. Death is not abnormal; it comes to all living creatures. As Leming and Dickinson (2011) wrote, "Dying is a human activity that is carried out in a normative manner. Each individual learns from society the meaning of death and the proper ways to die. One hopes to die what one's culture considers to be a good death" (p. 172).

Avoiding Talk of Death

For an older person, death is expected and becomes a normal event (Leming & Dickinson, 2011). The problem of death for older people is not so much death itself, but how and under what circumstances death will take place (Gates, 2007).

Until recently, Americans tended to be willing to discuss death in the abstract but were uncomfortable discussing their own deaths. Death in American society tends to be hidden in hospitals and nursing homes, and few Americans see their relatives die. They are told that death has occurred. Most people say they want to die at home, but most do not die there.

As so many people in American society are not comfortable discussing death other than in the abstract, many euphemisms are used to refer to death or dying, such as *the departed, passed on, expired, passed away, succumbed, croaked, cashed in, checked out,* and *six feet under*. As a result, many people are ill at ease talking to someone about the death of a close relative or about a patient's imminent demise.

In our death-denying culture, it is an unfortunate fact that even professionals, who regularly work with those who are aging, such as physicians, nurses, health professionals, and clergy, often lack education regarding issues related to death, dying, and bereavement. This point is further explored in the Practical Application at the end of Part II of this textbook.

History of Funerals

At one time in American history, most people died at home. Now approximately 70% die in an institutional setting. In keeping with banishing death from the homes of America to hospitals or nursing facilities, funerals (including paying respects and sharing grief with relatives, friends, and neighbors) have been moved from the family parlor to funeral homes (Leming & Dickinson, 2011). Following the Civil War, middle-class Americans began to replace the formal parlors in their homes with what were called "living rooms." Corpses were no longer laid out in family living rooms. All of this has made death more distant to the family setting and more removed from the normal life cycle (Auger, 2007).

FEAR OF DEATH

Similar to people of all ages, older people have some fears and concerns as they become closer to death. Research has indicated that older persons think about death more than younger people do, but the elderly seem to be less fearful and have less anxiety about it (Leming & Dickinson, 2011). Research over the years is not clear as to why older people seem to fear death less than younger people do. Kalish (1987) pointed out that there may be at least three reasons. The old may believe that they have lived their lives to the fullest, and as a result, they have a sense of completion and realize that death is the next natural part of the life cycle. Some are in a painful, prolonged, hopeless illness where they see death as a release from pain and suffering. Others have lost so many friends and relatives that they increasingly feel isolated from others. They have seen their spouses and close friends die and have "less to live for." One of the results of living into the oldest-old years is that one loses most of one's friends to death at a time when physical disabilities can make it hard to make new friends.

Fear of the Dying Process

Older people do have some anxieties as to how and under what circumstances they will die. Many years ago, Balfour Mount (1976) found that there are several concerns people have about the dying process. Many people fear that they may die alone, have considerable pain, become a burden to their loved ones, and become a financial burden for their family. In addition, some have indicated a fear of death itself, of the unknown, of what happens after death.

Neimeyer and Van Brunt (1995) discussed the fears of dying that people may have as a result of their religious beliefs about a life after death: concern about punishment for what they have done; fear of being abandoned; fear of pain and indignity; and fear of being nonexistent. Women seem to have more fear about death than men, or they may be more open in expressing their fears. The authors also indicated that research does not show that education about death reduces the fear of death. In fact, there is some evidence that death education may increase the fear of death.

SUSTAINING LIFE: A THORNY ISSUE

Over 30 years ago, the President's Commission for the Study of Ethical Problems in Medicine and Biomedical and Behavioral Research (1981) stated that there is little debate over the fact that the human body can be kept alive almost indefinitely with intravenous fluids, tube feedings, and various advanced medical technologies. This commission also stated that humans can be kept physically alive whether or not there is any brain function.

Refusing Treatment

Once they go to a hospital, people can become "trapped" in a situation of complex technology in which their bodies continue to survive even if there is no lucidity and no hope of recovery. At that point, the hospital staff may prefer to discontinue treatment, but they are caught in a maze of legal requirements and therefore continue the treatment because they fear litigation. A federal law, enacted on December 1, 1991, called the Patient Self-Determination Act requires hospices, nursing homes, hospitals, and home health care agencies to provide patients with information about their right to determine whether they want "extraordinary" means used to keep them alive if they become comatose or hopelessly ill. The law requires that each person entering an institution be given information about his or her right to refuse treatment.

By 1986, the American Medical Association declared that whenever the question to sustain life becomes an issue, the patient's choice should prevail. In that spirit, Barbara Bush, wife of the former first President Bush, acknowledged that she signed a living will, commenting "I had a dog I loved put down because I didn't want the dog to suffer; I certainly hope that someone would do the same thing for me" (cited in Burnell, 1993, p. 8). Burnell (1993) stated the dilemma as follows:

> Part of the confusion over the concept of dying lies in the fact that many people are not aware of the new ways of defining death. Formerly, a person who stopped breathing and had no heartbeat was considered dead. Now, brain function is also considered in the definition of death. In recent years, we have come to recognize that there is more to a person than just a body. The brain plays a major role in providing each of us with a personality, a set of unique behaviors and traits. These, in essence, are what distinguish us from others and give us what we call our identity. (p. 16)

A patient's choice may be determined by a legally chosen advocate through something called a *durable power of attorney for medical decisions*. Although the American Medical Association has been strongly opposed to a doctor taking an active role in helping people die, not all doctors agree. Surveys of U.S. physicians' attitudes reveal that about one third would participate in physician-assisted suicide if it were legalized (Dickinson, Clark, Winslow, & Marples, 2005). In *Dying with Dignity*, Patrick Sheehy (1981) wrote:

> We can also predict what the quality of the remaining time will be for the patient. If death is imminent, and if there are only the throes of physical pain and struggle left, I believe that a doctor should be allowed to give you a drug that will painlessly release you to death. As society matures, I foresee a time when this will be possible. (p. 236)

In some countries, that time has arrived. Current evidence seems to indicate that the desire of most people to die with dignity is becoming a national dialogue involving a definition of terms such as *death with dignity, uncontrollable pain, extraordinary methods to keep people alive*, and the meaning of *alternative methods of treatment*. In addition, there will be continuing theological and philosophical disputes about the meaning of life as well as arguments about the medical costs of sustaining life in comatose patients who are in a vegetative state.

LIVING WILLS

Through a living will, Americans can make their wishes known regarding whether heroic methods should be used to keep them alive. In a living will, prior to an emergency situation, people can indicate to medical staff and their family, in a written document, their wishes about the type of medical care they wish to have, or not to have, under certain conditions. It essentially spells out a refusal of certain types of treatments, but it usually cannot be used for stopping treatment that has begun. As a result, a person with a living will could be taken from a nursing home in a medical emergency and given treatment that seems reasonable. However, during the treatment the person may suffer a severe stroke. If the staff reacts quickly and gives life-sustaining care, and the person then drifts into permanent subconsciousness, at that point the staff will not usually withdraw treatment that has begun. The reason for this is that they probably fear a lawsuit because if they remove the treatment, they may be charged with killing the person. In addition, family members, because of feelings of guilt, love, or other reasons, may not permit the staff to remove the artificial life-sustaining equipment. It is not uncommon for a living will to contain vague terms such as *no extraordinary means*, or *no heroic methods*, which the family will be asked to define, and they may disagree among themselves as to their meaning.

Durable Power of Attorney

For many people the living will is a desirable statement, but in itself it is often inadequate. As a result, many experts also recommend a *durable power of attorney for medical care*. The durable power of attorney for medical care designates an individual to make treatment decisions for a person who no longer has the mental capacity to do so. The living will, then, tells the person designated by the durable power of attorney for medical care the wishes of the person who is no longer mentally competent to make those decisions.

EUTHANASIA

Euthanasia is a word so filled with emotional reactions that it probably should no longer be used. In its original derivation, it means will (*eu*) and death (*thanatos*). The emphasis is on a "good," painless death. The term became despised by many because of its use by the Nazis under Hitler's orders to exterminate certain categories of people such as the retarded, the mentally ill, Jews, political dissidents, homosexuals, gypsies, and others. The word *euthanasia* is inappropriately used in that context, because these persons were murdered. They did not choose "good" deaths. They were eliminated because of the criminal acts of Adolf Hitler.

In some ancient societies, euthanasia was socially acceptable. In Athens of ancient Greece, for example, judges had a supply of poison available for those who wished to die. The evidence indicates that permission to use the poison was not difficult to obtain (Burnell, 1993).

The term *active euthanasia* is commonly taken to mean purposely and deliberately taking action to end an individual's life. The term *passive euthanasia* refers to deliberately not taking any action to prolong the life of someone who is dying or existing in a vegetative state.

Euthanasia in Holland

There is much misunderstanding about euthanasia in Holland. It is a topic that has been debated much longer there than in the United States. The Dutch do not require that terminal illness be the only permissible grounds for assisted death. They consider death with dignity to be an important consideration. It must also be understood that the doctor–patient relationship in the Netherlands is based on more trust and personal interaction than is the case in the United States. The typical Dutch patient in assisted death is usually a person in his or her early 60s who has an advanced case of cancer. About 85% are cancer patients in their last few weeks of life. The remaining patients typically have AIDS, multiple sclerosis, or other neurological diseases that cause paralysis.

Research on Euthanasia

Current research in the Netherlands has found that physicians grant 44% of adults requesting euthanasia. They turn down 12% of the requests. In 13% of cases where the request has been granted, the patients died before the euthanasia occurred. In another 13% of cases, the patients changed their minds about euthanasia. In the rest of the cases, the decision was not made at the time of the study. This research provides a beginning indication of how physicians might react to such requests. Much more research will need to be done before the above types of questions will have some empirical answers. Outside of the philosophical and theological questions involved in euthanasia, much more study needs to be done as to what type of persons will request euthanasia and how the medical community will respond. Of the 136,000 annual deaths in the Netherlands from 1985 to 2005, 1.7% were by voluntary euthanasia (*USA TODAY,* 2007).

U.S. Legal Positions on Euthanasia

In the United States, some states allow terminally ill people to engage in assisted suicide. The Oregon Department of Human Services' Annual Report of 2010, which details the Oregon Death with Dignity Act, indicated that 65 people died in 2010 under the terms of the Act. This report showed that the dire predictions by the opponents of the Act—that it would lead to coercion, excessive use, or acting because of depression—did not occur. Indeed, there was not one report of abuse of the Act. The report also indicated that for the 11th year in a row, Oregon's Death with Dignity Act had proven to be effective (*USA TODAY,* July 20, 2009).

The United States Supreme Court has upheld Oregon's law, and Judge Sonia Sotomayor, in her Supreme Court Confirmation Hearings, stated that she would follow precedent (*USA TODAY,* July 20, 2009). The state of Washington in March 2009 became the second state to have a voter-approved assisted suicide law. This law requires a 15-day waiting period between the first oral and first written request for a lethal medication, and an additional 48 hours before a prescription can be written. This delay is intended to prevent someone from acting hastily and without adequate thought. A majority of Americans (56%) in a Gallup Poll have indicated support for doctors to be allowed to assist terminally ill persons to die (*USA TODAY,* July 20, 2009).

THE PROCESS OF DYING

Having looked at some of the current major issues and debates surrounding death and dying, it is important to examine the process of dying as well as some of the approaches that have been developed to begin to understand and cope with this process.

The Stages of Dying: Kubler-Ross

Kubler-Ross (1969, 1975, 1981) found that people tend to go through five stages in the dying process. When they are first diagnosed with a terminal condition, they refuse to accept the situation. They *deny* the reality of their situation and live in a condition of unreality in which they believe that the situation will change, that there is a misdiagnosis, and that new developments will help them. In the second stage, *anger and resentment,* they curse their fate, feel that the situation is unfair, and may project their anger and resentment onto medical staff or family members. In the third stage, *bargaining,* they may plead with God, promise that they will change their behavior, devote themselves to religious or worthwhile causes, and promise that they will no longer engage in certain types of questionable behaviors if they get a "second" chance at life. In the fourth stage, *depression*, they admit that their condition is terminal, that death is imminent, and that they are not going to be cured. They may then go into a stage of grief and isolation. Relatives and friends may find it difficult to communicate with them, and they may reject visits. In the final stage, *acceptance*, they accept their death. This is not a stage reached by all dying persons. It is a stage in which some feel that their life is going to end soon and that they have done all that they could regarding the situation. It is a stage achieved by those who have been able to relate their feelings to others and who have a sense of completion regarding their life's journey.

It is important to note that not everyone goes through all of these stages. Nor do the persons who go through all of these stages go through them in the same order (Bonanno, 2009; Bryant, 2003). Medical personnel or family members should not try to force dying persons into any one of these specific stages.

Educating Medical Staff

In recent years, there have been some attempts to educate medical personnel about death and dying, especially about the needs of the dying patient. With a greater emphasis on the practice of holistic medicine by many of the nation's medical schools, a greater awareness of the needs of the dying patient and his or her family and significant other should be expected. Without this awareness and approach, a sort of "social death" occurs when the attending medical staff no longer see the dying patient as a unique person with specific psychological needs, relationships, and spiritual dimensions. Given the current interest in death and dying, it is likely that the treatment of terminally ill patients will improve.

THE HOSPICE MOVEMENT: ORGINS AND GOALS

An international trend in the care of the dying is the hospice movement. Dr. Cicely Saunders played a key role in the development of the modern hospice movement when she started St. Christopher's Hospice in 1967 in London, England. The goal at St. Christopher's Hospice was to make an assessment of the spiritual, physical, social, and psychological needs of the dying person and of his or her support network. It was based on a belief that dying can occur best at home or in a specialized institution where there is a concerted attempt to reduce pain and to give the person supportive care that allows him or her to maximize relationships with others during their dying process. It is a program for persons who cannot be cured of their physical illnesses, so the emphasis is not on curing the condition, but on enabling the person to die "in comfort" with a caring, supportive staff and with friends and relatives. To define this approach further, Buckingham (1983) wrote:

> Hospice is a medically directed multidisciplinary program providing skilled care of an appropriate nature for terminally ill patients and their families to allow the patient to live as fully as possible until the time of death. Hospice helps relieve symptoms of distress (physical, psychological, spiritual, social, economic) that may occur during the course of the disease, dying, and bereavement. (p. 3)

It is important to note that the goal in the hospice movement is to maximize the quality of life for the dying patient and to make the best use of the time remaining with relatives, friends, and acquaintances. In addition, there is a focus on the comfort of the patient.

Key Aspects: Patient Care

Even though there are different types of hospice programs, they are all unified by their general philosophy of patient care (Leming & Dickinson, 2011). Hospice care is focused on patients with life-threatening illnesses. About 95% of the hospice patients in the United States suffer from cancer.

The Spread of Hospice in the United States

The first modern hospice program in the United States grew out of Dr. Cicely Saunders' lecture in 1963 at Yale University in New Haven, Connecticut, and her subsequent contacts with personnel from Yale nursing and medical schools. Representatives of various disciplines became involved in the development of Hospice Incorporated in 1971, which was later changed to the Connecticut Hospice (Leming & Dickinson, 2011).

VITAL ORGAN DONATION PROGRAM

The death of one human being can mean the gift of some key bodily functions or even life itself to another—in some cases several others, if multiple vital organs are utilized.

Federal law now requires hospitals to inform patients and family members about organ donations. There are many misconceptions about organ donations. To correct these misconceptions, Burnell (1993) pointed out:

- Donating organs will not interfere with receiving medical treatment in a hospital. Doctors are not more interested in obtaining organs than in providing their patients with proper treatment.
- Organ donation is considered only after all attempts to save a life have been made.
- Organ donation will not take place until the heart has stopped beating or brain death has been established.
- For viable organs, such as the heart, the lungs, the liver, the pancreas, and the kidneys, to be harvested, brain-dead individuals must be maintained on a respirator. However, the donation of eyes, bone, skin, and other tissues does not require maintenance on a respirator. These tissues can be obtained from 6 to 24 hours after breathing and the heartbeat have stopped.
- The body will not be disfigured by organ donation. After the removal of the donated organs, the surgical team will leave the body intact for proper funeral or burial arrangements.
- The family does not receive any compensation or fee for the donation. It is illegal to buy or sell organs or tissues.
- There is no charge or fee connected with the removal of organs or tissues.
- All major religions support the concept of organ and tissue donation as well as the concept of brain death.
- Organ donation does not interfere with funeral arrangements. Funeral directors can direct embalmers to prepare the body appropriately.
- The most common organ and tissue transplants are skin, lungs, hearts, livers, kidneys, corneas, certain bones, pancreases, and middle ears.
- Time is of the essence in most organ transplants, except for skin and corneas, so the removal of most organs is likely to occur in an acute care hospital.
- Even if a person has indicated his or her wish to donate organs, the medical transplant team may not automatically accept the donation. Many variables must be considered, such as the health of the donor.

- Generally speaking, organs are more suitable if they come from people under 70 years of age. Also, the organs of cancer patients (except in some cases of brain cancer) or of patients with infections or other serious diseases are not suitable for donation.
- Transportation and other incurred costs are usually covered by the organizations procuring the organs for transplant. There are many organizations that coordinate organ donations.
- Whether or not a person decides to donate his or her organs, there is a federal law that requires hospitals to inform the families of deceased patients about the option of organ donations.
- Organ donation does not interfere with a living will, which refers to one's wishes while one is still alive. (pp. 299–301)

FUNERALS

Anthropologists have found that all the cultures they have studied have some form of funeralization process—a rite or ritual recognizing death and a final disposition of the dead body (Leming & Dickinson, 2011). All cultures have ritualistic aspects to mourning death and some type of public ritual that families and friends go through. Aspects of these rituals vary from one culture to another. In the United States, funerals vary enormously according to social class, race, ethnicity, religious affiliation, and geographic location, but it is the funeral that becomes the focus of ritual.

Social Roles of Funerals

The funeral is a social event that brings the chief mourners and community members to the reality of death. In addition, it allows people to express their sympathy and give support to the relatives and friends of the deceased. It develops a context in which people are expected to come and greet the family. It is an event that one attends even though one does not receive an invitation. Even though a person may find it difficult to express his or her feelings of sympathy and support to the relatives, just being there makes a statement of support (Leming & Dickinson, 2011).

Another function of the funeral is to provide a theological or philosophical meaning for one's life. For a religiously oriented person, a cleric usually speaks about the purpose and meaning of life, along with a eulogy about the deceased (Leming & Dickinson, 2011).

The funeral enables members of the community to express their regards to the living by sending sympathy cards or flowers or by giving to charities named by the relatives of the deceased.

Making Decisions About Funerals

Funeral directors (undertakers, morticians) at times have been accused of taking advantage of people who are in a state of shock and depression at the death of a family member or close friend. The most scathing attack on the funeral industry was first made by Jessica Mitford in 1963. She accused funeral directors of inflating prices, misleading grieving family members, overselling unneeded services, and generally being dishonest in their dealings. She contended that they could do this because many persons are in unfamiliar surroundings at a mortuary and are too trusting of funeral directors. Since the publication of her book and the intense publicity it received, national legislation has been implemented to regulate the funeral industry more closely. Even so, an updated edition of Mitford's book (2000) entitled, *The American Way of Death Revisited*, sheds light on new trends in what she terms the *death-care industry*, including the rising costs of cremation, which used to be a less expensive alternative to burial, and new organizations dedicated to keeping costs in tow. The industry contends that Mitford exaggerated the number of dishonest funeral directors and that it now is better at regulating itself. Others argue that self-regulation of an industry is always suspect because of vested and conflicting interests, cronyism, and a reluctance of members of any industry to publicize its problems.

More and more Americans are choosing cremation over traditional funerals. Forty-one percent of Americans now choose cremation compared to 21% in 1995. This change, in part, is the result of a significant difference in price as a basic cremation costs about $1500, while a traditional funeral costs about $10,000 (*The Week*, 2011, p. 10).

BEREAVEMENT AND GRIEF

Diana Harris (2007) states that "there are three distinct phases in the bereavement process. In the first phase, there is a period of shock that lasts for several days. This is followed by a second phase of intense grief, which can even have physiological effects including loss of appetite, insomnia, loss of weight, etc. In the third phase one begins to recover and resume social interaction" (p. 125).

Some persons have anticipatory bereavement in which they grieve as they watch a spouse or a parent lose any sense of self-awareness because of Alzheimer's disease, or some other disease causing a lengthy dying process. For some, death then produces a feeling of relief as there is finally closure for which the grieving has already taken place.

Most grieving persons eventually begin to adjust to the reality of the death and begin to work their way back into their social world without their deceased spouse, child, sibling, or friend. At that point, the person begins to get back into their normal routine, although grieving for some brings about a psychological condition that needs professional counseling (Roos, 2002). There are processes that grieving people go through, but the length and stages of grieving, and the intensity of the grieving process, vary tremendously depending on the personality, the relationship with the deceased, and the way the death occurred.

WIDOWHOOD

There are millions of widowed persons in the United States, with widows (women) outnumbering widowers (men) by a ratio of five to one. Most older women are widowed, while most older men are married, the result of the reality that women live longer than men, and that men tend to marry younger women.

Helen Lopata's (1979) classic study on widowhood, *Widowhood in an American City*, found that there are widely different reactions by widowed persons. Some become isolated, while others seek out new friendships and experiences; some may develop new talents or find or rediscover abilities that were repressed; and some may become very passive and struggle over a long adjustment time, while others are able to adjust rather quickly.

The AARP founded the Widowed Persons Service (WPS) back in 1973 to meet the emotional and practical needs of newly widowed persons of both genders. There are thousands of WPS volunteers located in hundreds of sites across the United States, serving tens of thousands of newly widowed persons each year by telephone calls, visits, and WPS-support group meetings.

Mourning for a deceased spouse usually takes more that just a month or two. For some people the mourning process is never totally over, while for others, mourning may involve 2 or 3 years of grieving (Gibala, 1993). Becoming a widow or widower usually results in severe stress, typically more stress than is involved in losing a job or having a major illness.

The WPS outreach volunteers function as support persons, as "bridges over troubled waters," and for some, as new friends:

> In addition to one-to-one outreach, WPS sponsors group meetings. Because warmth and caring are primary needs of the widowed, WPS meetings first offer hugs, more hugs that you can count.... The participants share their stories, discuss their worries, offer coping skills, and receive accolades for meeting personal challenges. A guest speaker may talk about a range of topics such as crime prevention, cooking for one, or adjusting to widowed life. (Gibala, 1993, p. 7)

SUGGESTED RESOURCES

Coping with Grief and Loss: http://www.helpguide.org/mental/grief_loss.htm
> This website is dedicated to health challenges in general and has a page solely for grief and loss understanding. The site offers information about the stages and symptoms of grief, with suggestions for coping with grief, when to seek counseling, and support group options.

End-of-Life Issues: http://www.usa.gov/Topics/Seniors/EndofLife.shtml
> This federal government website offers information on grieving, funerals, hospice care, caretaking, and living wills. There is a link to a hospice care locator, which has a search tool for palliative care, hospice care, grief counseling, and in home services in your area.

National Hospice & Palliative Care Organization: http://www.nhpco.org
> This organization has a website for services that offer everything related to palliative care, hospice care, and grief. You can fi nd links to other sites and organizations that offer services such as grief counseling, help witih hospice, end of life services, and after life services.

Oregon Death with Dignity Act, available through http://public.health.oregon.gov
> This organization has a website for services that offer everything related to palliative care, hospice care, and grief. You can fi nd links to other sites and organizations that offer services such as grief counseling, help with hospice, end of life services, and after life services.

The Realities of Growing Older

Michael A. Faber

INTRODUCTION

The five chapters in this section provide a detailed description of the aging process, aging-related physical changes, health and wellness, mental health and abilities, and sexuality and aging, as well as death and dying. The focus of this Practical Application will be on healthy aging, motivation for wellness, adaptation to aging-related loss, independence versus interdependence, mental health stereotypes and stigma, as well as reflection on life and death.

Healthy Aging

Healthy aging is a topic that should concern us all, since we are all aging. By now, in our information-laden age, most everyone is aware of the right things to do to take care of themselves. It's not rocket science after all. Healthy aging involves eating right, exercise, no use of tobacco, moderation of alcohol, avoiding stress, and adequate sleep and relaxation. Knowing this, why is it that most of us don't do the right things?

Lifestyle choices, long-established habits, changed life patterns (where in the past people either didn't know better or didn't make time for physical activity), changes to our food sources, and a lack of knowledge regarding what constitutes proper nutrition have all contributed to a large number of individuals aging in unhealthy ways. Therefore, let's examine the factors that help to motivate older individuals to do the right things in regard to their health and wellness.

Motivation for Wellness

Everyone knows the right things to do, so why don't they do them? For those choosing to enter the field of gerontology, this is an important question and issue to address. One way that we can help to improve, and perhaps even extend, the lives of those we serve is by learning to understand personal "motivation" and help identify ways to motivate and encourage those we serve to make healthier lifestyle choices.

According to the *Encarta Dictionary: English* (North American edition), *motivation* is defined as "giving of reason to act" or "the act of giving somebody a reason or incentive to do something." Using this definition, an informal survey was administered to a group of older individuals at a local senior center by this author. Those identifying themselves as exercising regularly were asked what motivated them to do so—their responses included the following:

- An urgency brought about by specific chronic diseases/conditions (heart, fibromyalgia, arthritis, stroke, high cholesterol, etc.);
- Fear based on family history (life-limiting genetic conditions);
- A desire to maintain balance and mobility;
- Wanting to control their weight; and
- Probably even more telling, those who identified themselves as *not* exercising regularly, when asked *why not*, said it was due to laziness, discouragement, or conditions such as shortness of breath that made it difficult to exercise.

Understanding the motivations of an older person is the starting point for positive intervention through education, encouragement, and the provision of appropriate supports.

Aging, Loss, and Adaptation

Far too often, the aging process is described in terms of loss and decline. In reality, the majority of older persons live happy, healthy, active, and productive lives. Yet, for many in the oldest-old age category (85+) aging-related losses are commonplace. Therefore, it is important to understand these losses and how to help older adults adapt to these aging-related challenges.

In order to accomplish this it is important to realize:

- Most older persons are flexible and used to adapting to change;
- Educating older persons and their caregivers about aging-related losses and how to cope with losses increases the probability of adapting to life's changes; and
- Relating to the older persons as adults and not children involves including them in any care planning or problem-solving discussions.

Older adults often experience a number of aging-related changes and losses including but not limited to decreased physical abilities (i.e., changes in mobility, flexibility, vision, hearing, taste and smell, and sensitivity to hot and cold); loss of the "work" role through retirement; reduced income; changed social and familial roles; and the loss of family and friends due to death. Aging successfully involves adapting to such changes and losses. Listed below are a number of helpful tips on how to help older persons adapt to some of the more common aging-related changes.

Mobility

- Encourage regular exercise to maintain flexibility and strength—core strength is especially important to prevent falls.
- Make the home barrier free—eliminate potential causes of falls including clutter, slippery floors, throw rugs, extension cords, etc.
- Promote the use of assistive devices when needed (canes, walkers, etc.).

Vision

- Install proper lighting in the home—lighting should be bright, without glare or shadows, and should be brighter in areas used for reading.
- Use florescent tape or paint to delineate edges of stairs, platforms, and counter tops.
- Avoid walking in the dark at night—use night lights, flashlight, or other lighting options, and eliminate possible barriers in the home.
- Use specially marked larger knobs and dials on appliances.

Hearing

- Speak clearly, distinctly, and do not shout—shouting increases your pitch, and the higher pitches are most often lost first due to the aging process.
- Eliminate background noises.
- Face the person and look them directly in the eyes when speaking—this will help older adults who supplement what they hear by reading lips.
- Encourage the use of assistive devices, such as hearing aids and telephone amplifiers.

Touch

- Touch is an important form of communication—older persons, especially those who are isolated and alone, often crave appropriate forms of human contact/touch.
- Pay attention to extremes in temperature—older persons' internal thermostats do not work as efficiently as do those of younger people, and therefore they are at higher risk for hypothermia.

Taste and Smell

- Encourage the use of a variety of herbs and spices to season foods—many older adults must avoid the use of salt and are not very knowledgeable of the proper use of alternative seasonings.
- Make sure that foods served to older persons are colorful and attractive—the more appealing the food, the more likely it is to be consumed.
- Use safety devices, such as smoke detectors and timers, especially in areas of meal preparation, to prevent possible fires and the burning of food.
- Date and store all leftovers in the refrigerator—never leave meat or other pre-pared food items on the counter to defrost or cool.

Independence Versus Interdependence

Independence is highly valued in American culture. It is a learned behavior from a very young age, as demonstrated in a 2-year-old loudly and proudly declaring, "I do it myself!" Yet, in reality, people need people, and most of us are not truly independent as much as "interdependent" on one another. Popple and Leighninger, in their work *Social Work, Social Welfare, and American Society* (7th edition, Allyn & Bacon, 2008), define *interdependence* as "dependence on each other or one another; mutual dependence," and *dependence* as "a state of being in which one is not able to participate as a social being in rewarding ways and, thus, is a proper opposite of interdependent."

Unfortunately, far too often older persons only see things in terms of independence versus dependence, rather than thinking about the value of interdependence. Part of the role of a professional working with older persons is to help them to recognize their interdependence. If successful in doing so, the older adult often has a greater openness to accepting needed support and assistance. Another important rule of thumb is to never do for an older person what she or he is able to do herself or himself, for this may lead to unnecessary dependence and a sense of diminished value or worthlessness on the part of the older person.

Mental Health Stereotypes and Stigma

Many of those in the oldest-old generation grew up at a time when mental health issues were not socially acceptable. To suffer openly from even common mental health issues, such as depression and anxiety, an individual risked social isolation and stigma. Therefore, most individuals learned to keep these types of issues to themselves and/or quietly within their family, without seeking competent professional assistance. In other words, they would suffer needlessly in silence. Unfortunately, this means that many older adults today continue to suffer in silence. These same individuals fail to share their concerns related to depression, anxiety, memory loss, or other mental health issues with loved ones, a physician, or a mental health professional. What does this mean to those of us who choose to work with older persons? It is this author's opinion that it is the responsibility of those of us working in the field of gerontology to recognize the mental health issues of those we serve and educate and encourage them to seek appropriate treatment. In other words, we need to work to dispel the stereotypes and stigmas surrounding mental health conditions and their treatment.

Death, Life, and Possible Lessons

This section includes information on death and dying. In many ways, American culture is denying death. Not all professionals in medicine, health care, social service, or pastoral care have received extensive education or training in dealing with death, dying, and bereavement. Yet, if one is to work with older persons, a thorough understanding of death, dying, and bereavement is important. Therefore, it is recommended by this author that anyone choosing to work with this population include the study of thanatology (death, dying, and bereavement) as part of their education.

In studying death, dying, and bereavement, one not only becomes more understanding and empathetic toward those in our care, but one can also learn many powerful lessons about life, such as the value of living life to the fullest, embracing each new day, and recognizing one's true priorities.

PART III

THE DIVERSE LIVING CONDITIONS OF OLDER PEOPLE

CHAPTER 8

Living Environments
of Older People

The learning objectives of this chapter include understanding

- That where an older person lives has a great impact on the quality of her of his life.
- The range of living environments including metropolitan, rural, small town, suburban, and urban settings.
- How various environments impact the lives of older people.
- That factors such as aging in place, availability of services, transportation, living alone, living with a spouse, racial and ethnic characteristics, and household size impact the living characteristics of older people.
- The new trends in moving and staying in place, as well as the capacities of communities to accommodate aging residents.

JANE AND PETE: ENDING UP ISOLATED?

Jane and Pete moved to the suburbs of their medium-sized eastern city in 1954, when Pete got a promotion to sales manager and their three children were 2, 4, and 7 years old. The American dream of owning their own home in a new area with space for the kids and new schools was a goal they realized along with millions of other Americans in the 1950s and 1960s. Life, it turned out, was not paradise in the suburbs, but compared to many other settings, it was pretty good. But as they got older and the children moved away, Jane and Pete thought it might be good to try a new way of life after Pete retired. They had enough money from the sale of their house to buy a mobile home in Florida and a small cottage on a lake in the northern, rural part of their state.

This was great living as some of their friends moved to the same area of Florida for the winter months. In the spring, they moved up north to their cottage. This went well until they were in their early 80s. All of their friends had died or were too ill to go back to Florida. Pete could no longer drive very well to get to the bank or store. They gave up trying to go to church. It was too hard to get to and besides, they didn't know many people anymore. Up north at their cottage, things got pretty tough, too.

Pete had a heart attack one summer and he was 35 miles from the nearest hospital. The adult children were busy with their own lives and lived in different cities; the closest lived 40 miles away. After his hospitalization, Pete needed a range of services, some of which were not available in their rural area. When their neighbor was gone, there was no one to get their groceries. Jane felt isolated and helpless. Like so many of her generation, she had let Pete do all the driving. Their kids, helpful and caring, also felt helpless so far away.

ELLEN: WHERE WILL SHE GO?

Ellen had never married. She had a fine education and devoted herself to her profession of social work. She began working in the 1930s and for a time was paid in scrip (IOUs from her employer) because of a budget crunch. Her salary was never large; she worked at a time of relatively low wages in an area of the country that was not too prosperous. Ellen lived frugally and helped her brother send his three children through college.

In 1968, Ellen retired at the age of 65. She had lived in apartments ever since graduation from college and had moved only twice in all those years. Now her apartment building was being torn down as part of a new shopping center development. Where can Ellen move? What kind of living facility can she afford? The savings she accumulated are now quite modest, given the ongoing inflation since her retirement. The income she earns on this money has decreased dramatically with falling interest rates. In addition, Ellen's income from her pension and Social Security is very small because both are based on her prior wages, which were always rather meager, particularly by today's standards. Does Ellen have to move to substandard housing in a deteriorating neighborhood?

WHERE DO OLDER PEOPLE LIVE?

This chapter is the first in Part III, which focuses on where and how older people live. Included are chapters on where they live physically, their economic status, their work status, and, if applicable, their retirements. As with most aspects of older adult life, great diversity is common in all of these areas.

First, this chapter looks at where and under what circumstances older people live. What is the importance of living environments to older people? What are the factors that directly influence the satisfaction or happiness of older people in their living environments? What conditions make them unhappy or unable to function adequately, in particular living arrangements? Where can older people live? What are their options?

What does it mean for older people to live in urban or rural America? What are some of the implications of living in the suburbs as persons continues to grow older? These types of questions have important implications for older persons as well as for people who work with them in social agencies, health services, religious organizations, and businesses. They also have real implications for planners and policy makers on all levels in the public and private sectors.

This chapter concludes by examining some of the major factors of living arrangements that directly affect how older people are able to function. These factors affect the satisfaction and happiness of older people as well as their ability to carry on independent lives. What are the things about living environments that affect the ability of older people to survive with dignity and independence? What can be done to improve these conditions? What can people who work with older persons do to assist them in coping with some of these important factors?

IMPORTANCE OF LIVING ENVIRONMENTS TO OLDER PEOPLE

Where a person lives has a great impact on the quality of his or her life. The type and condition of a person's living unit and the general characteristics of the neighborhood make up a person's living environment. Until relatively recent times, a person's environment was not a very important consideration in the study of the social sciences (Howell, 1980; Lawton, 1983, 1985). Later research has shown the vital importance an older person's living condition has on his or her overall well-being, including physical and psychological health (Rieske and Holstege, 1996). It also relates to an older person's ability to interact and relate to other people. Indeed, going back to the 1971 White House Conference on Aging, it was determined that except for an older person's spouse, his or her living arrangement was probably the single most important aspect of daily life.

Aging in Place

It is generally agreed that living environments are vitally important to life satisfaction. This is particularly true for older people because they spend so much of their time in and around their homes. Most no longer go off to work anymore, at least on a regular basis. Many are limited in their ability to get in their cars and go somewhere else. As people continue to age, many are even limited in their ability to go to the grocery store, regional malls, their places of worship, or their doctors. As people continue to *age in place*—to become older in the places they have been living—they find themselves more and more confined to their immediate environments. Multiple factors should be considered in regard to an older person choosing to age in place. These factors are explored within the Practical Application at the end of Part III of this textbook.

Availability of Services

The living environments of older persons include not only the housing units in which they live, but also other aspects of living, such as the availability of shopping facilities, medical services, transportation, and access to relatives and friends. Good transportation and access to relatives and friends can be more important than the quality of the living unit itself. For an older person who does not drive, a home, apartment, or other type of living unit may become a virtual prison if transportation is not readily available. Accessibility to relatives and friends depends on the availability of transportation. In America's mobile society, with its fragmented family units, many older persons find themselves hundreds or even thousands of miles from their children, grandchildren, and friends. All of these factors have a great influence on the quality of life for older persons in our society.

As where older people live is so important to their happiness, their sense of well-being, their ability to feel secure, their ability to feel that they are still somehow in charge of their own lives, and their ability to relate to others, especially significant others in their lives, it is important to look at some of the major factors that contribute to their overall happiness in their living environments.

Metropolitan Areas

In reviewing the living environments and situations of older people in the 21st century, it is important to note that 81% of people over age of 65 live in metropolitan areas (Administration on Aging, U.S. Department of Health and Human Services). This is a percentage and numerical increase from the 1990 census. And the oldest-old population (aged 85 and older) is three times as likely to be living inside metropolitan areas as outside these areas.

Of those in metropolitan areas, 60% live in the suburbs. This continues a trend that began in 1980 when, for the first time, older persons in the suburbs outnumbered those in the central cities (U.S. Senate, 1991). The suburbanization of America became a major phenomenon in the 1950s. At that time, younger families moved to the suburbs for a variety of reasons: to live and raise their children in "ideal" conditions, thus "escaping" crime, pollution, congested traffic, and deteriorating housing.

Older Suburban Areas

In older suburban areas, the problems of aging in place continue to emerge. These problems will become the focus of growing older in America as they apply to housing. The American suburb was built around the automobile—its widespread ownership and use. The automobile revolutionized how Americans lived, worked, and played. Workplaces, shopping centers, recreational facilities, and many houses of worship were all built around the use of the automobile. As people grow older, physical changes occur that affect their ability to perform certain tasks, including driving an automobile. These changes are very gradual for most people and hardly noticed at first. However, they are real and in time will affect people who are dependent on their use of automobiles.

What makes this situation worse is that public mass transportation is minimal in most American suburbs. Much of what is available is geared toward moving suburbanites to central city business and financial districts. Advocates for the elderly are calling for ways to help them go to stores, doctors' offices, houses of worship, and other services when driving becomes difficult, particularly in the hours of darkness and on congested freeways and crowded streets.

Small-Town Living

Relatively few older persons live in small communities (less than 2,500 residents), reflecting the long-term trend toward urbanization (including suburbanization) in America. Early research has found that older persons in small towns have fewer services, lower income, and poorer health than older persons who live in metropolitan areas (Lawton, 1980). However, older persons in small towns tend to interact more with friends and neighbors—with younger people and with persons their age—than do their counterparts in metropolitan areas. For many older persons, small towns are much easier places to live in. Generally, things move slower, including traffic. Points of interest as well as other services (stores, houses of worship, banks, post offices) are closer. Change is usually less pronounced, and relatives, friends, and neighbors are not likely to move away. Knowing more people around town gives older people a sense of security. If they become ill, a neighbor, friend, or even a store owner or manager will deliver food. Knowing where everything is in a small town and being able to move around are great comforts. However, services to deal with crises or prolonged-illness situations usually are limited. With the closing or threatened closing of many rural hospitals, this is particularly true of emergency medical care, a real crisis for many people in rural and small-town America.

TRANSPORTATION AND OLDER PEOPLE

Transportation is a major problem facing older people in all types of settings—rural, urban, and suburban. This is particularly true of the older suburbs where so many older people live. Most activities older people participate in, and most services they need to access, require some form of transportation, typically a private car, or public transportation, which is limited in many areas of the nation (Walljasper, 2009). The impairments that so many older persons experience as they continue to age can hinder their use of either public or private transportation without special assistance. And without adequate and appropriate transportation, many older persons are at risk of losing their independence (Cox, 2005). They become trapped in their houses when they are not able to access programs and services as well as attend and engage in activities that are vital to their lives—religious services, shopping, movies, doctors' appointments, and so on.

Attempts to meet the transportation needs of elders as well as the younger disabled go back to the amendments to the Urban Mass Transit Act of 1964. Funds were to be allocated to modify transportation for those who are frail and disabled as well as to develop new transportation services. Later, legislation provided reduced fares on public transportation for the elderly and handicapped along with federal funds for transportation in nonurban areas—small towns and rural areas (Cox, 2005). Currently, there exists a wide array of transportation programs at the local, state, and federal levels including the purchasing of vehicles and the installation of assistive devices and wheelchair lifts. The Federal Transit Administration in the Department of Transportation and the Administration on Aging in the Department of Health and Human Services are developing a plan to coordinate the available programs to facilitate transportation for older persons and the disabled. As it is with all assistance programs, adequate funding is essential. More information about funding for transportation services and the unmet needs for transportation is presented in Chapter 13.

IMPACTS OF LIVING ENVIRONMENTS/LIVING ARRANGEMENTS

The living arrangements and living environments of the older population are important indicators because they are linked to income, health status, and the availability of caregivers. For example, older people who live alone are more likely than older people who live with their spouses to be in poverty (*Older Americans 2010*).

As Baby Boomers Retire

As they have had at each stage of their lives, Baby Boomers will continue to have a significant impact on the kinds of living environments and housing arrangements they will choose as they move into the later stages of their lives (Mellor & Rehr, 2005). It is predicted that Baby Boomers will reinvent retirement in almost all aspects of their lives including living environments, living arrangements, moving patterns, issues of working, and literally all social and economic issues that relate to growing older.

LIVING ALONE

In 2009, 11.4 million people aged 65 and older lived alone. Almost three quarters of these were women (Administration on Aging, U.S. Department of Health and Human Services). Between 1990 and 2009, the proportion of older women living alone actually declined. In the same period, the proportion of older men living alone increased (Taeuber, 1993).

The living arrangements and living environments of the older population reflect factors other than their health status, socioeconomic situations, family caregiving, and cultural ties. Research has found that independent living arrangements—living alone or with a spouse—are considered most desirable for older adults in the United States because they offer more autonomy. However, these living arrangements (in particular living alone) can increase social isolation and reliance upon formal social supports.

Baby Boomers Living Alone

Overall, the proportion of older persons who live alone increases with age. This trend has been of some concern to aging specialists looking at the aging of the Baby Boom generation because as they grow older, larger numbers of elderly people are projected to live alone (Mellor & Rehr, 2005). But some experts have pointed out that this may not be as big a problem as some have anticipated as Baby Boomers are more practiced at living alone than their parents or grandparents. This is because of an increase in the numbers of those who never married, higher divorce rates, and later marriages translate into many Baby Boomers having had more experiences in living alone than earlier generations. As such, it is speculated that it will be less difficult for many Baby Boomers to cope with living alone.

Living With a Spouse

Men aged 65 and older are more likely than women the same age to live with their spouses (*Older Americans 2010*). As they move into the later years—aged 85 and older—more than half of older men still live with their spouses while less than one eighth of older women live with their spouses. Far more women in this oldest age category live alone than live with their spouses or live with others (children, friends, etc.).

Living Arrangements by Race

The living arrangements of the older population also vary by race. Only 13.4% of non-Hispanic White women live with relatives, while more than 30% of older Black American, Asian, and Hispanic women do so (*Older Americans 2010*). And this pattern is similar for men—only 5.8% of non-Hispanic White men live with relatives while more than 10% of older Black American, Asian, and Hispanic men do. The proportion of older men living with their spouse is lowest among Black Americans (54.9%) and highest among Asians (76.9%; *Older Americans 2010*). Many studies have shown that cultural differences play an important role in determining the living arrangements of older people.

A New Trend in Not Living Alone?

As indicated earlier, living alone increases with advancing age, particularly among older women. And living alone, particularly for women, can be a significant factor in going into poverty or near poverty. According to U.S. Census Bureau data and an AARP Foundation Women's Leadership Circle study, 500,000 women aged 50 and older live with a nonromantic housemate, and more than a third of the women aged 45 and older who were surveyed said that they would be interested in sharing a house with friends or other women as long as they could have their own private space (Mahoney, 2007).

The main reason women may be interested in sharing a home with another woman is a financial one. An obvious concurrent benefit is having companionship available, which has real value for many older women. And according to Mahoney (2007), many of the 25 million single women aged 45 and older are proud of their status, at least for the present time. But at the same time, many of these single women realize that they are not as prepared for their retirement years as are married women their same ages. In addition, a good percentage of single women have not been able to earn as much money from working as most men earn from working.

Many single women who are divorced or widowed understand firsthand how difficult it can be to maintain a one-income household. Mahoney (2007) pointed out that these financially strained women may be willing to consider any housing option as long as they can keep their freedom. "After all, we're from the generation who lived in communities back in the 1960s," stated Connie Skillingstad who founded Golden Girls Housing in Minneapolis (Mahoney, 2007, p. 49). This nonprofit service helps women look at nontraditional options for housing that meet their financial, social, and emotional needs. Skillingstad pointed out that it is difficult for some women to seriously consider shared housing. She went onto say that in our culture it has been difficult to incorporate the concept of living communally as a normal way of life. For women to seriously consider nonromantic shared living, there is usually a compelling financial need brought about by a divorce, a job loss, an illness, or simply realizing they do not have enough money to purchase and maintain their own single residences.

Indeed, Skillingstad predicted that this type of housing arrangement may be the wave of the future due to the following factors: (a) financial security for many single women who can pool their resources to provide and maintain housing arrangements that meet the necessities of their lives; (b) time to contemplate one's next or final move after the death of a spouse, a divorce, or any major life changing event; and (c) peace of mind knowing that one is not alone in a residence is a motivator for many women, especially as they age in place (Mahoney, 2007). Companionship can enhance the mental and physical aspects of life.

Factors in Choosing Shared Living

Mahoney (2007) pointed out that in spite of the obvious benefits of this possible new trend, there can be significant downsides. Sometimes the other person can appear to be friendly and compatible and turn out to be the opposite. "Even women who have known each other for years can discover that living together is very different from meeting each other for lunch and a chat," said Jane Portman, an attorney and coauthor of *Every Landlord's Legal Guide* (8th edition; cited in Mahoney, 2007, p. 81). She went on to state that it is important to discuss each other's expectations before making any shared housing decision.

STAYING IN COMMUNITY

Most of today's older people and Baby Boomers want to continue to live in their communities during their older years (Mellor & Rehr, 2005). Indeed, an AARP (2006) study entitled, *Aging, Migration, and Local Communities: The Views of 60+ Residents, and Community Leaders*, points out that nine out of 10 persons aged 60 and older (41.5 million) do not want to move from their general location. They may move from a larger residence to a smaller one if they downsize (move from the large house in which they raised their children to a smaller house, apartment, or condominium). It is a myth that most or even many persons pack up and move to Florida or Arizona or some other sunny place once they retire. The AARP study cited previously clearly indicated that older people make essential contributions to their own communities including volunteering, voting, mentoring, and generally being an asset to the area in which they live (Ryers, 2006).

Naturally Occurring Retirement Communities (NORCs)

As so many older people (as well as Baby Boomers) choose to remain in their own homes and communities, this results in something known as Naturally Occurring Retirement Communities (NORCs; Mellor & Rehr, 2005). These are communities wherein there are groups or clusters of persons who aged in place—stayed in the same residence where they lived while working and raising their families. Recently, there has been increasing interest in providing the services these older people need to remain independent in their own homes.

Baby Boomers and NORCs

As the nation's Baby Boomers move into their older ages in the early decades of the 21st century, much focus has been put on their impacts on the nation's major entitlement programs—Social Security and Medicare. But another older-age factor is also a major concern—where and under what circumstances will they live out their 60s, 70s, 80s, and beyond? Will most of them want to move to a warmer climate if they do not already live in one? Will most of them want to move to some fancy retirement village or home? Will many want to move in with their relatives—adult children, grandchildren, or some other kinfolk? As noted previously, the answer to all these questions is a resounding "no." Most want to remain in their communities so the real question is how are they going to be able to do this?

In a report by the AARP entitled, *These Four Walls...Americans 45+ Talk About Home and Community* (Greenwald & Associates, 2003), more than four out of five of those surveyed wished to remain in their existing residence with 82% of them wishing to obtain the services they may require to remain there—even after they are not able to care for themselves. The key is the availability of services they may require to stay in their own homes. And this is where NORCs come into play. NORCs are a way to organize communities in which clusters of people can naturally grow old together. They:

- Provide ways for older people to retain or develop positive roles as opposed to viewing elders as only a bunch of people with needs;
- Empower older people as civically engaged;
- Promote social connections—keep current ones and develop new ones; and
- Develop an assortment of supports for older people that are flexible and available.

MOBILITY AND MIGRATION OF OLDER PEOPLE

As noted earlier, most older people do not move. Among all the older people in the United States in 2011, 94% lived in the same place they lived the year earlier ("2011 American Community Survey"). By comparison only 6% of people aged 65 and older moved while 16.6% of people aged 1 to 64 moved. And among the small percentage of older people who moved, almost 60% moved within the same county.

Reasons for Moving

Research has shown that these relatively few older people who make an "amenity move" (move for better climate; fiscal characteristics that might include favorable property, sales, or income taxes; or specialized health care access) tend to move soon after retirement, when economic, social, and health resources are adequate to support such moves.

One in five older persons moves for family reasons other than a change in marital status. Research has shown that the older population's domestic migration is typically due to older parents' wish to live closer to their children or to move back to their former communities if, when younger, they were among the few who left their communities (*65+ in the United States*, 2005).

Newer Trends in Moving

Some research has pointed out that there are a couple of new trends for moving in older age—although not widespread. One is the development of various types of retirement housing options on or near college and university campuses. This is particularly attractive to those college graduates who want to return in retirement to their respective college/university campuses to become connected once again to college activities including taking or auditing classes, attending lectures, and enjoying sporting events. For those universities that have medical schools, such living arrangements can also provide older people with direct access to excellent medical care, often benefiting from cutting-edge medical research. Some 50 colleges and universities have university-linked retirement communities (URLCs) on or near their campuses (Abrahms, 2008). An added bonus is the opportunity for intergenerational living, which can be very stimulating for both young and old.

Another mini trend is the moves of affluent Baby Boomers, or even older people, to town centers. Some affluent older persons are moving to the downtowns of numerous cities across the nation into refurbished older buildings (including old factories) and newly built upscale condominiums. These areas typically include specialty shops and cafes—kind of like town squares of earlier times. By the early 21st century, there were more than 150 of these "lifestyle centers" from Virginia to Oregon (Diament, 2007).

Why Some Older Persons Resist Moving

The question can be asked, "Why are some older persons opposed to moving when a move could greatly improve their living accommodations?" One reason is money, or the lack of it, as was discussed before. To move from deteriorating housing into a better housing unit costs money, both in the form of higher housing costs and moving expenses. Insufficient funds, real or perceived, is often the cause of an older person not wanting to move. Second, some people, young or old, simply resist change, especially a change that affects so much of their lives. Fear of the unknown is a limiting factor for people of all ages, but particularly for the old who no longer have the physical or emotional resources to cope with unknown changing life conditions. Third, relocation is a traumatic event, especially when a person's life centers on his or her place of residence. Relocation means leaving behind the old neighborhood, familiar surroundings, old friends and acquaintances, and neighborhood ties built over the years. Familiar surroundings in old neighborhoods give older persons a sense of stability and security. These losses are mourned, both physically and psychologically, by many elderly people.

Before the mass movement of people to suburban areas, living in older residential areas offered conveniences for many older persons because these areas were close to facilities such as stores, physicians, and dentists. As services of all types continue to move toward the suburbs, many older people are left without them unless they have access to reliable, cheap transportation.

In evaluating their existing housing situations, most older people refer to distances from medical and shopping facilities as a key factor, followed by distance from relatives, the climate, and assistance with housekeeping and meal preparation. When these factors become more remote and inaccessible, older persons are bound to feel the negative results of isolation in their lives.

Types of Moves

Moves may be required because of the inadequacy of an older person's present living arrangement, the closing of a retirement home or some type of supportive facility, or the physical or emotional deterioration of the elderly person. In addition, some older people move after they retire to enjoy recreational areas or beneficial climates. Some move to be near their adult children who can interact with them socially and look after them if and when they need assistance.

FINANCIAL STATUS AND HOUSING

One of the major factors that affects where and how older people live is their finances, including income and resources. The financial status of older people is discussed in Chapter 10. This section briefly examines what an older person's financial status means to his or her living arrangements.

As with other segments of the population, an older person's financial status has a direct relationship to his or her ability to live in a housing unit that adequately meets the needs of daily living. For some, this may mean upgrading and remodeling existing single-family homes to adapt them to the changing needs of older people, including such things as bathroom and washing facilities on the ground floor, new insulation for warmth in the winter or cooling in the summer, and adequate lighting to accommodate vision limitations. For others, it may mean the ability to move to a new neighborhood when essential services leave the old neighborhood or when the neighborhood becomes less safe. For still others, financial resources may mean the ability to leave their old home location to move to a retirement area in another section of their state or the nation. Included in these are the "snowbirds" who migrate to warmer climates upon retirement. For others, as they continue to age, it may mean moving to some form of congregate living arrangement when they need additional support services on a daily basis.

Losing Homes

For many older people, finances are a matter of survival in housing. Keeping a roof over their heads becomes a major struggle. Some do not win that struggle; they join the ranks of the homeless. This has become a major issue since the collapse of the housing market, which began in 2006 and became a crisis in the Great Recession of 2008 to 2009 (Fleck, 2008). This will be discussed further in Chapter 9. "I'm shocked by the numbers of elders who succumbed to predatory refinancing—interest only loans and adjustable-rate mortgages. More than half of my clients are facing displacement," said Len Raymond, founder of the nonprofit Homeowner Option for Massachusetts Elders in Boston, which counsels people aged 50 and older who are facing foreclosure—losing their homes (cited in Fleck, 2008, p. 13).

SOLVING LIVING ARRANGEMENT PROBLEMS THROUGH MEDIATION

A movement has developed across much of America that is already offering, and has greater potential to offer, services for older people to help them cope with their surroundings (neighborhoods/environments). It was identified by various labels including *community mediation, alternative dispute resolution, reconciliation center, neighborhood justice center,* or just *mediation.* The goal has been to resolve disputes without going through the formal legal system by coming to a resolution of problems so that all parties to the dispute can live together in peace. Having one party "win" and the other "lose" has not been the objective. Reaching a negotiated agreement that reflects the best interests of both parties has always been the overriding objective (Hoffman & Wood, 1991–1992). A "win–win" result to disputes is the goal. Community mediation is being used by older people in a wide array of living environments, from neighborhoods with single- and multiple-family homes to nursing facilities.

Mediation in Neighborhoods

In neighborhoods, alternative dispute resolution centers are handling a range of cases that involve older people. Disputes between neighbors over property use, driveways, trash, barking dogs, loud music, noisy parties, lot lines, unruly children, and a number of other issues are being mediated by some 450 mediation centers in communities across the nation. In addition, the AARP's Standing Committee on Dispute Resolution has looked for ways to include mediation in disputes that involve some types of criminal activity. This has been particularly useful with neighborhood youth who engage in activities that affect the homes and lives of older people. Community mediation has been particularly effective in landlord/tenant disputes. This can involve the older person either as a landlord or as a tenant.

Episode 7: Support Systems

High Bandwidth:
http://raidercast.grcc.edu/flash/2011_2012/grcctv/successful_
aging/success_aging_7_large/grcc_player.html
Low Bandwidth:
http://raidercast.grcc.edu/flash/2011_2012/grcctv/successful_
aging/success_aging_7_small/grcc_player.html

To learn more about older adults using mediation to solve disputes and disagreements without involving attorneys, watch Video 7.

ARE COMMUNITIES READY FOR OLDER PEOPLE?

According to a major study in 2006 entitled, *The Maturing of America—Getting Communities on Track for an Aging Population,* by the National Association of Area Agencies on Aging, less than half of the nation's communities have begun preparing to cope with the various needs older people face trying to remain independent in neighborhoods. This is critical because in addition to the large numbers of older persons who already live in communities, the 77 million Baby Boomers began to turn 65 in 2011. Consequently, by 2030, the numbers of older persons (aged 65 and older) will double from the 2000 census. According to the chief executive of the National Association of Area Agencies on Aging,

Sandy Markwood, "The findings call for communities to begin planning now" (Powell, 2006, p. 1). The study indicated that

- One third of the communities have inadequate access to health care services.
- Only 25% of the communities provide nutrition education.
- Over one third of the communities have fitness programs for older persons.
- Only half of the communities have home modification programs to help physically challenged older persons stay in their own homes.
- Over 40% of the communities do not offer job training or retraining services.
- Many communities do not have a central information point to disseminate information regarding services.

Some specific recommendations of this study focused on simple things such as making larger, more light reflective street signs and increasing the time of pedestrian crossings (Powell, 2006).

SUGGESTED RESOURCES

Age Friendly Communities: http://afc.uwaterloo.ca
   This website, sponsored by the University of Waterloo, provides tools and resources to help guide communities towards developing solutions to become more age friendly, while recognizing the uniqueness of each community.
National Aging in Place Council (NAIPC): http://www.ageinplace.org
   The NAIPC is a senior support network dedicated to providing information and resources to assist older adults to remain independent in their own homes as long as possible. The website includes practical advice (e.g., on making homes senior friendly, transportation resources), financial options (e.g., home equity loans), and a search feature to find service providers ranging from elder law to travel.
Naturally Occurring Retirement Communities: http://www.norcs.org
   This initiative provides assistance to communities dedicated to supporting older communities and aging in place, focusing on support services for naturally occurring retirement communities.
"When Seniors Relocate": http://ohioline.osu.edu/ss-fact/0143.html
   This website includes a downloadable tip sheet to help older adults in relocating. Topics focus on how to be supportive of a move and adjusting to relocation.

CHAPTER 9

Housing Options for Older People

The learning objectives of this chapter include understanding

- The array of specific housing options available (depending on financial status) to older people.
- That homeownership as a type of housing option is the most common among older persons, and that the viability of this form of housing unit can have positive as well as negative consequences.
- How housing options—other than the single-family home—may offer advantages to an older person depending on each person's needs and wishes at a given point in her or his aging process.
- Why it may not be workable or desirable for older person to move into the homes of adult children.
- Housing trends for older people.

JOHN AND MAY: STAYING PUT

John and May were married in 1935. John was a painting contractor. Until the birth of their first child, May was in charge of an office for a large band instrument company. The goal of both John and May was to build a home across from a new park in a new section of the city. With lots of hard work, sacrifice, and worry, they were able to hang onto their house through the end of the Great Depression and World War II. They raised their three children there. Within six blocks from their house were churches, grocery stores, and other services including a dentist and a physician. The park across the street had baseball diamonds, a swimming pool, and acres of grass for everyone to enjoy in the summer. In the winter, there was an ice-skating rink that attracted a lot of young people.

Fifty years later, a lot of things have changed. John died. The children are all grown. May continues to live alone in the house she loves so much, a house filled with her possessions and memories. Her church moved to the suburbs in 1986. Most of the stores in the area have changed: The old movie theater only shows triple-x movies. The clothing store is now a massage parlor. Two liquor stores now occupy the old drug store and the old ice cream parlor. The dentist and the physician have moved to newer professional buildings. The park, once the center of outdoor recreation for the whole family, has attracted a large number of drug dealers and users. Police are regularly called to break up fights. May is reluctant to move, even though her children strongly encourage her to do so.

HOUSING OPTIONS FOR OLDER PEOPLE

This chapter outlines the types of housing available to older people. Although they are called *options*, in some important aspects they are not really options at all because (a) the vast majority of older persons, as well as almost half (48%) of the older Baby Boomers, want or plan to continue to stay in the housing unit they are living in and never move (Kravitz, 2011); (b) many older people are not willing to consider other types of living arrangements, even if another type of unit may be more suitable to their needs; and (c) many older people simply cannot afford to move to a different or more appropriate living arrangement. The overwhelming trend in America is to *age in place*, to continue to grow older in one's current residence regardless of the condition of the dwelling unit, the changing nature of the neighborhood, and the special needs an older person may have with the tasks of daily living. As a result, large numbers of older people in America are trying to cope with daily living while remaining in their single-family homes where they raised their families. A major aspect of aging in place that has gained a lot of attention is adapting existing homes to the particular needs of people that develop physical limitations.

HOME OWNERSHIP

The community-dwelling older population in the United States is primarily home owning. Of all the older households, almost 75% are single-family homes including manufactured/mobile homes (*65+ in the United States*, 2005). And the rate of home ownership varies by region of the nation. Home ownership rates also vary by family status and living arrangements. The majority of older married couples own their own homes (*65+ in the United States*, 2005).

Housing Costs

The amount of money spent on something called the *housing cost burden*, or the expenditures of housing and utilities combined, that exceeds 30% of all household income has increased somewhat for older people over the past decade. Since the 1980s, the housing cost burden has increased from 30% to 37%. In comparison, "The housing cost burden for all United States households has increased from 26 percent to 35 percent in the same period" (*Older Americans 2010*, p. 21). The difference in overall housing costs between the older population and the cost of the population reflects the reality that older people typically choose to remain in the homes in which they have lived for relatively long periods of time.

Housing Conditions

Older people tend to live in older homes. The median year in which the houses of older people were constructed was 1962 meaning that by now half of their houses are over 50 years old. An interesting sidelight is that older renters live in newer housing more often than do the rest of the population (*65+ in the United States*, 2005).

Overall, older people tend to live in adequate housing conditions, which means they have complete kitchens, washing machines, clothes dryers, air conditioning, warm air furnaces, and complete plumbing facilities.

About 40% of households with persons aged 65 and older experience one or more of the following types of housing problems: too costly, physically inadequate housing, and/or crowding. The rates of these problems are a little more than the rates of problems among all United States households (*Older Americans 2010*).

Physically inadequate housing, or housing with severe or moderate physical problems such as lacking complete plumbing or having multiple upkeep problems, has become less common. Only about 4% of households with persons aged 65 and older have inadequate housing compared to 8% in the 1980s. In contrast, 5% of all United States households report living in physically inadequate housing in the first decade of the 21st century compared to 8% in the 1980s (*Older Americans 2010*). Lack of financial resources is generally cited as the reason for the housing of older and younger people that had severe physical problems.

Another important component of the housing conditions of older people is the need to modify existing housing units to meet the changing physical needs of many people as they go through the aging process. As noted previously, most older people want to remain in their own communities in their own homes. Even if their health status changes, most still want to age in place in their own home. But in many cases, this requires home modifications—changing or adding some physical characteristics of the home—be it wider doors, access ramps, grab bars, and so forth. This is addressed in more detail later in this chapter.

Housing Energy Costs

Although it has been a persistent problem for many older householders for the past few decades, a housing problem that has gained national attention puts many older people at real financial and physical risk—the cost of energy. Since the first part of the 21st century, the price of energy has soared making it difficult for more and more older people to adequately heat, or in some cases, cool their homes. For example, the price of oil fluctuated from roughly $25 a barrel to over $100 a barrel from 2001 to 2011. This has translated into increasing energy costs—all of which greatly impact older persons as so many live on fixed and/or inadequate incomes.

Factors Influencing Energy Costs

The reasons for dramatic increases in the cost of energy are complex and varied but are not unrelated to instability in the Middle East as well as speculators investing in oil as a commodity; increased fuel usage in the United States due to some extent to the lack of a realistic national conservation program; and increasing demand for energy worldwide, particularly with the rapid economic development of major third world economies including India and China.

In a survey for AARP, nearly 90% of those questioned blamed the high profits of the oil companies for the spike in oil prices over the last few years (Povich, 2005). This survey also found that homeowners try to take some steps to cope with these soaring energy costs that can threaten the health of many older persons. For example, almost two thirds of the householders take steps to conserve energy, such as turning down thermostats to lower room temperatures. But room temperatures too low for the comfort of older people can result in hypothermia—a physical condition that if extended too long can result in physical harm or even death. More about hypothermia, and heat exhaustion, is discussed in Chapter 3.

Housing Concern: Safety

One of the key aspects of the housing conditions of older people is physical safety. This is particularly important in preventing falls. In northern climates, one typically relates falling to snow or ice-covered walkways and steps. And, indeed, thousands of people—including many older persons—fall every winter, resulting in severe consequences. But it is inside the home where large numbers of older people fall every year. ("Avoiding Slips and Falls in This Holiday Season," 2005).

According to home safety experts, there are key remedial steps that older house-holders can take to dramatically enhance their safety at home. One of the most dangerous rooms in an older person's home is the bathroom. Falls, slips, and scalding water are all major risks. Among recommendations to make bathrooms safer are adequate lighting, with some light on throughout the night; strategically positioned grab bars, especially around the bathtub, shower, and toilet; nonslip surfaces on the bottoms of bathtubs, showers and bathroom floors utilizing nonslip surfaces or bath mats with nonslip grippers; a cordless phone in bathrooms so those needing assistance can call for help; single-lever faucets; benches in shower stalls or showers with seats built into them; no clutter on countertops or on the floors; levers for door knobs on bathroom doors as well as all doors in the home (McClintock, 2006).

There are additional issues regarding safety addressed under "Aging in Place" in the Practical Application at the end of Part III of this textbook.

Staying Connected at Home

Another key factor for older people who live alone is staying connected with the outside world—particularly with close relatives or friends as well as emergency services. With 95% of people aged 75 and older wanting to continue living in their own homes, it is essential that they are able to stay connected for their own safety. Fortunately, continued developments in technology make this possible (Saltzman & Walker, 2008). It all started with Alexander Graham Bell who invented the telephone. The telephone is still important for keeping people connected, but wireless communications and computing power are also key in this objective. There is a new generation of gadgets that can summon aid, alert people to take their medications, help caregivers keep tabs on an older person's movements, and let doctors monitor vital signs from a distance (Saltzman & Walker, 2008). Experts predict that in the near future, additional technologies will converge to the point where older people, their families, and health care providers will be completely connected. Currently, technological devices used in a home setting by elders can address the following home-living issues:

- Emergency pendants that contain a button that can be pressed to reach a 24-hour dispatcher who will notify a relative, a caregiver, or emergency services.
- Problem Addressed: One third of all older adults suffer a fall each year. About a fourth of those who fall lose some independence due to injury.
- Pillboxes, pagers, vibrating watches, and dispensers that talk to the patient or alert a caregiver to ensure older patients take their medications.
- Problem Addressed: Up to 40% of nursing home admissions result from an inability to take medications at home unsupervised.

- Motion detectors and small TV cameras attached to computers or TV sets to reassure family members and caregivers that the older person needing assistance is carrying out his or her daily routine. The small TV cameras enable family members to visit via the Internet.
- Problem Addressed: About 7 million adults live at least an hour from a parent they are caring for, the National Institute on Aging estimates (Saltzman & Walker, 2008).

ADAPTING/BUILDING HOMES FOR OLDER PEOPLE

All of the concerns outlined previously relate to new ways to build new residences or adapt existing homes for the physical needs of people as they grow older. Increasingly the focus of architects, developers, homebuilders, and remodelers is building or adapting homes to address the needs of an aging population. In one survey of some 500 firms, 74% reported "greater accessibility" as a growing trend in home design (Olubayo & Brown, 2007). Americans aged 55 and older purchase one in five of all new homes built in the United States, according to the National Association of Home Builders (NAHB).

A voluntary certification process has been developed for builders committed to construction that makes a home cost-effective, accessible, and convenient for people of all ages. It is called the *Easy Living Home Program*. In addition, AARP and the NAHB have also created a joint awards program—the Livable Communities Awards for Builders.

REVERSE MORTGAGES

Reverse mortgages are loans to older householders that are secured by the value of their homes and do not need to be paid until the borrower dies, sells the home, or moves out permanently. In order to obtain one of these mortgages, a borrower must be at least 62 years old and own the home. The house must be a primary residence. There are no income requirements for this type of loan.

Types of Reverse Mortgages

There are two types of reverse mortgage loans: (a) the Home Equity Conversion Mortgage (HECM), which is backed by the federal government, and (b) private reverse mortgages that do not have federal mortgage insurance. "The HECM is still the gold standard," said Shelley Giordano of Wells Fargo Home Mortgage. "It's the most versatile product and the best for most people," (Gandel, 2008, p. 12). Older homeowners turn to reverse mortgages for a variety of reasons according to an AARP study released at the end of 2007. These include paying off existing mortgages, paying for prescription drugs, improving the quality of their lives, and paying for home health care, which is the top reason.

But a reverse mortgage is not for everyone. Some even call it the loan of last resort. Some experts think these loans may be best for persons in their 70s and 80s, but they may not be as good for persons in their 60s because they could outlive their resources in their later years that would leave them with little or nothing upon which to rely. In addition, these loans are expensive and the amount one owes increases every month. In fact, an AARP study found that the expense of this type of loan—between 8% and 10% of the home's value—is the main reason many potential borrowers decide against reverse mortgages (Gandel, 2008).

The market for these loans is expected to swell with the oldest Baby Boomers having reached age 65 in 2011. The U.S. Senate and House of Representatives both passed legislation in 2007 to 2008 to update the HECM program, which was designed to make these loans more accessible.

TAX RELIEF PROGRAMS FOR HOMEOWNERS

Most of the states have some form of property tax relief program for older persons. They may be called *circuit-breaker* programs or *homestead exemptions*. Circuit-breaker programs provide tax cuts or refunds to older homeowners when property taxes go above a certain percentage of their household income. Homestead exemptions are usually fixed-percentage reductions in the assessed valuation of an older person's primary residence. For example, when property taxes are raised by a special millage election for schools, many older homeowners pay just a little extra in taxes if these programs are in place.

THE SINGLE-FAMILY HOME

In the later years of the 20th century and the early years of the 21st century, single-family homes increased in value at a rather remarkable rate. But this upward trend came to an abrupt end beginning in 2007 and in the Great Recession of 2008 to 2009. Home prices fell generally across the nation, with rather dramatic declines in specific regions along with widespread home foreclosures. But for many older persons, home values increased because of the length of time they owned their homes—often 20, 30, 40 years, and more. In spite of the major housing crisis of 2008 to 2009, the single-family home has been one of the best investments the average older Americans have made. The true financial value of home ownership needs to be measured by the equity an older person has in a home. If older people were to sell their homes and invest the equity in secure investments, they might realize enough monthly return to pay for other forms of housing that are more suitable to their needs. The current tax laws permit a once-in-a-lifetime sale of a person's home after the age of 55 on which they do not need to pay any federal tax on a capital gain up to $500,000. The older person selling his or her home and investing the equity can have the benefit of a monthly (or quarterly or yearly) income and the security of having the money available. The only question is whether the equity market is a safe investment vehicle for older persons given what happened to equities when their value dropped by about 40% between October 2007 and January 2009.

The Impact of the Housing Bubble on Retirement Security

Between 2000 and 2007, house prices rose 60% before the housing bubble burst in the Great Recession (Munnell & Soto, 2008). A major study by the Center for Retirement Research at Boston College showed that an increase in housing prices as a result of the housing boom led to increases in debt and to increased consumption—people bought a lot more things. This was done by extracting equity from their homes—obtaining cash by taking out second mortgages and lines of credit. Indeed, older householders, with most other responsibilities out of the way, are more likely to take out equity from their homes than are other people (Munnell & Soto, 2008).

Impact of Extracting Equity From Homes

Taking money out of the equity in one's home, according to research, directly impacts retirement financial security in a period of declining home prices and fluctuating stock market values. It is estimated that for those householders who took equity out of their homes from 2001 into 2008 and continued to consume, their net worth was 36% less on average than the net worth of householders who did not extract home equity (Munnell & Soto, 2008). Overall, many householders reacted to the very large growth of the price of houses by increasing their debt. The danger is that when housing booms (with rapidly increasing house prices) are followed by housing busts (with falling home prices), too many homeowners will have borrowed against gains they may never obtain. That is why "bubbles" can negatively impact the retirement balance sheets of older persons.

As a result, Munnell and Soto pointed out that increases in mortgage debt have affected the retirement readiness of many householders. Some 30% of older household-ers took out money from their home equities. The housing boom provided some financial liquidity (ready cash) for many older householders, but, as the researchers stated, "a significant portion of those entering retirement today—and perhaps over the next several years—will have a fragile balance sheet in a time of depressed home prices and poor financial market returns" (Munnell & Soto, 2008, p. 8).

Fear of Foreclosure

The downward spiral of the housing market combined with the fluctuations in the finan-cial markets has led to the reality of older people facing the loss of their homes through foreclosure. Many older Americans refinanced homes using risky mortgage instruments. The founder of the nonprofit Homeowners Options for Massachusetts Elders pointed out that owners of homes who were aged 75 and older were the fastest-growing group of people who refinanced (Fleck, 2008). Many fell for predatory refinancing that included interest-only loans and adjustable rate mortgages. The same nonprofit organization noted that more than half of its clients face the loss of their homes. An AARP survey indicated that persons aged 50 and older hold 41% of all first mortgages in the United States. Of this group of persons, some 684,000 are delinquent on their mortgages, in foreclosure, or have already lost their homes (AARP Policy Institute, 2009).

Another downside of the collapse of home prices in so many areas of the nation is that many parents are being asked to help adult children who have been stuck with mortgages they could not afford (Fleck, 2008). For example, the executive director of the Las Vegas Area Legal Services said that 90% of her clients had mortgages that were as much as tens of thousands of dollars more than the value of their homes, a condition that has been com-mon across the nation (Fleck, 2008). The chief economist of Moody's economy.com said, "Not since the Great Depression [of the 1930s] have so many people had their homes worth less than they paid" (Fleck, 2008, p.14). The story was reported of a couple in Lawrence, Massachusetts, aged 64 and 62, who refinanced their home of 30 years to obtain cash to supplement their fixed income. They got behind in their payments on the loan and faced losing the home. As a result they said, "We're not eating well or keeping warm. We keep our heat at 50 to 55 degrees and stay upstairs because it's warmer. We eat eggs, canned soup, and potatoes. I only buy the cheap ham and cheap cheese" (Fleck, 2008, p. 14).

APARTMENTS

One of the options for older people who decide to move from their single-family home is to move to an apartment. Many styles of apartments are available in a variety of price ranges. For the older person, apartment living can be attractive because it transfers the responsibilities of property ownership to someone else. A person's commitment is usually for a fixed period of time, typically a year at a time. This can be an advantage or a disad-vantage. During the rental year, housing costs are fixed so the person can budget housing costs with no surprises, such as the need for a new roof or furnace or escalating taxes or utility costs. However, at the end of the year's lease, the price of the apartment may go up. If apartments have been overbuilt in an area, rents tend to be much more stable, so it is important to be familiar with the apartment market. It may be possible for an older person to get a longer term commitment for a fixed amount of rent, or, if not a locked-in price, at least a cap on the yearly increase. Because so many older people live on some form of fixed incomes, price stability for their housing can be a key factor in their ability to survive financially. On the other hand, if for some reason they become dissatisfied with their apartment, yearly leases give them the flexibility to move to a living unit that they like better.

Many elderly people feel they lose privacy in an apartment setting. Others feel loss of ownership or control. Still others cannot come to grips with a drawer full of rent receipts. They believe this is money "down the drain." However, for many older persons, apartment living can be an economical way to obtain tax-free equity from the sale of the old homestead, as well as to get out from under the escalating cost of taxes, insurance, utilities, and maintenance associated with keeping their own homes.

Possible Problems With Apartment Living

In towns and cities across the nation, developers have been buying buildings containing apartments by the tens of thousands in order to convert them into condominiums—"condo conversions." For example, the wave of these conversions began back in 2004 with more than a quarter of a million apartments taken out of the rental market by the end of 2005, according to the National Associations of Realtors (Basler, 2006).

Experts say that no matter how stable a rental apartment building may seem, the tenants are always vulnerable to the threat of a condo conversion. Sometimes the renters are able to stay in their rental/condo unit if they can afford to buy it. But many older renters living on fixed incomes with limited savings or investments cannot afford to buy their converted unit, which then forces them to move—some after many years in what they thought was a secure home. And research has shown that moving for many older people negatively impacts their physical and mental health. As William Apgar, a senior scholar at Harvard University, stated, "For seniors to face an unknown future, to have lives disrupted this way, literally makes some ill. And where do they go? Move in with their kids or a relative? Go to a nursing home? This is incredibly stressful" (Basler, 2006, p. 17).

There are no federal laws that regulate condo conversions. And state laws vary widely. Some cities have regulations, but these regulations often do not achieve the goal of keeping older renters in their homes. Most existing regulations only require the owners to notify the tenants of the changes, offer them the right to purchase their units, and give them adequate time to relocate. A Harvard University housing expert suggests that Baby Boomers need to plan ahead so that they do not get caught in this conversion bind. One way to do this is to have the tenants band together to buy the building while they are still younger and make it a cooperative effort with the stipulation that if they move, they will sell only to new residents at affordable prices. Otherwise, the next big wave of condo conversions will hit Baby Boomers and put some of them at risk (Basler, 2006).

CONDOMINIUMS

Condominiums, or "condos," are a form of real estate ownership. They can take almost any form of housing unit from detached single units on the ground level to "cubes" or apartments in high-rise buildings. They are housing units that are individually owned but part of a multifamily housing sitting on common grounds that typically have support facilities and recreational facilities. Condominium owners are real estate owners. They own (or are buying) the housing unit they live in, plus a fractional share of the common grounds and facilities. Owning a condominium is just like owning one's own house except the condo owner generally does not do the maintenance and repairs and is partial owner of the common areas. The condo owner pays a fee that covers the cost of ongoing maintenance and repairs. As a property owner, a condominium dweller can obtain a mortgage on his or her property, deduct the interest she or he pays on the mortgage from their tax returns, pay real estate taxes, and sell the property.

For many older persons, condominium living combines the benefits of living in an apartment-type setting with no responsibility for grass cutting, snow removal, and other chores (except for monthly and yearly fees) associated with home ownership. There are no rent receipts. The living unit is owned by the resident, which means it can appreciate or depreciate in value.

MOBILE HOMES

Mobile homes can be very appealing to some older people. They are an affordable housing option that gives them the feeling of a secure living environment if they are in a mobile home park that they enjoy, while at the same time allowing them the independence and privacy of a single-family home. The purchase price of the mobile or manufactured home does not typically include any of the costs associated with getting the home ready for occupancy.

A major problem in mobile home parks where the lots are rented by the residents has been the spiraling costs of monthly rentals. This has been particularly true for prime recreational areas of the South and Southwest. As these rentals prices tend to increase, many older persons have been forced to sell because they could no longer afford the monthly rental fees for their mobile home lots.

Most parks will not accept older mobile homes. Even if they were to find a park that would accept older mobile homes, many older persons on modest, fixed incomes simply cannot afford the expenses involved in moving a mobile home. Another major consideration for mobile home dwellers is restrictions. Most parks have some restrictions. Some are so restrictive that residents are not permitted to wash their cars or have visitors overnight.

Another type of mobile home park is one in which the residents own the lots on which their mobile homes are placed. These parks are generally co-operatively managed and have co-operatively owned recreational buildings and services. Some even have their own fire departments and emergency paramedical units, such as Trailer Estates in Manatee County, Florida. There the elderly residents participate directly in the decision-making processes of operating the park. There is no "rent" to pay each month beyond the service charges. This type of park cannot be sold unless there is a cooperative decision by the park's resident owners. As a result, resident owners of a co-operatively owned mobile home park generally are in a better position to control their own living environments.

COHOUSING

Cohousing can take two forms. One is homesharing where unrelated persons share one home. Another form of cohousing is where a group, typically made of strangers, develops a communal-type housing unit with separate units with shared common space (Abrahms, 2011).

Homesharing is a concept that is developing rapidly in some sections of the nation. It is economical because it significantly cuts the homeowner's housing costs. But it is not easy for many older (or younger) persons to have some strangers move into their homes. For some, it is a way to keep their home and have companionship at the same time. The most important part of homesharing is matching appropriate persons. Even for people who are generally compatible, inevitable differences and tensions may arise.

Information on homesharing can usually be obtained from a local Area Agency on Aging, or from the National Shared Housing Resource Center. Homesharing makes it possible for many older people to exchange an important resource they have—their home—for services they need.

In the other form of cohousing, a group may purchase the property, mutually design it, develop the rules, and manage it. The residents may sometimes eat together. In 2011, there were more than 112 intergenerational cohousing communities with an additional 40 to 50 in the planning stage. Over half were in California (Abrahms, 2011).

ACCESSORY APARTMENTS

Accessory apartments are private living quarters, which include a sitting and sleeping area, a kitchen, a bathroom, and sometimes a separate entrance in existing single-family homes. It is an independent apartment within a single-family home. These are sometimes referred to as *mother-in-law apartments*. Historically, some of the antebellum plantation homes of the South had mother-in-law apartments separate from the rest of the family. The object of this type of apartment is to provide secure living arrangements for older persons close to the family so that family members can help care for the older person, while still maintaining the privacy and independence of a person's own living space.

Residential zoning can be a problem in developing an accessory apartment in single-family zoned neighborhoods. It may be possible to deal with zoning restrictions in communities through revised zoning ordinances, zoning variances, licensing, or special-use permits. Each community deals with this issue in its own way. Zoning ordinances for accessory apartments are usually more lenient in rural areas.

ECHO: ELDER COTTAGE HOUSING OPPORTUNITY

Elder Cottage Housing Opportunity (ECHO) refers to small, freestanding, removable housing units placed on the sides or backyards of single-family homes to provide private, independent housing for elderly parents to be close to the homes of adult children. This enables adult children to care for the daily needs of dependent elderly parents without leaving their own property. It has the advantage of maintaining the privacy and independence of each family unit. The older folks do not have to listen to their grandchild's stereo, be in the way when their adult children entertain, or deal with all the other inconveniences of two families living together in the same home. They can go to bed as early or late as they wish. The traumas and adjustments necessary when the old folks move into the home of an adult child are avoided.

PUBLIC HOUSING

The concept of public housing came about in President Franklin D. Roosevelt's New Deal with the passage of the Housing Act of 1937, 2 years after the passage of the Social Security Act. It was not until 1956 that the Housing Act was amended to provide public housing specifically for the elderly. Through its various sections, public housing for the elderly has been cooperatively provided through federal governmental loan programs to municipalities, religious organizations, private investors, and various social agencies.

Forms of Public Housing for the Elderly

Public housing has been developed primarily through two provisions. One is Section 202 of the Housing Act enacted back in 1959. Through this section of the law, long-term loans are made to nonprofit organizations to develop multifamily housing complexes for elderly and handicapped persons. The program was suspended in 1969 after much opposition. It was revived in 1974 as part of the Housing and Community Development Act.

Rents are limited to 20% of a person's income. Section 202 housing was designed to make sure that elderly residents had access to a variety of services that enable them to live independently, such as the availability of meals, transportation, personal assistance, and housekeeping (Cox, 2005). Residents need to be age 62 and older with income below 50% of the area's median income. A major problem is lack of supply of these types of units.

Section 8, created by the Housing and Community Development Act back in 1974, is a program designed to provide subsidized rent to low-income households, including elderly people. In this program, money is provided through the Department of Housing and Urban Development (HUD) to landlords for persons who can show financial need to make up the difference between 30% of a person's income and what is considered fair-market rent. In this program, the tenants can choose their own rental units (within price ranges) in a wide variety of rental housing styles, including apartment buildings, duplexes, single-family homes, and others.

SINGLE-ROOM OCCUPANCY

Single-room occupancy (SRO) is a living arrangement that many older persons would not choose. It refers to those single rooms that people of any age occupy in inner city hotels and rooming houses, usually with a shared or common bath and no kitchen. For many years, research has indicated that older persons typically occupy a large percentage of SROs (Harris, 1990). The development of urban renewal projects back in the 1960s first brought this population to light. Typically, SROs have been located in old hotels in the inner city or in rural areas. SROs can be undesirable housing units for many reasons. They can be generally substandard in quality, with no private bathrooms, no adequate cooking facilities, no common area, and no regular meal service. Many of these old rooms were designed for transient stays, not for long-term residences.

ADULT FOSTER CARE

Another housing option for the elderly is called adult foster care. It is primarily for functionally impaired older persons. Similar to foster care for children, these homes are typically operated by families in their own homes and provide care for a small number of older adults. The care provided usually includes room and board, assistance with activities of daily living, and overall supervision.

Licensing varies by state with some states having no provisions for licensing. Often adult foster care homes can be more flexible than nursing facilities and feel more like a family home.

LIVING WITH ADULT CHILDREN

Many people believe that families today are quite different from the families of earlier times. Obviously many things have changed, such as high technology applications, higher divorce rates, and fast-paced lifestyles; but contrary to common belief, what has not changed in American family life are intergenerational living arrangements. Many people feel that they have an obligation to automatically move their aging parents into their own homes when one parent becomes widowed or is not capable of maintaining his or her own home. Many people feel this is the way it was done in earlier periods of our history. One of the pioneers in gerontology, Clark Tibbitts (1968), noted that the three-generation family, where the old parents moved into the home of a nuclear family, has been relatively rare. Even in American colonial times, the three-generation family was an exception. The historical evidence for this comes from examining family wills in Plymouth Colony (Demos, 1965). Another study of family life in Massachusetts in the 17th century noted the difference between the family of residence, which was mostly nuclear, and the family of interaction or obligation (Greven, 1966). This was a kinship group of two or more generations living in a single community, not a single house.

The Value of Independence

Whether people live in separate homes, apartments, condominiums, mobile homes, or any other type of housing units, most value some degree of independence with the ability to rely on family members living nearby. In our culture, for the most part, there has never been an emphasis on older people moving in with grown children and their families unless it was really necessary. Arranging for an independent living situation for older parents is not abandoning them. In most instances, it is best for both parties, the older people and their adult children.

Key Questions Before Moving a Parent Into an Adult Child's Home

Before an elderly parent is invited to move into the home of an adult child, it is helpful to raise the following questions:

- Can they tolerate each other's lifestyle? Different generations have different tastes in food, music, TV watching, and a range of other activities.
- Can they relate to each other as mature adults? The aged parent and the middle-aged child have lived apart for many years. The adult child is not the same person who left his or her parents' home years before. In a close living situation, differences can become evident and tensions can surface easily.
- Does the home have enough space? Physical space and adequate privacy are essential if an aging parent is to live successfully with an adult child.

RETIREMENT COMMUNITIES

For many years, retirement communities have been described as places where people move when they retire. This does not mean that no resident in a retirement community works, but rather that the residents typically have retired from their primary job and have relocated to a retirement community.

Types of Retirement Communities

Retirement communities typically have included mobile home parks, high-rise senior housing complexes, leisure villages, or other forms of housing units. Among the largest and most elaborate retirement communities are Sun City, Arizona, and Leisure World, California, which have been in existence for many years. An elaborate range of amenities and services to meet the wishes and needs of retired persons continue to be found in these villages. Housing options, recreational facilities, medical assistance, houses of worship, and a range of educational opportunities seem to have had no limit in this type of retirement environment (Stevey & Associates, 1989).

As Baby Boomers continue to move into their later years (aged 65 and older), experts contend that they will shape the future of retirement housing. As John McIlwain, senior fellow at the Urban Land Institute, stated, "They [Baby Boomers] have changed expectations for every decade they've gone through; I don't think it will stop now" (Abrahms, 2011, p.10).

One variation is something called *niche communities* where "people live with others who share similar lifestyles, backgrounds or interests" (Abrahms, 2011, p. 12). In 2011, there were some 100 of these communities across the nation. They range from RV parks for artists and university-/college-based housing units, to the pricey Rainbow Vision in Santa Fe, New Mexico, focusing on—but not exclusively—lesbian, gay, bisexual, and transgender (GLBT) residents (Abrahms, 2011). With some 3 million GLBT older Americans, a number projected to nearly double by 2030, this type of housing focus can provide vital supports as these older persons may not have adult children to care for them (Abrahms, 2011).

SUGGESTED RESOURCES

Elder Cottage Housing Opportunity (ECHO): http://www.seniorliving.about.com/od/housingoptions/a/echo.htm
This site describes what ECHO housing is, its benefits and challenges, and where to get more information about it.

National Association of Housing Cooperatives (NAHC): http://www.coophousing.org
Incorporated in 1960, the NAHC is a nonprofi t national federation of housing cooperatives, mutual housing associations, and other resident-owned or controlled housing, professionals, organizations, and individuals interested in promoting the interests of co-operative housing communities.

National Shared Housing Resource Center (NSHRC): http://nationalsharedhousing.org
The NSHRC is a clearinghouse of information for people looking to fi nd a shared housing organization in their community or to help get a program started. The site has a directory of programs by state, and a list of regional representatives with contact information.

Reverse Mortgages: http://www.ftc.gov/articles/0192-reverse-mortgages
The Federal Trade Consumer (FTC) is the nation's consumer protection agency. This website provides information on how reverse mortgages work, the types of reverse mortgages available, and how to get the best deal.

CHAPTER 10

Economics of Aging: Work and Older Persons

The learning objectives of this chapter include understanding

- That the economic status of older people varies greatly depending on income levels, personal wealth, savings, and sources of income.
- How poverty and near poverty are still threats to some older people.
- That Social Security as a federal program has been, and continues to be, a key component in the economic lives of a majority of older persons in the United States.
- That the attacks on Social Security, Medicare, and Medicaid have existed since the inception of these programs and how they continue as part of ongoing political debates.
- Why more older persons are continuing to work or trying to find paid employment and the significant obstacles they encounter as a result of the Great Recession and myths about older workers.

ESTHER: THE UNPAID WORKER

Esther was the second of six children. Her fondest dream as a youngster was to be a schoolteacher. But her family was a working family and she was expected to contribute to the family income as soon as she was able, which in her case was after completing 10th grade at age 16. This was how it was for working-class families in America in 1920. Only a privileged few actually went on to college.

Esther got a job in an office and by the age of 21 was the manager of the accounting section. By the age of 23, Esther married and she continued to work until the birth of her first child. She helped her husband start his own business, a small contracting firm. Esther kept all the records, paid the bills, computed the taxes, and managed the payroll when the company added employees as time went on.

She continued to do this even after the birth of two more children. The Great Depression of the 1930s sent their business reeling for a few years, with very little work and income. World War II also interrupted the contracting business as Esther's husband entered a war plant for 3 years and left the business for a time.

After World War II, things began to pick up and the business flourished. Once again, Esther was key to all the office procedures of the business. In addition, she managed a store that she and her husband started to furnish needed household products to returning servicemen and their new families (the beginning of the Baby Boom).

Because their businesses were small and often struggling, Esther was never a paid employee. No Social Security taxes were ever withheld for her. Because they lived and worked at a time when wages and prices were very low by today's standards, Esther and her husband never were able to save any amount of money that could produce income in their later years—especially extended later years, as she and her husband lived into their 90s.

During all her busy years, Esther was a homemaker, raised her three children, volunteered in the community and in her church, cared for her elderly parents until they died in their early 80s, and worked in the family business. For all of these activities lasting over 45 years, she received no public or private pension. Her only reward was to get 50% of her husband's Social Security benefits based on his earnings and work record, which ended years ago. Needless to say, she and her husband ran out of money as they continued to grow older, spending increasingly more money on medical expenses in spite of Medicare, and spending more on personal assistance as they did less and less for themselves.

Esther was one of the more fortunate elderly Americans. If she had been member of a minority group, widowed earlier, never married, or divorced, her financial situation would have been more desperate.

PARADIGM SHIFTS IN THE ECONOMICS OF OLDER PEOPLE

If ever there were a chapter that highlighted major paradigm shifts in the status of older Americans, this is one. Overall, the elderly population has experienced significant gains in overall economic status since the inception of the Social Security Act of 1935. Widespread poverty, unemployment, and economic vulnerability in the Great Depression of the 1930s provided the stimulus to develop programs that would provide some economic stability to the lives of older Americans. A detailed discussion of Social Security is provided later in this chapter.

New Threats to Income Security

Tremendous gains in the overall economic status of older persons have been evident since the implementation of Social Security and the cost of living adjustments that were included in the Social Security Amendments of 1972. But once again, in spite of the overall economic gains of older people since the Great Depression of the 1930s and the still high poverty rate for the elderly as recent as 1959, many older persons again face economic hardships as the result of the Great Recession of 2008 to 2009. With the plunge of equity markets (stocks, bonds, and other investments) in 2008 to 2009, and the collapse of the housing markets in most sections of the nation, many persons in their early to middle 60s have been forced to postpone their retirement plans if they are able to keep their jobs, or drastically scale back their standard of living. One bright spot in all the economic downturns of this 2008 to 2009 era is the reality that President George W. Bush was not able to privatize Social Security funding following his pledged objective in the 2004 presidential election. As a result, the Social Security Trust Funds were not negatively impacted by the collapse of the equity and housing markets in 2008 to 2009.

Numerous stories, as well as statistics, describe the economic plight of many Baby Boomers and elderly (those aged 65 and older) persons as a result of the Great Recession. The story is told of Jeanne Phillips of Badon, Pennsylvania, who planned to keep working as long as she could, even after two heart attacks, because she needed the money to survive

(Fleck, 2009). And Frank Wilkinson, 89, of Clearwater, Florida, worked about 25 hours a week to maintain himself because he lost his pension from the airline he worked for after it went bankrupt (Fleck, 2009). David Sinclair, 62, of Rio Rancho, New Mexico, who retired in 2007, was confident that his savings of $500,000, in addition to a government pension, would be enough to support him and his wife throughout their retirement years. But the value of his investment savings dropped 33%, and he has ended up back at work (Carpenter, 2009).

In fact, Standard & Poor's 500 lost 55% of its value from October 2007 to March 2009 (Carpenter, 2009). Millions of people in their 60s, 70s, and 80s found the reality of retirement changed because of economic reasons (Fleck, 2011b). They continued to work if they were able to retain or find jobs because they needed the money to support themselves. Using data from the Bureau of Labor Statistics, Whoriskey (2012) reported that the percentage of workers over 65 has increased faster than any other age group.

DIVERSITY OF ECONOMIC STATUS

In spite of what has occurred since the Great Recession of 2008 to 2009 (many trace its onset to the decline in housing prices in 2007), there is real diversity in income and overall wealth (or lack of wealth) among older people (aged 65 and older) and the emerging old (aged 55 to 64). There is obviously a long list of elderly persons in the United States who are among the wealthiest people in the nation and the world. This would include persons who have developed, owned, and/or run major corporations and equity firms. On the other end of the spectrum are many impoverished older people, who in spite of Social Security, Medicare, and other specific age-related benefits, still struggle to pay for the basic needs of life.

Although net worth or overall wealth is an important concept in assessing the economic status of older persons, determining the levels and sources of incomes of elders is vital to understanding their ability, or lack of ability, to cope with the costs of daily living throughout the aging process. Diversity of income levels among older persons in the United States prevails. Some older persons have high incomes, some have poverty-level incomes, and many are somewhere in the middle ranges. In 1959, 35% of older adults lived below the poverty line (*Older Americans 2010*). But looking just at the percentage of older people living below the poverty line, for example, does not provide a complete picture of their economic situations. Looking at the income distribution of persons aged 65 and older and their median income gives a better view of their economic well-being. Since 1974, the proportion of older people living in poverty and in the low-income group generally declined so that by 2007, 10% of the older population was in the low-income category (*Older Americans 2010*). At the same time, people in the middle-income group made up the largest share of older people according to income groupings (33%). And the proportion of those in the high-income category increased from 18% in 1974 to 31% by 2007 (*Older Americans 2010*). The following chart (Figure 10.1) illustrates the distributions of income by categories among the elderly.

Income Differences

Among older people, poverty rates vary greatly according to sex, marital status, work history, and race. The roles of wives, homemakers, nurturers of children, caregivers for ill family members aging parents, and volunteers in the community, the church, and the school have occupied the lives of countless American women who are currently elderly. Unless wives who do not work outside the home inherit a large amount of money or win the lottery, their retirement income is typically dependent on their husbands.

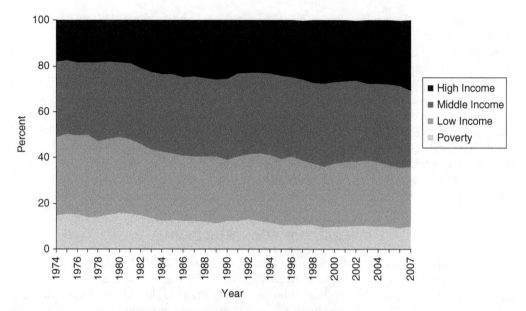

FIGURE 10.1 Income Distribution of the Population 65 and Over, 1974–2007.

Note: Income categories are derived from the ratio of the family's income (or an unrelated individual's income) to the corresponding poverty threshold. Being in poverty is measured as income less than 100% of the poverty threshold. Low income is between 100% and 199% of the poverty threshold. Middle income is between 200% and 399% of the poverty threshold. High income is 400% or more of the poverty threshold.

Reference population: These data refer to the noninstitutionalized population.

Source: Older Americans 2010, Table 8a.

Although the percentage of women who work outside the home has increased dramatically in the last four decades (from 43% in 1970 to 60% in 2010), research indicates that there are still major pitfalls for women as they begin retirement today, or contemplate it in the future (Fleck, 2011a). Women who are in the paid labor force earn about 77 cents to a man's dollar. For those who interrupt their work histories to raise children, care for aging parents, or volunteer, there is less work time to build up Social Security credits or 401(k) pensions (Locke, 2011). Not surprisingly then, women generally start saving later in their lives, and then do not have enough savings to finance their retirement years (Choi, 2008). As women generally have more retirement years to finance, all these, as well as other factors, put them at a financial disadvantage in their later years.

Race and ethnicity are also directly related to income differences among older persons. For example, older non-Hispanic White men are far less likely than older Black American men and Hispanic men to be living in poverty—about 5% compared to 17% for older Black American men and 13% for older Hispanic men (*Older Americans 2010*). And significantly, older non-Hispanic White and Black American women have higher poverty rates than their male counterparts (*Older Americans 2010*).

A major study by the National Academy on an Aging Society points to specific indicators that threaten the retirement security of people of color (Hudson, 2005). These include low wages, spotty work histories, family responsibilities, inadequate pension coverage, poor financial literacy, and discrimination. Working people of color are more likely to be forced out of the labor market due to not being able to keep or find work. And according to the National Academy report, at the same time, people of color are often less able to retire because of a lack of adequate savings or pension income. In short, they, too, often cannot work, but they cannot afford to retire.

Another Measure of Poverty

Overall, the official poverty rate for older Americans has been about 10% for many years, which has been the lowest rate among all age categories. But according to a formula created by the National Academy of Sciences, the real rate is 15.1% for older Americans because the existing formula does not account for the rising costs of medical care as well as some other factors (Short, 2012).

SOCIAL SECURITY

A common denominator of income for the elderly in today's America is Social Security monthly cash. This program has expanded greatly since 1940, when less than 1% of older people received Social Security benefits. By the end of 2011, some 55 million Americans received Social Security benefits with 16% relying on it for at least 90% of their total income (Quinn, 2011).

History of Social Security

Social Security was developed to be a "floor" or base of income for retired, older persons, to be supplemented by other sources of income, such as assets, pensions, or some continued earnings from work. But since the 1960s, Social Security has provided the largest share of total income for older Americans. Indeed, the share of income from pensions increased rapidly in the 1960s and 1970s but has declined since the mid-1980s. The share of income from working has been the opposite—declining until the mid-1980s and increasing somewhat since then (*Older Americans 2010*). Social Security came out of the Great Depression of the 1930s as one of the most, if not *the* most, important achievement of President Franklin Roosevelt's New Deal. This type of program traces its roots to Europe in the 1880s, where Otto von Bismarck of Germany developed a program to require employers and employees to contribute to a fund, first for disabled workers and then for retired workers at age 65. It should be noted that not many people lived to age 65 at that time. As a result, not much money was paid out in extended benefits during that era.

By 1905, France had enacted a similar program for unemployment. In 1911, England also adopted both old age and unemployment insurance plans. Roosevelt followed the outlines of the European plans with these key components:

- Government sponsored
- Compulsory
- Independently financed

Intergenerational Aspects of Social Security

It is an error to view Social Security only as a program for older people. From the beginning, it had intergenerational aspects. By providing a base of financial income for retired workers and their spouses, Social Security relieves younger family members from needing to support their elderly parents. Younger workers also gain financial security by having income in place for their spouses and dependent children in the event of their death. In 1956, Disability Insurance (DI) was added to Social Security to replace a portion of a worker's income when he or she becomes disabled and is unable to work. The Old Age and Survivors Insurance (OASI) and the Disability Insurance (DI) programs together form the OASDI program, which is intended to replace a portion of a worker's income upon retirement, disability, or death. Generally referred to as *Social Security*, monthly benefits are based on a person's work record (years of covered employment), earnings history, and the age at which the first benefit is claimed.

Scope of Social Security

Social Security payments amount to 37% of the total income of the population aged 65 and older. Earnings provide 30% of total income; pensions come to 19% of total income; and asset income (dividends, interest on savings, etc.) amounts to 13% of total income with 3% coming from other sources (*Older Americans 2010*).

Studies over the past several decades clearly show that Social Security has improved the economic status of older Americans and helped to alleviate poverty among them (*Older Americans 2010*; Social Security Administration, 2003). The majority (64%) of OASDI funds goes to retirees, while the remaining portion is split between survivor benefits and disability benefits (Quinn, 2011). And over half (56%) of those receiving Social Security benefits are women.

Importance of Social Security

Many people believe that they would be better off investing their own money for their retirement incomes. The director of research for the Pinnacle Advisory Group has calculated that the average wage earner would need to have at least $580,000 in savings to provide a monthly income of $2,170—the average monthly income from Social Security plus inflation adjustments for this worker (Quinn, 2011). And this private-based income might last only 30 years.

Attacks on Social Security

In recent years, serious questions have emerged regarding the viability, fairness, and desirability of the Social Security program. These questions relate to the following issues:

1. The national debt and annual national deficits.
2. The large number of people living longer.
3. The prospect of the Baby Boomers overwhelming the retirement systems, including Social Security, as they continue to retire in the 21st century.

Ever since the Social Security program was enacted in 1935, various politicians, pundits, and so-called experts have opposed and attacked it. Writing in 2011, James Roosevelt, Jr. stated, "Social Security critics have been casting the same aspersions on the program for 75 years" (p. 32). Attempts to alter the program's basic structure, reduce benefits, increase the age to receive benefits, privatize the funding, or eliminate the program altogether go back to the 1926 presidential election in which Franklin D. Roosevelt (James' grandfather) was running for reelection against Republican Alf Landon who labeled Social Security a "hoax" (Roosevelt, 2011). The 1926 Republican platform dismissed the program as "unworkable" and stated that it would not be able to pay benefits to two thirds of retirees.

Specific elites in Washington and Wall Street have made it a goal to reduce, greatly modify, or eliminate support programs such as Social Security, Medicare, and Medicaid. These include some "think tanks," media figures, propagandists posing as economic experts, and billionaires such as Peter Peterson, a financier who made his money doing corporate takeover deals (Greider, 2009). To do this, Peterson has launched a media blitz and assembled a coalition of think tanks and tax-exempt foundations to produce a report that would lead to caps on Social Security benefits. It would also "provoke conflict between the generations" (Greider, 2009, p. 14).

One of the major criticisms that has been misleadingly leveled against the Social Security program is that it is running out of money, or already out of money, and that it cannot be counted on by future retirees. James Roosevelt, Jr. (2011) and others have pointed out that Social Security is funded out of its own dedicated revenue system—the Social Security Trust Fund—which by the end of 2011 had a positive fund balance of $2.7 trillion, and is expected to increase to $3.7 trillion by the end of 2021. After 2021, the fund balance is expected to decline but still be able to pay full benefits through 2033. According to the 2012 Annual Report of the Board of Trustees of OASDI, the program could still pay 75% of benefits after that, if no changes are made to its funding. And, Social Security has added nothing to the national debt. In fact, "the Social Security surplus…makes the federal deficits seem smaller than they are—around $200 billion a year smaller" (Greider, 2009, p. 13).

Ignorance About Social Security

Many political discussions, at least since President Roosevelt's New Deal of the 1930s have focused on the size and role of government—especially the federal government—in the lives of everyday Americans. The presidential election of 2012 certainly was no exception, in part due to the rise of the Tea Party, a group opposed to government programs, particularly entitlements, and various forms of welfare and supports—especially for other people. Professor Suzanne Mettler of Cornell University pointed out in her research that 44% of Social Security beneficiaries, 43% of those persons receiving unemployment benefits, and 40% of those on Medicare say that "they have not used a government program" (Krugman, 2012, p. 17A). This ties in with the famous cry at a Tea Party rally when someone yelled, "Keep the government out of my Medicare," apparently not knowing that Medicare is a federal government program.

Paul Krugman (2012), in a *New York Times* article, based on research by Aaron Carroll of Indiana University pointed out that "the regions in which government programs account for the largest share of personal income are precisely the regions electing those severe conservatives" (p. 17A). These severe conservatives are the leaders trying to reduce or eliminate government programs such as Social Security and Medicare. Ignorance about the Social Security program, including not appreciating that it is indeed a federal government operation, makes it easier for politicians to foment opposition to "government handouts" by persons who do not know the facts.

Privatization

Even though President George W. Bush failed in 2005 to privatize Social Security funding, there are ongoing attempts to revive such a plan. Jane Bryant Quinn (2011), a professional finance expert and prolific writer, has noted that "if young people switched their payroll taxes into private accounts, the government would have to borrow $6.15 trillion or more (depending on the details) to keep paying out benefits to current retirees—which means higher deficits, higher income taxes, further slashes in spending, or all three" (p. 22).

The Social Insurance Concept

Noted experts in the field of gerontology, such as James H. Schulz and Robert H. Binstock (Schulz & Binstack, 2006), have argued that it is essential to maintain and even strengthen the social insurance programs already in place (such as Social Security, Medicare, and Medicaid) rather than promote radical changes. They have contended that our political leaders and policy makers should be supporting programs that spread the risks people face, instead of making the individual person in our society primarily responsible for taking on the many uncertainties of work and retirement.

These experts have gone on to point out that the public needs to understand that radical changes in our safety-net programs would bring dire consequences for older people, extended families, and accepted lifestyles that are key to the lives of so many Americans (Binstock, 2007). For example, many older people would likely become financially dependent on their families and their local communities without these basic programs. This could result in many more families forced to live in three- and even four-generational households. Many adult children could be financially wiped out by policy changes that would lead them to pay for the daily needs, health care, and long-term care of their parents. People need to understand that providing social insurance programs for older people is really a family and an intergenerational benefit as these safety-net programs alleviate much of the need for adult children to support their older parents, freeing their incomes to support themselves and their dependent children.

Social Security, as constituted, is considered a right for most workers—rich, middle class, and poor. There is no test to determine if one needs benefits upon retirement. Everyone who works and contributes into the system (which is now mandatory for most U.S. workers) earns benefits. So the dates each month Social Security benefits are recorded are "paydays" for Social Security recipients. They are not welfare payments. Politicians from time to time (including some prominent current ones) think they have a ready answer to the national debt and the annual budget deficit by controlling and limiting Social Security benefits through capping cost of living adjustments (COLAs), or by means testing—making benefits available only to the poor. But means testing would destroy one of the most successful programs of the U.S. Government. Social Security is a contract workers have with their government as well as a contract between generations. With proper management and minor adjustments, it will be a major component of younger workers' financial future.

Supplemental Security Income

The Supplemental Security Income (SSI) program was authorized as Title XVI of the Social Security Act of 1972. It went into effect 2 years later. It is a cash-assistance program designed to provide a nationally uniform, guaranteed, minimum income for eligible old, disabled, and blind persons. SSI replaced federal assistance to old state-administered poverty programs for the elderly, the permanently and totally disabled, and the blind. Three congressionally mandated goals were part of SSI:

1. Construct a coherent, unified income assistance system.
2. Eliminate large differences between the various states in eligibility and benefits.
3. Reduce the stigma of being on welfare by having the program administered by the Social Security Administration rather than state-sponsored welfare offices (U.S. Department of Health, Education, and Welfare, 1972).

PENSIONS

Pensions are another major source of income for many elderly Americans, but the coverage is uneven. Five categories of pension plans cover a range of American workers and retirees:

1. Private pensions (private industry and business)
2. State and local public employee pensions
3. Federal civilian employee pensions
4. Military retirement pensions
5. The Railroad Retirement System

Changes in Pensions

Private pensions are undergoing major changes. Not introduced in the United States until the end of the 19th century, pensions covered very few workers until the 1940s and 1950s in the post–World War II industrial boom. The typical pension plan was the *defined-benefit* plan where the worker is guaranteed specific retirement benefits by the employer. The real change in pension coverage has been a retreat from the defined-benefit approach to *defined-contribution* plans. Defined-contribution pension plans are those that allow employees to set aside part of their wages in tax-sheltered accounts for their retirement. Employers may contribute to these plans, but they are not required to do so. The level of a worker's pension under these plans depends on the amount he or she is able to set aside during working years, as well as the performance of the investment funds. Often these plans are referred to as *401(k) plans*, named after the section of the Internal Revenue Code that authorizes them (Lewis, 1992). The defined-contribution plans will affect retirees in the future, as they are rapidly outpacing the older defined-benefit plans.

Defined-Contribution Plans

The number of defined-contribution pension plans has been increasing. Defined-contribution plans give workers flexibility and portability, and provide generally lower costs and fewer investment risks for employers (Campbell & Munnell, 2002). Defined-contribution pension plans involve a specified payment out of each paycheck into an employee-specific account, to which an employer may or may not contribute a partially or fully matched contribution. Common types of defined-contribution pension plans include "401(k)," a profit sharing "403(b)," and "457" plans. The percentage of the paycheck that is contributed to the account is set out in advance. The exact amount of the pension is not predetermined but depends on many factors, including the amount contributed and the rate of return on the investment of the pension funds. The total amount collected is typically available as a lump-sum payment at the time of retirement, and sometimes may be taken as an annuity (spread out over many years) (Campbell & Munnell, 2002).

Problems With 401(k) Pensions

During the Great Recession, significant problems emerged with the rapid expanse of the 401(k) pension plans. When Congress changed the Internal Revenue Code to include Section 401(k), it believed that this was a way for workers to supplement their companies' traditional defined-benefit plans and Social Security. These new plans were not expected to become the only source of pension income. However, as time went on, more and more employers looked for ways to get out of funding their defined-benefit plans

(Rutten, 2009). Not many employers bothered to ask their employees if they wanted to swap retirement plans. And not many employers realized that very few employees have the background or ability to manage investments.

Employers rushed to abandon their traditional retirement plans for the 401(k) variety. As a result, more than 60% of all workers rely on 401(k) plans for their pension. The problem is that since the peak of the equity markets in October 2007, 401(k)s have lost a collective $1 trillion in value, which was fully a third of the value of all 401(k)s (Rutten, 2009). In addition, another $1 trillion has been taken away from workers who lost or changed jobs and rolled their 401(k)s into individual retirement accounts (IRAs). In addition to that, 20% of American workers stopped contributing to their retirement accounts and 401(k)s due to the hardships of the Great Recession. And millions of others were forced to make early withdrawals from their accounts due to economic hardships, including possible foreclosure on their homes, debts, and living expenses. What makes this very serious is the fact that the collapse of the 401(k) experiment is occurring as Baby Boomers are beginning to retire in large numbers. As one observer noted, "welcome to hard times" (Rutten, 2009, p. A15).

The Pension Benefit Guarantee Corporation

For workers fortunate enough to have remained in defined-benefit plans, there is a remedy if their company files for bankruptcy. It is a federal government insurance agency that takes over pension payments when a company with a defined-benefit pension plan goes bankrupt. In 2009, the maximum pension benefit it paid was $54,000 a year for workers who retired at age 65. This amount is adjusted with inflation. Some 84% of retirees fall at or under this amount (Hawthorne, 2009).

WORK

Among all the paradigm shifts in the aging of America in the 21st century, the trend toward older persons continuing to work beyond what was considered the "normal" age of retirement is a major component. In fact, the percentage of workers over age 65 is increasing faster than any other age group (Fleck, 2009; Whoriskey, 2012). The number of older workers aged 65 and older grew by 24% from 2006 to 2011; more than half of those worked full time (Carpenter, 2011).

A Pew Research Center report stated, "As people live longer, public expectations with retirement are in a period of transition. Given the demographic changes afoot . . . this evolution in attitude is likely to continue for years to come" (Fleck, 2009, p. 18).

Reasons for Older Persons to Continue to Work

The reasons why older Americans are continuing to work or attempting to work vary:

■ The Realities of Retirement Income. Many older persons are facing the harsh realities of declining pensions, lower than needed retirement savings, rising health care costs, and mounting debt due to a number of factors (Whoriskey, 2012). As the book *Working Longer: the Solution to the Retirement Income Challenge* states, "Workers have not saved enough money to offset these contractions [the contractions of retirement income]. The only two options are to eat less or work longer" (Fleck, 2009, p. 20).

■ The Option to Work Longer. Policy changes, such as the demise of mandatory retirement laws and the elimination of the Social Security earnings penalty for those who are at full retirement age, have made it more realistic for older persons to continue to work or go back to work as full- or part-time workers. According to the Center for Retirement Research at Boston College, 52% of Baby Boomers born between 1948 and 1954 are at risk for being unable to maintain their standard of living when they retire (Fleck, 2009). In addition, 64% of the Boomers born between 1955 and 1964, as well as 71% of Gen X-ers born between 1965 and 1974, may not be able to retire with much degree of comfort in their lifetimes. As a result, "most people will be able to spend 15 years in retirement, not 30 years," according to Richard Johnson, a senior fellow who specializes in older-worker issues at the Urban Institute (Fleck, 2009, p. 20). But because life expectancy continues to increase, most people will simply need to work longer.

■ The Vulnerability of Retirement Savings. It is widely concluded that most retirement investments, including the 401(k) plans that have supplanted the older retirement-benefit plans described previously, will continue to be vulnerable to investment market downturns. This is in the context of rising drug and health care costs, which have consistently outpaced inflation (Fleck, 2009). The Great Recession of 2008 to 2009 has resulted in the loss of some 40% of savings (in investments) for retirees and those about to retire. And even though some investment values regained much of what they lost, these types of fluctuations are hardest on older workers nearing retirement because they have a short time to recover market losses (Fleck, 2009).

■ Accumulated Debt. Recent studies have revealed that many workers are moving toward retirement with lots of debt. One report entitled, *Debt: the Detour on America's Road to Retirement*, pointed out that in the Great Recession, those Baby Boomers who had debt of $25,000 or more rose from 28% to 38%, and those with debt of $50,000 or more rose from 12% to 22% (Fleck, 2009). "Even though you've done all the right things, you could still be in trouble," said Harvey Sterns of the Institute for Lifespan Development and Gerontology at the University of Akron. He went on to say that "We're in a reset period, where people are going to think very differently about retirement from now on because of the sense of vulnerability" (Fleck, 2009, p. 20).

■ Personal Satisfaction/Sense of Worth. In addition to the economic issues associated with older persons continuing to work or seek reemployment, there are other significant reasons for people to work in their later years. Many older persons simply enjoy working—being productive (Stengle, 2011). These people have taken real satisfaction in being productive workers throughout their lives, some having begun work in their teen years. As Sara Rix, an AARP strategic policy advisor, stated, "Work is how many of us define ourselves and stay engaged with the world…and also how we give back" (Slon, 2007, p. 4). A Rand study found that workers aged 65 and older are healthier than people the same age who are not in the workforce. To many older persons, as well as those Boomers looking ahead in life, stopping work means disengagement, not just from work, but from life (Slon, 2007).

■ Changes in Pension Plans. In various studies, Baby Boomers have indicated that a large percentage of them have not saved enough money or do not have adequate pensions or income to stop working by traditional retirement years because, in many cases, the responsibility for funding retirement is shifting from businesses and the federal government to the workers themselves (Magnusson,

2006; Whoriskey, 2012). This is happening as traditional defined-benefit pensions, which are based on salaries, are being replaced by more unreliable defined-contribution pension plans, which require employees to assume much of the risk of investing their pension funds. Only 20% of workers who have any sort of pension participate in a defined-benefit plan compared to a defined-contribution plan such as a 401(k) plan (U.S. Census Bureau, 2011). "That shift in retirement financing, combined with the recession, has dramatically increased the incentives to work into old age and appears to be reshaping how Americans ride out the later part of their lives" (Whoriskey, 2012).

Realities Facing Baby Boom Workers

In spite of all the trends promoting workers to stay employed into their later years, current realities of the job market make it difficult for many would-be older workers to keep or find suitable employment. This is particularly applicable to Baby Boomers. The reason is that older workers, especially Baby Boomers who have lost their jobs or who want to change jobs or move to part-time work, are encountering a world of work that is in transition.

Many economists have predicted a significant labor shortage with 10 million unfilled jobs in the future, as millions of Baby Boomers reach retirement with fewer younger workers ready to take their place (Pope, 2007). But until this predicted shortage becomes a reality, many older workers are unable to obtain the kind of employment they want. For example, many older workers who have had good jobs, even some middle- and upper-level managers, can only find jobs that "may not utilize their skills or abilities" (Fleck, 2011b).

Ways to Help Older Workers

Another hurdle for older workers is the reluctance of employers to seek older workers or put in place work practices that meet their needs. An Ernst and Young survey found that 6 in 10 companies expect that the retirement of the Baby Boomers will cause shortfalls of workers, but 85% had no formal programs to retain workers (Pope, 2007). Even though many employers say older workers are motivated, disciplined, and reliable, there is still a reluctance to hire them because many see older workers as more costly, unskilled in technology, and opposed to change.

Some forward-thinking employers have developed innovative strategies to keep and attract mature workers, including short-term projects, sabbaticals, telecommuting, job sharing, seasonal work, labor pools made up of older workers, two-location jobs to satisfy migrating "snowbirds," and phased retirement (in which work hours are scaled back).

Strategies for Older Workers to Keep or Obtain Jobs:

- Do not quit a job; line up a new job before leaving a job.
- Go back to school to acquire training in a needed skill.
- Retrain in a skill area so skills can transfer to another job, such as an auto mechanic retraining to be a marine repair mechanic.
- Think ahead to prepare for alternative jobs before leaving the workforce by improving skills or finding ways to diversify the current job (Pope, 2007).

Myths About Older Workers

There are many misconceptions about older workers that have been dispelled over the last 20 years (AARP, 2000). Many of these misconceptions persist into the second decade of the 21st century. These misconceptions include that "they get sick more, have poor attendance, expect high wages, lack ambition or are technology-impaired" (a particularly galling stereotype for a generation that invented computers; Fiore, 2011).

PROBLEMS FACING OLDER WORKERS

Older workers face a range of issues including:

Unemployment

Even though the jobless rate for older workers following the Great Recession was lower than the rate of the total workforce, mature workers lost jobs at a faster rate than the overall labor force (Fiore, 2011). In addition, joblessness for older workers has doubled since the recession began, according to data from the Bureau of Labor Statistics (Fiore, 2011). And once out of work, they remain unemployed longer than do younger workers—9 months for younger workers, about a year for older workers.

Unemployment Varies by Education and Race/Ethnicity

Older workers who do not have a high school diploma consistently face higher rates of unemployment than do those with diplomas. The rate of unemployment for older workers without high school diplomas is 12.4% compared to 5.4% for workers with college degrees (Harootyan & Sarmiento, 2011). In addition, studies show that unemployment rates of Black American and Hispanic older workers are nearly twice those of non-Hispanic White older workers (Harootyan & Sarmiento, 2011).

Older Women and Unemployment

According to 2010 U.S. Census Bureau data, women have surpassed men in earning college degrees—from bachelor's to advanced degrees. In spite of this, women still earn about one fifth less than men earn (Roelofs, 2011). Even more discouraging is their unemployment status. With a large proportion of working women employed by governmental units as teachers, health care providers, social workers, librarians, and legal aid staff, they have endured disproportional unemployment due to drastic slashes in state and local government budgets, particularly since the midterm elections of 2010 (Pollitt, 2011).

Indeed, one leading writer/commentator/professor—Melissa Harris-Perry (2011)—has claimed that since 2010 the U.S. House of Representatives majority has been clear "that belt-tightening deficit reduction is entirely compatible with an older social agenda committed to pushing American women out of the public sphere" (p. 12). She goes on to say that some Republican governors elected in 2010 have tried eliminating collective bargaining rights for public-sector employees, such as "nurses, teachers, and other pink-collar workers who are disproportionately women" (Harris-Perry, 2011, p. 12). Some of these rights have been eliminated.

In a study of female job seekers by Texas A&M University, it was determined that "companies were more than 40% more likely to interview a younger job candidate than an older one" (Fiore, 2011, p. 19). And once unemployed, older women workers face significantly higher wage losses compared to younger women (Van Horn, Corre, & Heidkamp, 2011).

Age Discrimination

Of all the barriers to the employment of older workers, age discrimination is one of the most pernicious and pervasive. Age discrimination in employment first came to national attention in 1965. At that time, a report issued by the U.S. Department of Labor documented that more than 50% of all available job openings were not open to persons aged 55 and older due to employers' policies (Schulz, 1992). In 1967, Congress enacted the Age Discrimination in Employment Act (ADEA) "to promote employment of older persons based on their ability rather than age; to prohibit arbitrary age discrimination in employment; to help employers and workers find ways of meeting problems arising from the impact of age on employment" (ADEA, 1967).

In its original form, ADEA prohibited employment discrimination against persons aged 40 to 65. Subsequent amendments were made. In 1974, age protection was extended to federal, state, and local government employees. The range of employees covered was also expanded. In 1978, ADEA increased the age covered to 70 (the first step to eliminating an upper age limit), and removed the upper age limit for federal government employees. In 1982, ADEA was amended to require employers to retain their workers aged 65 and older on the company health plan rather than automatically shifting them to Medicare. In 1984, ADEA was extended to U.S. companies in foreign countries. The 1986 legislation removed all age limits in protecting older workers, with the exception of college professors and state and local public safety officers. The age limit on college professors was lifted in 1994.

The enactment of the Age Discrimination in Employment Act of 1967 and all subsequent amendments and accompanying legislation would appear to be enough to solve the problem of age discrimination in employment in the American workplace. Such has not been the case. Although the more obvious and overt forms of age discrimination, such as age limits in newspaper ads and forced retirements at specified ages, have almost disappeared, more subtle and cleverly disguised forms of age discrimination against older workers are still evident.

The 2009 Supreme Court Ruling on Age Discrimination

In June of 2009, the U.S. Supreme Court handed down a 5 to 4 ruling that makes it more difficult for older workers who believe they are victims of age discrimination to prove it. The ruling was in response to a suit filed by a demoted worker under the ADEA. The Court said it is not sufficient to show that age is among the reasons for the bad treatment of an employee; age has to be the primary reason (Cose, 2009).

It should be noted that very few older workers have the resources to bring a case to court. "Most who do are white, male middle-managers or professionals," stated Joanna Lahey, an economist with the Rand Corporation (Cose, 2009, p. 26). The larger issue here is how society tends to view categories of people, such as older workers; how stereotypes are imposed on older-aged workers. To address this, laws are very important, but so is a new paradigm of aging in America—where workers are viewed according to their value, not their age.

Health and Older Workers

With all the forces motivating older people to continue to work in paid employment or seek to find work if not employed, the question is raised if they are healthy enough to work. Health directly impacts an individual's ability to work in old age. According to a study conducted by the Center for Retirement Research at Boston College, "life expectancy has been steadily increasing, but differences in health and mortality (death) outcomes have widened and improvement in health for the population in general may have slowed or reversed" (Munnell, Soto, & Golub-Sass, 2008, p. 1). Between 1970 and 2000, while life expectancy at age 50 increased by 4.2 years, disability-free life expectancy increased by only 2.7 years for men (Munnell et al., 2008). The improvement that was noted in people with more education. However, these overall averages do not tell the real story because health status as well as disability-free life expectancy vary dramatically by socioeconomic status, occupation, and income. How disability-free life expectancy will change in the future depends on the general health of the population, as well as increasing educational achievements (Munnell et al., 2008).

SUGGESTED RESOURCES

Bureau of Labor Statistics (BLS): http://www.bls.gov
> The Bureau of Labor Statistics of the U.S. Department of Labor is the principal federal agency responsible for measuring labor market activity and working conditions. Data available on this website include unemployment, employment, pay and benefi ts, and workplace injuries.

Social Security Trust Funds: http://www.socialsecurity.gov/OACT/TR/index.html
> Through this part of the U.S. Social Security Administration's website, annual reports on the financial status of the Trust Funds are available, including projections of future revenue and expenditures.

Supplemental Security Income (SSI): http://www.ssa.gov/pgm/ssi.htm
> Provided by the U.S. Social Security Administration, this website provides information on the SSI program, including how to apply for it and other resources available for current SSI recipients.

U.S. Department of Labor: http://www.dol.gov
> This federal government website has links and referrals to resources on age discrimination, adult training programs, and job searches.

Workforce50.com: http://www.workforce50.com
> Workforce50.com arms the older workforce with employment resources and career information to achieve their goals. It is committed to helping mature job seekers find meaningful employment opportunities.

CHAPTER 11

Retirement: A Changing American Institution

The learning objectives of this chapter include understanding

- The history of retirement and the reasons people retire.
- Current trends to delay retirement.
- Major shifts in the types of pensions and how they impact a person's ability to retire.
- The future directions of retirement.
- The effects of retirement on marriages, incomes, and psychological well-being.

THE CHANGING NATURE OF RETIREMENT

In a new paradigm of aging, retirement as an institution is in a state of change. Up until around the beginning of the 21st century, thanks primarily to the expansion of Social Security and the broad coverage of Medicare (income and health entitlements), it was generally believed that most Americans would enjoy—and look forward to—years of retirement. Books and articles that were written about older people toward the end of the 20th century assumed that most workers would spend years in retirement (Riekse & Holstege, 1996). But economic realities, social trends, lifestyles, and societal norms tend to change over time and retirement as an American institution has not been exempt from change.

Even before a variety of factors impacted the institution of retirement in the 21st century, retirement had many meanings as pointed out by Abraham Monk (1994), some years ago:

It refers to the termination of and formal withdrawal from a regular job under the provisions of a statutory pension system, a demographic category, an economic condition, a social status, a developmental phase in the human life span, the transition to old age, and a lifestyle dominated by leisure pursuits or at least by economically nonproductive activity. (p. 3)

In the 21st century, however, not all Americans take for granted that a good portion of their lives will be spent in retirement, even though retirement has become an established institution. Indeed, it was just a few years ago that retirement could occupy up to one third of a person's life. How and why this has changed will be explored later in this chapter. But first, it is important to look at how retirement became a prime feature of a working person's life, and examine how this history contributes to a new paradigm of retirement for middle- and younger-aged workers.

HISTORICAL PERSPECTIVE ON RETIREMENT

Retirement is not something that has always been part of the American scene. In 1900, when the life expectancy for men was 46.3 years, the average man spent only 1.2 years in retirement or in activities out of the labor force. This was only 3% of a man's life. By contrast, in 1900, women spent an average of 29 years working at home and in retirement out of an average life expectancy of 48.3 years, and averaged only 6.3 years in the labor force (U.S. House of Representatives, Select Committee on Aging, 1992). Societal roles typically mandated that a woman's work be confined to the home setting.

With dramatically longer lives, the passage of the Social Security Act of 1935, the advent of Medicare in 1965 (health insurance for persons aged 65 and older), and additional coverage of pensions in the private and public sectors, retirement became a reality for millions of Americans. At one point, early retirement entered the picture as a goal for many workers. By 1990, only 16% of men over the age of 65 were in the labor force. Decreased participation rates in the labor force applied to younger categories of workers as well, especially those aged 55 and older. Indeed, only about 2 in 5 (39.3%) men aged 55 and older were paid workers in 1990. On the other hand, women in their late 50s were more likely to be in the labor force in 1990 than in previous decades (Taeuber, 1993). Since that time, the percentage of both men and women in the labor force has increased, as will be described later in this chapter.

Why Retirement?

One way to understand retirement is to examine its historical trends. Another way to grasp the retirement concept is to understand why the goal of retiring has been so widespread. Schulz and Binstock (2006) explore the retirement concept in their book, *Aging Nation*. Why, they ask, is most of our workers' increased leisure bunched at the end of the life cycle? They explain this reality by quoting one of the early pioneers of gerontology, Clark Tibbits, who stated, "Retirement is a phenomenon of modern industrial society.... The older people of previous societies were not retired persons; there was no retirement role" (Schulz & Binstock, 2006, p. 145). When society became based on an industrialized economy, Schulz and Binstock point out that it was in the self-interest of employers to require long hours when workers were young and get rid of them when they became old. Another scholar, Juliet Schor, contends that the "key incentive structures of capitalist (market) economies contain biases toward long working hours.... The eventual recovery of leisure came about because trade unions and social reformers waged a protracted struggle for shorter hours" (Schulz & Binstock, 2006, p. 144).

But Schulz and Binstock point out that not all workers were treated the same. Instead of longer hours for older workers, employers promoted "retirement"—a way to get rid of those they thought were deficient workers. As a result, by 1900, long before public and private pensions were widely established, almost one third of workers 65 and older were "retired" due to poor health. But how could these workers afford retirement in the beginning of the 20th century? The reality was that too many of them could not. They had to rely on their own savings (which were typically small), support from relatives, or charity, which could be life on a county poor farm. As a result, there was a push for some types of retirement incomes, which led to the establishment of the Social Security system in 1935 and the growth of private pensions in the 1940s and beyond. (For more information about the history of Social Security, see Chapter 10.) In addition, Schulz and Binstock point out that industrial growth—spurred by new technologies—resulted in economic output and growth that increased living standards and options for greater leisure, including retirement.

A New Paradigm in Retirement

In his book, *The Longevity Revolution* (2008), the late Robert Butler, a renowned geriatrician, pointed out that in a new paradigm of aging in the 21st century, "it is time to overcome the factors that encourage early retirement, introduce shared work and more flextime and phased retirement, advance the age of eligibility for Social Security, and secure more effectively the employment and rights of older persons and the disabled" (p. 255). He went on to point out that being productive in the older ages will help to address the three greatest fears of a society in which people live longer—the fear that there will be too many dependent older people, the fear that older people will hinder economic productivity, and the fear that there will be more intergenerational conflict in the future.

Full (Normal), Early, and Late Retirement

In 1983, amendments to the Social Security Act introduced a gradual increase in "full retirement age" or "normal retirement age" from 65 years of age to a maximum of 67 years based on a beneficiary's year of birth (see Table 11.1). The purpose of raising the

TABLE 11.1 Age to Receive Full Social Security Benefits, by Year of Birth

YEAR OF BIRTH	FULL RETIREMENT AGE
1937 or earlier	65
1938	65 and 2 months
1939	65 and 4 months
1940	65 and 6 months
1941	65 and 8 months
1942	65 and 10 months
1943–1954	66
1955	66 and 2 months
1956	66 and 4 months
1957	66 and 6 months
1958	66 and 8 months
1959	66 and 10 months
1960 or later	67

age at full retirement was to extend the solvency of Social Security funds, given the fact that people are living longer than they were when Social Security was enacted, while at the same time recognizing that improvements in health are making it more feasible for people to remain in the labor force for longer periods of time

All those eligible for Social Security benefits can choose to retire as early as age 62, with a concomitant reduction in monthly benefits to offset the longer time period over which they will receive benefits. In addition, individuals can choose to begin receiving benefits later, at any time after their full retirement age up to age 70, with a concomitant increase in monthly benefits to compensate for the shorter time period over which they will receive benefits. The Social Security website (http://www.ssa.gov) provides current and future retirees with tools for calculating their projected benefits under these scenarios. Regardless of the age at which an individual opts to begin receiving Social Security benefits, the age for signing up for Medicare remains 65; waiting longer may result in higher costs for Medicare Part B and Part D.

THE RISE OF RETIREMENT COMMUNITIES

The big question in retirement (including early retirement) becomes "what should we do for the rest of our lives?" At the 1961 White House Conference on Aging, President John F. Kennedy spoke about how impressive it was that so many years had been added to persons' lives. But he said it was now important to "add new life to those years" (Lohr, 2005). Just a year earlier in 1960, Del Webb had opened his first retirement community, Sun City, near Phoenix, Arizona, as a destination to live out these retirement years. As the *New York Times* writer, Steve Lohr (2005), observed, Sun City tapped into a new vision of retirement where people could leave work and their old neighborhoods and move to a retirement community designed for endless vacationing for the rest of their lives—or at least until they became too frail or ill and needed the support of families. These years were termed the "golden years," which were affordable for many Americans born between 1900 and 1945. These retirement communities sprang up primarily throughout the sunshine states in the Southern and Southwestern areas of the United States with major concentrations in Florida, Arizona, and California. There is a question of whether these golden years' dreams (for many) could have been sustained over a longer time frame. But the reality is that for a number of reasons, what once seemed to be a realistic future for many American workers appears to be disappearing.

REASONS TO DELAY RETIREMENT

One reason some of these "golden years" dreams are changing is because many Baby Boomers are rejecting the concept of retirement as an endless vacation. Research has consistently shown that most Boomers do not see themselves giving up work after what has been a traditional retirement age. In fact, about 80% of them plan to engage in some kind of paid work into their 70s, and even beyond (Fleck, 2008; Lohr, 2005). And this trend is not confined to the United States. In one of HSBC's early global studies on retirement, 21,000 employees and 6,000 employers in 20 countries were surveyed. One quarter of the respondents said that the main reason they would continue to work past normal retirement age would be to earn money (HSBC, 2006). Others said doing something meaningful, keeping physically active, interacting with others, and promoting mental stimulation were their main reasons for working in retirement.

The Great Recession of 2008 to 2009

Another reason to delay retirement has been the Great Recession of 2008 to 2009. For example, in a survey conducted by the AARP early in the recession, about 1 in 5 persons aged 55 to 64, and nearly 1 in 4 persons aged 45 to 54, planned to delay retirement because of the economic downturn, which included falling home values and decreased personal financial worth of savings in investments (40% to 50% decrease). By 2014, it is estimated that the number of workers aged 65 and older in the labor pool will increase by 74% (Fleck, 2008).

Decreased Mobility

Still another reason retirement concepts and realities are changing relates to the decreased mobility of the American people. For a period of time in the late 20th century and the very first part of the 21st, America was thought of as a nation on the move—people moving from one place to another, from one region to another, and especially for older people, from cold areas to the Sun Belt, even though the percentages of older people that actually did move were rather low. For more than a generation, it was commonly thought that mobility would increase, with a resulting trend toward rootlessness. This idea was explained in a book by Vance Packard in 1972 entitled, *A Nation of Strangers*, and in Robert Putnam's book, *Bowling Alone*, in 2000. Putnam's view was that society was being undermined by suburbanization and increasing mobility. This mobility was particularly promoted by some of the large corporations such as IBM, whose initials were jokingly referred to as "I've Been Moved."

Scholars have noted a new trend that will likely impact retirement trends for some years. This trend is called the "new localism," which has the following premise: "The longer people stay in their homes and communities, the more they identify with those places and the greater commitment to helping local businesses and institutions thrive" (Kotkin, 2009, p. 42). Numerous factors are contributing to this concept including "(1) an aging population; (2) suburbanization; (3) the Internet; and (4) increased focus on family life" (Kotkin, 2009, p. 42).

By 2006, fewer people were moving around the nation than at any time since 1940 when the census started keeping track of population mobility. Most importantly for aging in the 21st century, it appears that the stay-at-home trend is especially strong among older Baby Boomers who are largely turning their backs on Sunbelt retirement in faraway condos and mobile homes. They want to stay in their own homes in their old regions. They are choosing to keep active with their families, friends, clubs, and churches in familiar surroundings (Kotkin, 2009). As an example, in Michigan, thousands of retired school personnel (teachers, administrators, etc.) could migrate to any region of the nation upon retirement, due to income security, being relatively young (many retiring in their mid-50s after 30 years of service), and generally being in good health. However, 87% still live in Michigan with 4% in Florida, 1% in Arizona, and lesser percentages elsewhere ("Where Do ORS Retirees Live?," 2009).

Rejecting a Permanent Vacation

Ken Dychtwald, a gerontologist and consultant on aging, said, "A life of leisure for most people is boring. Retired Americans watch an average of 43 hours of TV a week, akin to a full-time job. Traditional retirement has proved to be a failed experiment" (Lohr, 2005). This all contributes to the idea of changing the nature of retirement in the 21st century. Marc Freedman, a leader in Civic Ventures (an advocacy group that promotes older people as volunteers and paid workers) has said that just as the golden years concept was about freedom from work, the new concept of retirement could be about freedom to work in ways that are rewarding to older persons (Lohr, 2005).

BABY BOOMERS AND RETIREMENT

Between 1946 and 1964, about 75 million Baby Boomers were born in the United States. An additional 7.8 million born in other countries during these years have immigrated to the United States (U.S. Census Bureau, 1996). The first of the Baby Boomers turned 66 in 2012, making them eligible for Social Security's early retirement benefits. By 2020, the number of persons aged 60 to 64 is projected to nearly double from the 2000 census number.

Most Baby Boomers have expected that they will still be working during their retirement years—some because they enjoy the social contacts at work as well as the work itself, and others because they believe they will need the income. Baby Boomers do not want to depend on their children in retirement. But there has been speculation about how prepared the oldest Baby Boomers are for retirement.

Some negative factors increase the risks in retirement for many of the oldest Baby Boomers. The shift to more defined-contribution pension plans and away from defined-benefit pension plans, as outlined in Chapter 10, poses a real risk to retirement security. Defined-contribution plans depend on the value of 401(k) retirement accounts, and workers experienced large losses in their accounts during the Great Recession, thereby jeopardizing their future retirement.

FACTORS IN DECIDING TO RETIRE

In a new paradigm of aging, deciding if and when to retire is not determined solely by reaching a certain birthday in life's journey. The decision to retire involves a complex set of conditions and circumstances in each individual's life. Some of the experts in the area of retirement have looked at the key factors a person needs to consider regarding retirement. Among all the factors that are important in deciding whether and when to retire, the most important are a person's financial status and the condition of his or her health (Clark, Morrill, & Allen, 2012).

The Great Recession and Financial Security

Financial security has continued to be a key element in considering retirement, particularly since the Great Recession of 2008 to 2009. For example, in February 2009, the stock market, where so many workers have invested retirement funds such as 401(k)s, was down 45% from its October 2007 high, a $7 trillion loss in value of which $5 trillion was lost by persons aged 50 and older (Toedtman, 2009). In addition, housing values were down 20%, with most of the losses coming from persons aged 50 and older. And in that recession, 5 million jobs were lost, with unemployment doubling for workers aged 55 and older (Toedtman, 2009).

As a result, according to a survey by the Employee Benefit Research Institute, the percentage of workers "very confident" of a financially secure retirement dropped from 41% in 2007 to 13% in 2009. For many, working longer is no longer a choice but a necessity in times of economic downturns (Toedtman, 2009, p. 3). Turmoil in the equity markets, rising inflation, rising health care costs, and increased taxes all impact retirement planning.

Health Status

For a long time, it has been recognized that an individual's health influences their retirement decisions in various ways. Poor health can limit a worker's ability to carry out certain tasks. It may become difficult for a worker in declining health to keep up with the workload of a given work situation. In addition, a person's poor health may make work in general more difficult, resulting in a marked reduction in wanting to work. Going through the effort of getting to work and being there all day can simply become too difficult for some.

Health status can also directly impact a person's financial status when considering retirement. A study for AARP, using data developed some months before the stock market meltdown, found that persons aged 55 and older were the fastest-growing group to declare bankruptcy in 2007—almost 1 in every 4 cases. And these rates of bankruptcy increased with age (Kirchheimer, 2009). Elizabeth Warren, who headed the special congressional panel monitoring the bank bailout funds of the federal government prior to her election to the U.S. Senate, noted that "medical problems were a big reason [for the bankruptcies]" (Kirchheimer, 2009, p. 14).

PLANNING FOR RETIREMENT

One of the most important things people of all ages can do to have positive experiences in retirement is to prepare for it by planning ahead. Not until the years following World War II was there any organized effort to help people plan for their retirements. In 1948, Clark Tibbitts and Wilma Donahue of the University of Michigan, along with Ernest Burgess of the University of Chicago, began developing preretirement educational programs (Cooper, 1994). In 1956, Woodrow Hunter of the University of Michigan offered the first preretirement program that was sponsored by a union (Hunter, 1968). Since that time, planning for retirement has become

> **Episode 12: Retirement—Having a Plan**
>
> **High Bandwidth:**
> http://raidercast.grcc.edu/flash/2011_2012/grcctv/successful_
> aging/success_aging_12_large/grcc_player.html
> **Low Bandwidth:**
> http://raidercast.grcc.edu/flash/2011_2012/grcctv/successful_
> aging/success_aging_12_small/grcc_player.html

an integral part of a successful transition to another part of the life cycle. Older adults and professionals talk about planning for retirement in Video 12.

Working Longer for More Income

According to an analysis by for *The Retirement Project*, an initiative of the Urban Institute, "when people work longer, they produce additional goods and services for the economy...earn more income, usually save some of that income, allow their assets to grow, and increase their annual Social Security benefit" (Butrica, Smith, & Steuerle, 2006, p. 2). These economic advantages are even higher for lower- and middle-income Americans than they are for high-income Americans.

In addition, the analysis revealed that long-term differences between the benefits Social Security pays and the revenues it takes in would be cut dramatically if people continued working just one more year. Consequently, the need for other possible remedies to Social Security's projected shortfall, such as increasing Social Security taxes or decreasing benefits, would be reduced. Chapter 10 goes into detail about the history, current status, and long-term future of Social Security. The bottom line is that "added work leads to a more solvent and more financially secure retirement" (Butrica et al., 2006, p. 6).

MARRIAGE AND RETIREMENT

Research has shown that when both spouses are employed, married couples prefer to retire at approximately the same time so they can spend time with each other after retiring. However, the availability of Social Security benefits does affect couples' decisions about the timing of retirement (Gustman & Steinmeier, 2002). This pattern of retirement planning differs when one spouse is forced to retire because of a health problem or job loss; if a spouse has a long-term health problem, the other spouse is less likely to retire.

Marital Relationships and Retirement

Marriage and retirement can be a tricky combination. Although retirement can be a crisis point for marriages because there is a big adjustment for the two spouses spending so much time together, the retirement years can also be among the most rewarding years of a marriage, right up there with the newlywed years. The most stressful years are generally regarded as the child-rearing years.

However, the retirement of a spouse can have a major impact on a marriage. Two humorous quips partly describe what can result when a spouse retires: "For better or for worse, but not for lunch," and "Retirement is twice as much husband and half as much money" (Trafford, 2005). Postretirement difficulties can take different forms. A retiring husband may be at greater risk of getting ill than his wife is. Depression is a risk for a retiring spouse, particularly if the retiree does not have other interests or a network of friends outside of work.

Retired Spouse Syndrome

Retirement strains are not limited to men. As more and more wives enter the workforce, potential strains also apply to female workers who retire. Some balance between being independent and being together seems to work for many American couples. But these postretirement marital strains are not limited to the United States. So many Japanese couples reported physical ills to their doctors after the husband retired that this pattern of stresses was given a name—"retired husband syndrome." When applied to both husbands and wives, this stress pattern is called "retired spouse syndrome" (Trafford, 2005).

How widespread is the "retired spouse" syndrome in the United States? To find the answer to this question, AARP commissioned a survey of retired married (or living-as-married) couples aged 55 through 75. Unlike retirees in Japan, a big majority (71%) said they really did not mind having their spouses around them more (Koppen & Anderson, 2008). In fact, 96% said their relationship was as strong as, or stronger than, when they were working; 89% stated they were at least as romantic; and 84% said they spent more time doing things together. Overall, 78% said they were happier than when they and their spouse were still working. Perhaps some explanations for this perceived happiness include the fact that 80% of the retired men said that they increased their share of the housework (although only 47% of women said their spouses have done so), and 7% of the retired couples engaged in more sexual activities than they did when they were working (Koppen & Anderson, 2008).

WOMEN AND RETIREMENT

As in many financial areas of life, over the past decades women have been at a particular disadvantage regarding retirement. Going back many years, a study by the University of Miami's Center on Adult Development and Aging, found that under our economic system, men typically are able to retire earlier and with fewer cares than women have. According to one of the authors of the study, "Working women don't retire, or plan to retire, as early as men do unless they are married and their husbands have a good income or a lot of money stashed away" (Taft, 1991, p. 3E). The historical difference between the number of men and women seeking early retirement exists partly because women usually enter the labor force later than men do and, as a result, have fewer credits in Social Security or private pension plans.

Divorce and Retirement

According to the same study, divorced and separated women are particularly disadvantaged regarding early retirement. Divorced women need to plan to spend three more years being employed than do married women. Separated women need to plan to spend two more years in the labor force. On the other hand, divorce and separation have no negative effect on men's decisions for early retirement. This study reinforces others that clearly indicate that a woman usually comes out of a divorce or separation financially worse off than men do.

Vulnerable Financial Status of Women

Not too much has changed for women in the first decades of the 21st century. Two AARP studies, *Understanding Women's Financial Needs & Behaviors* and *Developing a Savings Habit*, have found that even though women had come a long way when it comes to their financial affairs, they still have a harder time making ends meet than men do, which directly impacts their retirement prospects (Reyes, 2007). These studies concluded that the financially disparity between women and men is primarily due to social issues that result in too many women earning less money than men do, women tending to drop in and out of the workforce because of their roles as caregivers (for the young and the old), and women constituting many single-heads of households (37 million in 2012, according to the U.S. Census Bureau, 2012), who are trying to survive in what has become for many a two-earner economy (Reyes, 2007).

As a result, almost a quarter of adult women say they struggle financially, with almost 40% reporting that they are just barely getting by. Xenia Montenegro, principle researcher for the first AARP study, stated, "The sad fact is, 96 percent of American women have problems to some degree with having enough money" (Reyes, 2007, p. 80). Jean Koppen, principle researcher for the second study, stated, "For low-income working women it's even more tenuous. They can limp along financially for years. But all it takes is one mishap to topple their financial house of cards: a divorce, a job loss or a major illness. Then they can spend the rest of their lives just catching up" (Reyes, 2007, p. 80).

A New Financial Future for Women?

It seems that all is not doom and gloom for many women in a new paradigm of aging in the 21st century. According to Rana Foroohar and Susan Greenberg (2009), economists, consultants, and other business types have looked at the rise of a new emerging market—women. A study by The Boston Consulting Group indicated that women may be in a position to drive the economy following the Great Recession of 2008 to 2009. The reasoning for this view includes (a) the prediction that the vast majority of new income growth in the years to come will go to women as a result of closing the wage gap (the difference between what men and women earn); (b) large improvements in women's education, documented by the fact that currently a majority of college students are women; (c) large increases in labor-force participation rates by women—including women in developing countries; and (d) dramatic improvements in health along with lower fertility rates. All of these factors can directly impact the prospects of retirement for women in the United States and around the world.

THREATS TO RETIREMENT SECURITY

For years, experts have warned about numerous possible threats to retirement including retiring too early, turmoil in the investment markets, increasing debt for older Americans, underfunded pension plans, and threats to the Pension Benefit Guaranty Corporation.

Retiring Too Early and Inflation

In a column on early retirement many years ago, Jane Bryant Quinn (1992) wrote a memo to workers who retired early or were planning to:

> You probably won't make it financially unless you find a part-time job. At 55 you could easily live another 30 or 40 years. If you're not working, you'll need more savings than most people ever see in a lifetime. (p. 13)

Quinn went on to point out that the early retiree's silent enemy is long-term inflation. If a retiree was living on $30,000 in 1992, by the year 2017, 25 years after retirement, the retiree might need $80,000 a year to pay for the same things. About one fourth of that amount might come from Social Security, which includes a cost of living adjustment, but pensions generally do not increase with inflation. The rest would have to come from savings or work, but it is usually difficult for most people to work 20 to 30 years after retirement.

Investment Market Turmoil

Because so much of the savings by current and future retirees is invested in the equity markets (stocks and bonds) due to 401(k) retirement plans, turmoil in these markets can be a major threat to financial security in retirement. This was pointed out early in the Great Recession when it was observed that older Americans with stock market investments were among the hardest hit by the big drops in the equity markets. In September 2008, just as the markets were falling, Alicia Munnell, Director of the Center for Retirement Research at Boston College, stated, "There's a terrified older population out there. If you're 45 and the market goes down, it bothers you, but it comes back. But if you're retired or about to retire, you might have to sell your assets before you have a chance to recover" ("Market Turmoil Slaps Retirees," 2008, p. A1). She went on to point out that today's retirees have less money in savings, expect to live longer, and are more vulnerable to the risks of the equity markets than are any retirees since World War II. The Benefit Research Institute of Washington found that even before the market fell in September 2008, some 39% of retirees thought they would outlive their savings, which was a 10% increase from the previous year ("Market Turmoil Slaps Retirees," 2008). By October 2008, the stock market's fall had wiped out almost $4 trillion of individuals' retirement funds, losses that were evenly divided between defined-benefit and defined-contribution plans (Munnell & Muldoon, 2008). "But in the future," Munnell and Muldoon (2008) cautioned, "individuals will bear the full brunt of market turmoil as the shift to 401(k)s [associated with defined-contribution plans] continues" (p. 1).

Increasing Debt for Older Americans

Even before the Great Recession, it was observed that older Americans and some of the Baby Boomers were piling up debts that could negatively impact their retirements or planned retirements. During the real estate boom, and prior to the Great Recession, substantial numbers of middle- and older-aged people borrowed against the value of their homes. For example, in 2006, Federal Reserve data indicated that while the value of household real estate climbed 71% in the prior 5 years, mortgage debt grew 75% as many persons cashed out part of the equity in their homes (Clements, 2006). During this same time period, outstanding consumer debt (including car loans and credit card debit) increased by 27%. The reasons for debts among older people include: (a) increasing life expectancy, which translates into longer years of life to finance; (b) health care costs that have continued to escalate, even for persons on Medicare; and (c) interest rates on savings that have turned lower, which means a lower monetary return on which to live (Clements, 2006).

Underfunded Pension Plans

Another threat to the financial stability of current retirees is the unsoundness of the pension plans under which many retire. To protect pensions and the retirees who depend on them, the Employee Retirement Income Security Act (ERISA) became law in 1974. ERISA was designed to expand the supervision and regulation of private pension plans by the federal government and to create tax-exempt individual retirement accounts for persons not covered by a qualified pension plan. Also established under ERISA was the Pension Benefit Guaranty Corporation (PBGC), part of the Department of Labor. This agency is designed to guarantee pension payments to retired workers and future payments to vested workers (workers who have worked long enough to collect under a pension plan) when a defined-benefits pension plan is terminated or runs out of money, which occurs frequently in turbulent economic times. In 2012, PBGC paid retirement benefits of up to $57,477 per year to 887,000 retirees whose employers (more than 4,500 of them) could not pay the benefits they had promised their employees (Pension Benefit Guaranty Corporation, n.d.).

Threats to the Pension Benefit Guaranty Corporation (PBGC)

The recent Great Recession was tough on the Pension Benefit Guaranty Corporation. In 2012, its total liabilities ($112 billion) exceeded its assets ($83 billion).

> Because PBGC's obligations are paid out over the lives of people receiving pensions, a deficit means we will have less money than we will need, over a period of decades. Without changes, at some point there is a risk that a program in a deficit position will run out of money. It will have paid out all its assets and still owe benefits. (Pension Benefit Guaranty Corporation, 2012, p. 4)

It should be noted that the PBGC receives no tax money. Its revenues come from insurance premiums paid by employers who offer defined-benefit pension plans ($35 annually per employee in 2012 for single-employer plans), earnings from its investments, assets from employers' failed pension plans, and funds recovered from these employers' bankruptcies. With the uncertainty of these revenues, as well as the potential for more bankruptcies in the fragile economy, the future of the PBGC is difficult to determine.

RETIREMENT TRENDS

The historic decline in people working into their older ages began around 1880 and continued until about the mid-1980s. Since then, the trend toward early retirement has ended, and in some respects, has reversed (Munnell, 2011). Over the course of the previous four decades or so, a number of policy, economic, and other factors have contributed to workers remaining in the workforce for longer periods of times.

Changes to Social Security and Private Pension Plans

Changes to Social Security in the year 2000 allowed individuals of full retirement age to continue working and collect full Social Security benefits, regardless of their earnings. Prior to that year, individuals under age 69 who continued working had their monthly benefit reduced by 1 dollar for every 2 dollars they earned, so many workers chose to leave the workforce. (Note that the amount lost in these reductions was restored when the person attained full retirement age.) In addition, workers now receive higher benefits if they wait until age 70 to claim them.

The dramatic shift by many employers to defined-contribution plans since the 1980s has contributed to the trend to stay in the workplace longer—workers with these plans retire on average 2 years later than do workers with defined-benefit plans (Friedberg & Webb, 2005). In Chapter 10, these pension plans and their advantages and disadvantages are described in more detail.

Declining Health Insurance Benefits

As health care costs have increased, many employers have decreased their support for health insurance, and some have completely dropped this benefit for retirees (Monk & Munnell, 2009). For those workers who might decide to retire but are too young to qualify for Medicare, eliminating retiree health insurance is a disincentive to retire. According to an analysis by the Center for Retirement Research at Boston College, approximately 7% of workers aged 55 to 64 would delay retirement if their employer stopped offering health insurance for retirees; in 2009 that would have amounted to over 1 million people remaining in the workforce (Monk & Munnell, 2009). This may be one of the main reasons why more workers have been delaying retirement until age 65 in the last few years—they are waiting until they are covered by Medicare.

Workplace Changes and Other Factors

There is some evidence that the workplace has become friendlier to older workers, but much progress is still needed to accommodate them (Centers for Disease Control and Prevention [CDC], 2012). In one inexpensive pilot program, the BMW car company modified the work environment for their older workers, for example, "replacing cement floors with wooden platforms to reduce the impact on knees [and providing] adjustable worktables to reduce physical strain and facilitate personnel rotation during shifts" (CDC, 2012, p. 5). These and other changes that were instituted after discussions with the company's employees resulted in a rise in productivity and a decrease in absenteeism, demonstrating the value of such programs not only for employees but also for employers. The opportunity for flexible schedules; for "bridge" jobs, which are transitional from full-time work to retirement; and for health education and physical activity programs are among numerous other ways to create more age-friendly workplaces.

In addition to changes in employment policies and practices, increases in workers' years of education, improvements in health, and couples coordinating retirement are all associated with working for extra years beyond normal retirement age (Munnell, 2011).

PSYCHOLOGICAL IMPACTS OF RETIREMENT

The major focus of this chapter has been on the financial implications of retirement. After all, financial security, or at least a perception of financial security, is what has made retirement possible. However, as noted earlier in this chapter, retirement is more than a financial consideration. It is a major life event, especially for people whose identities are tied to their life's work. In the past, this has been particularly true for men, whose lives have been mostly identified by the jobs they held, the professions they have had, or the work they have done. Increasingly, this type of personal job identity is true for women too as more and more are in the paid labor force for longer periods of their lives.

Leisure Opportunities

Opportunities for retirees' leisure are many, including returning to school, working part-time or temporarily, consulting, teaching, starting a business at home, becoming involved in the creative arts, traveling, and volunteering. The U.S. Bureau of Labor Statistics (2012) reports that 24% of persons aged 65 and older participate in volunteer activities. Some retirees volunteer to keep busy or out of a sense of duty. Most participate in volunteer activities because doing so gives them a sense of satisfaction.

The possibilities for volunteering among older people are endless. Matching talents and interests to needs is the key. Need exists everywhere in society, just waiting to be addressed by people with the time, interest, and ability. Chapter 13 presents information on the volunteer opportunities available to older adults through Senior Corps, a program of the Corporation for National and Community Service.

The Practical Application at the end of Part III of this textbook provides additional information on the changing paradigms of work and retirement, as well as the importance of helping older persons to rediscover their life purpose in retirement.

SUGGESTED RESOURCES

Center for Retirement Research at Boston College: http://crr.bc.edu
> The Center is a national leader in retirement research, including economics and behavior related to older workers, pensions, and health. The site provides access to research reports; the National Retirement Risk Index, which measures how prepared people are for retirement; and interactive tools to help people of all ages plan for retirement.

CNNMoney, Retirement: http://www.money.cnn.com/retirement
> This website, a service of CNN, Fortune, and Money magazines, has an "ultimate guide to retirement," which focuses on ensuring financial well-being in retirement. The site also offers a variety of topical news related to retirement.

Social Security Administration: http://www.ssa.gov
> The official website for Social Security offers information on all programs related to Social Security, including retirement benefits, disability and survivors' benefits, Supplemental Security Income (SSI), and Medicare.

What You Should Know About Your Retirement Plan: http://www.dol.gov/ebsa/publications/wyskapr.html
> This website from the U.S. Department of Labor includes information on types of retirement plans, payment of benefits, what happens to benefits during a plan termination or company merger, and what to do if there are problems.

Women's Institute For A Secure Retirement (WISER): http://www.wiserwomen.org
> Founded in 1996, WISER is a nonprofit organization that focuses on improving the long-term financial quality of life for women. It supports research, conducts workshops, and creates consumer publications on issues relating to women's retirement income, including Social Security, divorce, pay equity, pensions, savings and investments, home-ownership, and long-term care and disability insurance.

The Diverse Living Conditions of Older People

Michael A. Faber

INTRODUCTION

The four chapters in this section present detailed information on the living environments and housing options of older people, as well as the economics of aging including the impact of work and retirement on the lives of older persons. This practical application explores the realities of aging in place, and examines the changing meaning of work and retirement with a particular focus on helping older persons rediscover their life purposes.

Aging in Place

In the immortal words of Dorothy from the *Wizard of Oz*, "There is no place like home"; at least this is the opinion of the majority of older persons who wish to age in place. To this end, the role of the gerontologist should be to provide the support necessary to help those that they serve to remain safely within their home (however, they may define it) in the community. Is this always possible? Does everyone define *home* in the same way? What constitutes safety within the home? How does mental competency play into an older person's ability to remain in his or her own home and age in place? I would like to now address each of these questions.

Is it possible for everyone to age in place within his or her own home? Absolutely not. I think the best way to look at this is that there are no absolutes. Each person's situation is unique and needs to be examined on an individual basis. Over the years, I have heard from many family caregivers that their parent made them promise to never place them in a nursing home. It is my professional opinion that this promise should never be made. Why? Each individual's situation is different, and in many cases, a nursing home or some other type of long-term care placement might be in the best interest of the individual. It is possible that this level of care is what would be most beneficial to the individual based on their care needs, need for social stimulation, finances, and/or availability of qualified and capable family caregivers. It is important to keep in mind that not everyone has the right personality, patience, and/or ability to provide care for an older loved one.

The concept of home is different for different people. It may be a house, apartment, condominium, trailer, or even a joint living arrangement with a friend, family member, or significant other. No matter where someone chooses to live, home is usually the one place where an individual feels most comfortable and in control of their own life. Therefore, it is no surprise that most individuals wish to age in place within their home and would resist any change that would take them away from that "home."

The issue regarding what is safe and when it is no longer appropriate for someone to remain in his or her home is a complex issue with no easy answer. The professional or family member contemplating this issue needs to take a number of factors into consideration, including but not limited to, the following:

- Is there evidence of memory loss or other mental factors resulting in an individual's vulnerability to scams/financial exploitation, potential for wandering/elopement from the home, falls, and/or other safety/fire hazards?
- Is the physical structure of the home and/or immediate neighborhood/environment unsafe?
- Is the individual's condition impaired to the point that they cannot care for their basic needs, even with available assistance?

Each individual's situation needs to be carefully assessed, and even then if the older adult in question remains mentally competent, he or she has the right to continue to live anywhere that he or she chooses, even if we as the professional and/or family member feel that this is not in his or her best interest. Oftentimes, the most difficult issue is the determination of mental competency. If as a professional working with older persons you ever question someone's mental competency and feel that they may be vulnerable or unsafe, pursue an in-home assessment from a competent professional. If you are that professional and are still uncertain, make a referral to state adult protective services. No matter what the situation, try not to project your personal preferences and/or value system on the older persons that you may serve. It is important to remember that one person's shack may be another person's castle.

The Changing Paradigms of Work and Retirement: Work Versus Retirement

In the traditional view of aging, individuals viewed work and retirement as two separate life events with work preceding a time of leisure in retirement. However, as discussed earlier in this section, this paradigm is not necessarily true today, especially for Baby Boomers, the majority of whom wish to continue to work in later life. In the new paradigm of aging, traditional "retirement" is changing from a time of ongoing leisure, to a time for learning, self-discovery, and meaningful work. For those who embrace this new paradigm of aging, it is a time of redirection, reinvention, rejuvenation, rewiring, and renewal. It can be time to revisit and renew the interests, dreams, and passions of one's youth, which for many were set aside earlier in their lives due to the pressures of making a living and raising children.

Helping Older Persons to Rediscover Their Life Purposes

According to Jim Emerman, former researcher with the American Society on Aging, in the September/October 2006 edition of *Aging Today*, "To be successful in the aging process one needs purpose in life; whether one finds that in faith-based organizations, political activity, involvement in the arts and humanities, or in volunteerism. Purpose resonates with health and creativity."

It is estimated that many older persons have lost sight of their life purposes. This can be the result of the many ageist stereotypes and myths held in society. As individuals age, they often feel pushed aside and undervalued in a youth-oriented culture. As a result, many older persons buy into these stereotypes and lose their sense of purpose.

As an experiment, in speaking to groups of both young schoolchildren and older adults, this author has asked the question, "What do you want to do when you grow older?" The children readily respond with a wide range of hopes and aspirations, where few, if any, older persons respond to that inquiry.

What Is Life Purpose, and Why Is It Important?

According to Merriam-Webster's Collegiate Dictionary (2008), *purpose* "something set up as an object or an end to be attained" (page 104). In other words, in order to have purpose one must take intentional action toward a goal or an end to be attained. This requires knowledge of one's goal, as well as planning and action toward that goal.

On the other hand, *life purpose* might be defined as

- The primary reason for one's existence;
- What one is here to do while they are alive;
- The overall meaning of one's life that shapes who they are and all that they do; or
- One's own personal mission statement.

Having life purpose is important to the health and well-being of older persons. Those who have a clearly defined life purpose tend to have improved physical and mental health, positive and meaningful relationships with others, the ability to rekindle the passions of their youth, and an optimistic outlook on life. Far too often, for those lacking life purpose, the old adage remains true...if you fail to plan, then you plan to fail.

Those who choose gerontology as a profession should recognize as part of their role the need to help older persons rediscover their life purposes. How might this be accomplished? First, as outlined in detail in the Part I Practical Application, work diligently to dispel and counteract ageist stereotypes and myths. Second, utilize opportunities to encourage older persons to identify their life purposes, and then guide them to create short- (6- to 12-month) and long-term (3- to 5-year) goals and to take appropriate action toward these goals, periodically evaluating their progress toward them.

When it comes to life purpose, I believe that Victor Hugo said it best, "There is nothing like a dream to create the future."

PART IV

SUPPORT SYSTEMS

CHAPTER 12

Primary Support Systems

The learning objectives for this chapter include understanding

- The roles and importance of friends to older persons.
- The various roles that grandparents play in the life of their grandchildren.
- The stresses and strains that adult children and their parents experience in relating to each other.
- The dynamics that develop between siblings in regard to parental care.
- The importance, for older persons, of support groups.

Section A: The Family—Nuclear and Extended

HELP FROM THE FAMILY

Mary has had a stroke and needs a lot of supervision and help in everyday living. She has three children, but only one, a daughter, lives in her small town. That daughter, Jane, is 60 years old, is employed full time, and has a husband who is thinking of retiring in 2 years to a Southern state. Jane is increasingly angry, stressed, and filled with guilt over her feelings. She is also feeling guilty over not having more time for her own children and grandchildren. In addition, her mother is very controlling and does not accept assistance graciously.

Glen, who is 74, has been a widower for 2 years. He has a very close relationship with a 66-year-old widow. He is thinking about marriage but is concerned about what his two children will think. His significant other has four children who believe that Mr. Diamond is too old for their mother. Both sets of children are concerned about who will get the estates if the parents marry.

Mary is taking care of her father who was, and continues to be, an alcoholic. He abused her when she was small. They have never talked about the abuse, but Mrs. Murphy deeply

*resents taking care of her father whom she does not like. Out of religious convictions and feel-
ings of guilt, she provides care, but is suffering from insomnia and anxiety attacks. Her sisters
and brothers—there are five—will not help in taking care of their alcoholic, abusive father. They
want to put him into a nursing home, which is an idea he vehemently rejects.*

IMPORTANCE OF FAMILY SUPPORT

There is little doubt that the family is the basic support system for most older Americans.
In spite of the changes that have occurred in the American family, and all the negative
things that fill the popular press concerning family relationships, the family is still the
backbone of support for most older people. For emotional support, social interaction (visiting, spending holidays together, etc.), and various types of assistance in times of health
problems or frailty in old age, the American family remains ready to help its older relatives. For married older couples, the family unit is the basic financial support structure
(Aronson & Weiner, 2007).

The type of family support an older person receives depends to a great extent on
his or her family situation—whether married, widowed, separated, divorced, never
married, has living children, is living alone, living with adult children, or living with
friends or other relatives. To some extent, the type of family support older people obtain
depends on whether they are living in the community or in an institutional setting such
as a group home, retirement village, or nursing facility (Levine, 2004; Piver, 2004).

MARITAL RELATIONSHIPS/SUPPORT

All of these various family characteristics have a real impact on the kind and amount of
family support an older person receives. Probably the best determinant of family support for older people is marital status. Whether a person is married, has great impact on
that person's support within a family setting—including emotional, financial, and physical support, particularly in times of illness or infirmity. Whether an elderly person lives
in a family setting or lives alone has much to do with their being in or out of poverty.

Emotional Support and Happiness in Marriage

Marriage is much more than a financial arrangement or organization for caregiving, at
least ideally. It might be noted, incidentally, that many young people going into marriage
are not aware of its wide-ranging financial implications. The question needs to be raised:
How happy are older people who have been married a long time? How happy are their
marriages? Generally, most older couples have reported that their marriages actually
improve over time (Fingerman, & Charles, 2010; Gilford, 1991). However, there are gender differences. Men tend to be more satisfied with their marriages and with the degree
to which their emotional needs are fulfilled than are women (Gilford, 1984; Rhyne, 1981).
Like marriages in any age group, not everything is perfect with older couples. Older marriages have their strengths and weaknesses.

Divorce and Older People

As has been pointed out, marital status can strongly affect a person's emotional and economic well-being. It influences living arrangements and the availability of caregivers for
older people with illness and or disability. The following chart (Figure 12.1) illustrates the
marital status of older people by age category.

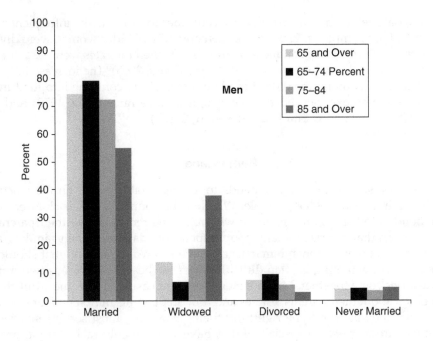

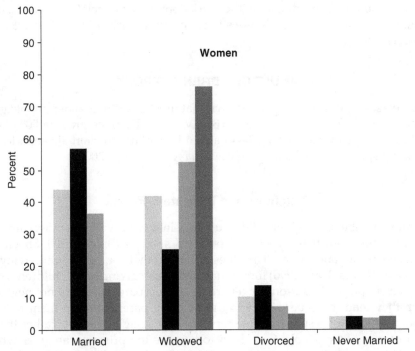

FIGURE 12.1 Marital Status of the Population Age 65 and Over, by Age Group and Sex, 2008.

Note: Married includes married, spouse present; married, spouse absent; and separated.

Reference population: These data refer to the noninstitutionalized population.

Source: Older Americans 2010, Table 3.

As ongoing research indicates, divorce continues to be relatively infrequent among older people. For example, in 2008, 8% of men and 10% of older women were divorced (*Older Americans 2010*). This is an increase from 1960 when the rates were 1.2% for older men and 1.5% for older women (*65+ in the United States*, 2005). The increase in the proportion of divorced among the older population is likely to continue into the future as younger adults who experienced relatively high divorce rates in the 1970s and 1980s grow older (Butrica, Iams, & Smith, 2003; Sheehy, 2010b).

Remarriage

The success of a second marriage depends to a considerable extent on the reaction of the adult children of the elderly couple. Whether the couple like their children or not, they are bonded to them. Adult children who reject the remarriage of their parents put a lot of stress on that marriage. Many people spend holidays with their families, and if the children reject their parents' remarriages, there is a real strain on what should be a happy event. Stepparenting is often difficult under the best conditions as two different family histories come together. Misunderstandings can easily arise. Some adult children are concerned about their parents' estates and how stepparents may spend, or eventually acquire, what they believe to be rightfully theirs. However, most second marriages of older couples are successful, especially if they have a similar cultural history, approval of their children, and can coordinate, without friction, their financial resources. The major reason for remarriage in old age is a desire for companionship (Brubaker, 1985; Sheehy, 2010b; Vinick, 1978).

ADULT CHILDREN SUPPORT

Over the years, study after study has shown that most of the help older people get when they need it comes for family members (Brody, 1990). Families provide 80% to 90% of personal care and help with various tasks around the house to maintain an older person, including transportation and shopping (*Caregiving in the U.S.*, 2009).

Daughters and Daughters-In-Law

Of all family members, daughters and daughters-in-law provide the most care for older adults, even more care than do elderly persons' spouses (Brody, 1990; Sheehy, 2010a; U.S. Department of Labor, 1986). This does not mean that sons do no caregiving. Perlin, Mullan, Stemple, and Skaff (1990) found that 16% of caregiving adult children were sons. As Brody (1990) pointed out, sons in general love their parents and do not neglect them. However, they tend to do tasks to help their elderly parents that to them reflect more gender-appropriate roles such as home repairs and managing money, rather than direct hands-on care of older people. Sons tend to become the primary caregiver when they have no sisters or none living near the elderly parent who needs help. When they do give aid, they are usually assisted by their wives.

Caregiver Stresses

There is increasing recent evidence that caregivers are at risk of physical and/or psychological burnout. Some caregivers experience a lack of sleep, and a continuing lack of sleep can lead to a decline of health (Sheehy, 2010b). In addition, studies have indicated "that long-term caregivers are at high risk for…immune system deficiency, depression, chronic anxiety, loss of concentration, and premature death" (Sheehy, 2010a, p. 72).

Detailed information on understanding caregiver behavior, caring for the caregiver, role reversal, and dealing with care recipient resistance is explored in the Practical Application at the end of Part IV of this textbook.

Racial Differences in In-Home Care

Black Americans and Whites have a different probability of moving into a nursing home. In addition, a study in the Sept/Oct (2006) issue of *Health Affairs* found that Black Americans are twice as likely as Whites to be in nursing homes that are closed by the Medicare and Medicaid programs because of their deficiencies in care (*65+ in the United States*, 2005). They also found that Black Americans are about 3 times as likely to be in nursing homes that predominantly care for poorer patients receiving Medicaid assistance. This means that those nursing facilities have much less funding to care for patients because of the low payments from the Medicaid program (Stephens, Townsend, & White, 2000).

GRANDPARENT SUPPORT

What is changing is the increased role older people are playing in the lives of their grandchildren. To put these changes in perspective, it is important to realize that the ranks of the young-old (aged 65–74) are growing rapidly with people who tend to be healthier, wealthier, and more mobile than persons of these ages in previous generations. Added to the young-old are many persons in the aged category (aged 75–84) who continue to have the health, vigor, and resources to play active grandparenting roles along with the millions of persons who are becoming older (aged 55–64), many of whom are already retired. This is part of the new paradigm of aging (Musil, 2010).

These growing ranks of active, energetic grandparents face requests for intergenerational assistance as a result of many changes in the American family. Some, such as the need to care for grandchildren as a result of the drug culture that has affected much of the nation, are leaving many children with no effective parental support. Other changes are the result of changing lifestyles, which lead to changing cultural norms. The rise of single-parent families by choice or as the result of the high national divorce rate has resulted in additional care of children by grandparents. In addition, the dramatic change in the number and percentage of women working outside of the home has had an impact on the need for direct grandparent help with young children (Simmons & Dye, 2003).

The Changing Roles of Grandparents

Grandparenting is not a new role. For decades, there have been endless stories and anecdotes about grandparents who take pleasure in "spoiling" their grandchildren. Grandparenting has been portrayed as an opportunity to indulge children's children in ways a person never could or would for her or his own.

As some of the popular media have pointed out, times, social roles, and expectations continue to change. With the multigenerational family (including the four-generation family) becoming more prevalent, many of today's grandparents are taking on roles that are more complicated and difficult than the old stereotypes would have us believe (Larsen, 1990/91).

Grandparents as Substitute Parents

One of the most significant shifts that has occurred in American society in recent years is the rapid growth in the number of grandparents who have taken on the role of raising their grandchildren. They have become stand-ins or surrogate parents for these children due to various factors including divorce, drug addiction, illness, and, at times, abandonment of their children. These situations are sometimes referred to as *skipped generation households* where a generation of parents is missing. The following data further illustrates this situation:

- A 2003 Supreme Court decision gave foster care benefits to grandparents raising their grandchildren. The Court ruled that benefits could not be denied to relatives if they would otherwise be eligible to be foster parents. Older grandparents, no matter how motivated, can find caring for grandchildren to be very tiring.
- Although the research is limited, there seems to be an emerging category of great-grandparents who are raising great-grandchildren, often ending up in a situation in which the very old are raising the very young.
- Society will increasingly be faced with political questions of how to support grandparents raising children. What financial subsidies should low-income grandparents receive? Should they receive housing subsidies? Should they receive social work support assistance? If so, what type or assistance should that be?

Grandparent Support Groups

Support groups have played important roles in assisting grandparents who find themselves in these difficult roles. *Grandparents Raising Grandchildren*, *Grandparents as Parents*, *Grandparents Against Immorality and Neglect*, *Second Time Around Parents*, *Grandparents United for Children's Right, Inc.*, and *From Generation to Generation* are examples of these types of support groups. "For sure it helps us—we've all learned to laugh again," said Paula Browne of *Grandparents as Parents* in California. "But it also helps the kids" (Larsen, 1990/1991, p. 34). Support groups for grandparents raising their children's children are helpful because people come to them in different stages of acceptance and are able to draw emotional support from the participants who have already worked their way through many of the situations that arise in this difficult role.

Grandparents as Babysitters

Unlike most European countries, the United States does not have a coordinated, state-supported system of child daycare. Essentially, each family is responsible for its own childcare. Specific childcare programs are established for specific groups of people or in conjunction with some specific programs. In the main, childcare is the responsibility of each family. It can be very expensive. Child day care can be so expensive for a family that the cost effectiveness of a parent's participation in the paid labor force may come into question depending on how much a parent earns. This question especially applies to single mothers on AFDC (Aid to Families with Dependent Children) who, if they return to the workforce, are stuck in minimum-wage jobs and loses income and benefits that come with staying on welfare and not going back to work. Why return to work if income and benefits from welfare are lost, and in addition, they must spend a considerable amount of money on childcare?

Section B: Other Support Systems

HATTIE'S FRIENDS

Hattie has lived most of her adult life in the same house. Her husband built it when they were first married. She raised her three children there. Her church and doctor's office were in a shopping center four blocks away. Hattie is now 89 years old. One of her three children died over 10 years ago, and the other two live on opposite sides of the nation. She had a lot of friends over the years, but many of them are either dead, confined to nursing homes, or living with or near their children. With the loss of her husband 2 years ago, and with her children living great distances away, increasingly Hattie has relied on her friends for mutual support in facing the changes and losses in her life. In the past 6 months, Hattie's church has announced it is relocating to the suburbs, where most of its members live. Her doctor's office, along with other offices and stores in the neighborhood shopping center, is being demolished for a new urban freeway. Last week her only remaining friend, who was still driving in the daylight hours, suffered a stroke.

Hattie's children, who have been providing for some home-help services for their mother, are encouraging her to move to a congregate living facility for older people that has a continuing-care option, meaning she can be provided any level of assistance she needs as she grows older.

Feeling all alone in her old house and neighborhood, Hattie is willing to consider moving, but she is afraid because she doesn't know anybody in the facility her children have suggested. How can she survive without her old friends? Will she still be able to see those friends if she moves to the new facility? Will she be able to make new friends at age 89? With her husband dead the past 2 years and her children many hours away, friends have been a key component of Hattie's life. She has passed the time with them when they have been able to get together, and she has been able to confide in them in times of happiness and times of stress and loss.

FRIENDS

As important as families are in the support systems of older people, most people throughout their lives have an important source of mutual assistance that adds to their quality of life—friends. Few things are more important than good friends (Cacioppo & Berntson, 2005; Cacioppo, Hawkley, & Berntson, 2003; Cacioppo & Patrick, 2008; Giles, Glonek, Luszcz, & Andrews, 2005). Friends are important at any age from toddlers making their first attempts at personal interaction in the sandbox to 99-year-olds recalling past events and reacting to today's news. The only problem for the 99-year-olds is that many of their old friends are no longer around. So, new friends of various types often take on the roles of companions and confidants.

Roles of Friends

It is important to note the roles of friends, companions, and confidants. A companion is someone with whom a person can share activities and pastimes—go to the movies together, share a ball game, build and fly model airplanes together. A confidant is someone to confide in and share personal problems with—a person to lean on in times of stress and joy.

Friendship and close personal relationships enable one to age with better physical and psychological health (Cacioppo & Patrick, 2008; Chao, 2012; Eisenberger, Jarcho, Lieberman, & Naliboff, 2006). Research continues to accumulate that being human means that there is a need to live in a network of relationships (Cacioppo et al., 2003; Giles et al., 2005). Daniel Goldman argued from his research that friendships are needed to function well. There is evidence that in addition to bringing about feelings of joy and contentment, friendships enable people to function well psychologically (Fingerman & Charles, 2010). In addition, friendships seem to lead to increased longevity. James Coan of the University of Virginia argued that persons who are friendless have an increased probability of developing more chronic health problems, more accidents, and even more psychiatric problems (Coan & Allen, 2004, 2007). He stated that friendlessness can be compared to the added health risks brought about by obesity, smoking, and a lack of exercise.

Friends and Feelings of Well-Being

Research has shown that having close ties with friends is more important to an older person's well-being than are family ties (Crohan & Antonucci, 1989; Eisenberger, 2006). Friendships tend to help people maintain a positive self-image even in the face of major problems. A positive self-esteem is important for happiness and contentment as well as for the ability to care for others (Antonucci, 1990; Cagley, 2009). John Cacioppo, in his research, argued that we are "hard-wired" from birth to need personal relationships (Cacioppo & Berntson, 2005). He stated that in people who are lonely, the body increases secretion of the hormone cortisol. Prolonged excessive cortisol production can increase cardiovascular disease (Cacioppo et al., 2003). He also stated that his research showed that with loneliness there can also be a heightened danger of loss of sleep, and increasingly, research has shown the need of the body for at least 7 hours of sleep a night. Social networking and relationships have an impact on the neural circuitry in the brain, and as Daniel Goldman has stated, friendships have a very positive impact on the brain, and in addition to other positive affects, it increases the functioning of the immunological system (Goldman, 1996, 2006). Capioppo stated that loneliness, isolation, and a lack of interaction with others can lead to physical and emotional decline (Cacioppo & Berntson, 2005; Cacioppo et al., 2003; Lester, Mead, Graham, Gask, & Reilly, 2012; Schnittger et al., 2012).

Friends and Coping With Life Changes

In addition to helping older people cope with isolation and loneliness, such as that brought about by loss of a spouse, friends can help older people with some of the major life changes they face (Goldman, 1996, 2006). For example, social support from friends is very helpful for women at the time of their retirement (Francis, 1990). Friends can play a crucial role in older people adjusting to a congregate living situation, such as moving into a retirement community or even a nursing facility (Atchley, 1994). Moving into a retirement living environment where a person already has a friend can be a great advantage, but even in these kinds of facilities, new friendships can be developed that can make a real contribution to a person's adjustment. Lynn Giles in her research has found that an extensive network of close and intimate friends may increase life expectancy by as much as 22% (Giles et al., 2005). She believes that the evidence indicates that friends can help one get through difficult times and increase one's optimistic moods.

RELIGION/SPIRITUALITY

Not all support systems are available to all older people. On the whole, family and friends are vital support mechanisms, as indicated previously. Economic supports, along with medical and long-term care, play key roles in meeting the basic needs of older people.

Some people, because of previous experiences, cultural backgrounds, or personal encounters, tend to rely heavily on religion to help them cope with the changes and challenges of old age (Mackinlay & Dundon, 2012).

For many older persons, religion and/or spirituality enable them to cope, and give them reasons for survival (Sun et al., 2012). A particular church may give a chronically ill older person both support and a process by which they can continue to see themselves as contributing persons. Studies have indicated that many persons who are religiously involved have more psychologically close contacts than do others. Religion enables one to focus beyond oneself by being a part of a circle of relationships. Being a part of this social group enables a person to have a sense of purpose and to believe that they are neither totally isolated nor abandoned (Sloan, Bagiella, & Powell, 1999).

SUPPORT GROUPS

One form of support that has grown rapidly is support groups. Support groups have developed across the nation to deal with almost any problem people might have or think they have. Older people, and those moving toward the older ages, are included. As some writers have observed, in localities across the nation, people are streaming to churches and synagogues. A religious revival? Not really. Instead of sitting in the pews, they are going off to meet in rooms throughout the building sharing their innermost thoughts, darkest fears, deepest secrets, confounding frustrations, and strangest cravings (Leerhsen, Lewis, Pomper, Davenport, & Nelson, 1990).

Many people have discovered that sharing feelings, frustrations, and problems through talking and listening to people who are facing the same situations has a soothing and healing effect (Andrews, Clark, & Luszcz, 2002). They can motivate people to work out solutions through suggestions and encouragement. Most professionals see these types of groups as effective ways to cope with isolation—a condition that tends to make all other problems worse. "Just the sight of your fellow sufferers tends to make your pain a little more bearable," said one self-help group organizer (Leerhsen et al., 1990, p. 50).

Support Groups and Older People

Support groups have proven to be very helpful to older people and the people who help them—particularly their caregiving family members. There are a number of support groups that provide assistance to dependent older people and their caregivers. Many of these are coordinated on the national level, including: United Ostomy Association (for patients and family members of persons who have had an ostomy, an operation to make an artificial opening to empty the large or small bowel or the bladder), American Cancer Society, American Heart Association, Arthritis Foundation, Courage Stroke Network, Huntington's Disease Society of America, Leukemia Society of America, and many others. These support groups deal with a range of issues patients and their families face as they try to cope with their illnesses.

Support Groups for Caregivers

Some of the support groups focus on the people who take care of their elderly relatives and friends. One is the Alzheimer's Disease and Related Disorders Association. Until it was founded in 1979, there was little organized support for the caregivers of Alzheimer's patients. "The country was just barely becoming aware of Alzheimer's then," recalled

Dr. Robert Butler, former chair of the geriatrics department of Mt. Sinai Medical Center in New York City (cited in Barnhill, 1994, p. 15).

In order to survive the strains and stresses of being a caregiver to an Alzheimer's patient, experts say that people need a place to obtain advice, share experiences, let off steam, and know that they are not alone in what they're trying to do. Dr. Butler stated that, "exhaustion and burnout can make the caregiver a second patient. Support groups provide much-needed relief" (cited in Barnhill, 1994, p. 5), and more recent work has substantiated the value of these support groups (McFadden & McFadden, 2011).

SUGGESTED RESOURCES

Caregiving.com: http://www.caregiving.com
> This website comprises a community of family caregivers sharing their stories, support, and solutions. Weekly words of comfort, free webinars, articles specifi c to caregiving, and online support groups are featured.

Children of Aging Parents: http://www.caps4caregivers.org
> A national nonprofit, CAPS offers support to caregiving children of older adults. Its website includes a newsletter on current caregiving issues and links to other websites about caregiving, Medicare, and support groups for caregivers.

GrandCare Support Locator: http://www.giclocalsupport.org/pages/gic_db_home.cfm
> Providing a way for grandparents to access national, state, and local groups, programs, resources, and services to support caregiving, this website is a service of the AARP Foundation.

The New Old Age. Caring and Coping: http://newoldage.blogs.nytimes.com
> A blog focusing on the intergenerational challenges of caregiving for older parents; includes articles, resources, and links.

CHAPTER 13

Formal Support Systems

The learning objectives of this chapter include understanding

- The role of the Older Americans Act (OAA) in providing services and programs for older adults.
- The components of the National Aging Services Network.
- The types of services and programs, primarily offered through the Aging Services Network, focusing specifically on older Americans.
- Why services may be underused on the one hand, and ways in which programs stretch resources to reach more older adults than could otherwise be served, on the other.
- Senior Corps' opportunities for older adults to volunteer in their communities.

VALUING HOME- AND COMMUNITY-BASED SUPPORT

Helen Cosgrove has lived all of her life in State College, Pennsylvania. Helen recently celebrated her 90th birthday, but she still values her independence. However, she's had to give up driving and can't get around without the use of a walker. Her children and grandchildren live in Maryland, so Helen depends on the generosity of friends and neighbors and her caring volunteers from Meals On Wheels to help her complete the daily tasks so many of us take for granted. For Helen, Meals On Wheels means much more than a nutritious meal. For the past two years, volunteers have delivered peace of mind, a friendly smile and the comfort of knowing that she is not forgotten. ("Stories From the Heart," 2012).

Margaret Reilly, 89, is a walking testimonial for the Gulfport Multipurpose Senior Center. "It's the spice of my life," she says. "Whatever you want to do is there." Margaret should know since she has volunteered at the Center for more than 25 years. . . . Now, she volunteers two hours a day, . . . plays canasta, visits the Fitness Center twice a week and participates in the Wii Fit group Thursday afternoons. "There's no reason for anybody to feel lonely," Margaret says. "Everyone is so nice and so knowledgeable. I've learned a great deal being involved at the Senior Center." (Oatley, 2011)

SHOULD THERE BE SPECIAL PROGRAMS AND SERVICES FOR OLDER ADULTS?

This chapter examines the range of services and volunteer opportunities that are available to older people in the United States. When it comes to services and programs, there seems to be growing pressure to justify their existence. In the face of increasing needs across our society with limited and diminished resources, many people are asking why special programs and services are offered to people just because they have reached a certain age. Much of this type of questioning relates to a more general ongoing debate concerning the basic role of government. Is the role of the government limited to basic services to maintain order and provide for the national defense with some emergency relief to the neediest citizens? Does the government's role include providing programs, services, and resources to enhance the lives of various categories of people across America? Or, does the role of the government fall somewhere in between? Obviously, there is no easy or set answer to this ongoing debate. It is rooted in the politics of the nation and depends on the vitality of the economy. Politics is the art of making choices on a collective basis. In the United States, those choices are made democratically with input, pressure, guidance, and plain old-fashioned clout from a variety of sources. We will look at how this debate translates into formal support for older people in America.

NATURE OF PROGRAMS AND SERVICES FOR OLDER AMERICANS

Older people in America are the beneficiaries of two basic types of programs: one type is designed for people of any age, and the second type is designed specifically for older people. An example of the first type is the Supplemental Nutrition Assistance Program (SNAP), called the Food Stamp Program until 2008, originally established to alleviate malnutrition and hunger among low-income persons by increasing their food purchasing power. Any person can qualify if he or she meets income and asset guidelines. Relatively early in its history, the nation collectively decided that it was not a good thing to have starving people. Emergency aid to the poor usually included some type of starvation prevention, often in the form of distribution of excess commodities such as flour, peanut butter, eggs, and powdered milk. Following an eight-county experimental antihunger program in 1961, the Food Stamp Act was passed in 1964, making it available to all states as an option to giving out food commodities. In 2010, 40.3 million Americans were taking part in SNAP, nearly half (47%) were children, and 8% (3.2 million) were aged 60 or older (U.S. Department of Agriculture, Food and Nutrition Service, 2011). Eighty percent of older people who do receive SNAP benefits live alone and receive an average of only $119 per month in SNAP benefits.

Programs of the second type are designed specifically for older Americans. These programs arose out of collective decisions that it was in the best interests of the nation, as well as older people and their families, to design and develop programs and services specifically to meet some of the basic needs of older people and to offer them opportunities to serve their communities. From the beginning of the United States under its Constitution in 1789, it took a long time to come to a collective decision to organize a part of government to specifically assist older persons, particularly on the national level. Remember, it was not until 1935 that Social Security was enacted into law. Prior to that time, in cases of abject poverty the welfare of older people was the responsibility of families, and to some extent local governments. Of course, there were not nearly as many older people then as there are today. Not until 1965, when the OAA was passed, did we see a systematic, organized approach to providing services and programs on a nationwide basis to enhance the lives of older people.

OAA: NATIONAL LEGISLATION TO ASSIST OLDER PEOPLE

The Older Americans Act (OAA) of 1965 was enacted to address the social service needs of older people. The Act grew out of the deliberations of the first White House Conference on Aging, which was held in 1961, and continues to be the primary source of support for human and social services for older persons in the United States. Its mission is broad: to help older people maintain maximum independence in their homes and communities, to promote a continuum of care for the vulnerable elderly, and to avoid unnecessary and costly institutionalization. In successive amendments, Congress authorized targeted programs to respond to specific needs of the older population. While OAA programs are not entitlements, all people aged 60 and over—approximately 57 million individuals in 2010—are eligible for services regardless of income and need. To date, Congress has resisted any attempts to make the OAA programs and services means-tested, in other words, to require proof that income is low enough or that one has a demonstrated need. And yet, despite the broad sweep of services included in its mission, the OAA's reach is constrained by modest resources.

Objectives of the OAA

The language of the OAA concerning the objectives for older Americans provides insight into the societal decision that resulted in the legislation. It states:

> The Congress hereby finds and declares that, in keeping with the traditional American concept of the inherent dignity of the individual in our democratic society, the older people of our Nation are entitled to, and it is the joint and several duty and responsibility of the governments of the United States, of the several states and their political subdivisions, and of Indian tribes to assist our older people to secure equal opportunity to the full and free enjoyment of the following objectives:
>
> 1. An adequate income in retirement in accordance with the American standard of living.
> 2. The best possible physical and mental health which science can make available and without regard to economic status.
> 3. Obtaining and maintaining suitable housing, independently selected, designed and located with reference to special needs and available at costs which older citizens can afford.
> 4. Full restorative services for those who require institutional care, and a comprehensive array of community-based, long-term care services adequate to appropriately sustain older people in their communities and in their homes, including support to family members and other persons providing voluntary care to older individuals needing long-term care services.
> 5. Opportunity for employment with no discriminatory personnel practices due to age.
> 6. Retirement in health, honor, dignity—after years of contribution to the economy.

7. Participating in and contributing to meaningful activity within the widest range of civic, cultural, educational and training, and recreational opportunities.
8. Efficient community services, including access to low cost transportation, which provide a choice in supported living arrangements and social assistance in a coordinated manner and which are readily available when needed, with emphasis on maintaining a continuum of care for vulnerable older individuals.
9. Immediate benefit from proven research knowledge which can sustain and improve health and happiness.
10. Freedom, independence, and the free exercise of individual initiative in planning and managing their own lives, full participation in the planning and operation of community based services and programs provided for their benefit, and protection against abuse, neglect, and exploitation. (Title I, Sec. 101, Older Americans Act of 1965, as amended in 2006, Public Law 109–365.)

Structure to Implement the OAA

To achieve the objectives of the OAA and to provide the services that result from them, the Congress established the Administration on Aging (AoA), which is within the Department of Health and Human Services. AoA administers most of the programs that come under the OAA and is the primary federal agency to advocate for older persons. An important idea in developing OAA's framework was, when it comes to policy and program decisions, that decentralization of authority and the use of local control would make a more effective and responsive service system for those receiving services at the local level. Thus, AoA oversees an Aging Services Network (see Figure 13.1) consisting of State Units on Aging, Area Agencies on Aging (established under OAA in 1973), and Tribal Organizations (established under OAA in 1978).

The 56 State Units on Aging (state agencies), which are found in each of the states, the District of Columbia, Puerto Rico, American Samoa, Guam, the Northern Mariana Islands, and the Virgin Islands, are awarded federal funds to implement state plans on aging. The state agencies can be independent units of state government—for example, a state Department of Aging Services—or part of existing state agencies—for example, one of a state's human service departments. However constructed, each state office is responsible for developing a statewide plan to serve the elderly, and these plans are approved by AoA. AoA then distributes funding for programs and services through grants to the state agencies. Through these grants, states receive a set amount of funding and are given the flexibility to design and operate OAA programs within federal guidelines. Grant amounts are generally based on funding formulas weighted to reflect a state's aged 60 and over population.

Area Agencies on Aging (AAA, referred to as *triple As*) are offices established by the state units. Each AAA develops its own 2-, 3-, or 4-year plan, as determined by the state unit, to facilitate and support the development of programs to address the needs of older adults within a defined geographic region, and support investment in their talents and interests. State units approve the AAA plans and typically allocate the funding they receive from the AoA to their area agencies. At the discretion of the state, an area agency can be a unit of county, city, or town government. It can even be a private, nonprofit agency. State and local agencies are responsible for planning, developing, and co-ordinating an array of services within each state, though states also provide services to older adults through other funding, such as Medicaid, and through separate programs and departments. Local AAAs do not usually provide services directly to the elderly unless it is absolutely necessary to do so to ensure an adequate supply of such services. Instead,

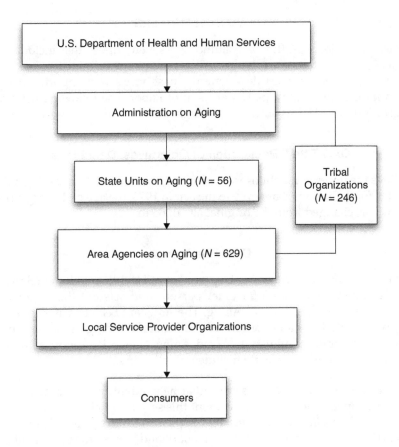

FIGURE 13.1 National Aging Services Network.

Source: Adapted from the National Association of Area Agencies on Aging, http://www.n4a.org

they contract with local providers for services in their areas. A few states (Nevada is one), have no AAAs, and so they allocate funds directly to local providers.

The AoA also awards grants to tribal organizations to provide supportive and nutrition services that maintain the unique cultural and other needs of older Native Americans. Two Native American Resource Centers, one in North Dakota and one in Colorado, address issues related to community-based long-term care among the Indian communities on reservations.

Approximately 20,000 local organizations provide services through all the sectors of the Aging Network (Government Accountability Office [GAO], 2011). For a humorous look at the difficulties seniors can experience with such a large bureaucracy, watch Video 4.

Episode 4: The Challenge of Bureaucracy

High Bandwidth:
http://raidercast.grcc.edu/flash/2011_2012/grcctv/successful_
aging/success_aging_4_large/grcc_player.html
Low Bandwidth:
http://raidercast.grcc.edu/flash/2011_2012/grcctv/successful_
aging/success_aging_4_small/grcc_player.html

OAA'S SEVEN TITLES

To implement its objectives, the OAA authorizes seven "titles" that include a series of formula-based and discretionary grants. All programs are administered at the federal level by the AoA, except for the Title V community service senior opportunities program, which is administered by the U.S. Department of Labor. The following titles reflect the basic programs of the OAA as amended through 2011.

OAA Title I: Declaration of Objectives; Definitions

Title I outlines the underlying philosophy of the legislation and its sweeping objectives. It also provides for definitions that apply to the act. In 1973, the age of the target population to be served was changed from the original age of 65 to 60.

OAA Title II: AoA

Title II establishes the AoA within the Department of Health and Human Services as the chief federal agency to advocate for older persons and sets out the responsibilities of AoA and the Assistant Secretary for Aging. The Assistant Secretary is appointed by the President, with the advice and consent of the Senate. Funding authorized under Title II goes toward program administration and Aging Network support activities. Aging Network support activities currently include the following:

- *National Eldercare Locator*, a service that helps identify community resources for older people (more information about this service is below);
- *Pension Counseling and Information Program* funds six regional counseling projects that help older Americans learn about and receive the retirement benefits to which they are entitled;
- *Senior Medicare Patrol Program* funds projects that educate older Americans and their families to recognize and report Medicare and Medicaid fraud;
- *National Long-Term Care Ombudsman Resource Center* provides training and technical assistance to state and local long-term care ombudsmen;
- *National Center on Elder Abuse* provides information to the public and professionals, and provides training and technical assistance to state elder abuse agencies and to community-based organizations;
- *National Center for Benefits Outreach and Enrollment* helps to enroll seniors and persons with disabilities into federal and state benefits programs for which they are eligible but not yet enrolled; and
- *Health and Long-Term Care Programs Initiative* helps older Americans plan for long-term care services and supports so that they can maintain their independence in the community.

Information about services that are available in communities is the key to the services being used by older people and their caregivers. Having an array of resources does little good if the intended recipients do not know about them or do not know how to access them. As such, information and assistance become community-based social services in their own right. In 1993, the National Association of Area Agencies on Aging, with funding from AoA, established the Eldercare Locator, a nationwide call center and website that connects older Americans and their caregivers with information on senior services in their area. The call center (800–677-1116) is available between 9:00 a.m. and 8:00 p.m., Eastern time, Monday through Friday. The website (www.eldercare.gov) allows users to search for services by zip code, by city and state, or by topic, or engage in an online chat with an information specialist. Information is provided about such resources as adult day care centers, legal assistance, home health services, and transportation resources. The Eldercare Locator taps into an extensive network of organizations that are familiar with state and local community resources.

Almost half of the funding for Title II goes toward health and long-term care programs, which include Aging and Disability Resource Centers (ADRCs). Nationwide, there are currently more than 200 ADRC sites, one-stop shop/single points of entry providing objective information and helping people access community-based services to help older individuals, and those of any age with disabilities, to continue to live at home.

OAA Title III: Grants for State and Community Programs on Aging

Title III provides funds for supportive services (Part B), nutrition services (Part C), health promotion (Part D), and family caregiver support (Part E), all with the goal of helping older people remain independent in their own homes and communities. (Part A addresses the purpose and administration for Title III.) The Government Accountability Office (GAO, 2011) estimates that in fiscal year (FY) 2008, about 2.9 million people, constituting approximately 5% of the nation's population aged 60 and over, received select home- or community-based services through programs authorized and funded by Title III of the OAA.

Part B: Supportive Services

A variety of supportive services are funded by Title III Part B, including transportation for those with or without mobility impairments; home care for those who have difficulty performing daily activities such as bathing; case management; adult day care; and senior center activities. Part B receives just over 19% of OAA's total annual budget ($367 million in FY2012).

Assuring the availability of transportation options for seniors was voted number 3 among 50 top policy priorities at the most recent White House Conference on Aging, held in December 2005. This top ranking reflects a growing understanding among aging-service professionals, transportation experts, and seniors themselves that transportation is a critical aspect in maintaining quality of life for older Americans. According to research reported in the *American Journal of Public Health*, both men and women are likely to live beyond the time they can drive safely, as much as 6 years for men and about 10 years for women (Foley, Heimovitz, Guralnik, & Brock, 2002). The Practical Application at the end of Part IV of this textbook includes a section on driving and excellent suggestions for dealing with an older adult's resistant to giving up driving.

Concerns about older drivers' safety, coupled with the need to maintain mobility in the community, are responsible for much of the growing interest in transportation options. Among the ideas that communities are implementing are subsidizing taxicab fares, community shuttle buses, and volunteer driver programs. A nonprofit organization dedicated to fostering "new ideas and options to enhance mobility and transportation for today's and tomorrow's older population," the Beverly Foundation has developed five criteria for evaluating the extent to which transportation options are senior friendly. Known as the *Five A's of Senior Friendly Transportation*, they are: availability, accessibility, acceptability, affordability, and adaptability. Table 13.1 provides a brief description of each criterion.

TABLE 13.1 The 5 A's of Senior-Friendly Transportation

CRITERION	DESCRIPTION AND EXAMPLES
Availability	Transportation exists and is available when needed.
Accessibility	Transportation can be reached and used (bus stairs can be negotiated, bus seats are high enough, bus stop is readable, vehicle comes to the door).
Acceptability	Standards relate to conditions such as cleanliness of vehicle, safety (stops located in safe areas), and user-friendliness (courteous, helpful drivers).
Affordability	Costs (fees) are affordable, comparable to or less than driving a car, and vouchers or coupons help defray out-of-pocket expenses.
Adaptability	Transportation can be modified or adjusted to meet special needs (wheelchair can be accommodated, trip chaining is possible).

Source: Beverly Foundation (2010).

Home-Based Services

Perhaps the most important services that enable older people to remain in their own homes and communities are in-home services. In recent years, in-home care has been one of the fastest-growing components of Medicare. Too often admission to nursing homes, chronic-care hospitals, and other long-term facilities is used to meet the needs of impaired older individuals when appropriate assistance at home, or in the home of an adult child or friend, would be a better solution. Not only is staying at home usually much more cost effective, but also most older people want to remain in the familiar surroundings of their own home.

In-home services may be provided by medical professionals, home health aides, or personal care aides. Nurses, physicians, and physical therapists, for example, can provide medical care. Home health aides are trained to provide routine health care such as changing bandages and dressing wounds, applying topical medications, and monitoring or reporting changes in health status to a supervising medical professional. They may also provide personal care such as bathing and dressing and, in some states, they may be able to administer medication. Personal care aides may assist with housekeeping (e.g., making beds, laundry), preparing meals, shopping, and running errands.

Being able to afford in-home services is a major problem for many older persons. Title III provides some support for in-home services through local AAAs or state units, with the primary purpose of keeping older people in their own homes and out of long-term care institutions for as long as possible. In-home services may also be covered by Medicare, Medicaid, and client fees. Medicare covers short-term health-related services and clients who meet Medicare eligibility requirements (Chapter 14 provides information about Medicare coverage for in-home services). Medicaid can also be used to pay for in-home services when the client and the service meet Medicaid eligibility requirements, which include strict income guidelines. Finally, there are proprietary (for-profit) in-home service agencies that offer services for fees paid by the clients. AARP has excellent guidelines for hiring a home care worker; they are available online through AARP's website (http://www.aarp.org/relationsips/caregiving-resource-center/providingcare).

Case Management Services

Case management services include assessing needs for an individual, developing a plan of care, locating appropriate services, coordinating services, authorizing and arranging for services, monitoring services, and monitoring and reassessing needs. They are usually done by a qualified person, often a nurse or social worker, or team. In the case management process, the case managers can help determine eligibility for various services as well as assist with applications for government-sponsored programs. Case management services are becoming increasingly critical as service delivery systems become more complex and the number of older people who need in-home services continues to grow.

Many caregivers are hesitant to call someone into their home to help with this kind of assessment. Most think they know what needs to be done, and most want to do what needs to be done by themselves. Many think it is their duty and their responsibility, but deep down they also know that they cannot do everything. They cannot continue to give around-the-clock care and continually worry about frail, elderly parents without paying the consequences in terms of personal health, family unity, and emotional well-being. With case management, there is usually no obligation after the initial assessment. Suggestions may be followed, rejected, or modified. Using any of the services and following some of the suggestions for help do not mean that caregivers are abandoning their responsibilities to their loved ones. It means that they are wise enough to know that they cannot do everything by themselves all the time. By using a case management approach, family caregivers can plug in the types of assistance that are needed so that they can continue to be effective caregivers. It means that they are using their own resources in more effective ways.

Case management services can provide adult children who live far away from their aging parents the opportunity to assist in the care of their elderly parents without having to move near them, or without moving their parents near them. Some agencies, such as the Jewish Family and Children's Agencies, have developed an Elder Support Network through which family members are able to arrange for case management and supportive services throughout the nation with fees based on a sliding scale determined by the family member's income. Private care managers are springing up across the United States and can be accessed through the National Association of Professional Geriatric Care Managers.

Adult Day Care

First organized in England in the 1940s, adult day care is a response to the need for family caregivers to have relief from caring for dependent older people on a regular basis. Unlike senior centers, adult day care programs and centers are usually not "drop-in" situations. They are generally offered Monday through Friday during the day, with clients attending a regular number of days each week for up to 8 hours per day. Adult day care centers offer family caregivers opportunities to continue to work outside the home or participate in any activity, free for some hours each day from the responsibilities of caring for a dependent older person.

The range of services provided by adult day care centers include: screening for physical conditions; medical care (generally arranged with an outside physician); nursing care; occupational, physical, and recreational therapy; social work; transportation; meals; personal care; educational programs; and counseling. Funding for these programs can come from OAA's Title III, Social Services Block Grants, Medicaid, and fees paid by users and their families. These centers may be located in an independent facility, a senior center, a neighborhood center, a hospital, or a religious organization. Day care has become an important component of community services available to older people and their families. It plays a key role in alleviating isolation, preventing or delaying institutionalization, and providing some relief for families from caretaking responsibilities.

Multipurpose Senior Centers

Contrary to popular misconceptions, senior centers are not places where older people can live, such as assisted living facilities or nursing homes. Instead, multipurpose senior centers are usually community focal points for older people to access resources and services funded through the OAA. Although the history of a center for older people goes back to a program developed in New York City in 1943, senior centers were not funded through the OAA until 1975. Now, nearly 11,000 senior centers serve 1 million older adults every day (National Council on Aging , 2012).

Senior center programming is usually of two types: (a) services, and (b) recreation and education. Common services, in addition to meals, are counseling and referral; assistance with living arrangements and employment; health programs, including screening clinics and health education; protective services; legal and income counseling; friendly visit outreach programs; homemaker assistance; telephone reassurance; home repair programs; and transportation assistance. In Malden, Massachusetts, for example, the Mystic Valley senior center offers programs that benefit "eight communities where 52,000 elders reside; delivers 1,700 meals every day, operates 15 senior dining sites, and provides referrals, services, and critical support to 10,000 individuals every year" (*The Beacon*, 2011). Senior centers also provide a place where seniors can gather for social interaction and recreational and educational activities, which may include arts and crafts; nature, science, and outdoor life; drama, music, and dance; physical activities; table games; excursions; and, speakers, lectures, and forums. Activities are usually designed to appeal to both men and women.

Often led by the active involvement of older adults in their communities, senior centers are incorporating programs to appeal to Baby Boomers, of whom more than 22 million are already 60 years of age or older, while continuing to serve present users. Some examples include tai chi and yoga classes, computer rooms, and coordination of volunteer opportunities. Extending center hours so that seniors who are still employed can participate, and better marketing to reach potential new users have also been suggested (Fitzpatrick & McCabe, 2008).

Part C: Nutrition Services

Nutrition services are the most well known of the services supported by the OAA. They receive almost 43% of OAA's funds ($811 million in FY2012). They are designed to provide balanced and nutritious meals in congregate settings, such as senior centers, community centers, and churches, or in the homes of those older adults who have difficulties that limit their ability to obtain or prepare food. The OAA identifies three purposes for the nutrition programs: (a) to reduce hunger and food insecurity, (b) to promote socialization of older individuals, and (c) to promote the health and well-being of older individuals by assisting them in gaining access to nutrition and other disease prevention and health promotion services. While improving the nutritional intake of older people, the congregate meals programs have addressed many other problems older people may face including social isolation, loneliness, and limited access to social and health services. Even homebound older people get a brief conversation along with their "meals on wheels." There are 5,000 senior nutrition programs, serving over one million meals per day (congregate and home-delivered). Professionals who work at the nutrition program sites are aided by approximately a million volunteers nationwide (Meals on Wheels Association of America, 2012).

Part D: Disease Prevention and Health Promotion

OAA grants "seed money" for programs whose purpose is to prevent or delay chronic conditions and promote health among older people. Part D receives barely more than 1% ($21 million in FY2012) of the total annual budget for OAA. State and area agencies are meant to use these federal funds to leverage other sources of funding. The types of activities that can be supported vary widely and include both group services, such as physical fitness and chronic disease management classes, and individualized services, such as medical and dental screening, nutrition counseling, pharmacology consultation, and immunizations.

Part E: Family Caregiver Support

The National Family Caregiver Support Program recognizes the extensive demands placed on family members and friends who provide primary care for their loved ones. It funds some assistance and support for these caregivers. Training for caregivers, home rehabilitation and adaptations (e.g., safety bars in bathrooms), and respite care to give temporary relief from caregiving responsibilities are among the services funded.

Closely related to day care, respite care generally offers more intensive care on a limited-time basis for elderly persons who require ongoing care. This care may be in the caregiver's home, or the dependent older person may be brought to a respite-care facility, which may be a nursing home or other long-term care facility. The length of the assistance may range from a few hours to a few days. In a second option for respite care, the elderly patient is brought to a group setting where he or she has the opportunity to socialize with others and participate in program activities. This type of service is increasingly being provided to Alzheimer's patients.

Respite care is relatively new and generally underfunded by social-support funding systems. Some are being developed on a fee-for-service basis. Respite care in communities is seen as an effective means of maintaining frail, dependent older people in their own homes for longer periods of time. This service helps the informal support system (family and friends) provide the care that dependent older people need. Overall, family caregiver support programs receive only 8% of OAA funds ($152 million in FY2012).

OAA Title IV: Activities for Health, Independence, and Longevity

Title IV provides authority for training, research, and demonstration projects in the field of aging. Its four major purposes are

1. To expand the nation's knowledge and understanding of the older population and the aging process;
2. To design, test, and promote the use of innovative ideas and best practices in programs and services for older individuals;
3. To help meet the needs of trained personnel in the field of aging; and
4. To increase awareness of citizens of all ages of the need to assume personal responsibility for their own longevity.

Title IV has supported a wide range of projects related to income, health, housing, and long-term care. Funds are awarded to a wide range of grantees, including public and private organizations, state and area agencies on aging, and institutions of higher learning. In recent years, funds have been awarded to support a national Alzheimer's disease call center, multigenerational civic engagement projects, and a number of national organizations serving older minorities (National Health Policy Forum, 2012).

OAA Title V: Community Service Senior Opportunities Act

Title V, sometimes referred to as the Senior Community Service Employment Program (SCSEP), subsidizes part-time community service jobs for unemployed, low-income people aged 55 and older who have poor employment prospects. The Department of Labor contracts with all 50 states, the District of Columbia, Puerto Rico, American Samoa, Guam, the Northern Marianas Islands, the U.S. Virgin Islands, and 18 national organizations that recruit and enroll workers who are then placed in community service jobs, in settings such as hospitals, schools, and senior nutrition sites. The 18 national organizations, which receive 78% of Title V funding, include the AARP Foundation, the Association National Pro Personas Mayores, Easter Seals, Experience Works, Goodwill Industries, the Institute for Indian Development, Mature Services, the National Able Network, the National Asian Pacific Center on Aging, the National Caucus and Center on the Black Aged, the National Council on Aging, the National Indian Council on Aging, the National Urban League, Quality Career Services, SER-Jobs for Progress National, Senior Service America, Vermont Associates for Training and Development, and the WorkPlace (National Health Policy Forum, 2012).

OAA Title VI: Grants for Services for Native Americans

This title, added to the OAA in 1978, provides grants for Indian tribal organizations, Alaskan Native organizations, and nonprofit groups representing Native Hawaiians to develop supportive and nutrition services for older Native Americans. Supportive services include information and referral, transportation, and home assistance. In 2010, for example, grants for these services were awarded to 254 Indian tribal organizations and two Native Hawaiian organizations. Family caregiver grants were made to 219 Title VI organizations (National Health Policy Forum, 2012).

OAA Title VII: Vulnerable Elder Rights Protection Activities

Title VII was added to OAA in 1992. It authorizes the long-term care ombudsman program as well as a program to prevent elder abuse, neglect, and exploitation. The purpose of the long-term care ombudsman program is to investigate and resolve complaints of residents of nursing facilities, board and care facilities, and other adult care homes. It is the only OAA program that focuses solely on the needs of institutionalized people. Complaints may relate to action, inaction, or decisions of long-term care providers or their representatives that adversely affect the health, safety, welfare, or rights of residents. Other functions to be carried out by ombudsmen include representing the interests of residents before governmental agencies and seeking administrative and legal remedies to protect their rights. In 2010, approximately 1,200 paid ombudsmen were responsible for oversight of more than 69,000 residential care facilities, with a combined total of 2.9 million beds (National Health Policy Forum, 2012).

Under the elder abuse program, states are required to carry out activities to make the public aware of ways to identify and prevent abuse, neglect, and exploitation, and to coordinate activities of area agencies on aging with state adult protective services programs. Although funds are allocated to states based on the state's share of the older population, ombudsmen are to serve all populations in facilities, regardless of age.

Legal Assistance

Legal assistance and elder rights programs work in conjunction with other AoA programs and services to maximize the independence, autonomy, and well-being of older persons. Legal programs under Title VII, as well as Title III-B and Title IV, provide and enhance important protections for older people.

Title VII requires each state to appoint a legal assistance developer (LAD). Similar to a state long-term care ombudsman, the LAD is responsible for developing and coordinating the state's legal services and elder rights programs. Legal assistance provided under Title III-B protect older persons against direct challenges to their independence, choice, and financial security. Areas of legal service may include assistance in: accessing public benefits (e.g., Medicare, veterans benefits), drafting advance directives, dealing with issues related to guardianship, accessing available housing options, handling foreclosure or eviction proceedings that jeopardize independence, and advising on elder abuse issues, including fraud and financial exploitation.

Title IV authorizes the National Legal Resource Center and Model Approaches to Statewide Legal Assistance Systems. The National Legal Resource Center (NLRC) serves as a centralized access point for a national legal assistance support system serving professionals and advocates working in legal and aging services networks. Core support functions include:

- Case consultation, through the National Senior Citizens Law Center, to assist in resolving complex legal problems impacting older people;
- Training, through the National Consumer Law Center, on a wide range of legal and elder rights issues;
- Technical assistance in developing efficient and effective legal and aging service delivery systems, through the Center for Social Gerontology, and for legal helpline professionals, through the Center for Elder Rights Advocacy; and
- Information and resource development and dissemination through the American Bar Association's Commission on Law and Aging.

Model Approaches is a discretionary grant program designed to help states develop and implement cost-effective, replicable approaches to broaden and integrate state legal service networks. One effective approach is the use of legal hotlines or helplines, which also overcome the problem many older people have with transportation. In 2010, 29 states, Puerto Rico, and the District of Columbia had statewide legal hotlines (Center for Elder Rights Advocacy, 2011).

NEED AND UNMET NEED FOR SERVICES

Measuring need and unmet need for services is difficult. Despite AoA's support and technical assistance, requiring agencies to complete surveys can be complicated, costly, and once gathered, the resulting information may become outdated quickly. Furthermore, states differ in how they are structured and how they administer diverse funding for home- and community-based services. In some states, funding is administered across multiple agencies and the state office on aging may not have access to information on older adults receiving services from sister agencies. Nevertheless, in preparation for the reauthorization of OAA, the U.S. Senate's Special Committee on Aging asked the GAO to evaluate what is known about the need for home and community-based services such as those funded by OAA and the potential unmet need for these services. In response, the GAO (2011) analyzed data from a variety of national surveys (e.g., Current Population Survey, Health Retirement Study). It also conducted its own survey of 125 area agencies on aging, made site visits to four states, and interviewed additional state and national officials involved in Title III programs gathering information on requests for and use of services, use of funds, and the impact of the economic climate on requests and availability of Title III services.

Nutrition

Many low-income older adults who are likely to need meals programs do not receive them. For instance, an estimated 19% of low-income older adults are food insecure and about 90% of these individuals do not receive any meal services. A survey by the GAO found that about 22% of agencies are unable to serve all clients who request home-delivered meals and the agencies noted that many older adults who would benefit from meal services do not know that they exist or that they are eligible to receive them (GAO, 2011).

Assistance With Activities of Daily Living (ADLs)

The GAO has also determined that many older adults who have difficulties with daily activities receive limited or no home-based care. For example, among older adults with three or more difficulties with ADLs, 11% (more than a quarter of a million people) do not receive any help and 68% (2 million) receive only some help. In 80% of the cases where older adults receive some help, that help comes from family members. The available data do not allow an assessment of the extent to which the help received is sufficient to meet a senior's needs.

Transportation

Approximately 8 million older Americans are likely to need transportation services due to circumstances such as being unable to drive or not having access to a vehicle. People aged 80 or older, women, and those living below the poverty threshold are more likely to need these services. In a GAO (2011) survey, 62% of state and local agency officials reported that transportation is among the most requested support services, and that the unmet need is substantial. Analyzing data from several national surveys and databases, the American Public Transportation Association (2010) determined that only half to two thirds of the estimated need for transportation services is being met. In some communities, lack of funding limits transportation to only essential medical treatments such as dialysis.

The reality is that the resources of most programs and services are not adequate to meet the demands for them by the rapidly growing numbers of older adults. Blazer and Sachs-Ericsson (2005) demonstrated that inadequately met basic needs, such as food, housing, and transportation, are significant predictors of mortality in community-dwelling older adults. Individuals who experience problems in meeting basic needs are likely to have difficulties "obtaining needed health care, using social support networks, and maintaining a safe living environment" (p. 303).

Stretching Resources

The actual appropriations for all the titles of the OAA have always been well under 1% of the federal budget, a proverbial "drop in the bucket." Indeed, Torres-Gil (1992), in his book on public policy on aging, written prior to his becoming Assistant Secretary for Aging, questioned how so few dollars (relatively measured) in the hands of one small agency (AoA) within the mammoth Department of Health and Human Services could meet its goals. In FY2010, appropriations for the OAA totaled slightly more than one half of 1% of the federal budget—$2.328 billion out of a total budget of $3.6 trillion. Table 13.2 shows the distribution of funding for FY2012 among the titles of OAA.

TABLE 13.2 Older Americans Act Funding for Fiscal Year 2012

TITLE	SERVICES	PERCENT (%)	AMOUNT (MILLIONS)
II	Administration	1.4	$ 27.3
III	State & Community Programs	71.0	$ 1,358.0
IV	Health, Independence, Longevity	1.2	$ 23.6
V	Community Service Employment	23.4	$ 448.3
VI	Native American Services	1.8	$ 34.0
VII	Elder Rights Protection	1.1	$ 21.8

Source: O'Shaughnessy (2012).

Requests for all Title III services are dramatically up since the start of the Great Recession. Most agencies are scrambling for other funds and resources to at least maintain services, and to increase services where they can (GAO, 2011).

> State and local community agencies across the country actively seek additional funding, more than doubling the funding received through the OAA. In addition, states leverage those funds with a variety of other funding sources, such as Medicaid. These organizations make concerted efforts and difficult choices in targeting those older adults and family caregivers in greatest social and economic need. Despite these efforts, states report that across programs they are not able to serve all other individuals in need. States believe OAA administrative flexibility is one tool that assists them in maximizing their resources. (GAO, 2011, p. 98)

As a member of Nevada's Commission on Aging, one of this textbook's authors (JAS) marveled at the ingenuity and frugality of local agencies in meeting as many of the needs of seniors in their communities as possible. For example, many community agencies in Nevada garnered food donations, volunteer drivers, and donated vehicles to augment their meager funding for meal and transportation services.

In FY2009, on average, OAA funds comprised only 42% of local agencies' Title III program budgets (GAO, 2011). Other sources of funding for Title III services come from other federal sources, state and local budgets, private donors, and in-kind and voluntary contributions, sometimes even from the clients themselves. The current law prohibits mandatory fees, but providers are allowed to ask for voluntary contributions for those receiving nutrition and supportive services. It is important to note, though, that seniors cannot be denied any service because they will not or cannot make a contribution for a service.

Recognizing its enormous responsibilities and limited funding to carry them out, the AoA follows OAA guidelines that require programs to target or make it a priority to serve older adults with the greatest economic and social need. This has come to mean primarily low-income persons, minority older persons, residents of rural areas, and the frail elderly. As the OAA is designed to provide services to all older persons regardless of income and need, Torres-Gil (1992) has noted that targeting services without alienating healthier, active, affluent older persons is a real challenge.

The OAA has provided somewhat of a safety net for older adults, especially for those who may need the services that many state agencies and area agencies try to provide. Nevertheless, the provisions of the OAA continue to be overextended and underfunded. Every time the OAA is reauthorized more responsibilities are added to AoA's portfolio without the increases in funding that would reasonably permit those responsibilities to be fully carried out. And, the number of older adults eligible for services is growing by leaps and bounds—every day 10,000 more Americans become eligible as they turn 60 years of age.

SENIOR CORPS: VOLUNTEER PROGRAMS FOR OLDER ADULTS

Many seniors certainly need the services that state agencies and area agencies on aging try to provide. Yet, it is also the case that a large proportion of older adults want to give back to their communities. There is no shortage of needs for their contributions. Of course, any individual can seek out ways to volunteer, but for older adults Senior Corps provides a means of easily finding and exploring options, and includes some perks, such as training and sometimes reimbursement for expenses such as transportation to volunteer sites.

Senior Corps is a program of the Corporation for National and Community Service, an independent federal agency created in 1993 to connect Americans of all ages and backgrounds with opportunities to give back to their communities and their nation. Senior Corps incorporated three long-standing programs—RSVP, the Foster Grandparent Program (FGP), and the Senior Companion Program (SCP)—that have linked Americans aged 55 and over with the people and organizations in their communities that need them most.

RSVP

Established in 1971 and now one of the largest senior volunteer organizations in the nation, RSVP offers a variety of volunteer opportunities to persons 55 years of age and older to share their knowledge, experiences, abilities, and skills for the betterment of their communities and themselves. These volunteers serve in many areas including youth counseling, literacy enhancement, refugee assistance, consumer education, crime prevention, housing rehabilitation, after-school programs, and respite care for older adults. Volunteers choose how, where, and how often they want to serve, with commitments ranging from a few hours to 40 hours per week. RSVP is open to all people ages 55 and over. Volunteers do not receive monetary incentives, but sponsoring organizations may reimburse them for some costs incurred during their service, including meals and transportation.

The Foster Grandparent Program

The Foster Grandparent Program (FGP), which began in 1965, provides loving and experienced tutors and mentors to children and youth with special needs that limit their academic, social, or emotional development. Working one-on-one and serving between 15 and 40 hours a week, Foster Grandparents provide support in schools, hospitals, drug treatment centers, correctional institutions, and child care centers. Among other activities, they review schoolwork, reinforce values, and care for premature infants and children with disabilities. Volunteers must be 55 years of age or older. Those who meet low-income guidelines receive a small stipend. All FGP volunteers receive accident and liability insurance and meals while on duty, reimbursement for transportation, and monthly training.

TABLE 13.3 Senior Volunteer Programs

	RSVP	FOSTER GRANDPARENTS PROGRAM	SENIOR COMPANIONS PROGRAM
Volunteers	296,100	27,900	13,600
Hours Served	60 million	24 million	12.2 million
Clients Served	837,000	232,300	60,940
Federal Funding	$50.2 million	$110.7 million	$46.8 million
Nonfederal Support	$42.9 million	$33 million	$22.9 million

Notes: Clients served by RSVP volunteers include 65,000 organizations, 96,000 children, and 676,000 frail elderly people. Statistical data from FY2010 and 2011. Federal funding shown was enacted for FY2012.

Source: Senior Corps (http://www.seniorcorps.gov)

The Senior Companion Program

The Senior Companion Program, which began in 1974, helps frail seniors and other adults maintain independence, primarily in the clients' own homes, and enables seniors to return to home care settings after hospitalization or rehabilitation. Senior companions serve between 15 and 40 hours a week and typically assist between two and four clients. Among other activities, they help with daily living tasks, such as grocery shopping; provide friendship and companionship; alert health care professionals and family members to potential problems; and, provide respite to family caregivers. Volunteers must be 55 years of age or over. Those who meet low-income guidelines receive a small stipend. All SCP volunteers receive accident and liability insurance and meals while on duty, reimbursement for transportation, and monthly training.

Through these three formal volunteer programs, each year more than 330,000 seniors contribute more than 96 million hours of service. Based on the estimated value of volunteer time —$21.79 per hour in 2011, according to the Independent Sector, (http://independentsector.org/volunteer_time) a coalition of charities, foundations, corporations, and individuals—seniors' volunteer service is worth over $2 billion to the U.S. economy. Table 13.3 gives details on the number of volunteers in each program, the number of clients served, and funding.

SUGGESTED RESOURCES

Eldercare Locator: http://www.eldercare.gov
> A public service of the Administration on Aging, this website connects older Americans and their caregivers with information on a wide variety of senior services, ranging from Alzheimer's to volunteerism. The ability to search by zip code or city/state makes it easy to find local help.

National Association of Area Agencies on Aging: http://www.n4a.org
> This Association supports the national network of AAAs and Title VI Native American aging programs, offering advocacy, training, and technical assistance. The website includes a directory through which all AAAs and Title VI agencies can be located.

National Association of Professional Geriatric Care Managers: http://www.caremanager.org/
> NAPGCM is an association with more than 2,000 members who provide a range of services for older adults, which may include assessment, support, and referrals for individuals and

families. In addition to a wealth of information about geriatric care management, the website has an asy-to-use feature to search for care managers by geographic region.

National Association of States United for Aging and Disabilities: http://www.nasuad.org

This Association, representing all 56 state and territorial agencies, seeks to design, improve, and sustain the delivery of home- and community-based services for older adults and individuals with disabilities. It provides many resources and information for these agencies, most of which is freely available to the public on their website.

Senior Corps: http://www.seniorcorps.gov/

Senior Corps connects today's 55+ with the people and organizations that need them most. Volunteers receive guidance and training in three programs: Foster Grandparent Program, Senior Companion Program, and RSVP.

CHAPTER 14

Medical Care, Medicare, and Medications

The learning objectives of this chapter include understanding

- The importance of health professionals being well versed in geriatrics, the medical treatment of older people.
- The major shift in the leading causes of death over the last 100 years, from acute to chronic health conditions, and the most common chronic conditions that older adults experience.
- Vision diseases and sleep disorders that can accompany aging.
- Basic facts about Medicare: who gets it, what it does and does not cover, and what it costs.
- The challenges for older adults of managing medications.

EVERYBODY IS A LITTLE DIFFERENT—EVEN THE OLD

Peter is 86 and is beginning to develop glaucoma. He needs assistance in using the drops that he says he has to put into his eyes several times a day to reduce the pressure on his optic nerve. In addition, he suffers from diabetes, which has resulted in severe pains in his legs because of inadequate circulation. He also has congestive heart failure, and as a result is frequently tired because of a lack of blood being pumped by his failing heart. Through all of these physical difficulties, Peter remains in his own home because of the assistance of his 79-year-old wife and daily visits from a nurse.

Jennifer is 78 and suffers from osteoporosis. She has a "widow's hump," a curvature of the spine caused by deteriorating vertebrae, which makes her walk with a stoop. Her spine is forcing her upper body to curve outward, bending her head and neck down. She is worried about falling and breaking her hip, as happened last year to her 83-year-old sister. Her physician has told her that she must be very careful because her bones are very brittle.

When it comes to aging, medical care quickly becomes one of the most important issues facing people. This is particularly true for those in the two groups of the elderly that include the more advanced years—the aged (75–84 years) and the oldest-old (85 years and older), who are less likely that the young-old (aged 65–74 years) to retain excellent health and independent functioning. As people grow older, they are more likely to have health conditions that require attention and that hinder their ability to perform the daily tasks of living. And yet, the number of health care providers prepared to deal with a growing population of older Americans is woefully inadequate, as pointed out by a key report from the Institute of Medicine (IOM, 2008), entitled *Retooling for An Aging America: Building the Health Care Workforce*. In addition to recruiting and retaining more health care specialists in aging and more caregivers, the report concluded that, "all licensure, certification, and maintenance of certification for health care professionals should include demonstration of competence in the care of older adults as a criterion" (p. 161).

As an example of the inadequacy of the health care workforce, according to the IOM report there are only 7,100 physicians trained in geriatrics, the branch of medicine that focuses on older adults and their care, to serve an elderly population of more than 40 million. To serve only a slightly larger population of children, the American Academy of Pediatrics reports there are approximately 60,000 pediatricians. A true primary-care specialty, geriatrics includes hospital care, office care, house-call medicine, day care, and nursing home care. Because geriatricians are trained to look at the whole person, they are able to differentiate between diseases and normal physiological aging processes, to manage symptoms that stem from multiple diseases, and to develop an appropriate care plan for each patient, a plan that can minimize emergency care and potentially avoid placement in an institution. Unless health care professionals go into pediatrics, a substantial proportion of their patients will be over the age of 65 once they begin practicing.

CHRONIC AND ACUTE HEALTH CONDITIONS

Improved medical care and prevention efforts have contributed to dramatic increases in life expectancy in the United States during the past century. They have also produced a major shift in the leading causes of death for all age groups, from infectious diseases and acute illnesses to chronic diseases and degenerative illnesses. Acute conditions are those that are expected to be of limited duration, and can range from simple bruises to heart attacks, pneumonia, or broken bones. They often require a hospital stay. Chronic conditions are those that are expected to be long-term and most often permanent, and may or may not require hospital stays. They include heart disease, high blood pressure, chronic obstructive pulmonary disease (COPD), diabetes, arthritis, hearing loss, and vision impairment. Chronic conditions are the leading causes of death for Americans aged 65 and older. Heart diseases (28.3% of all deaths), malignant neoplasms (cancers, 22.2%), cerebrovascular diseases (stroke, 6.6%), and chronic lower respiratory disease (6.2%) together account for 63% of all deaths in this age group (Heron, 2011).

Some chronic conditions can become disabling, threatening the person's well-being and independence. That is why it is important to learn and practice self-management procedures that can improve health outcomes and quality of life. Dr. Kate Lorig and her team at Stanford University have developed a Chronic Disease Self-Management Program (CDSMP, Stanford Patient Education Research Center, n.d.) that focuses on building problem-solving and coping skills as well as support to help people manage their own chronic conditions. CDSMP has been found to result in positive health outcomes and lower health care costs for people with a variety of chronic conditions, including arthritis, diabetes, and heart disease (Gordon & Galloway, 2007). Howard Falvey enrolled in a program.

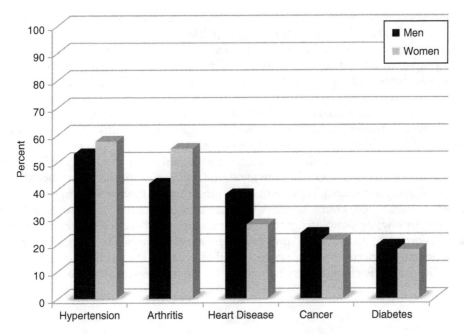

FIGURE 14.1 Percentage of People Age 65 and Over Who Reported Having Selected Chronic Health Conditions, by Sex, 2007–2008.

Note: Data are based on a 2-year average from 2007–2008.

Reference population: These data refer to the civilian noninstitutionalized population.

Source: Adapted from *Older Americans 2010*, Table 16a.

Now 64, he learned to control his diabetes without medication by adopting a healthier diet and exercising more frequently. "I learned to take charge of my own health....A doctor can't do that for you," he said (cited in Tergesen, 2012, p. R9). The National Council on Aging is leading a Self-Management Alliance to promote collaboration among government, business, and nonprofit organizations to make self-management an integral part of health care for people with multiple chronic conditions by 2020. Currently, 80% of older Americans are living with at least one chronic condition, and 50% have at least two such conditions. The top five chronic conditions of older adults and the percentage of people age 65 and over who report having them are depicted in Figure 14.1.

Hypertension and Stroke

People can have hypertension (high blood pressure) and still feel just fine. That's because signs of hypertension cannot be seen or felt. But, hypertension, sometimes called "the silent killer," is a major health problem. If it is not controlled with lifestyle changes or medicine, or both, it can lead to stroke, heart disease, eye problems, or kidney failure.

Blood pressure is the force of blood pushing against the walls of arteries. When blood pressure is measured, the results are given in two numbers. The first number, called *systolic pressure*, measures the pressure of the heartbeat. The second number, called *diastolic pressure*, measures the pressure while the heart relaxes between beats. Target blood pressure rates for older adults should be less than 140/90 mmHg, a rate that is a little higher than for level for younger adults, which is 120/80 mmHg (Aronow et al., 2011).

Anyone can get hypertension, but some people have a greater chance of having it, and one risk factor is age—the chance of having high blood pressure increases over time.

Hypertension is one of the main risk factors for stroke. In 2008, 114,508 people aged 65 years and over, died from a stroke (National Center for Health Statistics, 2012). A stroke, sometimes called a brain attack, occurs when a clot blocks the blood supply to part of the brain or when a blood vessel in or around the brain bursts. In either case, parts of the brain become damaged or die. The chances of survival and recovery are higher the faster emergency treatment takes place. Recovery can take months or years, and many people who have had a stroke never fully recover.

The good news is that blood pressure can be controlled in most people. To start, there are many lifestyle changes that can lower the risk, including: keeping a healthy body weight; exercising for at least 30 minutes a day most days of the week; eating a diet rich in fruits, vegetables, whole grains, and low-fat dairy products; cutting down on salt; keeping alcohol intake low; not smoking; and managing stress. If these lifestyle changes do not work well enough to control blood pressure, there are medications that can. These medications do not cure hypertension, so if necessary, they will need to be taken for the rest of the person's life. Lifestyle changes may help lower the dose of medication needed.

Arthritis

Arthritis is a disease that can attack joints in almost any part of the body, causing them to be painful and stiff. Some types of arthritis cause changes that can be seen and felt—swelling, warmth, and redness in joints—and may only last a short time, but be very uncomfortable, or there may be less pain, though joints are still being slowly damaged. Older people most often have one of three types of arthritis: osteoarthritis, rheumatoid arthritis, and gout.

Osteoarthritis starts when cartilage that pads bones in a joint begins to wear away. Once the cartilage has worn away, bones rub against each other. Osteoarthritis mostly occurs in the hands, neck, lower back, or the large weight-bearing joints of the body, such as knees and hips. Symptoms range from stiffness and mild pain that comes and goes to pain that does not stop, even when the person is resting or sleeping. Sometimes osteoarthritis causes joints to feel stiff after the person has not moved them for a while, for example, after riding in a car. The stiffness goes away when the joints are moved. Over time, however, osteoarthritis can make it hard to move joints, and it can cause disability if the back, knees, or hips are affected. Growing older is what most often puts people at risk for osteoarthritis, possibly because joints and the cartilage around them become less able to recover from stress and damage. Also, osteoarthritis in the hands may run in families. In the knees it is linked with being overweight, and in the knees, hips, or hands, it may be due to injuries or overuse.

Rheumatoid arthritis is an autoimmune disease, a type of illness in which the body attacks itself. It causes pain, swelling, and stiffness that lasts for hours (or longer), and it can happen in many different joints at the same time. While rheumatoid arthritis can damage almost any joint, it often occurs in the same joint on both sides of the body. It can also cause problems with the heart, muscles, blood vessels, nervous system, and eyes.

Gout is one of the most painful kinds of arthritis. It usually happens in the big toes, but other joints can also be affected. Swelling many cause the skin to pull tightly around a joint and make the area red or purple and very tender. Learning what brings on the attacks can help prevent future attacks. Eating foods rich in purines, such as liver and dried beans, can lead to a gout attack. Using alcohol and being overweight may make gout worse. Some blood pressure medications can also increase the chance of a gout attack.

The primary goals of treatment for arthritis are to prevent joint damage, manage pain, and maintain physical functioning in order to preserve a good quality of life. Getting enough rest; doing the right exercises; eating a healthy, well-balanced diet; and learning the right way to use and protect joints are keys to living with any kind of arthritis. Three types of exercises are best for arthritis: range-of-motion exercises, such as dancing, which relieves stiffness, maintains flexibility, and keeps joints moving; strengthening exercises, such as weight training, which enhances muscle strength to support and protect joints; and, aerobic or endurance exercises, such as bicycle riding, which make the heart and arteries healthier, help prevent weight gain, and may also lessen swelling in some joints. The National Institute on Aging has a free booklet, entitled *Workout to Go*, on how to start and stick with a safe exercise program. (It can be downloaded at www.nia.nih.gov/ health/publication.)

Along with exercise and weight control, there are other ways to ease the pain around joints. Examples include using a heating pad or cold pack, soaking in a warm bath, or swimming in a heated pool. The right shoes and a cane can help with pain in the feet, knees, and hips when walking. There are also gadgets to help with opening jars or turning doorknobs, for example. Some medicines can help with pain and swelling. When damage to joints becomes disabling or when other treatments do not help with pain, health care providers may suggest surgery to repair or replace affected joints with artificial ones. Pain and arthritis do not have to be part of growing older. Pain and stiffness can be lessened and more serious damage to joints prevented by working with health care professionals.

Heart Disease

The term *heart disease* actually refers to several types of heart conditions. The most common type in the United States is coronary artery disease (CAD), which can cause heart attacks, chest pain or discomfort (also called *angina*), heart failure, and arrhythmias. CAD happens when the arteries that supply blood to the heart muscle become hardened and narrowed due to atherosclerosis, the build up of cholesterol and plaque on the inner walls of arteries. It affects men and women equally.

Risk factors for heart disease include high cholesterol, hypertension, diabetes, cigarette smoking, being overweight or obese, poor diet, physical inactivity, and alcohol use. Risk can be determined by checking cholesterol, blood pressure, and blood glucose, and by examining family history of heart disease. The five major symptoms of a heart attack are pain in the jaw, neck, or back; feeling weak, lightheaded, or faint; chest pain or discomfort; pain or discomfort in the arms or shoulder; and shortness of breath (Roger et al., 2012).

For those who already have CAD, there are steps to take to lower the risk of worsening heart disease or of having a heart attack. Lifestyle changes such as eating a healthier diet, exercising, and not smoking are recommended. Medications may also be necessary. Prescription medications can treat risk factors such as high cholesterol, hypertension, an irregular heartbeat, and low blood flow. In some cases, more advanced treatments and surgical procedures can help restore blood flow to the heart.

Preventing or reducing risks of heart disease comes down to living a healthy lifestyle. A healthy diet, including plenty of fresh fruit and vegetables and foods low in saturated fat and cholesterol and high in fiber, can prevent high blood cholesterol. Limiting salt or sodium can lower blood pressure. Maintaining a healthy weight and engaging in moderate-intensity exercise for at least 30 minutes on most days of the week are also helpful, as are not smoking and limiting alcohol use.

Cancer

Cancer is not just one disease, but many diseases in which the genetic material in cells becomes damaged or changed for a variety of reasons, some of which are known (such as environmental toxins, radiation, and excessive alcohol intake), and others of which are not. Abnormal cells divide without control and are able to invade other tissues (National Cancer Institute, 2012). Due to advances in early detection and treatment, people are living many years after a diagnosis of cancer. Approximately 63% of people diagnosed with cancer live for at least 5 years after diagnosis, and more than 50% live at least 20 years (Keating, Norredam, Landrum, Huskamp, & Meara, 2005). As a consequence, what was once thought to be a death sentence is increasingly viewed as a chronic condition.

A majority of cancers (78%) are diagnosed in people aged 55 years and older, and breast, cervical, colorectal, and prostate cancers are the most common types in older adults (Alibhai, 2006). The Centers for Disease Control and Prevention supports comprehensive cancer control programs throughout the country. These programs provide an integrated and coordinated approach to reducing the incidence of cancer, morbidity, and mortality through prevention, early detection, treatment, and rehabilitation. These efforts encourage healthy lifestyles, promote recommended cancer screening guidelines and tests, increase access to quality cancer care, and improve quality of life for cancer survivors.

The number of new cancer cases could be reduced, and many cancer deaths could be prevented with early screening, especially for individuals at increased risk. Screening for cervical and colorectal cancers helps prevent these diseases by finding precancerous lesions so the lesions can be treated before they become cancerous. Screening for breast cancer also helps identify the disease at an early, often highly treatable stage. A person's cancer risk can also be reduced by receiving regular medical attention, avoiding tobacco, limiting alcohol use, avoiding excessive exposure to ultraviolet rays from the sun and tanning beds, eating a diet rich in fruits and vegetables, maintaining a healthy weight, and being physically active. In some cases, vaccines can help reduce cancer risk; for example, the human papillomavirus vaccine (HPV) helps prevent most cervical cancers and some vaginal and vulvar cancers, if administered in young adulthood. Making cancer screening, information, and referral services available and accessible to all Americans can reduce cancer incidence and deaths.

Type 2 Diabetes

Type 2 diabetes, also called adult-onset diabetes or diabetes mellitus, is the most prevalent type of diabetes, and results from difficulties in insulin production or action, or both. Diabetes can lead to serious complications and premature death. It can also be prevented, and those with diabetes can take steps to control the disease and lower the risk of complications. Black Americans, Hispanic/Latino Americans, American Indians, and some Asian Americans and native Hawaiians or other Pacific Islanders are at particularly high risk for type 2 diabetes and its complications. Among adults 65 years of age and older, 18.6%, have this type of diabetes (*Older Americans 2010*).

Diabetes can lead to serious complications, such as blindness, kidney damage, cardiovascular disease, and lower limb amputations. Controlling blood glucose, blood pressure, and blood lipids can lower the occurrence of these complications. Many people with type 2 diabetes can control their blood glucose by following a healthy meal plan and exercise program, losing excess weight, and taking oral medication. Others may also need insulin to control their blood glucose or medications to control their cholesterol and blood pressure.

Prediabetes is a condition in which blood glucose levels are higher than normal but not high enough to be classified as diabetes. People with prediabetes have an increased risk of developing type 2 diabetes, heart disease, and stroke. Studies have shown that losing weight and increasing physical activity can delay, or even prevent, the onset of diabetes and return blood glucose levels to normal. In a large prevention study of adults 60 years and older at high risk for diabetes, the Diabetes Prevention Program Research Group (2002) showed that over a three-year period, lifestyle interventions reduced the development of diabetes by 71%.

Osteoporosis

Another chronic condition that is of great concern, especially for older women, is osteoporosis. Osteoporosis, or "porous bone," is a disease of the skeletal system characterized by low bone mass and deterioration of bone tissue. It leads to an increased risk of bone fractures, typically in the wrist, hip, and spine. Bone mass declines with age, especially among White Caucasian women after menopause. In 2008, among the 65+ population, 26% of women and 4% of men reported having osteoporosis (*Older Americans 2010*). To maintain bone health throughout life, it is important to reach peak bone mass—the genetic potential for bone density—in early adulthood. People with high bone mass when they are young will be more likely to have a high bone mass later in life. Inadequate calcium consumption and a low level of physical activity early in life could result in a failure to achieve peak bone mass in adulthood.

One of the major worries of people with osteoporosis is falling, which can lead to devastating consequences. Fall-related injuries cause significant disability, loss of independence, early admission to nursing homes, and death. Each year as many as 12 million older adults experience a fall, and 2.6 million of those falls lead to some kind of medical attention, most frequently for fractures. Research has shown that medication management, tai chi (to improve balance), vitamin D supplements, and home modifications, such as removing hazards and installing safety features, can prevent many falls (Frick, Kung, Parrish, & Narrett, 2010).

Eye Diseases

A few serious conditions affecting vision can develop more readily in older people—macular degeneration, glaucoma, and retinopathy. Early detection can make a difference in the progression and prognosis for these conditions.

Age-Related Macular Degeneration

A leading cause of severe vision loss in adults over age 60 in the United States, age-related macular degeneration (AMD) occurs when the small central portion of the retina, known as the macula, deteriorates. The macula is the most important region of the eye because it is packed with light receptors that make focused, precise vision possible, such as that needed for reading, driving, sewing, and similar tasks. AMD can be detected during a comprehensive eye exam that includes a visual acuity test, which measures vision at various distances; a dilated eye exam, during which the pupils are dilated and the retina and optic nerve are examined; and tonometry, which measures pressure inside the eye. The causes of AMD are unknown, though some risk factors, such as smoking, obesity, hypertension, and family history, have been identified. There is no cure, but treatment may prevent severe vision loss or slow the progression of the disease. Treatments include laser therapy, drugs, and low vision aids. Researchers are currently investigating new surgical treatments and the use of stem cells too.

Glaucoma

Glaucoma is a group of diseases that can damage the eye's optic nerve, resulting in vision loss and blindness. The risk is much greater for people over age 60, though it can occur in younger people. It also occurs more frequently in Black Americans and Mexican Americans, and in those with a family history of the condition. For reasons that are still unknown, excess pressure builds up in the eye because fluid (aqueous humor) drains too slowly out of one or both eyes. Without treatment, people with glaucoma slowly lose their peripheral vision. Over time, straight-ahead vision may decrease, too, until no vision remains.

Although glaucoma cannot be prevented, regular eye check-ups are important because there are usually no early symptoms or pain, and the sooner glaucoma is diagnosed and treated, the better the outcome. In addition to the vision tests for macular degeneration, glaucoma is diagnosed with two additional tests: a visual field test, which measures peripheral vision, and pachymetry, which measures the cornea's thickness. Prescription eye drops or pills and laser surgery are the most common treatments.

Retinopathy

Retinopathy is a disease of the retina, the light-sensitive membrane at the back of the eye, that can also lead to poor vision and even blindness. Weakening blood vessels lead to blood leaking into the front of the retina, formation of scar tissue, and retinal detachment, as well as swelling of the macula. Causes include arteriosclerosis, diabetes, and hypertension so controlling cholesterol, blood sugar, and blood pressure can help prevent retinopathy. A dilated eye exam can detect retinopathy. With early detection, new laser treatments can minimize loss of vision, otherwise surgery can stabilize vision.

Sleep Disorders

Four sleep disorders are more common among older people: insomnia, circadian rhythm disorders, sleep apnea, and leg movements, though, according to renowned sleep researcher, Dr. Sonia Ancoli-Israel (2004), none are inextricably connected to healthy aging. Insomnia affects up to half of the older population. It occurs when a person has trouble falling asleep or staying asleep. There are many possible causes of insomnia, including changes in personal circumstances (losing a loved one, relocating), which may result in a temporary bout of insomnia, or pain associated with conditions such as arthritis or heartburn, which often leads to chronic insomnia. In addition, many medications produce insomnia. Alcohol can contribute to insomnia, too. A common belief is that drinking alcohol helps a person to fall asleep, which is true, but the problem is that a few hours later, it wakes the person up. Treatment for insomnia, of course, will depend on its cause, so it can range from counseling to pharmacotherapy.

Circadian rhythm disorders are another source of poor sleep. Older adults may not get a full night's sleep if they fight age-related changes in circadian rhythms that make them sleepy earlier in the evening and cause them to wake about eight hours after that sleepiness sets in. Naps in the early evening can also disrupt sleep/wake cycles. Exposure to bright light, from the sun or bright light boxes, late in the day or early evening is effective in resetting circadian rhythms.

Sleep apnea, or sleep-disordered breathing, is usually a chronic condition that disrupts sleep because it causes periodic pauses in breathing or shallow breaths. Symptoms include loud snoring and excessive daytime sleepiness. Untreated sleep apnea can increase the risk of hypertension, heart attack, and stroke, as well as accidents. Continuous positive airway pressure (CPAP), in which a device uses mild air pressure to keep the airways open during sleep, is the treatment of choice. Some people with sleep apnea can benefit from weight loss (if they are overweight or obese), avoiding alcohol, or even sleeping on their sides rather than on their backs.

Movement disorders, typically periodic involuntary leg movements during sleep, can involve as many as three movements per minute and, like sleep apnea, they disrupt sleep and result in daytime sleepiness. Up to 45% of older people suffer from some type of periodic leg movement problems. Although there are no cures for these disorders, medications are available to treat symptoms (Ancoli-Israel, 2004).

MEDICARE: HEALTH INSURANCE FOR OLDER ADULTS

Medicare is the nation's health insurance program for individuals aged 65 and over and certain disabled persons. Before Medicare was passed in 1965 and went into effect in 1966, approximately one in three older adults was living in poverty. That proportion has declined precipitously to less than one in 10 older people living in poverty (*A Profile of Older Americans 2011*). A part of President Lyndon Johnson's Great Society, Medicare goes a long way towards protecting the finances of older people and their families. Access to health care services is provided through Medicare's four distinct parts: Part A (Hospital Insurance), Part B (Medical Insurance), Part C (Medicare Advantage), and Part D (Prescription Drug Benefit).

Who Gets Medicare?

Medicare is an intergenerational program. To qualify for Medicare, a person must meet one of these eligibility requirements: be 65 years of age or older; be under age 65 with certain disabilities; or, be of any age with end-stage renal disease (kidney failure requiring dialysis or a kidney transplant), or ALS (amyotrophic lateral sclerosis, *Lou Gehrig's disease*). According to the 2012 annual report of the Medicare Board of Trustees (2012), 48.7 million people were enrolled in Medicare in 2011, 40.4 million older adults (aged 65 and over), and 8.3 milllion people with disabilities. Older adults who are receiving benefits from Social Security automatically get a Medicare card in the mail 3 months prior to their 65th birthday. Those who have not applied for Social Security benefits (e.g., because they are still working) need to sign up 3 months prior to turning age 65. Medicare's success is demonstrated in the 97% of older adults who reported in 2010 that they had a usual place to go for medical care, with only 3% saying that they failed to obtain needed medical care due to financial barriers. With 93% of the nation's noninstitutionalized persons aged 65 and older enrolled in Medicare in 2010 (*A Profile of Older Americans 2011*), the program's importance to the health of older Americans is clear.

Medicare Part A: Hospital Insurance

Part A of Medicare is hospital insurance that helps cover inpatient care in hospitals, skilled nursing care, home health care, and hospice. Most people do not pay a monthly premium to receive Part A benefits because they or their spouse paid Medicare taxes while employed for 40 or more quarters. People who do not meet this criterion may be able to pay for Part A coverage with a monthly premium ($451 in 2012). Medicare Part A benefits in 2012 are listed in Table 14.1.

TABLE 14.1 Medicare Part A Benefits 2012

HOSPITAL CARE	Inpatient hospital services & supplies (semi-private rooms, general nursing, meals, drugs); inpatient mental health care with 190-day lifetime limit.
	Days 1–60: $ 1,156 deductible
	Days 61–90: $ 289/day
	Days 91–150: $578/day*
	Days 150+: all costs
SKILLED NURSING FACILITY CARE	Skilled nursing & rehabilitative services; supplies. After 3 days or more of hospital stay.
	Days 1–20: no cost
	Days 21–100: $144/day
	Days 100+: all costs
HOME HEALTH SERVICES	Part-time skilled nursing care; physical & occupational therapy, speech-language pathology services, medical supplies, durable medical equipment. Must be homebound.
	Covered services: no cost
	Medical equipment: 20% coinsurance
HOSPICE CARE	Medical, nursing, & social services; drugs for pain relief & symptom management; some durable equipment; spiritual & grief counseling; inpatient respite care. For those with certified terminal illness & 6 or fewer months to live.
	Hospice care: no cost
	Prescriptions: $5 copayment each
	Respite care: 5% coinsurance

Note: All Medicare Part A services must be medically necessary.

*Days 91–150 are lifetime reserve days, a total of 60 additional days that can be used during a lifetime.

Medicare Part B: Medical Insurance

Part B of Medicare is a voluntary program for Part A recipients. Most older people choose to enroll. In 2012, enrollees paid a $140 annual deductible and a monthly premium of $99.90 (the standard for individuals who earn $85,000 or less, and joint tax filers who earn $170,000 or less; the premium for higher income consumers may be higher). For those who choose Part B, the premium is usually deducted from monthly Social Security benefits. Part B benefits in 2012 are listed in Table 14.2. Passage of the Affordable Care Act added free annual wellness check-ups and most of the preventive services as new benefits for Part B enrollees. Details about how often these services are covered and costs that may be associated with them, as well as updates on coverage, are available through Medicare's website (www.medicare.gov).

Medicare Part C: Medicare Advantage Plans

Medicare Parts A and B comprise what is called, *Original Medicare*. Original Medicare is a traditional fee-for-service (or pay-per-visit) coverage under which Medicare funds are used to pay health care providers directly for Part A and Part B benefits. Beneficiaries can go to any hospital, physician, or other health care provider who accepts Medicare. On the other hand, Part C plans, or Medicare Advantage plans, are offered by private companies that contract with Medicare to deliver Part A and Part B benefits, along with other coverage if they so choose, to those who enroll with them. Most plans also cover prescription

TABLE 14.2 Medicare Part B Benefits 2012

MEDICALLY NECESSARY SERVICES	Physician, ambulance, emergency department services; some physical & occupational therapy, & speech-language pathology services; cardiac & pulmonary rehabilitation; outpatient chemotherapy; supplies (e.g., for diabetes).
	20% coinsurance
DIAGNOSTIC TESTS & LABORATORY SERVICES	Diagnostic tests: CT scans, MRIs, EKGs, X-rays; lab services: certain blood tests, urinalysis, some screening tests.
	Diagnostic tests: 20% coinsurance
	Lab tests: no cost
HOME HEALTH SERVICES	Part-time skilled nursing care; physical & occupational therapy, speech-language pathology services, medical supplies, durable medical equipment. Must be homebound.
	Covered services: no cost
	Medical equipment: 20% coinsurance
OUTPATIENT MENTAL HEALTH CARE	Visits with a mental health care professional in office setting, clinic, or outpatient department for counseling or psychotherapy.
	Most services: 40% coinsurance (20% by 2014)
PREVENTIVE SERVICES	
Wellness visits:	*Welcome to Medicare* preventive visit within 12 months of enrolling; annual wellness visits thereafter
Vaccinations:	Flu (annual), hepatitis B, pneumonia
Screenings:	Abdominal aortic aneurysm, bone mass, cancer (breast, cervical, colorectal, prostate, vaginal), cardiovascular, diabetes, glaucoma, HIV, depression
Other services:	Screening & counseling for obesity, sexually transmitted infections; counseling for alcohol misuse & smoking cessation; medical nutrition therapy
	No cost for any of preventive services listed above.

drugs (Part D). The four types of Medicare Advantage plans are: HMO (health maintenance organization), local PPO (preferred provider organization), regional PPO coordinated care plans, and PFFS (private fee-for-service) plans. These plans can determine their own rules for providing services, for example, whether enrollees must have a referral to see a specialist, or whether they are restricted to using only those health care providers, facilities, or suppliers that "belong" to the plan's network of providers. Monthly premiums, deductibles, copayments or coinsurance, and limits on out-of-pocket costs are determined by each plan. In 2011, approximately 25% of Medicare beneficiaries chose to enroll in Medicare Advantage plans (Medicare Board of Trustees, 2012). One of the ways the Affordable Care Act contains Medicare costs is by shifting "from a policy that favors private plans [Medicare Advantage plans] relative to original FFS [fee-for-service] Medicare by providing subsidies of over $11 billion a year to one that treats private plans neutrally by paying plans nationwide at rates similar to average costs in the FSS Medicare program" (Biles & Arnold, 2010, p. 9).

Medicare Part D: Prescription Drug Coverage

The *Medicare Prescription Drug, Improvement, and Modernization Act of 2003* (MMA, P.L.108–173) established a new, voluntary prescription drug benefit under a new Medicare Part D, effective January 1, 2006. Up to that time, a lack of public and private insurance coverage for drugs and rapidly increasing drug prices had resulted in millions of older Americans not getting the prescription drugs needed to maintain their lives. Many seniors were forced to choose between buying enough food and paying for their prescriptions.

The Part D program helps cover the cost of prescription drugs. In general, to obtain their drug benefits, seniors must enroll in a plan when they first become eligible for Medicare, or pay a delayed enrollment surcharge that is effective for the entire time individuals are enrolled in Part D, usually for the rest of their lives. All plans must meet certain minimum requirements, but there are significant differences among them in terms of which drugs are covered and the costs (deductible, monthly premiums, and copayments/coinsurance). About 5% of Part D enrollees—people with individual incomes above $85,000 or joint incomes above $170,000—pay an income-related monthly adjustment amount in addition to their plan's premium. Some Medicare drug plans have a coverage gap (also called the *donut hole*), which, through the Affordable Care Act of 2010 initiated by President Barack Obama, will be decreasing until it is closed by 2020. This gap means that after the beneficiary and their drug plan have spent a certain amount of money for covered drugs, the beneficiary has to pay the full costs of their prescriptions up to an out-of-pocket spending limit ($4,700 in 2012). Thereafter, Medicare covers all drug costs for the rest of the year.

Medicare drug plans must also cover all commercially available vaccines (such as the shingles vaccine), except for those already covered by Part B. Medicare Part D enrollees may also be eligible to participate in a Medication Therapy Management (MTM) program. MTM programs include a free discussion and review of all a senior's medications by a pharmacist or other health professional to help achieve the most benefit from the medications.

Plans can change from year to year and individuals' needs may also change. To ensure that their plans continue to meet their needs, seniors should review them annually and switch plans or make adjustments to them during the open enrollment period from October 15th to December 7th. Many states and the U.S. Virgin Islands offer help in paying for drug plan premiums or other drug costs, or both. Information about these State Pharmacy Assistance Programs can be found at https://www.medicare.gov/pharmaceutical-assistance-program/state-programs.aspx

What Does Medicare Not Cover?

Medicare covers many health care expenditures, but it emphasizes acute care and does not cover everything. Among the services and items not covered are:

- Routine eye exams, hearing exams, dental care, and foot care (the latter may be covered for certain conditions, e.g., diabetes);
- Eyeglasses and contact lenses (except after cataract surgery), hearing aids and fittings, and most dental procedures (e.g., cleanings, fillings, tooth extractions, or dentures);
- Nursing home care or long-term care, private duty nurses, and custodial care (nonskilled personal care to help with activities of daily living), except for limited skilled nursing facility care under certain conditions; and,
- Health care outside the United States (with very limited exceptions).

In addition to assistance being available over the phone (1–800-MEDICARE) and online (www.medicare.gov), every state has a State Health Insurance Assistance Program

(SHIP) that provides free one-on-one health insurance counseling: This includes help in making health care decisions; information on programs for people with limited income and resources; and help with claims, billing, and appeals.

Medigap Supplemental Health Insurance Policies

Because Medicare has gaps in coverage and requires copayments, many Medicare-eligible people purchase Medigap insurance. A Medigap policy is health insurance sold by private insurance companies that can help pay for some of the costs of Medicare-covered services that Original Medicare does not cover (e.g., coinsurance, copayments, or deductibles), and may include certain additional benefits.

In most cases, insurance companies can sell only standardized Medigap policies (identified by letters *A* through *N*) so that consumers can compare them easily. Cost is usually the only difference between Medigap policies with the same letter sold by different companies. States determine the types of policies that can be sold to their residents, so there are variations among the states in the plans that are available. Any standardized Medigap policy is guaranteed renewable even for those with health problems, as long as the enrollee pays the premium. More information on Medigap policies is available on the Medicare website (at www.medicare.gov/medigap).

Help With Medical and Drug Costs

Low-income seniors may find that Medicare's costs are beyond their reach. Medicare Savings Programs administered by states may help pay Medicare premiums, and in some cases, the Part A and Part B deductibles, coinsurance, and copayments. Through the Qualified Medicare Beneficiary (QMB) program, states pay all Medicare premiums, deductibles, coinsurance, and copayments for seniors whose poverty-level incomes and resources make them eligible. For seniors with slightly more income and resources, the Specified Low-Income Medicare Beneficiary (SLMB) and Qualifying Individual (QI) programs will pay Part B premiums for those who are eligible, and for Qualified Disabled and Working Individuals (QDWI), the state will pay Part A premiums. Information about these Medicare Savings Programs can be found at local Social Security offices, and on Medicare's website (www.medicare.gov) under "Help with Medical and Drug Costs."

Funding Medicare

Medicare is paid for through two trust fund accounts held by the U.S. Treasury. These funds can only be used for Medicare. The Hospital Insurance (HI) Trust Fund pays for the Part A program and its administration (including paying benefits and combating fraud and abuse). It is funded primarily through payroll taxes on employees (1.45% of wages), which are matched by employers. Other sources of funds for the HI Trust Fund include interest earned on Medicare trust fund investments, income taxes paid on Social Security benefits, and Part A premiums from people who pay a premium. The Supplementary Medical Insurance (SMI) Trust Fund pays for the Part B and Part D programs and their administration. It is funded through a combination of premiums paid by enrollees in Part B and Part D, interest on SMI trust funds, and transfers from the U.S. Treasury's general fund. Beneficiaries can choose to receive all their Medicare services through managed care plans under the Part C program, in which case payment is made on their behalf in appropriate parts from the HI and SMI trust funds, and includes any premiums Part C enrollees may pay.

In recent years, there has been considerable discussion over the spiraling costs of the Medicare program—how much more it is costing each year; when the Medicare Trust Funds will run out of money without changes in funding; how costs can be curtailed; and, recently, whether there should even be a national health insurance program for seniors. In 1970, just 5 years after Medicare was introduced, the Medicare trustees' report projected insolvency for the Hospital Insurance Trust Fund by 1972, and in 1997 the trustees were projecting insolvency by 2001 (Zorn, 2011). Of course, changes to Medicare since its inception have kept it from running out of money, and changes will continue to be necessary to keep it so. Keeping rapidly growing costs in check is a problem for all health care entities. Medicare's coverage is more cost-effective than private insurance plans, in part because its administrative costs are much lower. In 2011, total expenditures for Medicare were $549 billion and total income was $530 billion, with assets held in the trusts filling the gap. Table 14.3 provides data on Medicare's income and expenditures, including total assets remaining in the trust funds as of the end of 2011. The Affordable Care Act extends Medicare's solvency from 2017 to 2024 (when there will no longer be any monies remaining in the trusts

TABLE 14.3 Medicare Trust Funds: Calendar Year 2011

		SMI		
	HI (Part A)	Part B	Part D	Total
Assets at end of 2010 (billions)	**$271.9**	**$71.4**	**$0.7**	**$344.0**
Total Income	**$228.9**	**$233.6**	**$67.4**	**$530.0**
Payroll taxes	195.6	—	—	195.6
Interest	12.0	3.2	0.0	15.2
Taxation of benefits	15.1	—	—	15.1
Premiums	3.3	57.5	7.7	68.5
General revenue	0.5	170.2	52.6	223.3
Other	2.4	2.7	7.1	12.2
Total Expenditures	**$256.7**	**$225.3**	**$67.1**	**$549.1**
Benefits	252.9	221.7	66.7	541.3
Hospital	132.7	35.1	—	167.8
Skilled nursing facility	32.9	—	—	32.9
Home health care	7.3	12.4	—	19.6
Physicians' fees	—	67.6	—	67.6
Private health plans (Part C)	64.6	59.1	—	123.7
Prescription drugs	—	—	66.7	66.7
Other	15.4	47.5	—	62.9
Administrative expenses	3.8	3.6	0.4	7.8
Net change in assets	**-$27.7**	**$8.3**	**$0.3**	**-$19.2**
Assets at end of 2011 (billions)	**$244.2**	**$79.7**	**$1.0**	**$324.9**

Note: Totals do not necessarily equal the sums of rounded components.

Source: Medicare Board of Trustees (2012), p. 10.

to fill funding gaps), giving us more time to address how to keep Medicare viable for future generations.

Trying to cope with this situation usually involves proposals to cut benefits, boost revenues, or raise taxes. Until the passage of the Affordable Care Act in 2010, little effort had been focused on how to keep older people healthier and thereby avoid costly hospitalizations and treatments. Now seniors can take advantage of new preventive services, such as cancer screenings and tobacco cessation programs. But much more needs to be done to maximize health and quality of life in the later years, and most such actions can lead to significant cost savings, too. For example, most cases of chronic kidney disease are caused by diabetes and high blood pressure, two preventable health conditions. And yet, Medicare's expenditures for end-stage renal disease alone, which results from a lack of prevention and early interventions for kidney disease, were $24 billion, more than $46,000 for each of the 514,642 patients in 2007 (*National Health Care Quality Report*, 2012). We are only beginning to scratch the surface in terms of our prevention efforts and making better use of our health care dollars for treatments that are demonstrated to be effective.

MEDICATIONS AND MANAGING PRESCRIPTION DRUGS

As important as affordable prescription drugs are for older people, the management of drugs (prescribing, giving, and taking medicines) is equally vital to their well-being. According to data collected by the Slone Epidemiology Center at Boston University, 28% of older men and women take five or more prescription drugs per week, about twice the percentage of 45- to 65-year-olds who take that many (*Patterns of Medication Use in the United States*, 2006). When combined with the normal body changes caused by aging, taking multiple medications, which is referred to as *polypharmacy*, can increase the chance of unwanted, and even harmful, drug reactions.

As a person ages, the way that medicines are absorbed and used can change. For example, changes in the digestive system can affect how fast medicines enter the bloodstream. Changes in body weight can influence the amount of medicine needed and how long it stays in the body. The circulatory system may slow down, which can affect how fast drugs get to the liver and kidneys. The liver and kidneys also may work more slowly, affecting the way a drug breaks down and is removed from the body. Because of these age-related changes, older adults are more susceptible to adverse drug reactions.

Adverse Drug Reactions

It is estimated that 30% of hospital admissions of older adults may be due to adverse drug reactions (Fick et al., 2003). The human toll in terms of morbidity, including increased depression, falls, and fractures, and mortality, as well as the economic impact of adverse drug reactions demand that more attention be paid to them.

Drug reactions can result when drugs interact with each other, with medical conditions, or with food or alcohol. Drugs can interact with each other, causing one of them not to work as well or even make one of them stronger than it should be. A medical condition, such as hypertension or asthma, can make certain drugs potentially harmful. Food in the digestive system can affect how a drug is absorbed, and some drugs may also affect the way nutrients are absorbed or used in the body. Mixing alcohol with some drugs may cause sleepiness, slow reactions, or even death. Many medicines do not mix well with alcohol, and older bodies may react differently to alcohol, as well as to the mix of alcohol and medicines. It is usually not easy to persuade a person using prescription drugs to stop drinking alcohol. It is, however, one of the most important things a family member, friend, or caregiver can do.

The causes of adverse drug reactions are many. Often elderly patients go to several different physicians and pharmacies and do not tell each one about all the medications they are taking. Clinicians who are not knowledgeable about geriatric patients can prescribe medications that should generally be avoided due to their lack of efficacy or unnecessarily high risks, given safer alternatives, including nonpharmacological therapy. To assist all health care providers, a panel of experts created a list of 66 potentially inappropriate drugs for older adults (Fick et al., 2003). Mixing prescription and other medications, including over-the-counter drugs, vitamins and minerals, and herbal/natural supplements, can also cause adverse reactions. For older adults living in the community, the mix of prescriptions and other medications is about 50–50 (*Patterns of Medication Use in the United States*, 2006).

> ### Episode 10: Geriatric Medicine
>
> **High Bandwidth:**
> http://raidercast.grcc.edu/flash/2011_2012/grcctv/successful_
> aging/success_aging_10_large/grcc_player.html
> **Low Bandwidth:**
> http://raidercast.grcc.edu/flash/2011_2012/grcctv/successful_
> aging/success_aging_10_small/grcc_player.html

A geriatrician discusses the use of pharmaceuticals, alternative therapies, herbs, antioxidants, and vitamins in Video 10.

Medication Management

Many programs for medication management are now available throughout the country. Older adults and their loved ones can obtain information about them through their local or state offices on aging (locate them via www.aoa.ogv/AOARoot/AoA_Programs/index.aspx). Medication management programs, sometimes called MTM or medication reviews, include a free discussion and review of all medications by a pharmacist or other health care professional who will check for possible interaction problems, correct dosages, and so forth. All over-the counter medications, as well as dietary supplements, vitamins, minerals, and herbals should be reviewed at the same time. Those who have more than one chronic health condition should contact their Medicare Part D plan to see if it includes such a program.

The U.S. Food and Drug Administration has developed a form called *My Medicine Record*, which can be downloaded (at www.fda.gov/Drugs/ResourcesForYou/ucm079489.htm), filled out, and shared with physicians, pharmacists, and other health care providers at all visits. *My Medicine Record* contains a chart to record the names of the medicines and dietary supplements that a person is taking; a page to record personal and emergency contact information, as well as physician and pharmacy contact information, and more. Also helpful is having a set of questions to ask health providers and pharmacists before taking medications—Table 14.4 gives a list of some good questions.

TABLE 14.4 Good Questions to Ask Health Care Providers and Pharmacists About Medications

• What is this medication supposed to do?
• How and when should I take the medication and for how long?
• When will the medication begin to work, and how can I tell if it is working?
• What should I do if I miss a dose?
• What are the side effects, and what should I do if they occur?
• What is the generic form of this medication, and can I take it?
• Will I have any testing to monitor the medication's effects?
• How should I store my medication?
• Should the medication be taken with food?
• Are there foods, drinks, other medications, or herbal supplements I should avoid?
• Am I able to drive while taking the medication?

Source: Department of Health and Human Services. Administration on Aging. Retrieved from http://www.aoa.gov/AoARoot/AoA_Programs/HPW/Med_Manage/index.aspx

SUGGESTED RESOURCES

Centers for Disease Control and Prevention, Healthy Aging: http://www.cdc.gov/aging/
> This part of CDC's website provides access to credible, reliable information, data, and statistics on healthy aging, including health topics relevant to older adults, chronic disease management, and clinical preventive services.

DailyMed: http://dailymed.nlm.nih.gov/dailymed/about.cfm
> This website, a public service of the National Library of Medicine, provides health information to providers and the public with a standard, comprehensive, up-to-date, look-up and download resource of medication content and labeling as found in medication package inserts for prescription and over-the-counter medications. AARP also has a website that provides a similar service, with simplified descriptions of key aspects of drugs (see http://healthtools.aarp.org/drug-directory).

Health in Aging: http://www.healthinaging.org/
> Created by the American Geriatrics Society Foundation for Health in Aging (FHA), this website provides consumers and caregivers with up-to-date information on health and aging.

Medicare: http://www.medicare.gov/
> This federal government website provides tools for signing up and managing Medicare coverage, creating and maintaining personal health records, and information on all things related to Medicare, including how to find health care professionals, facilities, and services.

NIH Senior Health: http://www.nihseniorhealth.gov
> A senior-friendly website from the National Institute on Aging and the National Library of Medicine, this website has health and wellness information for older adults. Special features make it simple to use, for example, the size of the type can be made larger.

CHAPTER 15

Assisted Living/Long-Term Care

The learning outcomes of this chapter include understanding

- How moving from some form of independent living to a dependent living arrangement impacts the lives of older people.
- The array of issues and circumstances older people and their family caregivers face in the fragmented system of assisted living/long-term care that exists in the United States.
- The burden caregiving places on families—especially female caregivers.
- How a seemingly sexist approach to caregiving developed and persists in the United States.
- The complexities and frustrations of financing long-term care in the political climate of contemporary America.

ESTHER'S NEED FOR CONGREGATE LIVING

Esther was the best cook in her family. Nieces and nephews always talked about Aunt Esther's chocolate cakes. Her dinners were also excellent. After she turned 80 years old, she began to develop macular degeneration (the loss of central vision). Gradually she lost more and more vision due to the deterioration of the retinas in her eyes. It became hard to read even the largest print. Her general health was quite good, with her high blood pressure controlled through aggressive medication. Her husband, so typical of their generation, never learned to cook nor did he want to try. His health too was quite good, but he could no longer drive for a variety of physical reasons. Esther and her husband had always been very independent. They did not rely on anybody. They helped lots of people in various ways. With Esther's limited vision, what were they to do? When they had some friends move into a congregate living facility that did not require an entry fee and rented on a month-to-month basis for $1,300 a month including *two meals a day, they saw that as an option for them, too. It was a new facility and really quite nice. Each unit had a living room, bedroom, bath, walk-in closet, and small kitchen to prepare meals they might choose to have in their own apartment. They thought they would try it. The biggest adjustment was eating with other people on a regular basis. At first, this was difficult for Esther because she was so used to being in charge of the food preparation and the eating arrangements, but she adjusted quite well after a time. Both Esther and her husband made many friends and actually looked forward to meals as a natural time to get together with their new friends.*

DIANE: FORCED TO BE A CAREGIVER?

Peter and Diane have a close-knit family. Peter's mother, who lives 2 miles away, has been widowed for 10 years and managed to take care of her own home. Everything was fine until she fell and broke her hip.

Peter's mother was hospitalized for a time, but being immobile and on medication made her chronic conditions worse. Her general health failed rather quickly, and Peter and Diane felt they should do something to help her until she was able to regain her strength. Peter's sister, Jane, lives on the other side of the state and spends most of her time caring for her injured husband. So where should Peter's mother go to recuperate? She can't go to Jane's, so are Diane and Peter expected to take her in?

Diane isn't ready to become a full-time caregiver. She wants to help, but she does not want to give up her job to stay home and care for Peter's mom. Peter and Diane need to find another solution, but they don't know where to look or whom to ask (Rieske & Holstege, 1992, pp. 158–159).

MOVING FROM INDEPENDENT LIVING

All of the housing options discussed in previous chapters, even those that involve sharing a home with others, are essentially independent living environments. This chapter looks at the types of living arrangements that involve various degrees of supportive services. Some of these facilities are chosen primarily for the benefits of interaction with people of similar ages and interests. Others are chosen as planned moves with continuum-of-care services built in as part of the environment, where levels of supportive care are provided as needed. Still others are chosen out of necessity when a person needs immediate assistance with daily living activities.

CONGREGATE/ASSISTED LIVING

Congregate/assisted living has many definitions and has many forms. It continues to take additional forms as the market expands because of the increase in the number of older persons in America. These living arrangements have been called *homes for the aged*, *retirement homes*, *old people's homes*, *sheltered housing*, and others. The common factors in all of these homes are housing units that have a common dining room in which meals are served on a regular basis along with access to social and recreational services.

The goal of congregate living is to provide services in a residential setting for persons who need some form of assistance with daily living but do not require continuing medical or nursing care. They generally do not require full-time personal assistance. In the past, many of these homes for the aged were developed and operated by religious institutions and fraternal or social organizations. Most of these were, and continue to be, nonprofit.

A Dormitory for the Elderly

For older persons, the "dorm room" of the home for the aged is where they spend much of their time. It is difficult for many older persons, after being active and in charge of their lives, to give up some of their independence and move into congregate living situations. This is particularly true for older persons who have a perception of homes for the aged from past experiences where the settings were often old, dismal, and generally oppressive. That is one of the reasons new approaches to congregate living situations are being developed, often by entrepreneurs who cater to more affluent older persons. They provide a sparkling physical environment with a range of entertainment and recreational options along with upscale services. They are designed to attract persons who are physically mobile, and want the security of a controlled, supportive environment.

Support for Congregate Living

Late in the 19th century, most old people had to look out for themselves only with the help of their families. For those who had no help, or no families to move in with, the alternative was to turn to the *poor farms* of America. These were common across the nation's landscape. With the beginning of Social Security in 1935, America began to look toward a different approach to providing for the needs of the elderly. But Social Security was only a beginning. It was not until a 1963 address to the Congress that President Kennedy proposed a basic concept that later became part of a national program for congregate housing. President Kennedy stated:

> For the great majority of the nation's older people, the years of retirement should be years of activity and self-reliance. A substantial minority, however, while still relatively independent, require modest assistance in one or more aspects of their daily living. Many have become frail physically and may need help in preparing meals, caring for living quarters, and sometimes limited nursing. (U.S. House of Representatives, 1963)

President Kennedy went on to recommend the enactment of housing programs that would include a variety of services. In 1970, Congress finally acted to provide funds for the construction of congregate housing for the elderly. In 1974, Congress authorized funds to include space for central kitchens and dining rooms. Congregate housing can be attractive to a cross-section of older people at a variety of income levels.

Assisted-Living Facilities

In addition to the many long-established congregate living institutions, a newer version of homes for the aged has sprung up in the past 15 to 20 years called *assisted-living facilities*. Services in these types of residences are supposed to be provided according to individual needs (Cox, 2005).

The goal of assisted living is to enable persons to live in a homelike environment. These facilities typically have a housekeeping service, serve at least two meals a day, provide recreational programs, and have some method of 24-hour supervision. The residents typically live in individual apartment units—from small to relatively large—which often have a kitchen. But standards of care vary widely from facility to facility and from state to state. Some form of health care monitoring is usually offered.

An investigation by *USA TODAY* of 5,300 assisted-living facilities in 12 states, including Michigan, indicated rather widespread lapses in care services (McCoy & Hansen, 2004). Specifically, this investigation found that among the facilities surveyed, more than 1 in 5 had been cited by state monitors for at least one significant medication error.

CONTINUING CARE RETIREMENT COMMUNITIES (CCRCs)

For those who want the assurance of being in an environment that will meet all of their needs as they continue to move through their later years regardless of the status of their mobility and health, there are CCRCs. They are also called *life-care* or *continuum-of-care communities*. They usually provide housing, personal care, supportive care, nursing care, congregate meals, and a range of social and recreational services. The key feature is that incoming residents enter into contractual agreements to pay entrance fees and monthly fees that will provide for their care for the rest of their lives. There are more than 1,800 CCRCs in the United States, most of them affiliated with nonprofit organizations (Government Accountability Office [GAO], 2010).

The continuum of on-site services that are needed by older persons as their status changes means that the residents are not at risk for being evicted if they become impaired or their impairments become worse. A study of persons who have moved into these types of facilities found that the main reasons for such moves are planning ahead for possible changing physical and mental needs, freedom from maintaining their own homes, and a wish not to be a burden on their loved ones (Krout, Moen, Holmes, Oggins, & Bowen, 2002).

Costs of CCRCs

In general, these facilities are geared for the middle and upper income older population—with some exceptions. The entrance fees for CCRCs generally range from $20,000 to more than $500,000, with monthly fees varying from $600 to more than $3,000, depending on regions of the nation, type of buildings, size of individual residences, and levels of services provided, which typically relate to the amount of health care needed (Cox, 2005). An exception to the typical middle and upper income tone to CCRCs would be those operated by religious and/or charitable organizations, such as the Holland Home of Grand Rapids, Michigan. Although accommodating upper income older persons with rather opulent suites and apartments, in 2009 it provided $5,000,000 of financial assistance to 40% of its 3,100 residents. Many of those persons simply outlived their resources. It also offered a *Home Buy-Out Program*, which actually bought the homes of would-be residents, so they could afford to pay entry fees. This is a strategy to address the large downturn in the housing market during the Great Recession of 2008 to 2009 (Claus, 2010).

Life in CCRCs

Many of the newer CCRCs have private apartments in duplex or townhouse arrangements, individual apartments in larger buildings, rooms in a "manor" type of building, supportive care rooms, and nursing facilities all on the same campus. As an older person's needs change, the resident can move within the same retirement community to the next level of assisted-living housing unit, including nursing home care. All of this is covered by a life-care agreement.

CCRCs can be ideal for older people who can afford the entrance and monthly fees, and who can adapt to living in an environment that is somewhat institutional and controlled. This approach can be a solution to guarantee long-term care. However, because of the relatively large fees involved, this approach does not address the public policy issues of long-term care for the majority of older Americans.

Regulations of CCRCs

Although there are no federal regulations for CCRCs, 38 states do regulate them. And standards and accreditation are provided by the Commission on Accreditation of Rehabilitation Facilities (CARF). But there is no requirement that facilities participate in such an accreditation process. As a result, it is important that older persons who contemplate moving into a CCRC understand the services provided, what services are available to meet current and future needs, the costs and the types of contracts offered, and the possible pitfalls in signing a contract for this type of facility. A report on CCRCs conducted by the GAO (2010) has pointed out that

> many older Americans sell their homes, which are often their primary asset, to pay the required fees, and, as a result, their ability to support themselves in the long-run is inextricably tied to the long-term viability of their CCRC. Further, many CCRCs may be financially vulnerable during periods of economic decline—such as the recent downturn—that can result in tight real estate and credit markets. (p. 1)

Things to Look for in Choosing a CCRC

Much of the decision in choosing a facility comes down to whether a prospective resident feels "at home" after a period of adjustment. The place chosen will become "home" and all that means to the life of an older person. Although it may appear that these living arrangements (CCRCs) are primarily for the well-to-do elderly, some contracts can be purchased for reasonable amounts of money considering the number of older people who own their homes free and clear of mortgages.

BOARD-AND-CARE HOMES

These types of homes generally focus on serving persons with lower incomes than those who reside in assisted-living facilities, which are often owned by large corporations and specifically target upper middle-class people. The residents of board-and-care homes typically lack other options if they wish to remain in the community.

It is difficult to determine exactly how many older persons live in board-and-care homes, as many of these facilities are not licensed, and their definitions differ among states. It has been estimated that the need for this type of facility will increase dramatically due to the projected large increase in older persons with functional limitations (doubling from 1990 to 2020).

The Operators of Board-and-Care Homes

Although they vary in size, the majority of board-and-care facilities are for-profit "mom and pop" operations. Some of the "moms and pops" are operated by individuals—a "mom" or a "pop." This type of manager usually plays an important role in the facility and in the lives of the residents. In fact, this person (or couple) is typically the key to the overall well-being of the residents. Whether the operators need to have any special training to operate a board-and-care home varies from state to state. Some operators hire outside help to manage the home. In these types of arrangements, there is potential for abuse and neglect of the residents.

Board-and-care homes, according to experts on aging, can provide a real service to many impaired elderly persons as an alternative to being institutionalized (Cox, 2005). The smaller settings of these facilities, along with more informality, can meet the needs of many older people if they are run properly.

LONG-TERM CARE FACILITIES

In addition to the various types of congregate facilities outlined previously, two types of living arrangements available for many frail, dependent, and chronically ill older persons are nursing homes/nursing facilities and dependent home care. Home care patients are cared for by friends or family members—usually wives or adult children (most often daughters or daughters-in-law)—in someone's home.

Nursing Homes/Nursing Facilities

One of the most difficult decisions to make is whether to put one's parent or loved one in a nursing facility. Many older people and their families perceive nursing homes as warehouses where old people just wait to die. There is a widespread perception of nursing homes as places where abuse and neglect can occur. The 1960s and early 1970s, a period of rapid growth of nursing homes, was also a time of well-publicized nursing home scandals (Vladeck, 1980). Despite nursing home reform legislation (*Omnibus Budget Reconciliation Act*, 1987), there is reason for continued concern about the care and safety of nursing home residents. Although the prevalence of serious deficiencies seems to have declined significantly (from 29% to 16%), in its most recent report on nursing homes, the GAO (2005) still found "a small but unacceptable proportion of nursing homes repeatedly caused actual harm to residents, such as worsening pressure sores or untreated weight loss, or placed residents at risk of death or serous injury" (p. 2). Tremendous variability exists, with 10 states reporting less than 10% of their nursing homes with serious deficiencies, but 15 states reporting more than 20% of homes with such problems.

Institutions classified as skilled nursing homes care for some of the oldest and frailest members of society. While most people aged 65 and older live in households, the probability of living in a nursing home increases with age; less than 1.1% for 65- to 74-year-olds, 3.5% for 75- to 84-year-olds, and 13.2% for those age 85 and older (*A Profile of Older Americans: 2011*).

Who Lives in Nursing Homes?

It is important to note that all the percentages of older people living in nursing facilities have declined since 1990. This decline may be due to the improved health of older people, or the substitution of other kinds of caretaking, such as assisted living, in-home health care, and hospice organizations (*65+ in the United States*, 2005).

The majority of older people residing in nursing homes are women. In addition, male nursing home residents tend to be younger than female residents. This difference is partly due to the longer life expectancies of women. Men also have higher rates of serious and permanent injury rates at relatively younger ages, which may lead to permanent nursing home stays and would slightly lower the average age of male residents. After entering nursing homes in old age, women tend to stay longer, further extending the average age of female nursing home residents (*65+ in the United States,* 2005).

Regional differences exist in the percentage of the older population living in nursing homes. The proportion of the population aged 65 and older residing in a nursing home ranges from a low of 2.7% in the West to a high of 5.5 in the Midwest (*65+ in the United States,* 2005). The smaller proportions of the older population who reside in nursing homes in the South and West may be partly due to migration. Healthy members of the older population may move from the Northeast and the Midwest to retirement areas in warmer climates, such as the South and West. This leaves behind a frail older population that is more likely to enter nursing homes. In addition, when these older people who move to the South and West experience illness or become frail, they may move back to their original regions to be closer to family members who can provide caregiving or oversight on health issues and decisions.

Current Trends in Nursing Home Living

The reasons the nursing home population has become smaller, older, and frailer are varied, but might in part be attributed to two trends. First, older people now have more options for long-term care, enabling more people to live outside a nursing home in an assisted, but nonmedical, environment. Second, older people with severe disabilities may not be able to live in alternative care settings (such as assisted living), so larger proportions of this group must rely on more traditional and intensive nursing home care.

Long-term care is now frequently provided in a variety of settings that, apart from nursing homes, are difficult to define. Nursing homes that receive Medicare and Medicaid funding are regulated by the federal government and must meet defined standards, which include developing a comprehensive care plan for each resident, maintaining the dignity and respect of each resident, and ensuring that residents have the right to choose activities, schedules, and health care. Assisted-living facilities and residential care, on the other hand, are overseen by state and local jurisdictions with differing standards (Stone, Bryant, & Barbarotta, 2009). Traditional nursing homes continue to be a component of caring for the oldest and frailest members of society, but other creative approaches to formal and informal care situations will likely continue to develop.

In-Home Long-Term Care

Long-term care in one's own home is mostly provided by family members, primarily women (wives, daughters, and daughters-in-law). In-home care is provided weekly, daily, or around-the-clock, depending on the condition and needs of each disabled older person.

An array of services is available in many communities to assist disabled older persons as well as caregivers in carrying out their tasks. No government program provides for 24-hour, in-home care. Paying for specific in-home services can be tricky. Some are available at little or no cost depending on the service, how it is accessed, and whether the recipient qualifies through programs of the Older Americans Act, Medicare, Medicaid, or state social service departments. Usually local Area Agencies on Aging can assist in finding services that meet the needs of specific disabled older persons. These services include care management, home health services, homemaker/home care services, friendly visitor programs, and telephone reassurance programs.

Additional Services Outside the Home

Some additional community-based services are offered to dependent older persons and their caregivers. These include adult day care, respite care, congregate meals, transportation, home delivered meals, and home repair. Some of these services may be funded by the Older Americans Act (OAA), and available through agencies accessible through state government departments that serve the elderly. More information on OAA-funded services is presented in Chapter 13.

In-Home Care Trends

Increasingly, older people and their caregivers are looking for options to formal institutional care. These options may include family or home-based caregiving, community-based paid care, self-care using assistive devices, or some combination of all of these.

Home- and community-based care are the most common care arrangements for older Americans. Among community-dwelling older people with long-term care needs, over 80% depend on unpaid help (Kaye, Harrington, & LaPlante, 2010). For older people who remain in the community, studies show an increase in paid care, especially at the higher rates of disability, when informal care (from friends or family) is supplemented by formal care (Langa, Chernew, Kabeto, & Katz, 2001).

The use of assistive devices, either alone or in combination with other care arrangements, is becoming more common among older people (Freedman, Agree, Martin, & Cornman, 2006). The use of assistive devices improves functioning, enhances independence, decreases caregiver responsibilities, and reduces the hours of personal care needed.

While there is real need and value for nursing homes for older persons with severe impairments, the overall goal of in-home care is the diversion of people from nursing homes when they can be served at home and in the community (Scripps Gerontology Center, 2008). This goal builds upon what most older people want as they go through the aging process—to stay at home as long as possible. To hear older adults talk about the importance to them of aging in place, watch Video 1.

> **Episode 1: Aging in Place**
>
> **High Bandwidth:**
> http://raidercast.grcc.edu/flash/2011_2012/grcctv/successful_
> aging/success_aging_1_large/grcc_player.html
> **Low Bandwidth:**
> http://raidercast.grcc.edu/flash/2011_2012/grcctv/successful_
> aging/success_aging_1_small/grcc_player.html

Reasons to Choose In-Home Long-Term Care

Many reasons are given by older persons and their families for choosing long-term care in a home-based setting. According to experts, these include:

Familiarity

Most people are familiar with the feelings of independence and security they have in the familiar surroundings of a home (Salamon & Rosenthal, 2004). They just simply like to be in a setting they have lived in throughout their lives—a single-family home, whether it is their own old home or the home of a relative. They feel that the warmth of caregiving from loved ones is far superior to what they might receive from strangers. But it is pointed out that the wish to stay in familiar surroundings may overshadow a better choice of care. This is particularly true for the family caregivers, usually daughters or daughters-in-law, who have their lives severely changed—usually in negative ways.

Fear of Institutions

People living in many forms of confinement in a range of institutions—prisons, mental hospitals, drug rehabilitation centers, and nursing homes—are often viewed as needing to be kept away from healthy society. In addition, many people have read about the really bad conditions in some nursing facilities—many of which are based on state investigations. This contributes to the feeling by many that nursing homes are "hellholes" or "snake pits." Also, many in the general public believe that nursing homes do not provide the personal care patients need (Salamon & Rosenthal, 2004).

Guilt

Many persons feel a sense—sometimes an overwhelming sense—of guilt if they do not personally assume the primary care of an aging parent. They simply feel the need to care for aging parents because the parents cared for them when they were young. They think it is their family obligation to care for aging loved ones (Riekse & Holstege, 1996).

Costs

Many—too many—simply cannot afford nursing home care (Gleckman, 2008). There is no federal entitlement for such long-term care outside of Medicaid, which is a federal-state program designed for the poor or those persons who are forced to become poor before they can qualify for benefits under this program. Many middle-class older persons, in order to receive assistance through Medicaid to pay for long-term care, become impoverished for the first time in their lives—a humiliating condition for proud persons who worked hard all their lives while supporting schools, cities, towns, states, and the U.S. government through their taxes, as well as serving all sorts of community support systems, and, for many, serving in the military (Riekse & Holstege, 1996).

ISSUES IN LONG-TERM CARE

There are a number of specific issues/decisions that relate to long-term care in the United States. These include, but are not limited to:

The Context of Long-Term Care

Defining the need for what is commonly called *long-term care* is linked to what is referred to as *functional ability*, which is also tied to the term *frail elderly*. Back in the 1970s, the Federal Council on Aging provided one of the first definitions of the term *frail elderly*. Frail elderly persons are "usually, but not always, over the age of 75, who because of the accumulation of various continuing problems, often require one or several supportive services in order to cope with daily life" (Cox, 2005, pp. 18–19). Frailty has also been defined as the "loss of a social support system to the extent that the person is unable to maintain a household or social contacts without continuing assistance" (Cox, 2005, p. 19).

All of the definitions relate to something called *functional status*, which is generally used to measure the need for long-term care services. Functional status is typically based on an older person's ability to complete what are called *activities of daily living* (ADLs).

These are the things persons do to maintain independent living including bathing, dressing, toileting, transferring between bed and chair, continence (controlling bladder and bowels), and eating.

In addition to measuring ADLs, there are also measurements of something called *instrumental activities of daily living* (IADLs). These include tasks people commonly do in the community as part of normal living. They include using a telephone or cell phone, shopping, housekeeping, doing laundry, taking medicines, transporting themselves (by car, bus, cab, etc.), and managing finances.

Caregiving: A Family Affair

In her book entitled *Helping Yourself Help Others, A Book for Caregivers*, Rosalynn Carter (1994), Former First Lady of the United States, quoted a colleague's perspective on caregiving, saying,

> There are only four kinds of people in the world: those who have been caregivers; those who are currently caregivers; those who will be caregivers; and those who will need caregivers. (p. 3)

In the United States, long-term caregiving is mostly a family affair. And in the family, it is the women—the spouses of those with disabilities and especially the daughters—who assume most of the burden of caregiving, according to Elaine Brody (2004). More than ever before, daughters (and daughters-in-law) are providing this care, while they probably have careers of their own in the workplace; may have debts from loans for their own education; and typically have families of their own with all that implies. They are facing competing demands from husbands, children, parents, and work, which often put them in the middle emotionally between elderly parents and husbands and children. The negative results of these tasks and conflicts, according to a wide range of research, typically include poor mental and physical health, threats to family well-being, problems and situations with paid work as well as other aspects of their lives, including their social lives.

Based on projections of people currently alive, as well as projected life spans, the number of older people is expected to increase to 70 million, or 20% of the total U.S. population by 2030. As a result, the number of elderly persons that may need caregiving is staggering. This is particularly evident if one realizes that the fastest growing sector of older people is the oldest-old (85 years and older) who generally need the most amount of caregiving. It is projected that by 2050, the oldest-old will number some 19 million. With care for these elders mostly provided by families—particularly daughters and daughters-in-law as they outnumber caregiving by sons 3 to 1 (4 to 1 when the parents are extremely disabled)—the burdens

---

Episode 3: Caregiving Part 1

High Bandwidth:
http://raidercast.grcc.edu/flash/2011_2012/grcctv/successful_
aging/success_aging_3_large/grcc_player.html
Low Bandwidth:
http://raidercast.grcc.edu/flash/2011_2012/grcctv/successful_
aging/success_aging_3_small/grcc_player.html

---

on female caregivers will increase substantially (Brody, 2004). To hear from caregivers about issues they have faced and how they have dealt with them, watch Video 3.

Passages in Women's Lives

Gail Sheehy, who has written extensively on the various passages in people's lives, has stated that many years ago in her earlier writings on passages in life, she thought that the age of 50 would be the gateway to the most liberating phase in a woman's life (Sheehy, 2010a). She thought that after age 50 women could climb mountains, rediscover romance, pursue a new career, and so forth. Now, with so many women having older and older parents, Sheehy has discovered a second round of caregiving (the first raising children) "that has become a predictable crisis for women in their midlife" (Sheehy, 2010a, p. 71). She points out that nearly 50 million Americans are caring for an adult who earlier had been independent.

Sheehy notes that men are caregivers, too (about one third of family caregivers), but they usually do so from a distance or it is administrative in nature. It is women who do the real, hands-on care. The average caregiver is 48 years old, has at least one child at home, and has a paying job. And, according to her data, the average caregiving role lasts about 5 years (Sheehy, 2010a).

Negative Results of Caregiving

Numerous recent studies have shown that long-term caregivers are at a high risk for sleep deprivation, immune deficiency, depression, anxiety, loss of concentration, and even premature death (Sheehy, 2010a). Dr. Esther Sternberg, a stress researcher, puts caregivers at the same risk for burnout as nurses, teachers, and air traffic controllers. When caregiver burnout occurs, typically the only option is to put the dependent family member in a nursing facility, which is usually everyone's last choice, the most expensive, and almost sure to promote guilt in the caregiver (Sheehy, 2010a). See additional information on caregiving in the Practical Application at the end of Part IV in this textbook.

Historical Role for Women

Women's free labor in family caregiving has been seen by some conservatives as a means to reduce the cost of care that is financed publicly. It has also been interpreted as a way to maintain the patriarchal family and women's traditional role in it (Rosenbury, 2007). Estes and Swan (1993) have pointed out that in the patriarchal family, the basic role of women is caregiving, and their status in the family is one of dependency. They went on to argue that because so much of women's work is not visible in terms of pay and benefits, American social policy continues to reflect the idea of women as dependents living in a stereotypical nuclear family. In this approach, women primarily fill domestic and reproductive roles with participation in the workforce a secondary consideration. The enormous amount of work women perform as caregivers and the sacrifices they make are often unrecognized because work within the family is seen as free labor, if it is recognized as labor at all.

Betty Friedan's "The Feminine Mystique" and Today's Caregivers

Writing in *The Nation* magazine, Ruth Rosen described how housewives in the 1950s faced the realities of unhappy and unfulfilled lives by saying, "that's life," whatever the troubling circumstance might be. Betty Friedan's bestseller, *The Feminine Mystique*, exposed "the problem that has no name" and the belief that a woman should find identity and fulfillment exclusively through her family (Rosen, 2007).

Rosen pointed out that it took the women's movement to identify and name hidden experiences many women faced including domestic violence, sexual harassment, economic discrimination, and date rape. The women's movement turned these experiences into public problems that were then debated, addressed by new policies and laws, or changed by new social customs. Rosen went on to point out that although much attention has been devoted to work/family problems, the nation has not named the burdens that currently affect so many women—the care crisis. For the most part, society has done little to restructure the workplace or family life. "Today, the care crisis has replaced the feminine mystique as women's 'problem that has no name'" (Rosen, 2007, p. 11). Rosen goes on to say that the care crisis is a problem of national importance.

Rosen contends that the use of the term *family values* by the political right ("conservatives") in the United States is cynical. She points out that the obstacles to solving the care crisis are "formidable, given that government and business—as well as many men—have found it profitable and convenient for women to shoulder the burden of housework and caregiving" (Rosen, 2007, p. 11). The health care reform bill enacted by the Obama administration in 2010 has what could be described as an opening for long-term care support—the Community Living Assistance Services and Supports (CLASS) Act. Unfortunately, this provision of the 2010 health care reform bill has not been implemented.

"The care crisis exposes how much of the feminist agenda or gender equality remains woefully unfinished," according to Rosen (2007, p. 13). America's family policies are quite far behind those in other parts of the world. Of 173 countries surveyed by Harvard and McGill universities, 168 have paid maternal leave, but not the United States (Rosen, 2007).

DEALING WITH TRANSFER TRAUMA

When a caregiver becomes burnt out, or when the patient can no longer be cared for in a community setting, placement in some form of nursing facility may be needed. Being placed in a nursing facility can be the most difficult change one can make in a lifetime. This has been called "transfer trauma." It has been thought to even cause death. However, more recent reviews of the relocation of elderly persons have suggested that this is not as serious a problem as has been previously indicated. This is especially true if the person being relocated is involved in preparations for the transfer (Salamon & Rosenthal, 2004).

Questions to Ask and What to Look for in Choosing a Nursing Facility

In choosing a nursing facility, a range of questions should be addressed including:

- Is the facility licensed?
- Is the home eligible for Medicare and Medicaid reimbursement?
- Does the home have Medicaid residents?
- What are the basic costs of the facility?
- Does the home make extra charges for special diets or feeding a patient?
- Are there special charges for walkers, crutches, or canes?
- Are bills itemized?
- What about physician services?
- What are the visiting policies?
- What are the living arrangements?
- What is the food like?
- Are private physicians allowed?

- Who provides eye care, dental care, and mental health care?
- Are rehabilitation services available?
- Are clergy encouraged to visit?
- What is the ratio of staff to patient?
- What are the rules concerning personal possessions, including some personal furniture?
- Is the location convenient?
- What happens to residents when they become ill?
- Does the staff try to get to know the resident?
- Does the home encourage the participation of a resident council?
- Is there a way to effectively address the questions and complaints of residents and relatives?

Being a Caregiver for Someone in a Nursing Home

Even after a loved one is in a nursing home, an adult child or friend can still continue to be a caregiver. Relatives and friends who are responsible for elderly persons can have important roles and functions in the care of their institutionalized relatives and friends. There are some positive steps these people can take. These include: visiting, monitoring care, participating in decision-making on behalf of the patient, acquainting the staff with the patient, knowing the rights of nursing home patients, encouraging the patient to participate in resident councils, and participating in family councils (Riekse & Holstege, 1996).

PAYING FOR LONG-TERM CARE

Paying for long-term care is one of the greatest financial threats to older Americans. As a result, some politicians and public policy experts have called for relief for family caregivers in the form of financial support for long-term care. This is in part due to the reality that according to Georgetown University's *Long-Term Care Financing Project*, about two thirds of persons who turned age 65 in 2005 will require some form of assistance for an average of 3 years (Komisar & Thompson, 2007).

Almost half of long-term care is paid for by Medicaid—a federal-state program that offers relatively wide coverage for people who are poor. About 20% of long-term care costs are paid for by the Medicare program, the universal health care program available to all U.S. citizens age 65 and older. But Medicare long-term care benefits are very limited, focusing on rehabilitative, short-term services. Almost all of the rest of long-term care is paid for "out of pocket" (meaning self-paid) or with private insurance (Komisar & Thompson, 2007). So far, the demand for private long-term care insurance is quite limited due to its high cost, complexity of policies, and the hesitation of younger people to buy such policies for their old age (Brown & Finkelstein, 2008).

Additional information on the importance of careful planning when shopping for long-term care options is included in the Practical Application at the end of Part IV in this textbook.

Proposed Changes to Funding Long-Term Care

Three approaches have been proposed to fund long-term care: (a) increase the use of private long-term care insurance by providing tax subsidies and other incentives; (b) develop a new social insurance program based on the same principle as Social Security and

Medicare where everybody pays a modest percentage of payroll tax (1.7% in Germany) or a new value-added tax (VAT), or a modest increase in the income tax (about 1%) for such a program; or (c) blend private and public insurance, creating a hybrid public-private system that would require persons to buy private long-term care insurance through a government program (Gleckman, 2008).

The CLASS Program: A New Paradigm of Paying for Long-Term Care

Since these wide-ranging proposals were offered in 2008, a significant development occurred on the national level—the passage in 2010 of the Patient Protection and Affordable Care Act under the leadership of President Obama. Although the main objectives of this legislation were the financial protection of all Americans and the extension of health insurance coverage to the uninsured, a key component, often never mentioned, was the inclusion of the CLASS Act. According to Lisa Shugarman in an article in *Public Policy & Aging Report* (2010), the CLASS Act "fundamentally reframes the concept of long-term care from one of poverty, sickness, and loneliness to one of choice, community and personal responsibility in the face of functional impairment" (p. 3).

In describing this new legislation, Kathryn Roberts (2010) stated that the Act provided Americans with "the possibility to change the paradigm of how we provide pay for long-term care services in major ways" (p. 36). She went on to point out that CLASS would give Americans a long-term care insurance option, which is particularly important for those who have none and are not able to afford or qualify for private insurance. It also would enable more older people to remain in their own homes—where most want to stay—when they experience disabilities and long-term illnesses. It also would keep Medicaid in place for those persons who could not get out of poverty. Unfortunately, in part due to the projected costs of implementing the components of the CLASS Act, it has been shelved, at least for now.

SUGGESTED RESOURCES

The Family Caregiver Alliance: http://www.caregiver.org/caregiver/jsp/home.jsp
> The Alliance, a national community-based nonprofit organization, addresses the needs of families and friends providing long-term care at home. The website is full of information and publications for caregivers, including a care navigator and technical assistance center.

LeadingAge: http://www.leadingage.org/data.aspx
> Formerly The American Association of Homes and Services for the Aging (AAHSA), LeadingAge includes 6,000 not-for-profit organizations in the United States, as well as state and business partners and a broad global network of aging services organizations that reach over 30 countries. The website provides information and links to services, many focused on housing.

National Association for Home Care: www.nahc.org/
> This association connects the interests of care organizations, hospice organizations, medical care agencies, and in-home care aides. Resources offered on their website include an agency locator for assisted living facilities, legal advocacy for the elderly, and information on individuals' rights in assisted living homes.

National Association of Professional Geriatric Care Managers: www.caremanager.org/
> NAPGCM is a collaborative association connecting individuals with care managers who are registered though the association. Geriatric care managers provide assessment and support, referrals, and overall care for individuals and families. The website features an easy to use search for care managers in different regions.

Support Systems

Michael A. Faber

INTRODUCTION

The four chapters in this section explore a wide array of issues related to the primary, formal, and informal (family, friends, caregiving, religion, spirituality, and support groups) support systems of older people; medical care including Medicare and prescription drugs; and long-term care. This section focuses on critical real life issues related to caregiving including understanding and caring for the caregiver; role reversal; dealing with resistance, manipulation, and feelings of guilt and anger; and planning for long-term care.

Caregiving: The Ostrich Effect

This author has had the privilege to work with hundreds of family caregivers over the years. Unfortunately, one disturbing fact that I have encountered time and time again is that family caregivers often fail to plan for the inevitable and wait until they are in crisis to do anything. Thus, the above title, "the ostrich effect," is based on the fact that family members often bury their heads in the sand and do nothing until in crisis. The problem with this frequent reality is that it is difficult, if not impossible, to make good decisions when in crisis, not to mention the fact that one's options may be limited in time of crisis. Therefore, the old adage, "if you fail to plan, then you plan to fail" is often true.

How might this knowledge impact the work of a gerontologist? The obvious answer to this question is the need to educate and encourage family caregivers to recognize what the future may hold for their loved one and help them to plan for the anticipated needs and issues of those they care for. Also, for those planning to work with older persons, it is important to realize that working in this field often requires one to work directly or indirectly with family caregivers. To have the greatest impact in the life of an older person may require addressing the needs and issues of the entire family system.

Caring for the Caregiver

It is very important for a caregiver of an older person to not only take good care of her or his older loved one, but also to take good care of herself or himself. Family caregivers often sacrifice their own work, relationships, recreation, and sleep in an effort to meet the needs of their care recipients. Family caregivers also tend to feel the need to do it all by themselves, often not taking advantage of the formal and informal supports available to them. It is these types of behaviors that put family caregivers at high risk for burnout. In these cases, the old adage, "you can't give what you don't have" truly applies. The good news is that professionals working with family caregivers can help them to avoid burnout by encouraging them to:

- Educate themselves about their loved one's condition;
- Take time off to restore themselves by taking breaks from caregiving;
- Ask others for help and join a caregiver support group;
- Understand and accept their feelings as normal and deal with any feelings of guilt they might be experiencing;
- Maintain meaningful relationships with family and friends;
- Take care of themselves physically, emotionally, and spiritually;
- Adjust their priorities and be realistic in their expectations and commitments;
- Explore available community resources and seek appropriate advice from professionals such as attorneys, financial planners, medical and mental health specialists, clergy, etc.
- Plan ahead for and utilize possible needed services, such as adult day care, respite, and other long-term care options;
- Celebrate even small successes, and find ways to reward themselves; and
- Recognize that no one is perfect, remain flexible, and use humor wherever possible.

Role Reversal and the Sandwich Generation

Many adult children, as well as their aging parents, find the role reversal which occurs as parents become more dependent upon their children, a very difficult adjustment. Not only do the adult children provide parent care, but also often they are "sandwiched" between the added responsibilities of a marriage, teenage children still at home, financial obligations, and careers. The pressures faced by individuals in the *sandwich generation* are often unbearable, yet surprisingly, research indicates that adult children overwhelmingly do contribute to their parents' care in old age.

Dealing With Resistance

At times, an older adult may be in denial that a problem exists, and therefore may be resistant to accepting or receiving needed assistance. Resistance might also be the result of fear, anxiety, significant amounts of change, or a sense of loss of control. Whatever the reason, resistance can be very difficult and frustrating for family and professional caregivers to deal with. In situations of resistance, it is important for all involved to remember that the resistant older adult

- May be reacting to underlying feelings (fear, anxiety, loss of control, etc.) and in need of emotional support and adjustment assistance;
- Has been making his or her own decisions, good or bad, for an entire lifetime;

- Has the right as long as he or she remains mentally competent (able to fully understand and accept the consequences of his or her own decisions) to continue to make his or her own decisions without interference, even if others disagree with those decisions, and fear for his or her safety; and
- Probably won't be in denial forever. Often mentally competent older adults, at some point, will begin to recognize their limitations and accept assistance. Therefore, it is important for family members involved in their care to be patient with, loving toward, and available to resistant older adults, always continuing to gently encourage them to accept needed help.

However, the previous list does not apply to situations where the older adult is no longer mentally competent. In these situations, professionals should assist families in acting to protect an older loved one from harm. Professionals can assist family caregivers to keep the resistant older adult safe by making the following recommendations:

- Take control, don't offer an option, just move into the situation, and do what needs to be done. This will sometimes be successful, but other times may lead to further conflict and difficulties.
- Contact Adult Protective Services through a county's Department of Human Services. This is a governmental agency mandated by law to protect vulnerable adults in danger of abuse, neglect (including "self" neglect), and exploitation. This agency may be able to mobilize community resources into the home or help the family build a case for a guardianship.
- Seek legal counsel and petition the probate court for guardianship. If granted by the court, the person named as guardian is given the right to make decisions on behalf of the older adult.

To Drive or Not to Drive... That Is the Question

A common situation occurs when an older adult is resistant to giving up driving. Determining the point at which an older adult should no longer drive is not always easy or clear-cut. However, this is a difficult and serious decision, which needs to be made on a case-by-case basis through careful assessment of a person's driving skills, coordination, and judgment.

Dealing With the Resistant Older Adult Who Should No Longer Drive

Once a determination has been made that an older adult should no longer drive, the following techniques may be used to deal with the resistance that may occur:

- Strongly encourage the person not to drive.
- Arrange for someone to drive the person to his or her destinations.
- Involve his or her physician in the decision to give up driving. A physician can require a formal assessment of the individual's ability to continue driving (through referral to a driver evaluation program, or special testing available through the Secretary of State office (in some states, such as Michigan, anyone questioning another's driving skills can confidentially complete a "Request for Reexamination" form at the Secretary of State office, which will require the individual to go to the Secretary of State office for special testing).

- Ask a respected authority figure (i.e., pastor, lawyer, friend) or family member to reinforce the message about the need to give up driving.
- Find ways to distract the individual from driving (e.g., "I'd like to take you for a drive in my new car."; "Why don't I drive today, since the route is familiar to me and new to you." etc.).
- Hide and/or control access to the car keys.
- Disable the car (i.e., remove the distributor cap, or possibly have your mechanic install a hidden "kill switch").
- Remove or sell the car.

Understanding Manipulation and Feelings of Guilt and Anger

Many individuals struggle with feelings of frustration, anger, and guilt while caring for an elderly loved one. Some adult children feel as though their parents are using guilt and manipulation to "push their buttons" in order to get a desired response. Others may feel angry or cheated by the fact that their parents have become old and frail. Still others may feel guilty for viewing their parents' care needs as an unwelcome burden in their lives. This, in turn, may result in not only feelings of guilt, but also anger and frustration.

There is no question that caring for an older parent or loved one can evoke a number of feelings and emotions. It is important to remind family caregivers that it is not wrong to have these feelings as long as they do not act upon them inappropriately. Professionals should assist family caregivers by providing them with education and access to available resources, as well as help them to maintain positive attitudes and keep themselves physically and emotionally healthy.

Caregiver Resource

An excellent online learning resource for both family and professional caregivers (which this author helped to develop and maintain) is the Caregiver Resource Network website (at www.caregiverresource.net). This educational website provides a wide range of caregiver information and resources designed for both family and professional caregivers including:

- Caregiver stories,
- Educational articles and fact sheets,
- A self-check survey on personal well-being designed to identify caregiver stress,
- A variety of professional tools including a number of caregiver curriculums that can be used for self-study or group presentation, and
- Free downloadable audio radio programs on topics of interest to both family and professional caregivers.

Planning for Long-Term Care

When it comes to paying for long-term care, for many this will be the single greatest financial investment in their lives. This being the case, why is it that so many individuals do not carefully plan and shop for needed long-term care? I like to compare this to someone going to shop for a new luxury vehicle and buying the first one that they are shown by the dealer, without ever taking a test drive, kicking the tires, or doing extensive comparisons of the costs and features of different models and brands. This just would not happen, so why does it happen with the purchase of the much more expensive long-term care placement and services? I believe that the answer to this question relates directly to the fact that family caregivers and many older adults themselves fail to plan ahead and be proactive. Instead, they are reactive when in crisis. This probably relates to the fact that it is difficult for individuals to ever think that they themselves or someone they love might grow old, frail, and dependent upon others for care. Therefore, the role of the professional working in this field is to support older persons and their family members in times of crisis, as well as work proactively to educate and encourage advanced planning for the successful aging of all.

PART V

OLDER PEOPLE AT RISK

CHAPTER 16

Elders at Risk: Older Women and Older Minority Group Members

The learning objectives of this chapter include understanding

- The demographics and life expectancy of older women, older minority group members, and lesbians, gays, bisexual, and transgender (LGBT) elders in America.
- The economic challenges of older women, racial/ethnic minorities, and sexual minorities.
- The role of caregiving responsibilities, partner status, and living arrangements on economic security among elders at risk.
- The self-assessed health and chronic health conditions of elders at risk.
- The use of preventive health services among elders at risk.

WHO IS AT RISK?

This chapter focuses on Americans at risk for poor economic and health outcomes as they age—women, racial/ethnic minorities, and LGBT individuals. At various points in the history of gerontology, intersections of age, gender, and race/ethnicity have been perceived as producing double or triple jeopardy for the well-being of older Americans. Now well into the second millennium, nondominant sexual orientation should be added to these identities, which leads to the possibility of quadruple jeopardy—old, female, racial/ethnic minority, and sexual minority.

Demographics: Women, Racial/Ethnic Minorities, LGBT

What are the demographics of American elders at risk? Women outnumber men at every age, but the difference increases with age. Thus, an aging society is an increasingly female society. Figure 16.1 displays U.S. Census Bureau (2012) data on the number of older women and men in 2011.

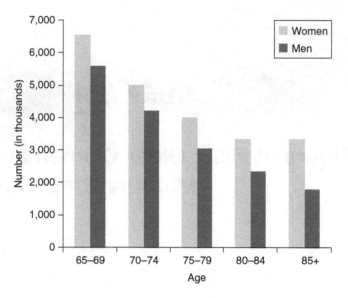

FIGURE 16.1 Number (in thousands) of Older Men and Women in the United States by Selected Age Groups: 2011.

Source: U.S. Census Bureau, Current Population Survey, Annual Social and Economic Supplement, 2011, Table 1.

Between ages 65 and 74, American women outnumber men by 15% (1.7 million); beginning at age 75, the difference increases to 24%. At age 85 and older, it is 46%, a ratio of just under two women for every man alive in that age bracket. In 2011, there were more than 22 million American women age 65 or older; 3.3 million of them were age 85 or older. It is projected that by 2060, there will be almost 50 million American women age 65 or older, and more than half a million of them (523,000) will be 100 years of age or older.

Figure 16.2 shows the proportion of our older population in each racial/ethnic group—White Americans, Black Americans, Hispanics, Asian Americans, and other races (the latter, alone or in combination) in 2010, and also the projected proportions in 2050 (U.S. Census Bureau, 2011). At 80%, White Americans are currently a large majority of the older population, with more than 32 million elders. Racial and ethnic minority elders represent just 20% of older Americans, with 3.4 million Black Americans, 2.8 million Hispanic Americans, 1.4 million Asian Americans, and 640,000 older Americans of other races.

The diversity of older Americans, however, will increase significantly over the next several decades. By 2050, racial and ethnic minority group members will grow to become 42% of older Americans. Though their numbers will grow (to 52 million), older White Americans will be a much smaller majority of the 65 and older population in the future. The number of Black Americans will increase twofold to 10.5 million. The largest increases will be in the number of Hispanic elders, who will increase more than fivefold to 17.5 million, and in the number of Asian American elders, who will increase more than fourfold to 7.5 million. This increase in minority elders is a consequence of two factors. One factor is improvements in the health of minority group members over their lifetime, leading to an increase in their longevity. A second factor is increases in immigration, especially among Asian and Hispanic people.

Data on the demographics of the LGBT population are scarce. Government agencies, such as the U.S. Census Bureau, have only just begun to include questions about sexual orientation and gender identity on their surveys, and it is uncommon to collect such data on older people. Of the five surveys described in the Institute of Medicine's (IOM) report on LGBT health, none included people over age 59 in their samples (IOM, 2011). One estimate is that there are 2 million people age 50 and older who self-identify as

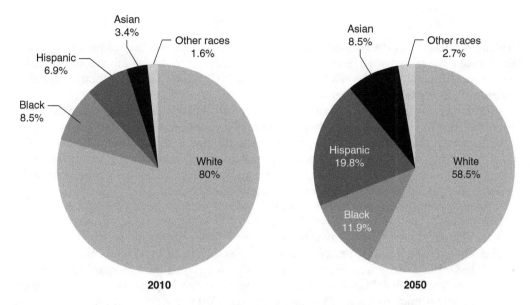

FIGURE 16.2 Percentage of Older Americans (65+) by Race and Ethnic Group: 2010 and 2050 (Projected).

Note: Other races includes all other races alone or in combination. Percentages do not add to 100% due to rounding.

Source: U.S. Census Bureau (2011). Projections of the population by sex, race, and Hispanic origin for the United States: 2010–2050. 2010 Census Summary File 1, Table 4.

lesbian, gay, or bisexual (LGB; Fredriksen-Goldsen, 2011). The National Gay and Lesbian Task Force estimates that there are 1.5 million LGBT people age 65 or older, which is expected to double to 3 million by 2030.

RISKS TO ECONOMIC SECURITY

Risks to the economic security of older women and minorities abound, and poverty is an all-too-common outcome. Among all older Americans, women and minority group members are the most likely to live at or near poverty levels. In 2010, the poverty threshold for a single American age 65 years or older was an annual income of $10,458, and for two people with a householder 65 years or older, it was $13,194. The "near poor" threshold is defined by an annual income between the poverty threshold and 125% of that threshold—$13,073 and $16,493 for one and two persons, respectively. People who are identified as living in poverty or near poverty are very likely to have inadequate resources for food, housing, health care, and other needs.

Based on the federal government's definitions of poverty, in 2010, over 17% of all older women were considered poor or near poor (U.S. Social Security Administration, 2011). For older men that proportion was 11.6%. Rates of poverty and near poverty for Black, Hispanic, and Asian Americans were 28.5%, 27.8%, and 20.6%, respectively, compared to 13% for White Americans.

A popular stereotype about LGBT people is that they are wealthy. Evidence to the contrary comes from a report by the first researchers to analyze data on poverty rates in this population. Albelda, Badgett, Schneebaum, and Gates (2009) found "clear evidence that poverty is at least as common in the LGB population as among heterosexual people and their families" (p. i). In fact, they said, "Gay and lesbian couple families are significantly more likely to be poor than are heterosexual married families" (p. i) and, as is the case for heterosexuals, women have much higher rates of poverty than do men. Older lesbians are twice as likely to be poor as different-sex married couples.

Income Inequities

One important reason for women and minorities' greater probability of being impoverished in old age is that their earnings throughout their years in the labor force are relatively low. Ultimately, the lower a person's wages, the less likely it is that they will be able
to accumulate assets and savings for retirement.

Women face cumulative discrimination in the workplace that begins when they first
enter the labor force, continues in their wages and promotions throughout their employment, and then affects their financial resources and benefits in retirement (Sugar, 2007).
Black and Hispanic Americans also experience discrimination in the workplace that
affects their lifetime earnings and retirement benefits. Figure 16.3 shows median weekly
earnings in 2010 for full-time workers, by sex and race/ethnicity.

Several patterns are apparent in Figure 16.3:

■ Women's earnings are lower than are men's for every racial and ethnic group.
■ On average, Asian Americans earn the most, followed by White Americans (11%
  less), Black Americans (an additional 18% less), and then Hispanic Americans
  (yet another 9% less). The difference between the highest and lowest earning
  racial/ethnic groups is 37%—an average of $320 per week in 2010.
■ There is an interaction between gender and race, a reminder that characteristics
  that contribute to elders being at risk are not simply additive. Even though Asian
  and White American women earn more than their Black and Hispanic sisters, the
  differences between their earnings and their male counterparts are 20% and 17%,
  respectively. Black and Hispanic Americans meanwhile earn just 7% and 9% less,
  respectively, than do their male counterparts. The smaller differences between
  female and male Black and Hispanic workers are likely attributable to the fact
  that these male workers' wages are low enough that the wages of their female
  peers cannot be that much lower.

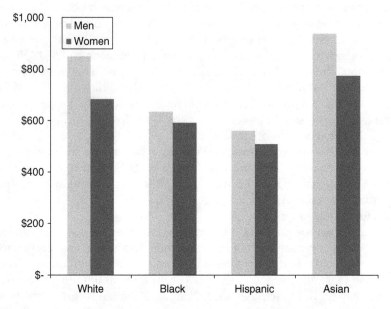

FIGURE 16.3 Median Weekly Earnings for Full Time Workers, by Sex and Race/Ethnicity: 2010.
Source: U.S. Bureau of Labor Statistics (2011).

One of the saddest commentaries on our society is that so many women live in poverty during their elder years. One "explanation" for this is that because women live to older ages than do men, women are more likely to outlive their financial resources. Although it is certainly true that, on average, women live longer than do men, it seems more than disingenuous to blame older women's poverty on their longevity. In fact, discriminatory policies and practices in the United States result in a substantial proportion of American women beginning their golden years with few, if any, accumulated financial resources.

To get a sense of just how much lower a woman's earnings could be over a lifetime of work, Sugar (2007) constructed a hypothetical case of a woman (call her *Sonia*) who begins full-time employment in 1975 and plans to retire in 2015. Using data from the U.S. Bureau of Labor Statistics on average sex differences in salary, Sonia's annual salary shortfalls were calculated for each of her hypothesized 40 years of full-time paid work between 1975 and 2015. The resulting total is a whopping $480,000 less in earnings than a male employee would receive over the same time period! This amount does not include the interest and potential other income that Sonia could accrue through investing the "extra" $480,000 she would have earned if she was a male employee. That amount for every older woman would go a long way toward ending poverty among older women.

Some good news about women's employment-related income is that the longstanding wage gap between women and men has been gradually closing. Both the women's movement in the 1970s, and its concomitant effects on the increased participation of women in the paid workforce, has helped to decrease sex differences in wages and salaries. In 1970, women on average earned 40% less than did men. By 2010, that gap had been reduced to 19%. The bad news is that women's wages are still significantly lower than men's. This is because, although women's wages have increased, men's wages have stagnated over that time period.

Although differences in salaries within occupational types do exist, what is clear is that female workers earn less than do male workers in all occupational categories (Sugar, 2007). So, occupational choices alone do not protect women from lower wages. Nor does a college education. In a study of male and female college graduates' pay, Judy Dey and Catherine Hill, researchers with the Educational Foundation of the American Association of University Women (AAUW), found:

> Controlling for hours, occupation, parenthood, and other factors [experience, training, etc.] normally associated with pay, college-educated women still earn less than their male peers earn.... As early as one year after graduation, a pay gap is found between women and men who had the same college major.... In biological sciences, a mixed-gender major, women earn only 75 percent as much as men earn. Female students cannot simply choose a major that will allow them to avoid the pay gap. (Dey & Hill, 2007, p. 9)

Thus, while some progress has been made in improving women's salaries relative to men's, women are still at a significant disadvantage in their paychecks. This disadvantage results in lower wages throughout their employment years, and a substantial risk of economic insecurity or poverty after they are no longer in the labor force.

And, if women stay in the labor force, or reenter it, after age 65, they can continue to expect lower wages than men receive. In 2010, the median earnings of full-time year-round female workers 65 years or over were $38,946, compared to $50,454 for their male counterparts (DeNavas-Walt, Proctor, & Smith, 2011), a gap which is larger than the overall average difference between women and men, regardless of age.

Caregiving

Taking on the role of a caregiver presents another notable reason for being at risk for economic insecurity and poverty in late life. As was pointed out in Chapter 12, the majority of caregivers in America are women. Caregiving responsibilities of any kind often lead women to cut back on their work hours, go from full- to part-time work, pass up promotions, change jobs for greater flexibility in their work schedules, take leaves of absence, quit their jobs, and take early retirement. Caring for a child usually brings about these interruptions in work history when women are younger, and caring for a parent, parent-in-law, or other relative has a similar impact on middle-aged and older women. Ultimately, these gaps in women's employment negatively affect not only their wages but also their retirement benefits, leading to long-term consequences for their economic security. The *MetLife Study of Caregiving Costs to Working Caregivers* (2011) estimated that the financial costs to female caregivers of exiting the labor force early totaled $324,000 in 2008—$143,000 from lost wages, $131,351 from lost Social Security benefits, and $50,000 from lost private pension benefits.

Work History

The role of work history in economic insecurity is also especially pertinent for women. It is impossible to understand the vulnerability of older women in American society without acknowledging the social roles that women have conventionally held. Traditionally, women's roles have focused on being wives, homemakers, mothers, community volunteers, and caregivers of ill and frail family members. For these roles, so important to any society, women have received no pay and no credits toward any retirement system. Their familial roles and less-than-full-time and intermittent participation in the labor force interact, frequently leading to economic and social dependency, costly for both them and society.

One of the main reasons women work part-time rather than full-time is to enable them to fulfill caregiving responsibilities for family members. Although more American women age 16 years and over are employed full-time than part-time (48 vs. 18 million), they are twice as likely to be part-time workers as are men (27%, and 13%, respectively, U.S. Bureau of Labor Statistics, 2011). In fact, during the critical years between 25 and 54 years of age, when employees are in the growth years of their careers for earnings, promotions, and accumulating retirement savings, only 75% of employed women are working full time compared to 89% of men.

Working part-time, as opposed to full-time, leads to several problems for women as they age:

- Their income will typically be too low to allow them to set aside savings for retirement.
- They are less apt to be offered promotions that would increase their incomes.
- Their contributions toward Social Security and other retirement vehicles, if any, will be lower.
- They are less likely to receive benefits, especially health care and employers' contributions to a pension fund.

Working part-time is one strategy women use to manage caregiving and other familial responsibilities. Another is taking leaves of absence. Due to concerns about young women taking leaves of absence and then potentially not returning to work, Sylvia Hewlett and Carolyn Luce (2005) conducted a survey to learn about ways to keep talented women on the road to career success. Among other questions, the nationally representative group of more than 2,400 college-educated women were asked about their experiences on returning to their jobs after taking leaves for various periods of time. The effect on their salaries was striking: compared to women who had not taken time out, those who took 1 year or less lost an average of 11% in their salaries, and those who took 3 years or more lost an average of 37% in their salaries. They were also significantly less likely to receive promotions after their return to work. The negative effect of the women's leaves, both in the short-term and the long-term, are examples of the costs women bear when they have an intermittent work history.

Partner Status

The likelihood of being impoverished is influenced by a person's partner status, including whether they are legally married. Compared to being single, having a partner, and thus two potential earners in a household as well as shared living arrangements, significantly reduces the chances of living in poverty. Unmarried folks (single, divorced, or widowed) who live alone have poverty rates between 2.5 and 5 times higher than their married counterparts. The rates of poverty for older men and older women who are married are very similar, ranging from 3.1 to 11.5%. Rates of poverty for older women who live alone range from 14.2 for White women to a shocking 41.5% for Hispanic women (U.S. Census Bureau, 2012).

In addition to adverse economic consequences, living alone means that as people continue to grow older and are more apt to need assistance at various times, if not on a long-term basis, help will not be readily available. Furthermore, being legally married bestows advantages on partners when it comes to health care and retirement benefits. Most employers do not provide benefits for an employee's partner unless the employee is legally married, and unmarried people cannot collect survivor benefits from Social Security. Couples in the LGBT community are at a distinct disadvantage in this regard because the federal government, and most states, have not legalized same-sex marriage, or civil unions that would grant same-sex couples the same rights as opposite-sex couples (read more on the status of legalized same-sex marriage in Chapter 6).

The modal partner status for older heterosexual men is married, whereas the modal status for heterosexual older women is widowed. In 2010, over three quarters (78%) of men age 65 to 74 were married, compared to a little over half (56%) of women in the same age group (*Older Americans 2012*). The proportion who are married is lower at older ages: 38% of women age 75 to 84, and 18% of women age 85 and over. For men, the proportion who are married is also lower at older ages, but not as low as for older women. Even among the oldest-old in 2010, the majority (58%) of men were married.

As they age, women of every racial/ethnic group are much more apt to live alone than are men, mostly due to their longer lives and the tendency for women to marry men some years older, which together bring about the greater prevalence of widowhood among women. In fact, older women are twice as likely as older men to live alone (37% and 19%, respectively). Figure 16.4 shows the living arrangements of older Americans in 2010 by sex and race/ethnicity.

Older White women and Black women have the highest rate of living alone, at 39% each, compared with 23% for older Hispanic women and 21% for older Asian women. Older Black men have a much higher rate of living alone—28%—than do other men.

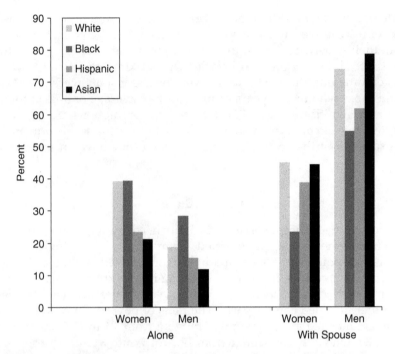

FIGURE 16.4 Living Arrangements of Older Americans (65+), by Sex and Race/Ethnicity, 2010.

Note: Numbers are percentages. (They do not total 100% because two additional categories for living arrangements [with other relatives, with nonrelatives] were excluded from this figure.) These data refer to the civilian noninstitutionalized population.

Source: Older Americans 2012, Table 5a.

Widowhood

Many older women live alone because, compared to older men, they are much more likely to be widowed, and the prospect of widowhood rises with age. Women age 65 and over are 3 times as likely as men of the same age to be widowed, 40% compared to 13% (*Older Americans 2012*). Nearly three quarters (73%) of women age 85 and over are widowed, compared to only 35% of men of the same age.

Widowhood presents especially serious economic problems for older women for several reasons. First, many older women rely on their husbands' retirement benefits. When their husband dies, Social Security benefits are reduced to the level of a single person. Private pension benefits are similarly reduced, and sometimes provide nothing for the surviving spouse. Women's accumulated savings throughout their lifetime are frequently inadequate to meet expenses without funds from their husband's retirement benefits. Secondly, a considerable portion of any savings may have been spent on medical bills prior to the husband's death. Thirdly, they lose the benefit of reduced costs from economies of scale for basic needs such as housing.

Retirement Pensions and Policies

Retirement benefits adequate to support older women and minorities in old age are rare. This is an especially challenging issue for women of all races and sexual orientation because their greater longevity means they need more financial resources in old age than do men.

The lifetime pattern of work that is often used as a standard or norm is a linear one in which a period of education is followed by a period of work, and then by a period of retirement. This has been the predominant pattern for American men, especially White men. Consistent with this lifetime pattern, all plans for pension income, including Social Security, are based on a model of full-time, and long-term, employment in the labor force, which is also the most common scenario for White American men.

Pension plans are based on earnings, and, as has been noted, on average, the earnings of women and minority group members are comparatively low. Remember the hypothetical case of Sonia presented a little earlier in this chapter? Both her Social Security benefits and private pension would be adversely affected by her lower income because both are based on employment earnings. And, because employers must match employees' Social Security contributions, and often match contributions to private pension plans too, Sonia's employer would also contribute considerably fewer dollars to her pension savings than would be the case if her paychecks were larger.

Policies regarding vesting periods for pensions also work against women's tendency to be in and out of the labor force. Vesting means that the employee has earned the right to keep pension contributions an employer makes on the employee's behalf. Regulations regarding vesting periods used to be highly advantageous to employers. For example, workers who left a company prior to an established 20-year vesting period would relinquish all contributions their employers had made to their pensions. (No matter how long a person works for a company, when they leave they always have the right to keep their own contributions.) Continuous employment for 20 years with a single company is not the norm for young women who may want to temporarily leave the labor force to bear and raise children, for example. Thus, long vesting periods discriminate against women, and, in so doing, contribute to the likelihood that they will be impoverished in their later years. This situation has improved as vesting periods have been reduced, and now the federal government requires employers to choose from two options, though employers can also provide more generous plans (e.g., shorter vesting periods). One option is for workers to be 100% vested after 3 years with the company. The other option is a 6-year graduated schedule through which workers become 20% vested after 2 years and 20% for each year until they reach 100% after 6 years with the company.

With the uptick in employers' use of 401(k) plans for pensions, married women face the possibility of new inequities. One example comes from the Pension Rights Center (n.d.):

> A wife will lose her right to a share of the money in her husband's 401(k) plan if her husband leaves the job that sponsors the plan and cashes out the account or rolls it over into an IRA. The wife's consent is not required. With 401(k) money increasingly becoming the largest asset of many marriages, this can result in a significant reduction of retirement income for women who work inside the home....Spousal consent is required to cash out benefits from defined benefit plans as well as defined contribution...plans.

RISKS TO HEALTH

Life expectancy is a basic measure of the overall health of a population. In Chapter 1, the average life expectancy of Americans was presented. How do elders at risk fare on this measure of health? Table 16.1 presents data on life expectancy at birth and also at age 65 by sex, race, and Hispanic origin.

It is a well-known fact of biology that the females of every species outlive the males, and humans are no exception. The differences between men and women at birth, which range from 4.7 to 6.3 years, narrow for all racial and ethnic groups to about 3 years by age 65. Thus, a significant proportion of the sex differences in life expectancy is a result

TABLE 16.1 Life Expectancy at Birth and at Age 65, by Sex and Race/Ethnicity

	AT BIRTH		AT 65 YEARS	
	Men	Women	Men	Women
Whites	76.4	81.1	17.7	20.3
Blacks	71.4	77.7	15.8	19.1
Hispanics	78.5	83.8	18.8	22.0

Note: Data for "At 65 Years" refer to years of life remaining for people who reach age 65.

Source: *Older Americans 2010: Key Indicators of Well-Being*, Table 14b.

TABLE 16.2 Percentage of Older Americans Rating Their Health as Good or Excellent, by Sex and Race/Ethnicity

	MEN	WOMEN
All	74.8	74.4
Whites	76.4	76.9
Blacks	65.2	60.7
Hispanics	64.8	62.5

Source: *Older Americans 2010: Key Indicators of Well-Being*, Table 18.

of conditions and events that lead to earlier deaths for men, for example, risky behaviors of young men that lead to deaths from traffic accidents. Reaching age 65 depends upon a person surviving all those health conditions and events that are more prevalent at younger ages. Of course, other health conditions, for example, heart disease, start to become more prevalent as a person ages.

As Table 16.1 shows, Hispanics have a greater life expectancy than White or Black Americans at birth, and at age 65. The better health outcomes of Hispanics compared to Whites has been deemed *the Hispanic paradox*, because the relatively low socioeconomic circumstances of many Hispanics should predispose them to poorer health outcomes (Markides & Eschbach, 2005). This paradox, and the greater life expectancy of female Asian/Pacific Islanders, suggest that there is much to be learned from studying life expectancy, health status, and the influences on them, in our increasingly diverse older population.

What do older people think about their own health? Chapter 4 included data showing that a majority of older people, including those over age 85, report good to excellent health. But what of the self-ratings of health among elders at risk? Table 16.2 presents the percentage of older Americans who rate their own health as good or excellent, by sex and race-ethnicity. Older White women and men self-ratings are equally likely to be high. However, Black and Hispanic women are less likely than their male counterparts to rate their health as good or excellent. A study by the IOM (2011) on the health of LGBT individuals found that cohabitors of the same-sex rate their health as poorer than married people of different sex.

Health Disparities and Health Inequities

The terms *health disparities* and *health inequities* are frequently used interchangeably, though they focus on different aspects of the fact that there are large gaps between population groups in the United States in access to health care, and the diagnosis, treatment, and

TABLE 16.3 Percentage of Older Americans With Selected Chronic Conditions By Race/Ethnicity

	WHITES	BLACKS	HISPANICS
Hypertension	54.3	71.1	53.1
Arthritis	50.6	52.2	42.1
Heart Disease	33.7	27.2	23.8
Cancer (any)	24.8	13.3	12.4
Diabetes	16.4	29.7	27.3

Source: Older Americans 2010: Key Indicators of Well-Being, Table 16a.

outcomes of health conditions. The term *health disparities* focus on differences between groups, and especially on groups with the poorest health. On the other hand, the term *health inequities* focus on the causes of such differences, especially the unfair distribution of health resources among population groups.

Health disparities and inequities among older Americans are a growing problem. The rapidly increasing population of older adults and the increasing diversity of that population are two reasons for concern, and escalating costs of health care are another. LaViest, Gaskin, and Richard (2009) at the Joint Center for Political and Economic Studies have determined that the costs of medical care and lost productivity as a result of racial and ethnic health disparities amounts to an alarming $309 billion per year. Considerable evidence exists that eliminating those health disparities will require improvements in "broader social, economic, and political inequalities alongside more downstream proximate factors that give rise to health inequalities" (Warren & Hernandez, 2007, p. 349). Furthermore, achieving a healthy nation is impossible unless all population groups are healthy and unless health inequities among these population groups are eliminated.

There are differences across the life span between the most prevalent health conditions in men and women, some of which, of course, are due to anatomical differences—for example, the prevalence of some types of cancers, such as uterine, cervical, and prostate. In addition, although breast cancer and osteoporosis occur in both men and women, they are much more prevalent in women. But other differences exist between older men and women, too. As age increases, so does the likelihood of developing a chronic condition, so it is not necessarily surprising that because women live longer than men do, they are also more likely to be affected by a chronic condition. Arthritis is almost twice as prevalent in women (35%) as in men (22%), and high blood pressure, the most common chronic condition in older adults, is also more prevalent in women (61%) than in men (54%). However, more men (36%) than women (27%) have heart disease. In general, older women (72%) are more likely to have two or more chronic health conditions than are older men (65%; Centers for Medicare and Medicaid Services, 2012).

Table 16.3 gives the percentage of older Americans with the top five chronic conditions by race/ethnicity. The differences among the groups are striking. Black Americans are more likely to have hypertension and diabetes; White Americans are more likely to have heart disease, and they are much more likely than Black Americans and Hispanics to have cancer; and Hispanics, like Black Americans, are more at risk for diabetes than White Americans. Consistent with the Hispanic paradox, the percentage of Hispanics with arthritis or heart disease is lower than other racial/ethnic groups.

It is one thing to be diagnosed with a chronic disease and another to die prematurely from one. A fine-grained analysis of data on coronary heart disease (CHD) reveals that Black women and men aged 45 to 74 years had much higher rates of death due to CHD than do White, Asian/Pacific Islander, or American Indian/Alaskan Native women and men. Premature death rates for Black women are higher (37.9%) than for White women

(19.4%), and higher for Black men (61.5%) than for White men (41.5%; Truman et al., 2011).

Although data on the health of American Indians, Native Alaskans, Native Hawaiians, and other Pacific Islanders are gradually becoming more readily available, these data seldom include information on older adults. Thus, there is limited knowledge about the health status and health disparities in these populations. The same is true for the LGBT community.

For American Indian and Alaska Native (AI/AN) elders, chronic diseases with high prevalence rates are arthritis, diabetes, and heart disease. The prevalence of arthritis among AI/AN elders is 43.5%, and, consistent with other groups, is more prevalent in women (50.2%) than men (35.4%; Center for Rural Health, 2006a). Among AI/AN elders with arthritis, 87% also have other chronic diseases, the most common of which are hypertension (59.2%) and diabetes (43.6%). Diabetes is more prevalent among AI/AN elders than among elders of any other racial/ethnic groups, with a rate of 31.3% (Kim, Bryant, Goins, Worley, & Chiriboga, 2012). Cancer rates in AI/AN elders are the lowest of all racial/ethnic groups in the United States, and one reason may be that the survival rate for in these elders is lower than it is for other groups (Center for Rural Health, 2006b). Poor survival rates are usually associated with late diagnosis and treatment.

A study of heart disease and its risk factors among Asians, Pacific Islanders, and Whites in Hawaii found that rates of heart disease, diabetes, and hypertension for Native Hawaiians were elevated relative to Whites (Juarez, Davis, Brady, & Chung, 2012). The researchers concluded that

> Our study highlights the importance of examining prevalence rates of disease and risk factors separately for API [Asians and Pacific Islanders] sub-groups and reveals the extent to which health disparities emerge at an early age.... By age 40, Native Hawaiians were at higher risk for diabetes and by age 50, they were at higher risk for heart disease than other groups. (p. 1008)

Little is known about the health of older LGBT individuals. The LGBT literature seldom includes information on older people, and the gerontology literature seldom includes information on the LGBT population. Due to experiences of stigmatization and their historically marginalized status in society, LGBT people often avoid or delay seeking health care, and even when they do they may not divulge their sexual orientation or gender identity to health care providers, all of which can jeopardize their health (IOM, 2011). Data from the Women's Health Initiative (Valanis et al., 2000) include information on lesbians and bisexual women. Compared to heterosexual women, breast cancer was found to be more common in lesbians and bisexual women, and the latter were less apt to have had a mammogram. Hypertension was found to be more common in heterosexual and bisexual women than it was in lesbians. In another study, the rate of hypertension in LGBT elders was reported to be 45%, which is lower than the rate for heterosexuals (IOM, 2011). The health effects of transgender individuals' long-term use of hormone therapy have not been studied, although it is thought that risks of cancers and cardiovascular disease may be elevated (IOM, 2011). HIV/AIDS is a concern in the LGBT community, especially for men who have sex with men and transgender women. Data on HIV/AIDS in older sexual minorities, however, are lacking. Although older adults, regardless of their sexual orientation, are largely ignored when HIV/AIDS is discussed, Chapter 6 presents information about the rates of HIV/AIDS among older adults and why they may be at a higher risk for HIV transmission than most people recognize, including older adults themselves. It is noted that HIV prevention programs rarely address older adults.

Preventive Services: Vaccinations and Screening Tests

Preventive services are one of the keys to preserving and extending the health of older Americans. With appropriate follow-up when necessary, services such as immunizations and screening tests are effective in preventing many health conditions and diseases, or detecting them in their early stages when treatment is more effective. Older adults' use of preventive services depends on a wide variety of factors including their access to health care professionals and preventive services, what they know about the services, as well as the actual costs of the services. Barriers for elders at risk, including poverty, discrimination, and health literacy, affect the use of preventive services. Racial and ethnic discrimination within health care settings have also been shown to affect whether, or how late, preventive services, such as cancer screenings, are provided (Crawley, Ahn, & Winkleby, 2008).

Vaccinations

Chapter 4 includes a discussion of the vaccinations that are most beneficial for older adults, which include influenza (flu), pneumococcal (pneumonia), and herpes zoster (shingles). Nevertheless, many seniors do not get vaccinated, including a disproportionately larger proportion of older minority group members. Of all vaccinations, the highest vaccination rates are for influenza—67.7% for White Americans, 66.8% for Hispanics, 67.9% for Asian Americans, and 68.7% for American Indians and Alaskan Natives, with a lower rate of 56.1% for Black Americans (Centers for Disease Control and Prevention [CDC], 2011). These numbers have substantially increased from very low rates prior to 1993, when Medicare Part B began covering the cost of annual flu vaccinations.

Pneumonia is one of the leading reasons that seniors go to hospital emergency rooms. It is also all too frequently a cause of death for them. Even though Medicare Part B has covered the cost of pneumonia vaccinations since 1981, a large proportion of older adults are not vaccinated for the disease, and there are health inequities between racial and ethnic groups here, too. White Americans have higher rates (63.5%), and Black Americans, Hispanics, and Asian Americans have lower rates of vaccination (46.2%, 39.0%, and 48.2%, respectively). A vaccine for shingles was first approved by the U.S. Food and Drug Administration in 2006, and subsequently all Medicare Part D plans started covering it. Unlike flu and pneumonia vaccinations, for which Medicare Part B covers all the costs, Part D plans may require cost-sharing, with the patient partially paying through their deductible or a copay. The newness of the vaccine and the potential cost undoubtedly contribute to the very low vaccination rates for shingles: 16.6% for White Americans, 4.5% for Black Americans, 4.4% for Hispanics, and 13.7% for Asian Americans (Greby, Lu, Euler, Williams, & Singleton, 2011).

Screenings

Lower rates are also found among women and racial/ethnic minorities in screening for preventable conditions and conditions that benefit from early detection. For example, for women between the ages of 50 and 74, White and Black Americans have the highest percentages of mammogram screenings (72.8% and 73.2%, respectively), and Asian Americans have the lowest percentage (64.1%; CDC, 2012).

A lot of attention has been focused on screening for colorectal cancer because, of those cancers that affect both men and women, it is the second leading cause of cancer-related deaths in the United States. Furthermore, when screening is done early enough the prognosis is very good. The CDC (2009) estimates that if everyone aged 50 years or older was regularly screened for colorectal cancer, at least 60% of deaths from this cancer could be avoided. Medicare Part B provides coverage for screening for many cancers, including colorectal cancer. Nevertheless, there are still significantly lower rates of screening for women and for racial and ethnic group members. Differences in screening rates suggest the need for further research to determine the reasons for these differences and then to find ways to address them, keeping in mind that reasons are likely to vary by gender and race/ethnicity (Jerant, Fenton, & Franks, 2008).

Research on health disparities is still in its infancy. Basic data collection on populations and subpopulations of elders at risk is critical for identifying and prioritizing the issues, for designing ways to ameliorate the disparities, and for evaluating the effectiveness of proposed solutions. There is also a

> need for community-based approaches that include policy, systems, environmental, and individual-level changes…and [a] need to tailor prevention strategies to the needs of specific communities to eliminate health disparities" (Liao et al., 2011, pp. 16–17)

Heterogeneity of Racial/Ethnic and LGBT Groups

Racial/ethnic and LGBT groups have been presented in this chapter as if they were homogeneous. Of course, within these groups there is much diversity. In the case of racial/ethnic groups, for example, Cuban Americans, Mexican Americans, and Puerto Ricans are all grouped with the ethnic label of *Hispanic* despite vast differences in their economic and sociopolitical backgrounds, which, in turn, can impact how much at risk they may be for different health conditions. The LGBT community is similarly diverse with respect to gender, sexual orientation, and race/ethnicity. Although some of the issues facing older adults in these groups have much in common, such as their historically marginalized social status, it is important to note that there are significant differences among subgroups within these populations. Such differences signal a need for more refined strategies and policies, including data collection, to improve the overall health of all older adults.

SUGGESTED RESOURCES

National Asian Pacific Center on Aging: http://www.napca.org
> Dedicated to ensuring resources and support for Asian American and Pacific Islanders as they age, the Center's website provides information on valuable resources, which include direct services, outreach, research, and advocacy.

National Caucus and Center on the Black Aged: http://www.ncba-aged.org
> The Caucus serves low-income elderly Black Americans. It works with policy makers, legislators, and the government to ensure that Black elderly communities are represented fairly. Information is available via the website for aging Black Americans on access to employment, health and wellness programs, and housing.

National Hispanic Council on Aging: http://www.nhcoa.org
> The Council works to educate, empower, and support aging Hispanic communities, through research, education, referrals to health care, and financial resources. They have information on a variety of health programs that they operate, such as an HIV/AIDS initiative, wellness programs, and immunizations for the aging Hispanic population.

National Indian Council on Aging: www.nicoa.org

    The Council's website provides resources on health care, conferences, advocacy, and employment for Native Americans and Alaskan Natives. Information is available on diabetes, long-term care, and elder abuse, among other topics.

National Resource Center on Lesbian, Gay, Bisexual and Transgender (LGBT) Aging: http://www.lgbtagingcenter.org

    The Center offers technical, educational, and training assistance to LGBT organizations, aging providers, and LGBT older adults. On the website are links to articles, publications, videos, webinars, slideshows, and audio programs, which can be searched by topic (more than 25, ranging from financial security to transgender issues). Website visitors can also search for resources in their communities.

Older Women's League (OWL): http://www.owl-national.org

    OWL is a nonprofit organization that serves to bridge the gap between women who are aging and groups that support aging communities. It focuses on research and advocacy.

CHAPTER 17

Elder Abuse: Crimes/Scams/Cons

The learning objectives of this chapter include understanding

- The definition and types of elder abuse.
- Characteristics of victims and perpetrators.
- Why older persons are vulnerable to abuse and/or neglect.
- Indications of physical abuse and/or neglect.
- The various types of scams perpetuated on older persons, and ways to prevent them.

OLDER VICTIMS OF ABUSE OR FRAUD

Mr. W had promised his wife that he would never put her into a nursing home. Even though she has severe Alzheimer's disease, he still tries to take care of her at home. He is 82 and she is 81. He has arthritis and has difficulty bending. He frequently shouts at his wife. Over and over he says, "Rose, don't do that. Rose, don't do that." He also slaps her hands. He told a visitor that he stopped trying to prevent her from eating the dog's food.

Mr. P is 62 years old, unemployed, an alcoholic, and lives with his 82-year-old mother. She is mentally alert but not able to get around without a walker. She depends totally on her son for groceries and for any transportation. Her son charges her $20 to take her anywhere. In addition, he demands that she give him "loans" of several hundred dollars. If she refuses, he becomes verbally and physically abusive. She usually gives him money, knowing he will use it for alcohol. She feels there is no alternative because she has no other children and is isolated from other people.

Ms. R is 72. Her mother is 92. Ms. R is suffering from congestive heart failure and is trying to take care of her aged mother. She is also suffering from depression, and over the last 4 months she has really neglected her mother's basic needs. On top of this, Ms. R is suffering from guilt feelings, because she has screamed at her mother, calling her a whiner. In the last week, she slapped her mother several times for her incontinence. She is thinking about suicide.

Ms. S has an income of over $300,000 a year by being involved in telemarketing scams. For years, she has been calling older people and is good at winning their confidence. She tells them she is interested in their financial future. She tells them about high-paying securities that she is selling, warns them that they will be sold out within the next 24 hours, and hopes that they will not lose an opportunity to buy these "gold-plated" financial instruments. Ms. S then asks for their savings account number and recommends that they not purchase anything less than $5,000 worth of these securities. Her voice sounds caring, soothing, confident, and trustworthy. Her financial instruments are virtually worthless and most of her clients lose most of their money.

Mrs. B received a call from a person offering a comprehensive physical exam, including state-of-the-art diagnostic testing, at "very little cost." The caller on the phone was so friendly and sounded so knowledgeable; it was a pleasure to talk to him. Mrs. B was not feeling ill at all, but after the friendly person called a number of times, she figured, given her age, why not give it a try. The 2-hour exam ended up costing Mrs. B $7,500.

ELDER ABUSE: A NATIONAL ISSUE

In the United States, elder abuse as a national issue first surfaced in 1978 when Congressman Claude Pepper, a tireless advocate for the needs and rights of the elderly, held hearings in the House of Representatives to expose the "hidden problem."

> Around the same time, an episode of *Quincy*, a late-1970s TV drama series, depicted a case of elder abuse, [which, it has been argued]...built support for the elder abuse agenda and contributed to public demands for changes in state and federal statutes. Also, *The Battered Elder Syndrome* was published by Block and Sinnott (1979) around this time. (Payne, 2009, p. 581)

A joint hearing by the U.S. Senate and U.S. House of Representatives in 1980 led to a report recommending that the federal government help the states deal with elder abuse by establishing a Prevention, Identification, and Treatment of Elder Abuse Act (Wolf, 1988). There was essentially no federal action until Congressman Pepper tried a new strategy, adding amendments to the 1987 reauthorization of the Older Americans Act (OAA) that defined elder abuse and authorized $5 million for program grants for elder abuse services and education. Nevertheless, Congress waited until 1990 to appropriate $3 million for fiscal year 1991 for these services. In the 1992 amendments to the OAA, $15 million was authorized to fund elder abuse programs, however, only $4.4 million was actually appropriated for fiscal year 1993 (Tatara, 1994). OAA appropriations for elder abuse prevention in fiscal year 2011 were $5 million, which is a reduction in funding of approximately $1.85 million relative to the value of the dollar in 1993.

Defining Elder Abuse

The World Health Organization defines elder mistreatment as "a single or repeated act, or lack of appropriate action, occurring within any relationship where there is an expectation of trust which causes harm or distress to an older person" (WHO, 2011). The OAA defines specific types of elder mistreatment, including elder abuse, neglect, and exploitation (learn more about the OAA in Chapter 13). Protection against these misdeeds is listed as part of the overall goals of the Declaration of Objectives for Older Americans of the OAA as amended back in 1972. State laws define elder abuse, but the definitions vary from one state to another. The National Center on Elder Abuse (NCEA) is one of the important gatherers of national data on elderly abuse and can be easily accessed via the Internet (see additional information on the NCEA in Suggested Resources at the end of this chapter). The NCEA has organized the definition of elder abuse into the following three basic categories:

- Domestic elder abuse
- Institutional elder abuse
- Self-neglect or self-abuse

Domestic Elder Abuse

Domestic elder abuse generally refers to forms of mistreatment of an older person by someone who has a special relationship (a spouse, a child, a sibling, a friend, a caregiver) in the older person's home or in the home of the person caring for the elder including:

- Physical abuse: Deliberate use of physical force that results in bodily injury, pain, or impairment.
- Sexual abuse: Nonconsensual sexual contact of any kind.
- Emotional or psychological abuse: Willful infliction of mental or emotional anguish by threat, humiliation, intimidation, or other verbal or nonverbal abusive conduct.
- Neglect: Willful or nonwillful failure by the caregiver to fulfill his or her caretaking obligation or duty.
- Financial or material exploitation: Unauthorized use of funds, property, or any resources of an older person. According to research conducted by Karen Roberto, director of the Center for Gerontology at Virginia Tech University, of the 1,128 news articles on elder abuse published from November 2010 through January 2011, 31% dealt with abuse of a financial nature, and older Americans are losing $2.9 billion annually to elder financial abuse ("The MetLife Study of Elder Financial Abuse," 2011).
- All other types: All other categories of elder maltreatment that do not belong to the above-mentioned five categories.

Institutional Abuse

Institutional abuse generally refers to the abuse that occurs in facilities designated for older people, such as foster homes, group homes, nursing homes, and board-and-care facilities. Persons inflicting institutional elder abuse usually are those who have a legal or contractual obligation to provide care and protection to the victims. They may include paid caregivers, staff, and professionals.

Self-Neglect or Self-Abuse

Self-neglect or self-abuse refers to neglectful or abusive behavior by an older person that is threatening to his or her own safety or health (Kelly, Dyer, Pavlik, Doody, & Jogerst, 2009). This type of activity generally results from the physical or mental impairment of the older person (Mosqueda et al., 2008). Most instances of physical, sexual, and financial/material abuses are classified as crimes in all states. Certain emotional abuse and neglect cases are considered criminal offenses depending on the perpetrator's conduct and the consequences for the victims (Connolly, 2008). On the other hand, self-neglect is not considered a crime in all states. Elder abuse laws in some states do not even address self-neglect (Naik, Teal, Pavlik, Cyer, & McCullough, 2008).

How Widespread Is Elder Abuse?

For the National Elder Mistreatment Study, Ron Acierno and his colleagues at the Medical University of South Carolina interviewed 5,627 community-residing people aged 60 and over who were cognitively intact (Acierno et al., 2010). They found that 11.4% of their interviewees reported that they had experienced at least one type of elder abuse in the past year—emotional, physical, sexual, or neglect. In addition, 5.2% reported financial abuse by family members. Note that the survey did not include cases of self-neglect or financial abuse by people other than family members. Furthermore, residents of nursing homes and other facilities were not interviewed, so the prevalence rates found in this research do not reflect the full extent of the problem of elder abuse.

Estimates put the number of elders who have been injured, exploited, or otherwise mistreated as high as 5 million. That may only be the "tip of the iceberg." Consistent with previous studies, the interviewees for the National Elder Mistreatment Study said that they seldom reported their experiences of abuse to police. The NCEA (2012) states that only 1 in 14 elder abuse incidents come to the attention of authorities.

Who Are the Victims?

Research has found that among confirmed cases of elder abuse, one third to one half are instances of self-neglect or self-abuse (Gray-Vickrey, 2004). It should be noted that while most states offer some protective services for elderly persons who neglect themselves, they are careful to consider a person's right to refuse these services (Connolly, 2008). This may result in a guardianship being established through court action, where a person appointed by the court can act on the behalf of the self-abused/neglected. Sometimes self-neglect results in placing the person in an institution, again through court action. These procedures usually are used only as last resorts for people in situations that are threatening to their health and safety.

Overall, low social support and isolation significantly increase the likelihood for elder abuse, as does having dementia (Bonnie & Wallace, 2003). Risk factors can also depend on the type of abuse. For example, for emotional, physical, and sexual abuse, as well as neglect, living with someone is a risk factor, while for financial abuse, living alone is a risk factor.

Who Are the Abusers?

Who is responsible for elder abuse? The NCEA reports that 90% of abuse is perpetrated by family members, most commonly spouses and adult children. Abusers often have mental illness or alcohol problems, and being financially dependent on an elderly relative is also a significant risk factor (Bonnie & Wallace, 2003). Data from state adult protective service units consistently find that women are more likely to be abused than are men, although these results may be skewed by the fact that there are more elderly women than men. According to the American Psychological Association (2012), "Elder abuse affects older men and women across all socioeconomic groups, cultures, races, and ethnicities" (p. 3).

CAUSES OF DOMESTIC ELDER ABUSE

A number of theories have been developed as to why elder abuse occurs. Why does a person become an abuser of an elderly individual? What are the circumstances that tend to lead to the abuse of an elder? The NCEA points out that elder abuse, similar to any type of domestic violence, is very complex and many factors are involved in its cause. Psychological, social, and economic factors that affect interpersonal and family relationships often combine with the physical and mental conditions of older persons and their potential abusers to result in domestic elder abuse according to this approach to analyzing the problem. When new stresses are added to already stressful situations that exist between elderly persons and the people around them, elder abuse may result. There is a mix of the existing situations between elderly persons and the people around them, their physical and mental conditions, and added stresses that enter their lives. The added stresses may be psychological, social, or economic, or a combination of these.

Theories to explain the causes of elder abuse include a situational model, which focuses on the affects of stress of the caregivers; an exchange theory, which focuses on dependency of elders on their caregivers; a social learning theory, which focuses on a repeated cycle of violence; and psychopathology, which focuses on mental or emotional problems of the abuser. In looking at these theories, it is important to note that they often combine to produce instances of abuse.

Stress of the Caregivers

As has been pointed out previously, caregiving for older people is a stressful role. This role is made more difficult when the older person being cared for is mentally or physically impaired, the caregiver has severe limitations because of his or her own problems or lack of knowledge of how to be a caregiver, and support from other family members is lacking. This theory stresses that a combination of internal factors in the caregiver—lack of coping skills, emotional problems—combined with external factors—mental or physical impairment of the older person being cared for, the financial burden of caregiving, lack of family or community supports—can result in elder abuse. This theory has wide support in the professional community.

Increased Dependency of Older Persons

This social exchange theory of elder abuse holds that abuse can occur when one person is contributing significantly more to a relationship than is the other person. The more powerful person in the relationship can manipulate the more dependent person, and being abusive may be an extension of that manipulation.

Cycle of Violence

Some families seem to be more prone to violence than others. Reacting to given situations in a violent way is a learned behavior that is passed from one generation to another. For these families, violence remains a normal behavior pattern throughout their lives—from child abuse through elder abuse. Clinical workers who have worked in both child abuse and elder abuse have observed these ongoing patterns of violence (Tatara, 1994).

Personal Problems of the Abusers

It has been found that persons who abuse older people usually have more personal problems than nonabusers. Adult children who abuse their parents often have mental and emotional problems, financial problems, or substance-abuse problems. As a result of these problems, these adult children are often dependent on their parents for support—the parents they end up abusing. This theory contends that the abuse of these parents by these dependent adult children is a response to their feelings of inadequacy (Tatara, 1994).

In looking at these and other possible theories to explain the causes of elder abuse, it is important to consider that no single theory can give a complete explanation. More research is needed to explore the causes of elder abuse as the aging revolution continues during the 21st century.

INSTITUTIONAL ABUSE AND NEGLECT

Up to this point, this chapter has focused on domestic elder abuse. It is important to describe briefly another setting in which elder abuse occurs—institutional settings, such as nursing facilities/homes or mental hospitals.

The rate of elder abuse is unclear for many institutional settings except community-based nursing facilities. In one study, 44% of nursing home residents reported that they had been abused (National Center on Elder Abuse, 2012). Psychological abuse, such as yelling at patients, has been observed by 81% of nursing home staff (Hudson, 2008). At least half of all nursing facility residents suffer from some form of dementia, mental illness, or impairment. These types of patients are particularly vulnerable to elder abuse and are unlikely to report instances of it.

Causes of Elder Abuse in Nursing Facilities

The reason for elder abuse in nursing facilities has been traced to four major underlying problems: (a) the lack of understanding of the cause of patient behavior, (b) dissatisfaction among the staff, (c) staff/patient conflict, and (d) burn-out among the staff. What these conditions result in is clear: a population of elder patients that is at high risk for abuse, as predicted by their multiple psychiatric and medical problems, cared for predominantly by young people who are poorly trained to work with the elderly population. They, in turn, are supervised by professional staff with limited experience in psychiatric diseases (Buzgová & Ivanová, 2009; Phelan, 2008).

POSSIBLE SIGNS OF PHYSICAL ABUSE AND NEGLECT

There are a variety of indicators that may point to elder abuse. For each category of elder abuse, these indicators include the following:

Physical Abuse

- Unexplained bruises and welts;
- Unexplained burns;
- Unexplained fractures, lacerations, or abrasions;
- Unexplained hair loss; and
- Evidence of past injuries.

Physical Neglect

- Consistent hunger, poor hygiene, inappropriate dress including soiled clothing, unexplained weight loss, dehydration;
- Consistent lack of supervision, especially in dangerous activities or for long periods;
- Constant unexplained fatigue or listlessness, or increased confusion;
- Unattended physical problems or medical needs, including urine burns or pressure sores;
- Lost or nonfunctioning aids, for example, glasses, dentures, hearing aids, walking aids, and wheelchairs;
- Over/under-medication; and
- Abandonment, immobility, hypothermia indicating possible isolation.

Sexual Abuse

- Difficulty in walking or sitting;
- Torn, stained, or bloody underclothing;
- Pain or itching in genital area;
- Bruises or bleeding in external genitalia, vaginal, or anal areas; and
- Unexpected and unreported reluctance to cooperate with toileting and physical examination of genitalia.

Emotional Mistreatment

- Habit disorder (e.g., sucking, biting, rocking);
- Conduct disorder (antisocial or destructive behaviors toward self or others);
- Neurotic trait (e.g., sleep disorders, speech disorders, inhibition of play); and
- Psychoneurotic reaction (e.g., hysteria, obsession, compulsion, phobias, hypochondria).

Note: It is necessary to assess whether symptoms and signs disappear in hospital or residential care over a period of time (Decalmer, 1993).

OTHER CRIMES AGAINST OLDER PEOPLE

In addition to elder abuse, older people are victimized by other forms of crime—the types that have become a focus of national attention in recent years. These include strong-arm robbery, murder, rape, aggravated assault, burglary, vandalism, purse snatching, theft of checks, and fraud.

Fear of Crime

It is important to note that older people tend to be more fearful of crime than are younger persons, and yet they are far less likely to be victims of violent crime—rape or sexual assault, robbery, aggravated assault, and simple assault. According to the 2011 annual report of the Bureau of Justice Statistics, rates for violent crime (which do not include homicide) were 4.4 per thousand for those 65 and older, and 49.0 for 18- to 24-year-olds (Truman & Planty, 2012). Data on homicides, which are collected by the *Federal Bureau of Investigation* (FBI), showed 607 homicides committed against those 65 and older, and more than 5 times that number—3,157—against 18- to 24-year-olds in 2011 (FBI, 2012). This does not mean that there are not many older people living in high-crime areas where it is dangerous for them to leave their homes. The fear and reality of crimes have resulted in many older people, particularly those who live in urban settings, becoming virtual prisoners in their own homes.

FRAUDS, SCAMS, AND CONS—RIPOFFS OF OLDER PEOPLE

A series of crimes that older people are not immune from, and indeed are often the prime targets for, are frauds, scams, and confidence schemes—all classified as consumer fraud. There are so many types of consumer fraud—the Federal Trade Commission tracks 30 types, and different ways that these types of fraud are committed, that it is difficult to calculate their full scope and impact. Fraud committed via the Internet has become such a problem, that in 2000 the FBI and the National White Collar Crime Center established the Internet Crime Complaint Center (IC3). According to the IC3's 2011 annual report, "Internet fraud has become one of the fastest-growing crime concerns facing the public. Nearly all crime that once was committed in person, by mail, or over the telephone can now be committed through

> ### Episode 9: Avoiding Cons, Scams, and Rip Offs
>
> **High Bandwidth:**
> http://raidercast.grcc.edu/flash/2011_2012/grcctv/successful_
> aging/success_aging_9_large/grcc_player.html
> **Low Bandwidth:**
> http://raidercast.grcc.edu/flash/2011_2012/grcctv/successful_
> aging/success_aging_9_small/grcc_player.html

the Internet" (Internet Crime Complaint Center, 2012, p. 19). The IC3 website lists and describes current and ongoing types of Internet crimes, provides prevention tips, and includes instructions for reporting such crimes (www.ic3.gov/default.aspx). Seniors are using the Internet more and more, so they, and future generations of seniors who have more lifetime experience with the Internet, will increasingly become targets for fraud committed through this medium. A discussion on how to avoid frauds, scams, and cons can be found in video 9.

Older People and Consumer Fraud

While people age 60 and over make up about 18.5% of the U.S. population, over 22% of consumer fraud was directed at them in 2011 (Federal Trade Commission, 2012). Research focusing on financial abuse has found that older people's annual losses amount to at least $2.9 billion ("The MetLife Study of Elder Financial Abuse," 2011).

There are a variety of reasons why older people are so often the victims of consumer fraud (Sharpe, 2004) including the following reasons:

- Older consumers are more easily contacted by telephone.
- Retired people and those who suffer from health problems or who have restricted mobility tend to spend much of their time at home, making them available to the swindler.
- Older people tend to be more trusting of salespeople.
- Older consumers tend to be less informed of their consumer rights.
- Many older persons welcome someone to talk with and are likely to let the con artists into their homes.

These factors do not mean older people are less intelligent. Older people experienced earlier times when trust was based on knowing the seller. In addition, older consumers often are inclined to rely on the expertise of salespeople who seem trustworthy and knowledgeable. This is particularly true for complex products about which an older person has little or no knowledge. Some are pressured by high-handed tactics of salespeople who get into their homes and will not leave until the older person agrees to sign on the dotted line. They literally become hostages in their own home. These predators of the elderly look for the most vulnerable older persons and then try to wear them down, play on their fears and needs, and increase their sense of helplessness. They end up robbing them of their money, dignity, and self-confidence (U.S. Senate Special Committee on Aging, 2005).

Telemarketing Scams

Telemarketing scams involve using the telephone to contact people in their homes with intent to defraud them. Older people are more likely to be targeted because the callers assume they may live alone, have a nest egg, and will be more polite toward strangers (Federal Trade Commission, 2012). In one version of these scams, older persons are asked to call an "800" or "900" number. They will then be offered prizes or low-priced trips, or an easily obtained loan. The "guaranteed" prize is one of numerous telephone-marketing scams. Often the caller will request a credit card number, and use that credit card information to make purchases, which are then charged to the older person. These callers often work from "boiler rooms," in which groups of persons will be calling constantly, trying to make "connections" with older people. They usually tell the person that the offer must be accepted immediately because it is only good for very short period of time (e.g., 24 hours or less). Some fraudulent telemarketing outfits contract with legitimate nonprofit organizations to raise funds but keep most of the funds for themselves to cover the "expenses" of calling. One version of this type of scam is to offer needed items such as trash bags, light bulbs, or birthday/holiday cards. These items usually are quite inferior and are priced very high. The telemarketing schemers then keep most of the profits.

Other telephone scams involve "cheap" trips, or "free" trips, or vacation housing at reduced prices, if the person acts immediately, which usually includes providing a credit card number. The swindlers will usually be willing to settle for a checking account number. Once the telemarketers have checking account numbers, they put them on "demand drafts," which function much like checks but do not require signatures. Often the victims are unaware that the bank has paid the drafts until they receive their monthly statements. As one older victim said,

> They called and told me I'd won an all-expense paid trip to Hawaii. All I had to do was purchase a round-trip ticket to Los Angeles. I gave them my checking account number and they took out $800 the next day. Two weeks passed and I hadn't heard from them. Turns out the company didn't exist. (Reyes, 1992, p. 72)

Con artists have found that it takes no more time to swindle $100,000 out of an older person than it does to swindle a younger person out of $3,000. Although persons 65 and over comprise about 12% of the population, they control over 30% of the wealth.

Mail Fraud

The mail service is frequently used to defraud older persons as well as persons of any age who are able to respond to mail-order advertisements. Some real-life examples of mail-order offers include:

- A "universal coat hanger" advertised for $3.99. What did consumers get stuck with? A sturdy 10-cent nail.
- A "solar clothes dryer" for only $39.99. Trouble is, it looked just like the clothesline and clothespin that were used years ago, and that was what it was.
- An ad for a 15-piece wicker set including a table, settee, two chairs, and a rocker guaranteed that the set would be exactly like the picture; that is just what the consumer got—a copy of the picture.
- An ad showing an actual photo of the product (a complete tool set and box for $40), so one couldn't be fooled, right? The ad was carefully worded to mention only the box—which was all the consumer got (Bekey, 1991; Morse, 2010; Steiner, 1989).

Medical Quacks/Frauds

Medical quackery is mostly targeted at older people. There is almost no limit to the fraudulent products and procedures offered to older people to reverse the aging process and treat or cure almost anything from athlete's foot to cancer. To pitch their quack remedies, the con artists use modern-day marketing techniques including ads in national magazines, supermarket tabloids, direct-mail flyers, television promotions that look like talk shows ("infomercials"), door-to-door salespeople, telemarketing, and the Internet. It is no surprise that anti-aging products flood the market promising new vitality and enhanced sexual vigor.

People with arthritis are especially vulnerable to medical quackery because most forms of arthritis go through periods in which the disease flares up, and then temporarily subsides. Knowing that, it is easy to claim that virtually any treatment will be effective because sooner or later the person will go into a natural remission, at which time the claim can be made that the treatment works. When the symptoms come back, as they are likely to do, it can be claimed that the person should either increase the treatment or just wait and the treatment will become effective. That is why many people who wear cooper bracelets for arthritis will claim that doing so is effective. In fact, scammers make these claims, because sooner or later anything will seem like it is effective. Not only are medical scams costly to the victims in terms of lost money and potential harm to the body, but relying on fraudulent products and treatments delays seeking diagnosis and treatment from reputable medical providers; and delays can be deadly in many instances.

Investment Fraud

With many older people trying to live on savings that they accumulated over years of work, they are natural targets for fraudulent investment schemes. Bank certificates of deposit are no longer paying the kinds of interest rates that made them attractive in the past, so older people across the nation have looked for higher returns from their investments so they could have a higher level of income. Fraudulent investment schemes may include phony artworks, gold, wines, gemstones, leveraged precious metals, rare coins, oil and gas leases, cellular telephone licenses, wireless cable and Internet licenses, and many more. They may include investments that are legal but simply not appropriate for older people because the risks associated with these investments are so high. In 2010, a survey conducted for the Investor Protection Trust found that "20 percent of Americans aged 65 or older—more than 7.3 million senior citizens—already have been taken advantage of financially in terms of an inappropriate investment, unreasonably high fees for financial services, or outright fraud" (Investor Protection Trust, 2010, p. 3).

One approach to getting seniors to invest their money is to offer "free lunch" seminars, often presented as opportunities to become more educated about investing choices. Concerned about escalating numbers of reports of financial scams being committed against seniors, federal and state regulators have been attending "free lunch" seminars to learn more about them. "In Arkansas, state agents…found that the dozens of seminars they attended all featured hard-sell pitches for financial products, many of which weren't appropriate for elderly investors" (Levitz, 2009). Of course, financial advisors are in the business of selling investments, but there are standards and rules set by the Financial Industry Regulatory Authority (FINRA), a private self-regulating organization. FINRA can and does adjudicate cases brought by investors. In addition to collecting $68 million in fines, in 2012, the FINRA recovered $34 million in funds wrongfully taken from investors.

Older people are especially vulnerable to investment fraud because they generally have more assets than younger people, live on fixed income, and may suffer from loneliness. Older widows can be more vulnerable because many have had limited experience in managing financial assets. Sophisticated, computer-generated lists provide the con artists with ways to identify newly retired employees, those receiving lump-sum pension payments, newly widowed older women, or older persons who sell their homes (Alt & Wells, 2004).

Living Trust Scams

Another scam largely targeted at older people is the high-pressure sale of living trusts. A living trust is a legal device to transfer real or personal property into something called a trust. The trust is managed by a trustee who may be the same person who set up the trust. It is an estate planning device that avoids probate. With this device, a person's property does not have to be processed through a Probate Court, which takes time and money.

This scheme takes advantage of the fact that between 30% and 50% of all the adults in the United States at any given time have not made adequate financial arrangements relating to their death (U.S. Senate Special Committee on Aging, 1993). As a result, slick-talking salespersons approach older Americans telling them how they can save purchasers of living trusts thousands of dollars in taxes and probate costs by "signing on the dotted line" and giving them what amounts to enormously inflated prices for what is often a very inferior service. They generally charge for something that may be inappropriate for an older individual's circumstances.

Phony Prizes

Either by telephone or by mail, these fraudulent schemes are used to notify potential victims that they have won a valuable prize such as a vacation, car, cash, or jewelry. Using various misrepresentations, these con artists lead the victim into buying items at prices that far exceed the value of the prizes. Through these schemes, it is easy for people to spend hundreds and even thousands of dollars on nearly worthless items. In many instances, the consumers never get the prizes that were promised.

Misuse of Guardianships

Another major area of fraud against the elderly is the misuse of guardianships. Guardianships are granted by court orders to manage the affairs of individuals who are judged incompetent to manage their own financial and personal affairs, including matters related to their health. A guardian can be a family member, a nonprofit social service agency, a public guardian, or a professional guardian. State or county offices may appoint a public guardian, and these offices also determine the conditions under which someone can be designated as a professional guardian. The appointment of a guardian typically means that the incapacitated person loses basic rights, such as the ability to sign contracts, vote, marry or divorce, buy or sell real estate, or make decisions about medical procedures (U.S. Government Accountability Office [GAO], 2010). Once a guardianship is granted by the court, it is not easy to reverse. Many people seek guardianship status to serve the best interests of their older clients. Unfortunately, many others take advantage of their authority, usually for financial gain, which can be accompanied by physical and psychological abuse.

In response to a request from the U.S. Senate's Special Committee on Aging, in 2010 the U.S. Government Accountability Office (GAO) was tasked with investigating the scope of allegations of abuse by guardians, looking into examples of abuse cases, and testing the processes by which states certify guardians. The federal government itself does not regulate or directly support guardians. The GAO's research could not draw conclusions about the extent of abuses by guardians because there is no entity—federal, state, or local government agency, or any other organization—that compiles data on allegations of such abuse. As a consequence, the number of abuses perpetrated by guardians is unknown. Examples of cases the GAO (2010, p. 7) did encounter include:

- In Arizona, court-appointed guardians allegedly siphoned off millions of dollars from their wards, including $1 million from a 77-year-old woman whose properties and personal belongings, such as her wedding album, were auctioned at a fraction of their cost.
- A Texas couple, ages 67 and 70, were declared mentally incompetent and placed in a nursing home after the husband broke his hip. Under the care of court-appointed guardians, their house went into foreclosure, their car was repossessed, their electricity was shut off, and their credit was allowed to deteriorate. The couple was allegedly given a $60 monthly allowance and permitted no personal belongings except a television.
- A 93-year-old Florida woman died after her grandson became her temporary guardian by claiming she had terminal colon cancer. He then moved her to hospice care, where she died 12 days later from the effects of morphine. The woman's condition was later determined to be ulcerative colitis, and the guardian's claims that she had 6 months to live were false. In addition, the guardian is accused of stealing $250,000 from the woman's estate.

In testing the guardianship approval process, representatives for the GAO applied to four states for guardianship certification using fake identities of someone with bad credit or the Social Security number of a deceased person. Guardianship certification was granted in all of these states—Illinois, Nevada, New York, and North Carolina (GAO, 2010). Even after appointing a guardian, most states do not demand much accountability from them. Most state courts are too busy to become very involved in examining in any great detail the activities of the guardians. The GAO found three consistent problems:

1. State courts failed to adequately screen potential guardians, appointing individuals with criminal convictions and/or significant financial problems to manage estates worth hundreds of thousands or millions of dollars.
2. State courts failed to adequately oversee guardians after their appointment, allowing the abuse of vulnerable seniors and their assets to continue.
3. State courts failed to communicate with federal agencies about abusive guardians once the court became aware of the abuse, which in some cases enabled the guardians to continue to receive and manage federal benefits. (GAO, 2010, pp. 7–8)

Proving financial exploitation is difficult because it usually requires the examination of financial records and following the flow of the victim's and the victimizer's funds. Added to these difficulties is the probability that if a guardianship has been granted, the victim is not able to provide testimony because of physical or psychological conditions. In other situations, the victimized person may die, and the guardian's exploitation of his or her estate may never become known.

These are some of the old as well as the newer frauds that are targeted at older people. The types and variations of scams and cons committed against older persons are endless. They continue to evolve, and marketing techniques continue to develop based on new technologies and strategies. What does not change is the fact that older people are exploited by greedy, ruthless con artists—exploitation that can result in financial ruin, loss of health, and even death.

PREVENTING CRIMES AGAINST THE ELDERLY

The con artist is often seen by the victim as a pleasant and caring person. They practice being friendly and try to project a kindly image. Not infrequently, the victim will state that they seemed to be such a nice person. Persons must always, unfortunately, be wary. They should never hurry in making a decision and should consult with family members and/or neighbors or others that they trust.

Many organizations and programs have been developed to educate older adults and their loved ones about warning signs and best practices for avoiding scams and other such crimes. For example, the National Council on Aging (n.d.) has created a list of "Top 8 Ways to Protect Yourself from Scams":

1. Be aware that you are at risk from strangers—and from those closest to you.
2. Don't isolate yourself—stay involved!
3. Always tell solicitors: "I never buy from (or give to) anyone who calls or visits me unannounced. Send me something in writing."
4. Shred all receipts with your credit card number.
5. Sign up for the "Do Not Call" list and take yourself off multiple mailing lists.
6. Use direct deposit for benefit checks to prevent checks from being stolen from your mailbox.
7. Never give your credit card, banking, Social Security, Medicare, or other personal information over the phone unless you initiated the call.
8. Be skeptical of all unsolicited offers and thoroughly do your research.

Some communities have formed something called *Triad/SALT organizations* in order to combat crimes against the elderly. Triads are organized when the local police and sheriff's departments agree to work cooperatively with senior citizens to prevent victimization of the elderly (Cantrell, 1994). The Triad concept began in 1987, when members of the AARP, the International Association of Chiefs of Police (IACP), and the National Sheriffs' Association (NSA) met to consider methods of reducing crime against the elderly.

SALT (Seniors and Lawmen Together) is the organization that the Triad usually creates when law enforcement personnel ask older persons, as well as people who work with them, to serve on an advisory council. The SALT organization typically conducts a survey to determine the needs and concerns of older people in their region regarding criminal activity. In describing the operation of the program, Cantrell (1994) wrote,

> Volunteers may staff reception desks in law enforcement agencies, present programs to senior organizations, conduct informal house security surveys, and become leaders in new or rejuvenated neighborhood watch groups. They may also provide information and support to crime victims, call citizens concerning civil warrants, or

assist law enforcement agencies in maintaining or property rooms of substations or in other areas. (p. 21)

In some areas, a Triad will create telephone programs in which older persons are called daily. In other areas, they have created shopping programs where grocery stores provide vans to transport older persons in regularly scheduled shopping trips. Triads also teach older persons safe ways to carry money and other valuables, as well as carjacking prevention.

Additional information on elder abuse, neglect, and exploitation as well as the ethical responsibilities of professionals working with older persons in reporting these forms of abuse can be found in the Practical Application at the end of Part V.

SUGGESTED RESOURCES

Center of Excellence on Elder Abuse and Neglect: http://www.centeronelderabuse.org/index.asp
This Center, located at the University of California, Irvine's School of Medicine, supports and disseminates research on innovative approaches to preventing elder abuse. It also conducts training activities and provides training materials via their website for home health aides and certified nursing assistants, nursing students, pharmacists, and pharmacy students, among others.

Elder Investment Fraud and Financial Exploitation (EIFFE) Prevention Program: http://www.nasaa.org/1733/eiffe
A variety of organizations have joined forces to create the EIFFE program to educate caregivers, including medical professionals, about financial abuse of elders. The website includes links to resources for seniors, service providers, and educators.

International Network for the Prevention of Elder Abuse (INPEA): http://www.inpea.net
Established in 1997, the INPEA's mission is to eliminate mistreatment of older adults globally. Members include individuals and organizations. Reports and resources from around the world are available via this website.

National Adult Protective Services Association (NAPSA): http://www.napsa-now.org
A national nonprofit organization, this association aims to improve the quality of services for older and vulnerable adults who have been mistreated, as well as to prevent mistreatment whenever possible. Among other resources, the site provides links to Adult Protective Services offices in all 50 states, Puerto Rico, and Guam.

National Center on Elder Abuse: http://www.ncea.aoa.gov
The Center's website provides descriptions and definitions of elder abuse, and laws concerning elder abuse. Resources, for families, caregivers, and individuals, include who to notify about elder abuse, how to contact authorities, and how to find state resources.

Older People at Risk

Michael A. Faber

INTRODUCTION

The two chapters in this section focus on the issues of older women and minorities, as well as elder abuse, neglect, and exploitation. This practical application will take a closer look at each of these issues, as well as examine the ethical responsibilities of the professional working with older persons.

Older Women and Minorities

As outlined in Chapter 16, older women and minority elders are economically and socially disadvantaged in many ways in American society. As a result, they are two of the highest need populations. Those who choose gerontology as a profession need to understand the needs and issues of older women and minorities in order to work effectively with these populations. This requires an open mind and a willingness to learn about different cultures, belief systems, and lifestyles.

For those considering a career in gerontology, this author recommends that they push themselves outside of their comfort zone through volunteerism. One can utilize volunteer activities to meet new people, experience different cultures and belief systems, and try new things to discover their potential niche within the field of gerontology.

Be Inspired...Be Inspiring

There is much one can learn from the wisdom of elders. This is one of the fortunate aspects of a career in gerontology; the fact that one has the opportunity to learn many important life lessons from the wit, wisdom, and life experiences of older persons. Those who choose to work with older persons should be open to the inspiration around them, and, in turn, use the knowledge and insight gained to inspire and teach others.

Elder Abuse, Neglect, and Exploitation

Families often get a bum rap with the common stereotype that they abandon their older loved ones. As noted throughout this text, families actually provide the majority of care for their elderly loved ones. American families often provide heroic levels of loving care including physical, financial, emotional, social, and spiritual support for their older loved ones. The sad reality, however, is that not all families provide such loving care, and, although not commonplace, elder abuse and financial exploitation do exist in America.

Another sad reality is the fact that elder abuse, neglect, and exploitation often go unreported. It is important to note that professionals working with older persons are required to report any suspicion of elder abuse, neglect, and exploitation. Many professions are legally required to report such abuse, including anyone licensed, registered, or certified to provide health care, education, social welfare, mental health services, and law enforcement. The role of the professional in helping to prevent elder abuse, neglect, and exploitation should not be underestimated. Through education, close observation, diligence, and when necessary, early reporting, the gerontology professional can help save the lives and well being of those older adults at risk.

The Ethical Responsibilities of the Professional

Financial exploitation of the elderly may be perpetrated by strangers such as con artists, but more often older adults are victimized by family, or other persons known to them including professional caregivers. Therefore, professionals working with older persons need to be ever vigilant, always know and practice ethical behavior, and remain above reproach doing everything they can to protect those who are vulnerable.

Gift giving is one area that professionals working with older persons may deal with in this regard. Older persons will on occasion offer personal gifts to those who provide them care and support. This can be a very delicate issue to deal with, because the last thing that anyone wants to do is to offend the giver and deprive him or her of the opportunity to express his or her gratitude. But it can also be a very tricky issue for the professional calling into question their honesty, integrity, and motivation. Was the older adult vulnerable due to lacking the mental capacity to make an informed and appropriate decision regarding the item that they gifted? Were they vulnerable due to physical or emotional intimidation or their reliance on the professional providing care? Let me provide an illustration. You are a professional providing regular in-home care to an elderly individual with whom you have developed a close relationship. On your last visit to their home, you mentioned how much you admired the painting hanging over their fireplace and jokingly hinted that your birthday was next week. Then on your visit to their home the following week, you were presented with this painting as a birthday present. If you accepted this gift, you might later find that it was worth thousands of dollars or a priceless family heirloom. The family, on discovering what happened, might even accuse you of theft. The good news is that most organizations/agencies that serve older adults have detailed policies on how to deal with this issue. It is this author's opinion that it is best to politely decline any such gift and to refrain from any comments that could be misinterpreted as a personal request for anything in their possession.

PART VI

PUBLIC POLICY ISSUES

CHAPTER 18

The Policies and Politics of Aging: A New Paradigm

The learning objectives of this chapter include understanding

- What public policy decisions are, and how they are made.
- The history of age-based public policies since the New Deal of President Franklin D. Roosevelt.
- The range of debates over entitlement programs and the political forces that impact these issues.
- The need for a new approach to making public policies in light of a new paradigm of aging.
- The politics of aging including senior power, the continuing development of the antigovernment New Right, and a new focus on an intergenerational approach to making public policies particularly as they pertain to health care, income supports, housing, transportation, long-term care, and overall quality of life issues.

POLITICS AND RETIREES: A CASE STUDY

In November 2010, Michigan, as did some other Midwestern states, elected a Republican governor, Rick Snyder. During the long primary and general elections, he portrayed himself as a rather benign, likable older middle age "nerd," a multimillionaire who wanted to cut taxes and regulations to help a state that was devastated by the loss of jobs in the car industry as well as those businesses that rely on making cars.

One of the first things this new governor did upon taking office was to promote legislation to cut taxes for businesses—big tax cuts, over a billion dollars. To make up this lost revenue he proposed major cuts to education, especially K-12 schools, and taxing the pensions of older people for the first time in the history of Michigan. Indeed, most of the reduction in business taxes was to be made up by taxing the pensions of retirees, and eliminating the earned income tax credits for lower income people, old and young.

*For the first time in the memory of some seasoned reporters in Michigan, big protest ral-
lies were held at the state capitol in Lansing with some signs saying, "Don't tax grandma." In a
front-page article about one of the largest rallies, one 40-year-old worker was quoted as saying,
"it was about time the older generation chipped in" (Roelofs, 2011, p. A1). A 21-year-old Calvin
College student in Grand Rapids said that the governor's plan to tax older people "makes sense"
to her. She went on to say that "she sees a government that is saddling those in a younger generation with a debt burden they didn't create" (Roelofs, 2011, p. A1). A professor at the same college
added, "Around West Michigan, what I am hearing is more, 'Every person for themselves. I have
to take care of myself because government isn't going to take care of me'" (Roelofs, 2011, p. A8; It
should be noted that Grand Rapids prides itself as a city of churches—The Grand Rapids Press,
April 13, 2011).*

A NEW PARADIGM OF AGING POLICIES

A new paradigm of aging directly impacts public policies and the politics of aging in
the 21st century. How society views its older members influences political decisions that
determine resource allocations as well as a wide range of societal policies that local, state,
and federal governmental units make on an ongoing basis.

To better understand what all this means, it is important first to look at what public
policies are, and why they are important to people of all ages—young, middle-aged, old,
and oldest-old.

WHAT ARE PUBLIC POLICY ISSUES?

Much of what is discussed and reviewed in some of the previous chapters directly relates
to the development of public policy issues and the political process in America. For many
people in contemporary America, including students, this seems to be either a dull subject or something that is not too relevant to their lives. In reality, nothing could be further
from fact. The development of public policy and the political process in American life are
simply ways of defining social decision making. Who makes decisions in a free society?
How are they made?

Public policy decisions are ongoing. They deal with important questions all of us
face on a daily basis. If Aunt Francis has to go to a nursing home, who will pay the
$75,000 bill she will ring up in a year? Why do I have to pay FICA tax each week when
I have real doubts that there will be any money in the Social Security trust fund when I
retire in 35 years? Why is it important to have entitlements specifically for older people
when so many kids in our country are so poor? How did the "greedy geezers" get so
greedy anyway? These are but a few of the questions and public policy issues people of
all ages raise, which ultimately get translated into political issues and become part of the
political process.

How Do Public Policy Issues Develop?

In a democracy, the development of public policy and the political process are the means
by which we address the pressing issues that many of us face in our daily lives. One
might argue that it really is not necessary to do very much, if anything, in a political way
to address many of the problems and issues most people face. But in reality, this approach
in itself is a way of dealing with issues. In fact, this has been a common approach throughout American history to many policy issues—a hands-off approach. Let each individual

take care of himself/herself or rely on family or immediate social institutions, such as one's church, to do so.

When specific problems and issues begin to grow larger, either because more and more people experience them, or the problems themselves become more complex and involved, it has been the American experience that they then become the subject of public policy debates and find their way into the political process.

The health care delivery debate is a ready example. Although health care delivery for all Americans was promoted by President Harry Truman in the late 1940s and early 1950s, not until the presidential campaign of 1992 did it become a primary public policy issue and end up as a centerpiece of Bill Clinton's political campaign. During the George W. Bush presidency, health care for all was not only unimportant, it was opposed by Bush and his top aides. With the campaign and election of Barack Obama, universal health care once again became a key issue. With the economic downturn of the late 1980s and early 1990s, and the Great Recession of 2008 to 2009 substantially leading to the Clinton and Obama presidencies respectively, increasing numbers of people—up to 47 million—found themselves with no health care coverage at a time when medical care was becoming more and more complex and increasingly expensive. Following the presidential elections of 1992 and 2008, the issue became how to achieve universal health coverage, not *whether* the United States should have health care coverage for all its citizens. Thus, health coverage became a public policy issue that ultimately entered the political arena.

AGING AND PUBLIC POLICY DEVELOPMENT

Dealing with public policy issues that end up in the political process can be looked at similarly. In his book, *The New Aging: Politics and Change in America*, Fernando Torres-Gil (1992), head of the Administration of Aging in the Clinton administration and professor of gerontology at the University of California at Los Angeles (UCLA), pointed out that the history of aging in America can be divided into three basic periods as it relates to public policy. The first period, "Young Aging," covers the history of America until 1930. The second period extends from 1930 to 1990 and is referred to as "Modern Aging." The third period, "New Aging," began in 1990.

Young Aging Period

The first period, "Young Aging," extended from the beginning of the nation to the Great Depression era. In this long span of time, the needs of older people were seen as the responsibility of the family and the local community. The family was, of course, the key element. For those poor elderly persons whose families could not or would not provide for them, many local communities established "poor farms" or some such institutions in which they could take refuge. However, it is important to note that there were not that many older people in the general population. With the average life expectancy of some 47 years in 1900, and with older people comprising only 4% of the population, caring for older people was not an enormous issue during most of our early history. Coupled with the agrarian, rural nature of our society at that time, with a large percentage of the people rooted to the land or small towns, providing for the needs of elderly people was relatively manageable.

With the coming of the Great Depression in late 1929, America took a more active role in dealing with its major social issues and problems. Many businesses and industries collapsed, resulting in large numbers of unemployed people across America. Economic survival became a key concern for most Americans and many problems of daily life became public policy issues, resolved through the political process. The political process resulted in the coming of the New Deal of President Franklin Roosevelt in 1933. The federal government played a whole new role in developing policies, structures, and institutions to deal with the pressing needs of people. In this period of Modern Aging, the pressing needs of the elderly, as well as the pressing needs of many persons of other age categories, became public policy issues that found their way into the political process (Torres-Gil, 1992).

The economic demands of the Great Depression of the 1930s were not the only forces that brought about a shift in public policy approaches in addressing the needs of older people in the Modern Aging period. Andrew Achenbaum (1983) noted four major shifts that resulted in the coming of the "Modern Aging" approach. These are: (a) demographic trends (increase in life expectancy as well as the numbers and percentage of older people in society); (b) changing images of old ages (older people increasingly looked at as a social problem); (c) group action among older persons (interest group activities and political action); and (d) new directions in social welfare (activist policies and programs as a result of the Great Depression).

THE MODERN AGING PERIOD

This analysis of how America got into the Modern Aging activist period follows our earlier illustration of how problems people face in their daily lives become public policy issues and enter the political arena for possible solution in a democratic process. The numbers of older people began to increase in the 20th century with more and more people living longer. In addition, the problems of this age group became more complex during the Great Depression; families were not able to meet the support needs of a growing elderly population due to their own pressing economic needs, and the reality that increasing numbers of families were dependent on an industrial economy, which was primarily urban based and in a state of collapse.

The Rise of Senior Citizen Activism

Added to the basic components needed to elevate issues and problems to the status of public policy issues was the development of citizen activism for and by older people—the beginning of senior power. The foundation for this citizen activism was developed in the 1920s, prior to the beginning of the Great Depression in October 1929. Three organizations emerged that promoted the adoption of old-age pensions. They were the American Association for Old Age Security, The American Association for Labor Legislation, and the Fraternal Order of Eagles (Day, 1990). Although all their efforts failed, they were the trailblazers for other movements that would follow.

One of the major efforts to develop public policy to improve the economic lives of older people was the Townsend Movement of the 1930s. This movement was headed by Dr. Francis E. Townsend who was motivated by the plight of so many older persons who became destitute as the result of the Great Depression. Dr. Townsend was a 60-year-old physician who had lost his job as assistant medical officer in Long Beach, California, during the Depression. He originally outlined his pension idea in a letter to the *Long Beach Press-Telegram* on September 20, 1933, at the depth of the Depression. His idea grew into a nationwide movement of 2 million people who organized 7,000 clubs. Although the movement never achieved its objective, it stirred public debate and elevated the economic security of older people into the public policy arena. It is credited with paving the way for proposals that became part of the Social Security Act of 1935 (Schulz, 1992).

It is important to note that professionals working in the field of gerontology also have a role in advocating for the rights and needs of those aging individuals that they serve. To this end, additional information on the role of professionals can be found in the Practical Application at the end of Part VI of this textbook.

A New Approach to Active Government

With the Townsend Movement of 1933 and the enactment of the Social Security Act in 1935 as a part of President Franklin Roosevelt's New Deal, a whole new approach to dealing with the basic needs of older persons in America was launched. In commenting on his 53 years of working in jobs relating to aging, including his early years in the Roosevelt administration at the beginning of the New Deal, Clark Tibbits, one of the pioneers in the field of aging, stated:

> I agreed with the late professor, Fred W. Cotrell's appraisal that enactment of this Social Security legislation represented the most radical extension of government into the private lives of citizens ever taken by the American government. (Cited in Schulz, 1992, p. XIV)

With this new approach to the role of the federal government in providing for the needs of citizens, especially older citizens, senior citizen interest groups and the Aging Enterprise emerged (Torres-Gil, 1992). Over this 60-year period, a whole range of programs, agencies, and benefits emerged to assist older people in meeting many of their needs. A variety of providers of services to the elderly emerged. For many of these services and benefits, age was the only criterion for eligibility. These are called *age-segregated programs*, or *entitlements*. A person receives benefits when he or she reaches a certain age, usually 60, for most of the programs of the Older Americans Act. Torres-Gil has pointed out that it is this series of programs and benefits for older people that comprise the system upon which the elderly of the nation and their families have depended for support. Some social policy experts back in 1990, such as Harry Moody (1990), have contended that these age-segregated programs are based on a view of the elderly that is outdated—a view that portrays older people as a vulnerable or needy group with nothing much to contribute.

IS THE AGING ENTERPRISE ENDING?

With very large annual federal deficits, the multitrillion dollar federal debt, escalating health care costs reflected in rising Medicare and Medicaid expenditures, and the suspicion of younger workers that they are supporting benefits for older persons that they themselves may never receive, there is intense pressure to reevaluate the programs and benefits of the aging enterprise that have been developed since the 1930s. Fernando Torres-Gil contended that the Modern Aging period has ended.

Former Colorado Governor Richard Lamm caused a public uproar when he agreed that too much is done for the elderly at the expense of younger persons. Organizations such as Americans for Generational Equity and the American Association of Boomers have contended that programs and benefits for the elderly should be reduced so that more money could be spent on groups that are needier.

Intergenerational Conflicts

The view of the elderly as needy and dependent began to shift in the 1980s (Torres-Gil, 1992). *Greedy geezers* became a phrase that portrayed these people as well-off, healthy, enjoying high retirement pensions (including Social Security), and living in luxury and leisure, much at the expense of poorer, younger people in America (Fairlie, 1988). With rising budget deficits and difficult economic conditions for millions of job seekers, including recent college graduates, many viewed the benefit programs for older persons as luxuries the nation could no longer afford (Torres-Gil, 1992).

Spokespersons for the elderly have for a long time contended that most older people are not *greedy geezers*. They have pointed out that older people have worked all their lives for the benefits they receive, including Social Security income. They also have shown that benefits such as Social Security, Medicare, and other age-related benefits actually ease the burden on younger members of the families of older people who traditionally assume the burdens of caring for aging parents in American society. Some advocates of the elderly have also claimed that many of the complainers of the younger generation are unwilling to work hard for their own successes. Some have contended that the younger complainers are spoiled. "They lived the good life with their parents, and they just expected that to continue," said Jim Wolverton, an advocate for seniors (quoted in Kellogg, 1993, p. A8).

Some senior advocates have also pointed out that older people have few opportunities to improve their lots in life. Young people may be able to get a job. It may not be the best job, or even a job for which they were trained. Many older people, especially the oldest-old, those with physical limitations, and those particularly discriminated against because of gender or minority status, have few if any opportunities for meaningful employment to improve their economic status. Their incomes are basically fixed for the rest of their lives, usually based upon earning and economic conditions of an earlier period.

Attacks on Entitlements

Pressures began to surface that indicated tensions between the generations for equal governmental support that led to the questioning of the scope of the entitlement programs for older people. The portrait of *greedy geezers* was one of the pressure points, meaning that some younger people felt that older people received too big a piece of the government support pie. Some of this pressure seemed to ease toward the end of the Clinton Administration when the policies of the government and business prosperity led to large federal surpluses—to the point that there was widespread talk of totally paying off the federal debt owed to private entities by 2012.

All of that dissolved with the coming of the Bush Administration in 2001. Not only did the policies and practices of this group lead to historic government debt (partly brought about by large tax cuts, primarily for the wealthy), but by a growing recognition that this Republican administration, unlike even previous Republican administrations (especially the Eisenhower, Ford, and George H. W. Bush administrations) had an agenda to dismantle the foundation entitlement programs that formed the basis of Modern Aging.

Nowhere was this clearer than in the Bush Administration's assault on Social Security—considered by many experts to be the most successful U.S. government program in history. Bush's plan to privatize Social Security by establishing private accounts dependent on the ups and downs of the equity markets was seen by many as a way to really change and ultimately weaken—and in the long-run, destroy—Social Security. This was the top priority of Bush's domestic policy following his reelection in 2004. But for a variety of reasons, in spite of tours to key American cities to promote this plan, Americans became less supportive of changing Social Security as time passed. A large percentage of the American people saw through Bush's motives and were not willing to radically change a system that needs some adjustment but is not broken nor really in "crisis" as they were told.

A Crossroad of Values

But in spite of the realization of the true facts about Social Security, the United States is truly at a crossroad in terms of public policy and the politics of aging, which is really part of the larger question of what is the role of government in the problems people face in everyday living. Should we be concerned about the fact that some 47 million Americans across all ages (especially children and young adults) had no health insurance before President Obama succeeded in passing health care reform? Does it matter to Americans that a 2009 Harvard University study determined that over 44,000 Americans die needlessly every year because they have no health insurance (Wilper et al., 2009)? Or does it only matter to those who have no insurance? Does it matter than most older Americans have no long-term care resources, and that caregiving for the elderly is mostly assigned by default to American women, the burdens of which are clearly detailed in this textbook?

As we move further into the 21st century, these and other basic questions need to be honestly and openly addressed if we are truly to be a just nation. Many politicians have talked endlessly about family values, but the issues outlined above, as well as many other social justice issues, are the real issues that determine our values as a people who live in the richest country in the history of the world.

Political Options

Much of the gloom and confusion surrounding the impact on society of having so many more people reaching old age directly relates to the almost constant drumbeat of too many politicians, policy makers, and pundits who continually predict disastrous results for the nation with the retirement of Baby Boomers. Dr. Robert H. Binstock (2007), a nationally recognized gerontologist, outlined what a new paradigm of aging means politically.

Binstock pointed out that the discussions of many politicians and pundits in regards to old-age policies are worrisome and confusing to most Americans. Much of this chatter about the aging and retirement of the 76 million Baby Boomers would lead one to believe that a demographic tidal wave and economic disaster are approaching the United States. These doomsayers continue to suggest that the aging of Baby Boomers is a real political threat as it will lead to greedy intergenerational conflicts over government benefits.

Binstock went on to point out that these doomsayers continue to predict that our present entitlement programs, particularly Social Security, Medicare, and Medicaid, will not survive the aging of the Baby Boomers unless radical changes are made to them—which usually means greatly reduced benefits. These radical changes would include (a) privatizing Social Security, (b) age-based rationing of healthcare, and (c) requiring people to work longer and retire much later. In regard to the last point, as outlined in an earlier chapter, there appears to be a trend developing for people to work longer into their later years. Research has shown that many of these older workers want to continue to work for a variety of economic, personal, and social reasons. But studies have also indicated that many of those who wish to work beyond normal retirement years are among the more educated and well-off categories of workers. This is quite different from all those categories of older workers who, because of physically demanding jobs, declining health, family caregiving demands, or loss of jobs for various reasons, need to retire. If the retirement support programs, such as adequate Social Security benefits and adequate health insurance provided by Medicare, are not available, this will present great hardships to these workers and their families.

Other proponents of reducing entitlement benefits for older people argue for the following:

Program-by-Program Cuts

Some congressional leaders have proposed other approaches to deal with the spiraling governmental expenditures they attribute to ever-growing entitlements, many of which have been developed for older persons. One such congressional approach is program-by-program cuts. This would involve going through mandatory spending programs one by one, trying to find ways to cut benefits, limit eligibility, or require recipients to pay more in the way of premiums, fees, or other payments. In this approach, federal, civil, or military retirees might have their cost-of-living adjustments cut.

Entitlement Caps

Another approach to curtailing federal spending for older people is to cap, or put a ceiling on, entitlements. If Congress is unable to make program-by-program cuts, across-the-board spending cuts on entitlements could be devised. Some have singled out entitlements, and the Americans who receive them, as the target for reducing the federal deficit. The primary entitlements affecting older people in this approach include Social Security, Medicare, Medicaid, and veterans' health benefits. Horace Deets (1993), a former Executive Director of the AARP, contended that this approach is off target. Entitlement caps, he argued, "would hit the poor, the middle-class, the young, the disabled, and the elderly with both barrels—by lowering income and increasing health care costs. Hardest hit would be low- and middle-income Americans" (p. 3).

Means Testing

Another approach to curtailing federal expenditures for a growing elderly population is to means-test benefits for the recipients. In this approach, benefits would be scaled back or denied to anyone of more than modest income and resources. Benefits would be targeted at the truly needy (Hager, 1993).

Fernando Torres-Gil (1992) has argued that means-testing Social Security would result in the loss of its support as a system. "It cannot be means-tested without losing the political support of those who pay into it through payroll taxes" (p. 112). He went on to contend that in means testing, "the more affluent and educated will depend on personal savings, asset accumulation, and private pensions. They will lose interest in preserving the basic structure of the Social Security system" (p. 112). He argued that this approach will only put future poor elderly persons in a more precarious situation.

Binstock (2007) described these situations—if they were to occur due to drastic changes and cuts to present-day entitlements—"as a return to a poverty-ridden old age for increasing numbers of people. Also, the uncertain and spotty health care of earlier generations of older Americans may again become a reality" (p. 33).

Some older adults' opinions about Social Security can be heard on Video 2.

Episode 2: Social Security and You

High Bandwidth:
http://raidercast.grcc.edu/flash/2011_2012/grcctv/successful_
aging/success_aging_2_large/grcc_player.html

Low Bandwidth:
http://raidercast.grcc.edu/flash/2011_2012/grcctv/successful_
aging/success_aging_2_small/grcc_player.html

IS THERE HOPE FOR PRESERVING BENEFITS?

If dismantling major benefit programs for the elderly is not the way to treat older people, and not politically feasible anyway, or if cutting programs across the board, capping them, means-testing them, or freezing them is unfair to the needy older people and counterproductive to their stability, are there any approaches to the benefit/entitlement dilemma that take into account the real needs of the growing number of older people as well as the pressing needs of persons in younger age groups in a nation with a growing national debt? Some approaches to these tough issues have been offered for review and debate by responsible policy makers.

Social Insurance

More recently, Schulz and Binstock (2006) contended that it is essential to maintain and strengthen the social insurance programs we already have rather than initiate some radical changes. These social insurance programs spread the risks people face in their everyday lives—risks from loss of income and risks from health problems and the real costs associated with medical treatments. Social insurance programs spread these risks among a very large pool of people instead of making the individual responsible for all the uncertainties of living. On an individual basis, it has been shown that many citizens simply cannot afford basic protections. We only need look at the millions of Americans who do not have any form of health insurance, compared to most older citizens who now have Medicare as significant health insurance once they reach 65 years of age.

Intergenerational Approaches

This intergenerational approach to the key issues and risks facing society as cited by Torres-Gil (1992) and Binstock (2007) is an integral outcome of a new paradigm of aging—looking at the basic needs of older people in the context of the whole society. Using this approach, for example, the health insurance needs of millions of Americans without insurance coverage could be addressed by implementing Medicare (presently only for people aged 65 and older) for all as in a single-payer financing system.

Reimagining America

In the first decade of the 21st century, AARP has taken bold steps to address the major health and income security issues facing Americans of all ages—not just older people or AARP members (membership eligibility begins at age 50). The first of these is an intergenerational approach called *Reimagining America: AARP's Blueprint for the Future*. It contends that the nation "can afford to grow older without economic train wrecks and without pitting the needs of the old against the young" (Novelli, 2005, p. 30).

Divided We Fail

Another effort of AARP to effectively address the pressing needs all Americans face was their *Divided We Fail* movement. Beginning as a joint effort of AARP, The Business Roundtable, and the Service Employees International Union, and quickly joined by the National Federation of Independent Businesses (representing 600,000 small businesses) and the Entertainment Foundation, this movement focused on the major domestic issues facing every American—not just older people or Baby Boomers (Novelli, 2007).

This movement tried to cope with the realities of contemporary American life where most of our political leaders are—and continue to be—stuck in gridlock, where "partisanship trumps problem solving just about every time; where millions of Americans also struggle for lifelong financial security, and most older people worry about their children, who for the most part are even worse off when it comes to health coverage and pensions and savings" (Novelli, 2007, p. 32). The AARP's *Divided We Fail* agenda was for everyone. Its thrust was to unite millions of voices to press political leaders to overcome partisanship and solve the real problems people face daily.

Family Values

Robert Binstock (2007) pointed out that even from a selfish point of view, the general public needs to understand that major changes and cuts to the existing entitlement programs would negatively impact adult children of the elderly and their families. If these entitlement programs were cut or eliminated, many more elderly persons would likely become financially dependent on their own families and their local communities. One only has to recall the county "poor farms" of pre–Social Security days when needy older persons who could not obtain support from their families (typically because these families were poor) were sent to a "poor farm." Binstock pointed out that without adequate entitlements, many families would be forced to live in three- and four-generation households, and also be responsible for the hospital and medical costs of their parents.

Binstock (2007) contended that these basic issues facing older people and their families are not divorced from communities and society at large. As he put it, "perhaps the best way to gain intergenerational political support for old-age policies is to frame options as family policies" (p. 33). Put this way the beneficiaries of these programs in the future "will be all of us" (p. 33).

In their book, *Aging Nation,* Schulz and Binstock (2006) suggested that one of the most effective strategies to counter what they term *the merchants of doom* (those politicians and pundits who proclaim economic disaster due to the aging of the population) and lessen conflict among the generations is to have AARP form a coalition that would advocate for all age sectors of society from children (such as the Children's Defense Fund) to older persons—and everyone in between. This focus would be on the basic needs that persons of all ages face, such as the need for universal health care.

They went on to point out that the merchants of doom promote the idea that "we are a country of age groups, divided from one another…engaged in intergenerational political conflict, young against old" (Schulz & Binstock, 2006, p. 234). They contended that the issues that confront older people are not isolated from the rest of society. One of the best ways to obtain popular support for policies and programs (such as Social Security and Medicare) would be to promote them as family policies because, in reality, that is what they are.

Robert N. Butler, a medical doctor and noted gerontologist who in 1968 coined the term *ageism* to describe discrimination against the old, wrote extensively on family values and public policies for an aging society. In his landmark book, *The Longevity Revolution*, he pointed out that, "although rooted in biology, the human family is more than a biological unit. It is a powerful, cohesive, emotional, economic, and social *centripetal* force that binds people together" (Butler, 2008, p. 60). Butler went on to point out that the term *family values* has been taken by the extreme right in the United States to include contraception, homosexuality, abortion, and school prayer, not social insurance, which can actually help families meet their real, and in too many instances unmet, basic needs. Indeed, the authors might note that these divisive issues of the extreme right have for many years formed the major policy planks of what has become of the Republican Party and the Religious Right, which has been a key component of that political party. Dr. Butler stressed that social insurance programs (also known as "entitlements") for older people in the United States are in reality family-based policies benefiting family members of all ages.

The Role of Taxes

Dr. Butler (2008) pointed out that the United States has one of the lowest tax rates in the world. And for those who think that taxes are higher now than in earlier eras, a look at the facts is illuminating. For example, when Dwight D. Eisenhower was president back in the 1950s, the top tax rate was 90%. And when President John F. Kennedy lowered the top rate for the wealthy, it went down to 50%, fully 10% higher than the rate President Obama proposed to become effective in 2011 (Harrop, 2009). In addition, President Obama proposed raising the capital-gains rate to 20% from the 2009 rate of 15% for families making $250,000 or more a year. Again, some cried a "War on Prosperity" (Harrop, 2009, p. 20A). Actually, President Ronald Reagan, known as an opponent of high taxes, instituted a capital-gains tax rate of 20% and raised it to 28% for high earners.

E. J. Dionne (2009), a noted writer for the Washington Post Writers Group whose work appears in many newspapers across the nation, stated that "the debate on the budget is phony, the howling on deficits a charade" (p. A13). He went on to say that debates about "entitlements reform" (changing and/or lowering social security benefits) are more important than ever because so many 401(k) retirement funds decreased as a result of the crashing equity markets in 2008 to 2009.

Toward a New Paradigm of Aging

Tom Brokaw (2007), former NBC *Nightly News* anchor, has pointed to his own family when his mother was in an assisted living facility in Southern California. He and his brothers were appreciative that he could afford to pay for her care. But more importantly, he pointed out that the nation cannot live with this lottery type of society where some people can afford to pay for care and have peace of mind, while so many others "are living in a state of terror about how they are going to take care of each other" (p. 35). He continued by saying that it is his (everybody's) obligation as a citizen to help the general welfare of this nation. All of this is integral to the new paradigm of aging for America.

Coping Strategies

In his book, *The Longevity Revolution*, Robert Butler (2008) provided a comprehensive plan to transition to a paradigm of aging, which he termed *The Longevity Revolution*. His political activist agenda includes, among others:

- Supporting equitable distribution of resources across generations.
- Working to reduce the widening gap of income and wealth and the inequity of longevity.
- Supporting universal health care.
- Sustaining Social Security.
- Establishing geriatric departments or equivalents in all medical schools.
- Strengthening public education.
- Protecting the human rights of older persons and the disabled (and all persons) against abuse and other forms of discrimination.
- Maintaining progressive taxation and estate taxes to avoid dynasties and promote a level playing field for the newborn.
- Strengthening unions, since labor is the true basis of society and prosperity, and to counterbalance the excess of capital. (pp. 318–319)

In the preface to their book, *Aging Nation: The Economics and Politics of Growing Older in America*, James H. Schulz and Robert H. Binstock (2006), leading gerontologists in the United States, contended that with the aging of the 76 (or more) million Baby Boomers, the nation faces many challenges in the 21st century. They state that:

- The Social Security program will require some adjustments—not a major over-haul or significant reductions in benefits.
- Employer-sponsored pensions need to be rethought.
- The Medicare program needs to be sustained so that older persons can share in the medical advances that will come in the decades ahead.
- The nation's health care system must be overhauled to contain spiraling costs.
- New policies will be needed to assist functionally dependent older persons and their families in dealing with the huge financial costs and other burdens of long-term care.

Robert Butler (2008) pointed out that for the first time in history the United States and the world's developing nations are beginning to see the entire lifecycle unfold for a majority of the population. Nearly all people in these nations expect to experience infancy, childhood, adolescence, early adulthood, middle age, and old age. But in addition to all the challenges older people—as well as people of all ages—face in defining and addressing what we call a new paradigm of aging for the 21st century, one hurdle continues that is difficult to overcome through public policies and political decision making, although they can help. That is the mind-set toward older people that Robert Butler defined as *ageism*. It is prejudice against those in society who are older. Butler pointed out that ageism is identical to any other prejudice in its outcomes. The prejudice of ageism takes many forms in numerous settings—economics (including work places), elder abuse, health care settings (including many medical schools), nursing homes, age-based health care rationing, and research protocols (health studies), to name a few.

As Eleanor Roosevelt stated, "Beautiful young people are accidents of nature, beautiful old people are works of art" (cited by Butler, 2008, p. 59).

SUGGESTED RESOURCES

AARP: www.aarp.org
> AARP is a nonprofit, nonpartisan organization that helps people age 50 and over improve the quality of their lives. It supports staffed offices in all 50 states, the District of Columbia, Puerto Rico, and the U.S. Virgin Islands.

Franklin D. Roosevelt American Heritage Center Museum: www.fdrheritage.org/new_deal.htm
> The museum holds one of the finest collections of primary source and other materials related to the New Deal.

Reimaging America: AARP's Blueprint for the Future: www.allhealth.org/briefingmaterials/aarpagingamerica-129.pdf

The Townsend Plan Movement: www.ssa.gov/history/towns5.html
> This website contains the plan, an issue of the plan's newsletter from 1934, editorial cartoons, decorative stamps, and other items related to the plan.

U.S. Tax Rates: www.taxpolicycenter.org/taxfacts
> Made up of nationally recognized experts in tax, budget, and social policy who have served at the highest levels of government, the Tax Policy Center is a joint venture of the Urban Institute and Brookings Institution. Among many other topics, find the Historical Top Tax Rate from 1913 to 2012 and Capital Gains and Taxes Paid on Capital Gains from 1954 to 2008.

Practical Application VI

Public Policy Issues

Michael A. Faber

INTRODUCTION

The chapter in this section outlined a new paradigm related to the public polices and the politics of aging in 21st century America. This new paradigm of aging stresses advocacy in the public policy arena for all age cohorts within the population. This approach is designed to decrease intergenerational tension and conflict, which further divides the nation and contributes to increased age-related bias. Another goal is to overcome ageism so prevalent in our society, as previously discussed in the Part I Practical Application.

Advocacy: A Personal Responsibility?

Serving as an advocate on behalf of the needs and issues of older persons has been a long-established role for many working in the field of gerontology. One cannot effectively work with older people if one is unwilling to advocate for the rights and needs of those one serves. Does the need for advocacy change in this new paradigm of public policy and aging, and, if so, in what way? If anything, the need for continued advocacy exists. The only difference is that one now needs to work for justice and equality in meeting the needs of all members of society and no longer advocate exclusively for the needs of older persons at the expense of other sectors of the population. If one works, through advocacy, toward the common good of all, we will improve the lives of those older persons we serve. Following this paradigm should help to alleviate intergenerational conflicts and dispel ageist stereotypes such as that of the "greedy old geezers."

If one chooses to work in the field of gerontology, it is important to stay informed on issues of concern to older persons and society as a whole. It is equally important to recognize and fulfill one's personal responsibility as an advocate. This can be accomplished in a variety of ways including:

- Helping to educate others on key issues of concern to older persons;
- Coordinating letter-writing campaigns on causes of significance (e.g., letters to the editor to local newspapers, letters to politicians, and other public policy decision makers, etc.);
- Writing letters of support on behalf of valuable community services in jeopardy of losing their funding or in support of needed programs or services;
- Joining an advocacy group or movement (e.g., AARP); and
- Becoming involved in the political arena (e.g., helping to get out the vote, assisting with a political campaign or cause, or running for office).

Becoming a Model of Lifelong Learning

As noted above, advocacy requires one to remain informed of the issues and concerns of older persons and society. In order to remain informed, one needs to become a lifelong learner. This is just one reason why those working in the field of gerontology should embrace and model lifelong learning. In the longstanding traditional model of learning, work, and retirement, it was thought that learning occurred primarily in youth, that work occurred primarily in mid-life, and that a recreation-based retirement occurred primarily in later life. This traditional paradigm has been challenged, especially by Baby Boomers, and is rapidly changing to a more integrated model of learning, work, and recreation equally disbursed throughout one's life. This new paradigm supports the concept of lifelong learning.

Personal Comments

One of the things that attracted this author to gerontology over a quarter of a century ago was the fact that it was a relatively new field where one could be a pioneer and make significant contributions to the lives of older persons. As a teaching professional, this author has always felt a responsibility to not just teach aging curriculum, but also to inspire and ignite students' passion for working with older people. This includes an effort to open students' minds to the many possibilities that exist in this "pioneer" field.

This author is reminded of an experience that he had during the junior year of his undergraduate gerontology studies. He had decided to take an *Introduction to Television Production* course, as an elective, with the intention of learning how to use the television/video medium within the field of aging. During the first class session, the instructor went around the room asking each student to share his/her reason for taking the course. When it came to the author's turn, he shared the belief that there was a connection between the TV/video medium and the field of gerontology. Everyone in the room, including the instructor, laughed. They just didn't understand. As it turned out, this writer had the privilege to be involved in both the production and distribution of a television series and nationally distributed educational videos on aging. This is shared to encourage students to continually and creatively think about how they might impact the future of gerontology.

As the aging population continues to grow in the United States and around the world, careers in gerontology will continue to evolve. Many future jobs in the field probably will not be today's established careers. Many may not be defined as gerontology jobs, but gerontology knowledge and skills in working with older people will be a key component of countless service occupations. A new paradigm of aging offers exciting opportunities to students with gerontology knowledge in all kinds of work situations as we move further into the 21st century with the aging of Baby Boomers.

References

2011 American Community Survey. *Geographical mobility in the past year by age for current residence in the United States.* Washington, DC: U.S. Census Bureau. Retrieved from www.factfinder2. census.gov

65+ in the United States. (2005). U.S. Census Bureau, Current population reports (P-23–209). Washington, DC: U.S. Government Printing Office.

A Profile of Older Americans: 2011. (2011). Administration on Aging (AOA), U.S. Department of Health and Human Services. Retrieved from www.aoa.gov/aoaroot/aging_statistics/Profile/index. aspx.

AARP. (2006, September). *Aging, migration, and local communities: The views of 60+ residents and community leaders.* Washington, DC: Author. Retrieved from www.assets.aarp.org/rgcenter/il/ migration.pdf

AARP Public Policy Institute. (2009, March & April). Mortgaging our future. *AARP Magazine,* p. 59.

Abrahms, S. (2008, January & February). Dorms beyond the norm. *AARP Magazine,* p. 13.

Abrahms, S. (2011, April). Happy together. *AARP Bulletin,* pp. 10–14.

Abrahms, S. (2011, September). The caregiver's dilemma. *AARP Bulletin,* pp. 10, 12.

Acevedo, B. P., & Aron, A. (2009). Does a long-term relationship kill romantic love? *Review of General Psychology, 13*(1), 59–65.

Achenbaum, W. A. (1983). *Shades of gray: Old age, American values, and federal policies since 1920.* Boston, MA: Little, Brown.

Acierno, R., Hernandez, M. A., Amstadter, A. B., Resnick, H. S., Steve, K., Muzzy, W., & Kilpatrick, D. G. (2010). Prevalence and correlates of emotional, physical, sexual, and financial abuse and potential neglect in the United States: The National Elder Mistreatment Study. *American Journal of Public Health, 100*(2), 292–297.

Administration on Aging, U.S. Department of Health and Human Services. (2010). *A profile of older Americans: 2010.* Washington, DC: Author. Retrieved from www.aoa.gov/aoaroot/aging_statistics/Profile/index.aspx

Age Discrimination in Employment Act of 1967. Pub. L. 90–202. Retrieved from www.eeoc.gov/laws/ statutes/adea.cfm

Aging in Michigan. (1992, January/February). *Prevent hypothermia, stay warm.* pp. 1–2.

Albelda, R., Badgett, M. V. L., Schneebaum, A., & Gates, G. J. (2009, March). *Poverty in the lesbian, gay, and bisexual community.* Retrieved from http://williamsinstitute.law.ucla.edu

Alibhai, S. M. H. (2006). Cancer screening: Applying the evidence to adults beyond age 70. *Geriatrics and Aging, 9*(3), 164–170.

Alt, B. L., & Wells, S. K. (2004). *Fleecing grandma and grandpa: Protecting against scams, cons, and frauds.* Westport, CT: Praeger.

Alzheimer's Disease Medications. (2008/2012). National Institutes of Health Publication No. 08–3431. Retrieved from www.nia.nih.gov/alzheimers/publication/alzheimers-disease-medications-fact-sheet

Alzheimer's Association. (2012). 2012 Alzheimer's disease facts and figures. *Alzheimer's & Dementia, 8*(2), 131–168.

American Association for Suicidology. (2010). *Elderly suicide fact sheet.* Retrieved from www.suicidology.org

American Association of Retired Persons. (AARP, 2000). *American business and older employees.* Washington, DC: Author.

American Medical Association and Council of Education Attitudinal Affairs. (1986). *Withholding or withdrawing life prolonging medical treatment.* Dearborn, MI: AMA.

American Optometric Association. (n.d.). *Dry eye.* Retrieved from www.aoa.org/dry-eye.xml

American Psychological Association. (2012). *Elder abuse & neglect. In search of solutions.* Washington, DC: Author.

American Public Transportation Association. (2010, March). *Funding the public transportation needs of an aging population.* Washington, DC: Author. Retrieved from www.apta.com

Ancoli-Israel, S. (2004). Sleep disorders in older adults. A primary care guide to assessing 4 common sleep problems in geriatric patients. *Geriatrics, 59*(1), 37–41.

Andreae, D. C. (1992). Alzheimer's disease: The family affliction. In F. J. Turner (Ed.), *Mental health and the elderly* (pp. 53–82). Toronto, Ontario, Canada: The Free Press.

Andrews, G., Clark, M., & Luszcz, M. (2002). Successful aging in the Australian longitudinal study of aging: Applying the MacArthur model. *Journal of Social Issues, 58*(4), 761–762.

Antonucci, T. C. (1990). Social supports and social relationships. In R. H. Binstock & L. K. George (Eds.), *Handbook of aging and the social sciences* (3rd ed., pp. 205–226). New York, NY: Academic Press.

Aronow, W. S., Flegg, J. L., Pepine, C. J., Artinian, N. T., Bakris, G., Brown, A. S.,...Wesley, D. J. (2011). ACCF/AHA 2011 expert consensus document on hypertension in the elderly: A report of the American College of Cardiology Foundation Task Force on Clincial Expert Consensus Documents. *Journal of the American College of Cardiology, 57*(20), 2037–2114.

Aronson, M. K., & Weiner, M. B. (2007). *Aging parents, aging children: How to stay sane and survive.* New York, NY: Rowman & Littlefield.

Arts, I. M. P., Pillen, S., Overeem, S., Schelhaas, H. J., & Zwarts, M. J. (2007). Rise and fall of skeletal muscle size over the entire life span. *Journal of the American Geriatrics Society, 55*(7), 1150–1152.

Atchley, R. C. (1985). *Social forces and aging* (4th ed.). Belmont, CA: Wadsworth.

Atchley, R. C. (1991). *Social forces and aging* (6th ed.). Belmont, CA: Wadsworth.

Atchley, R. C. (1994). *Social forces and aging* (7th ed.). Belmont, CA: Wadsworth.

Auger, J. A. (2007). *Social perspectives on death and dying.* New York, NY: Paul Co.

Austad, S. N. (2009). Making sense of biological theories of aging. In V. L. Bengston, D. Gans, N. M. Putney, & M. Silverstein (Eds.), *The handbook of theories of aging* (2nd ed., pp. 147–161). New York, NY: Springer.

Avoiding slips and falls in this holiday season. (2005, December 8). *Supplement to the Allegan County News and Union Enterprises,* p. 3.

Barker, J. C. (2003) Lesbian aging: An agenda for social research. In G. Herdt & B. de Vries (Eds.), *Gay and lesbian aging: Research and future directions* (pp. 29–72). New York, NY: Springer.

Barnhill, W. (1994). Self-help groups bolster Alzheimer's families. *NRTA Bulletin, 35*(3), 1, 15–16, 117.

Basler, B. (2006, July & August). Condo mania. *AARP Bulletin,* pp. 16–18.

Bekey, M. (1991, April & May). Dial S-W-I-N-D-L-E. *Modern Maturity,* pp. 31–41.

Beverly Foundation. (2010). *Fact sheet series,* Vol. 2(4). Retrieved from http://beverlyfoundation.org

Bickel, C. S., Cross, J. M., & Bamman, M. M. (2011). Exercise dosing to retain resistance training adaptations in young and older adults. *Medicine & Science in Sports & Exercise, 43*(7), 1177–1187.

Biles, B., & Arnold, G. (2010). *Medicare advantage payment provisions*. Washington, DC: The George Washington University School of Public Health and Health Services.

Binstock, R. H. (2007, March). The doomsters are wrong. *AARP Bulletin*, p. 33.

Blazer, D., & Sachs-Ericsson, N. (2005). Perception of unmet basic needs as a predictor of mortality among community-dwelling older adults. *American Journal of Public Health, 95*(2), 299–304.

Block, M., & Sinnott, J. (1979). *The battered elder syndrome*. College Park, MD: University of Maryland Center on Aging.

Bonanno, G. (2009). *The other side of sadness*. New York, NY: Basic Books.

Bonnie, R. J., & Wallace, R. B. (Eds.). (2003). *Elder mistreatment. Abuse, neglect, and exploitation in aging America*. Washington, DC: National Academies Press.

Brody, E. M. (1990). *Women in the middle: Their parent-care years*. New York, NY: Springer.

Brody, E. M. (2004). *Women in the middle: Their parent-care years* (2nd ed.). New York, NY: Springer.

Brokaw, T. (2007, December). Beyond self interest. *AARP Bulletin*, p. 35.

Brown, J. R., & Finkelstein, A. (2008). The interaction of public and private insurance: Medicaid and the long-term care insurance market. *American Economic Review, 98*(3), 1083–1102.

Brubaker, T. H. (1985). *Later life families*. Beverly Hills, CA: Sage.

Bryant, C. D. (2003). *Handbook of death and dying*. Thousand Oaks, CA: Sage.

Buckingham, R. W. (1983). *The complete hospice guide*. New York, NY: Harper & Row.

Burnell, G. M. (1993). *Final choices: To live or to die in an age of medical technology*. New York, NY: Insight Books.

Butler, R. N. (2008). *The longevity revolution*. Philadelphia, PA: Public Affairs, Perseus Books Group.

Butler, R. N. (2008, April). It's time for new age thinking. *AARP Bulletin*, p. 34.

Butler, R. N., & Lewis, M. I. (1976). *Love and sex after sixty*. New York, NY: Ballantine Books.

Butrica, B. A., Iams, H. M., & Smith, K. E. (2003). *It's all relative: Understanding the retirement prospects of Baby-Boomers*. Center for Retirement Research at Boston College (CRR WP 2003–21). Retrieved from www.crr.bc.edu/category/working-papers/

Buzgová, R., & Ivanová, K. (2009). Elder abuse and mistreatment in residential settings. *Nursing Ethics, 16*(1), 110–126.

Cacioppo, J. T., & Berntson, G. G. (Eds.). (2005). *Social neuroscience: Key readings*. New York, NY: Psychology Press.

Cacioppo, J. T., & Patrick, B. (2008). *Loneliness: Human nature and the need for social connection*. New York, NY: W. W. Norton.

Cacioppo, J. T., Hawkley, L. C., & Berntson, G. G. (2003). The anatomy of loneliness. *Current Directions in Psychological Science, 12*(3), 71–74.

Cagley, M. (2009, June). Social support, networks, and happiness. *Today's Research on Aging: Program and Policy Implications, 17*. Retrieved from www.prb.org/TodaysResearch.aspx

Campbell, S., & Munnell, A. H. (2002, May). *Sex and 401(k) plans*. Just the Facts on Retirement Issues, Number 4. Boston, MA: Center for Retirement Research at Boston College.

Cantrell, B. (1994). Triad: Reducing criminal victimization of the elderly. *FBI Law Enforcement Bulletin, 63*(2), 19–23.

Caregiving in the U.S. (2009, November). Bethesda, MD: National Alliance for Caregiving. Retrieved from www.caregiving.org/press-room-2

Carpenter, D. (2009, September 21). Meltdown serves as financial wake-up call. *The Grand Rapids Press*, pp. A1, A10.

Carpenter, D. (2011, October 30). 5 hot job sectors for older workers. *The Grand Rapids Press*, pp. F3, F4.

Carter, R. (1994). *Helping yourself help others. A book for caregivers*. New York, NY: Random House.

Center for Elder Rights Advocacy. (2011, November). *Senior legal helplines annual report. Calendar year 2010*. Lansing, MI: Author. Retrieved from www.legalhotlines.org/productivity.php

Center for Rural Health. (2006a, Summer). *Arthritis in American Indian and Alaska Native elders*. Grand Forks, ND: University of North Dakota. Retrieved from http://medicine.nodak.edu/crh (or www.raconline.org)

Center for Rural Health. (2006b, Winter). *Cancer screening practices among American Indian and Alaska Native elders*. Grand Forks, ND: University of North Dakota. Retrieved from http://medicine.nodak.edu/crh (or www.raconline.org)

Centers for Disease Control and Prevention. (2004). *National nursing home survey.* Hyattsville, MD: National Center for Health Statistics.

Centers for Disease Control and Prevention. (2006). *National health interview survey.* Hyattsville, MD: National Center for Health Statistics.

Centers for Disease Control and Prevention. (2009). *Heat stress in the elderly.* Retrieved from www.bt.cdc.gov/disasters/extremeheat/elderlyheat.asp

Centers for Disease Control and Prevention. (2009). *Colorectal cancer screening. Basic fact sheet.* Atlanta, GA: Author. Retrieved from www.cdc.gov/screenforlife

Centers for Disease Control and Prevention. (2010). *Health, United States, 2009: With special features on medical technology.* Hyattsville, MD: National Center for Health Statistics.

Centers for Disease Control and Prevention. (2010). Vital signs: Current cigarette smoking among adults aged ≥18 Years—United States, 2009. *Morbidity and Mortality Weekly Report, 59*(35), 1135–1140. Retrieved from www.cdc.gov/mmwr/preview/mmwrhtml/mm5935a3.htm

Centers for Disease Control and Prevention. (2011). *The CDC healthy brain initiative. Progress 2006–2011.* Atlanta, GA: Author. Retrieved from www.cdc.gov/aging

Centers for Disease Control and Prevention. (2011). *Final state-level influenza vaccination coverage estimates for the 2010–11 season-United States.* Atlanta, GA: Author. Retrieved from www.cdc.gov/flu/professionals/vaccination/coverage_1011estimates.htm

Centers for Disease Control and Prevention. (2012). *Breast cancer screening rates.* Atlanta, GA: Author. Retrieved from www.cdc.gov/cancer/breast/statistics/screening.htm

Centers for Disease Control & Prevention. (2012). *HIV surveillance report, 2010* (Vol. 22). Author: Atlanta, GA. Retrieved from www.cdc.gov/hiv/topics/surveillance/resources/reports/

Centers for Disease Control and Prevention and National Association of Chronic Disease Directors. (2008). *The state of mental health and aging in America. Issue Brief 1: What do the data tell us?* Atlanta, GA: National Association of Chronic Disease Directors.

Centers for Disease Control and Prevention. (2012, July). *Older employees in the workplace* (National Healthy Worksite Progam, Issue Brief No. 1). Atlanta, GA: Author. Retrieved from www.cdc.gov/nationalhealthyworksite/join/resources.html

Centers for Disease Control and Prevention and National Association of Chronic Disease Directors. (2009). *The state of mental health and aging in America. Issue Brief 2: Addressing depression in older adults: Selected evidence-based programs.* Atlanta, GA: National Association of Chronic Disease Directors.

Centers for Medicare and Medicaid Services. (2010). *Medicare current beneficiary survey.* Baltimore, MD: Author.

Centers for Medicare and Medicaid Services. (2012). *Chronic conditions among Medicare beneficiaries, Chartbook.* Baltimore, MD: Author. Retrieved from www.cms.gov

Cerf-Ducastel, B., & Murphy, C. (2003). FMRI brain activation in response to odors is reduced in primary olfactory areas of elderly subjects. *Brain Research, 986*(1–2), 39–53.

Challa, S., Sharkey, J. R., Chen, M., & Phillips, C. D. (2007). Association of resident, facility, and geographic characteristics with chronic undernutrition in a nationally represented sample of older residents in U.S. nursing homes. *Journal of Nutrition, Health and Aging, 11,* 179–184.

Chao, S. F. (2012). Functional disability and psychological well-being in later life: Does source of support matter? *Aging and Mental Health, 16*(2), 239–244.

Chappell, N. L., & Badger, M. (1989). Social isolation and well being. *Journal of Gerontology, 44*(5), S169–S176.

Charles, S. T., & Carstensen, L. L. (2010). Social and emotional aging. *Annual Review of Psychology, 61,* 383–409.

Chien, W., & Lin, F. R. (2012). Prevalence of hearing aid use among older adults in the United States. *Archives of Internal Medicine, 172*(3), 292–293.

Choi, C. (2008, July 9). Women fall short on saving. *The Grand Rapids Press,* pp. A1–A2.

Clark, R. L., Morrill, M. S., & Allen, S. G. (2012). The role of financial literacy in determining retirement plans. *Economic Inquiry, 50*(4), 851–866.

Claus, H. D. (2010, Winter). President's message. *New Horizons,* p. 2. Retrieved from www.hollandhome.org/PDFs/NewHorizons2010–1.pdf

Clements, J. (2006, March 9). Debt likely to derail boomers' retirement. *Bradenton Herald-Tribune,* p. 3D.

Clunis, D. M., Fredrikson–Goldsen, K. I., Freeman, P. A., & Nystrom, N. M. (2005). *Lives of lesbian elders: Looking back, looking forward*. Binghamton, NY: Hayworth Press.

Coan, J. A., & Allen, J. J. B. (2004). Frontal IEEG asymmetry as a moderator and mediator of emotion. *Biological Psychology, 67*, 7–49.

Coan, J. A., & Allen J. J. B. (Eds.). (2007). *Handbook of emotion elicitation and assessment*. New York, NY: Oxford University Press.

Cohen, G. D. (2000). *The creative age. Awakening human potential in the second half of life*. New York, NY: HarperCollins.

Cohen, G., Perlstein, S., Chapline, J., Kelly, J., Firth, K., & Simmens, S. (2006). The impact of professionally conducted cultural programs on the physical health, mental health and social functioning of older adults. *The Gerontologist, 46*(6), 726–734.

Collerton, J., Davies, K., Jagger, C., Kingston, A., Bond, J., Eccles, M. P., ... Kirkwood, T. B. L. (2009). Health and disease in 85 year olds: Baseline findings from the Newcastle 85+ cohort study. *British Medical Journal, 399*, b4904. doi:10.1136/bmj.b4904.

Commonwealth Fund. (1991). *New findings show why employing workers over 50 makes good financial sense for companies*. New York, NY: Author.

Connolly, M-T. (2008). Elder self-neglect and the justice system: An essay from an interdisciplinary perspective. *Journal of the American Geriatrics Society, 56*(S2), S244–S252.

Cooper, J. W. (1994). Getting ready to retire: Preretirement planning programs. In A. Monk (Ed.), *The Columbia retirement handbook* (pp. 59–80). New York, NY: Columbia University Press.

Cose, E. (2009, November 9). Fired is the new retired: The idiocy of axing older employees. *Newsweek*, p. 26

Costa, P. T., & McCrae, R. R. (1980). Still stable after these years: Personality as a key to some issues in aging. In P. B. Baltes & O. G. Brim (Eds.), *Life-span development and behavior* (Vol. 3, pp. 66–102). New York, NY: Academic Press.

Cowgill, D. O., & Holmes, L. (1972). *Aging and modernization*. New York, NY: Appleton-Century- Crofts.

Cox, C. B. (2005). *Community care for an aging society: Issues, policies, and services*. New York, NY: Springer.

Cox, H. G. (1994). Roles for aged individuals in postindustrial societies. In H. Cox (Ed.), *Annual editions, aging* (9th ed. pp. 62–66). Sluice Dock Guilford, CT: Dushkin.

Crawley, L. M., Ahn, D. K., & Winkleby, M. A. (2008). Perceived medical discrimination and cancer screening behaviors of racial and ethnic minority adults. *Cancer Epidemiology, Biomarkers & Prevention, 17*, 1937–1944.

Crews, D. (1993). Culture lags in social perceptions of the aged. *Generations, 17*(2), 29–33.

Crohan, S. E., & Antonucci, T. C. (1989). Friends as a source of social support in old age. In R. Adams & R. Blieszner (Eds.), *Older adult friendships: Structure and process* (pp. 129–146). Beverly Hills, CA: Sage.

Cumming, E., & Henry, W. E. (1961). *Growing old: The process of disengagement*. New York, NY: Basic Books.

Cutler, N. E., Whitelaw, N. A., & Beattie, B. L. (2002). *American perceptions of aging in the 21st century*. Washington, DC: The National Council on Aging.

Day, C. (1990). *What older Americans think: Interest groups and aging policy*. Princeton, NJ: Princeton University Press.

Decalmer, P. (1993). Clinical presentation. In P. Decalmer & F. Glendenning, (Eds.), *The mistreatment of elderly people* (pp. 35–61). Newbury, CA: Sage.

Deets, H. B. (1993). Attack on entitlements mock shared sacrifice. *NRTA Bulletin, 34*(7).

Demos, J. (1965). Notes on life in Plymouth Colony. *William and Mary Quarterly, 22*(3), 264–286.

DeNavas-Walt, C., Proctor, B. D., & Smith, J. C. (2011). *Income, poverty, and health insurance coverage in the United States: 2010*. U.S. Census Bureau, Current Population Reports, P60–239, Table A-6. Washington, DC: U.S. Government Printing Office.

Dey, J. G., & Hill, C. (2007). *Behind the pay gap*. Washington, DC: American Association of University Women Educational Foundation. Retrieved from www.aauw.org

Diabetes Prevention Program Research Group. (2002, February 7). Reduction in the incidence of Type 2 diabetes with lifestyle intervention or metformin. *The New England Journal of Medicine, 346*(6), 393–403.

Diament, M. (2007, June). Affluent boomers flock to town centers. *AARP Bulletin*, p. 9.

Dickinson, G. E., Clark, D., Winslow, M., & Marples, R. (2005). U.S. physicians' attitudes concerning euthanasia and physician-assisted death: A systematic literature review. *Mortality, 10,* 43–52.

Dionne, E. J., Jr. (2009, March 29). A deficit of truth about the need for taxes. *The Grand Rapids Press,* p. A13.

Dowd, J. E., & Stafford, D. (2008). *The vitamin D cure*. Hoboken, NJ: Wiley.

Edwards, B. A., O'Driscoll, D. M., Ali, A., Jordan, A. S., Trinder, J., & Malhotra, A. (2010). Aging and sleep: Physiology and pathophysiology. *Seminars in Respiratory and Critical Care Medicine, 31*(5), 618–633.

Eisenberger, N. I. (2006). Identifying the neural correlates underlying social pain. *Human Development, 49*(5), 273–293.

Eisenberger, N. I., Jarcho, J. M., Lieberman, M. D., & Naliboff, B. (2006). An experimental study of shared sensitivity to physical pain and social rejection. *Pain, 126,* 132–138.

Elder, T. E., & Powers, E. T. (2006). The incredible shrinking program—Trends in SSI participation of the aged. *Research on Aging, 28*(3), 341–358.

Estes, C. L., Swan, J. H., & Associates. (1993). *The long-term care crisis: Elders trapped in the no-care zone*. Newbury Park, CA: Sage.

Fairlie, H. (1988, March 28). Talkin' 'bout my generation. *The New Republic*, pp. 19–22.

Federal Bureau of Investigation. (FBI, 2012). *Crime in the United States, 2011*. Retrieved from www.fbi.gov/about-us/cjis/ucr/crime-in-the-u.s.

Federal Trade Commission. (2012, June). *Telemarketing scams*. Retrieved from www.consumer.ftc.gov/articles/0076-telemarketing-scams

Fick, D. M., Cooper, J. W., Wade, W. E., Waller, J. L., Maclean, J. R., & Beers, M. H. (2003). Updating the Beers criteria for potentially inappropriate medication use in older adults. *Archives of Internal Medicine, 163,* 2716–2724.

Fingerman, K. L., & Charles, S. T. (2010). It takes two to tango: Why older people have the best relationships. *Current Directions in Psychological Science, 19*(3), 172–176.

Fiore, F. (2011, October). Will I ever work again? *AARP Bulletin*, pp. 18–19.

Fischer, D. H. (1977). *Growing old in America*. New York, NY: Oxford University Press.

Fitzpatrick, T. R., & McCabe, J. (2008). Future challenges for senior center programming to serve younger and more active baby boomers. *Activities, Adaptation & Aging, 32*(3–4), 198–213.

Fleck, C. (2008, April). Fear of foreclosure. *AARP Bulletin*, pp. 12–14.

Fleck, C. (2008, July & August). Retirement on hold. *AARP Bulletin*, pp. 10–11.

Fleck, C. (2009, September). No rest for the weary. *AARP Bulletin*, pp. 18–20.

Fleck, C. (2011a, June). When any job must do. *AARP Bulletin*, pp. 16–18.

Fleck, C. (2011b, December). Surviving recession. *AARP Bulletin*, pp. 20–21.

Foley, D. J., Heimovitz, H. K., Guralnik, J. M., & Brock, D. B. (2002). Driving life expectancy of persons aged 70 years and older in the United States. *American Journal of Public Health, 92*(8), 1284–1289.

Folstein, M. F., Folstein, S. E., & McHugh, P. R. (1975). "Mini-mental state". A practical method for grading the cognitive state of patients for the clinician. *Journal of Psychiatric Research, 12,* 189–198.

Foroohar, R., & Greenberg, S. H. (2009, November 2). Hear her roar. *Newsweek*, pp. B2–B5.

Francis, D. (1990). The significance of work friends in late life. *Journal of Aging Studies, 4*(4), 405–424.

Fredriksen-Goldsen, K. I. (2011). Resilience and disparities among lesbian, gay, bisexual, and transgender older adults. *Public Policy & Aging Report, 21*(3), 3–7.

Freedman, V. A., Agree, E. M., Martin, L. G., & Cornman, J. C. (2006). Trends in the use of assistive technology and personal care for late-life disability. *The Gerontologist, 46*(1), 124–127.

Frick, K. D., Kung, J. Y., Parrish, J. M., & Narrett, M. J. (2010). Evaluating the cost-effectiveness of fall prevention programs that reduce fall-related hip fractures in older adults. *Journal of the American Geriatrics Society, 58,* 136–141.

Friedberg, L., & Webb, A. (2005). Retirement and the evolution of pension structure. *Journal of Human Resources, 40*(2), 281–308.

Gaffney-Stomberg, E., Insogna, K. L., Rodriguez, N. R., & Kerstetter, J. E. (2009). Increasing dietary protein requirements in elderly people for optimal muscle and bone health. *Journal of the American Geriatrics Society, 57*(6), 1073–1079.

Galenson, D. W. (2010). Understanding creativity. *Journal of Applied Economics, 13*(2), 351–362.

Gandel, C. (2008, January & February). Making your house work. *AARP Bulletin*, pp. 10–13.

Gates, T. (2007). *You must live a dying life: Reflections on human mortality and the spiritual life.* Boston, MA: Beacon Hill Friends House.

Gibala, J. (1993, May & June). Widowed persons service: 20 years serving all generations. *Highlights AARP*, pp. 6–7.

Giles, L. C., Glonek, G. F. V., Luszcz, M. A., & Andrews, G. R. (2005). Effect of social networks on 10 year survival in very old Australians: The Australian longitudinal study of aging. *Journal of Epidemiology and Community Health, 59*(7), 574–579.

Gilford, R. (1984). Contracts in marital satisfaction throughout old age: An exchange theory analysis. *Journal of Gerontology, 39*(3), 325–333.

Gilford, R. (1991). Marriages in later life. In H. Cox (Ed.), *Annual editions:* Aging (7th ed. pp. 37–41). Sluice Dock Gilford, CT: Dushkin.

Gleckman, H. (2008, June). *How can we improve long-term care financing?* Issue in Brief, Number 8–8. Chestnut Hill, MA: Center for Retirement Research at Boston College. Retrieved from http://crr.bc.edu

Golden, F. (2004, January). Still sexy after 60. *Time Magazine*, pp. 1–3.

Goldman, D. (1996). *Emotional intelligence.* New York, NY: Bantam Books.

Goldman, D. (2006). *Social intelligence.* New York, NY: Bantam Books.

Gopinath, B., Schneider, J., McMahon, C. M., Teber, E., Leeder, S. R., & Mitchell, P. (2012). Severity of age-related hearing loss is associated with impaired activities of daily living. *Age and Ageing, 41*(2), 195–200.

Gopinath, B., Wang J. J., Schneider, J., Burlutsky, G., Snowdon, J., McMahon, C. M., Leeder, S. R., & Mitchell, P. (2009). Depressive symptoms among older hearing impaired adults: The Blue Mountains Study. *Journal of the American Geriatrics Society, 57*(7), 1306–1308.

Gordon, C., & Galloway, T. (2007). *Review of findings on Chronic Disease Self-Management Program outcomes: Physical, emotional, and health-related quality of life, heathcare utilization and costs.* CDC and National Council on Aging. Retrieved from http://patienteducation.stanford.edu/research

Government Accountability Office. (GAO, 2005, December). *Nursing homes. Despite increased oversight, challenges remain in ensuring high-quality care and resident safety.* Washington, DC: Author. Retrieved from www.gao.gov/assets/250/248869.pdf

Government Accountability Office. (GAO, 2010, June). *Older Americans. Continuing care retirement communities can provide benefits, but not without some risk.* Washington, DC: Author. Retrieved from www.gao.gov/assets/310/305752.pdf

Government Accountability Office. (GAO, 2011, February). *Older Americans Act. More should be done to measure the extent of unmet need for services* (Report to the Chairman, Special Committee on Aging, U.S. Senate. GAO-11-237). Washington, DC: Author. Retrieved from www.gao.gov/products/GAO-11-237

Gray-Vickrey, P. (2004). Combating elder abuse: Here's what to look for, what to ask, and how to respond if you suspect that an older patient is a victim. *Nursing, 34*(10), 47–51.

Greby, S. M., Lu, P-J., Euler, G., Williams, W. W., & Singleton, J. A. (2011). *2009 Adult vaccination coverage*, NHIS. Atlanta, GA: CDC. Retrieved from www.cdc.gov/vaccines/stats-surv/nhis/2009-nhis.htm

Greenwald, M., & Associates. (2003). *These four walls ... Americans 45+ talk about home and community.* Washington, DC: AARP.

Greider, L. (2003, July & August). Shazaam! *AARP Bulletin*, pp. 16–18.

Greider, W. (2009, March 2). The man who wants to loot Social Security. *The Nation*, pp. 12–16.

Greven, P. (1966). Family structure in seventeenth century Andover, Mass. *William and Mary Quarterly, 23*(3), 234–356.

Griffin, W. S. T. (2011). What causes Alzheimer's? *The Scientist, 25*(9), 36–44.

Gustman, A. L., & Steinmeier, T. L. (2002). *Social Security, pensions and retirement behavior within the family.* Working Paper 8772. Cambridge, MA: National Bureau of Economic Research. Retrieved from www.nber.org

Haber, C. (1983). *Beyond sixty-five: The dilemma of old age in America's past.* New York, NY: Cambridge University Press.

Habermann, S., Cooper, C., Katona, C., & Livingston, G. (2009). Predictors of entering 24-h care for people with Alzheimer's disease: Results from the LASER-AD study. *International Journal of Geriatric Psychiatry, 24*(11), 1291–1298.

Hacker, S. S. (1990, June & July). The transition from the old norm to the new: Sexual values for the 90's. *SIE CUIU, 18*(5), 1–8.

Hager, G. (1993, January 2). Capital entitlements: The untouchable may become unavoidable. *Congressional Quarterly,* 2.

Hampel, H., Lista, S., & Khachaturian, Z. S. (2012). Development of biomarkers to chart all Alzheimer's disease stages: The royal road to cutting the therapeutic Gordian Knot. *Alzheimer's & Dementia, 8*(4), 312–336.

Hand, R., Antrim, L. R., & Crabtree, D. A. (1990). Differences in the technical and applied nutrition knowledge of older adults. *Journal of Nutrition for the Elderly, 9*(4), 23–34.

Harootyan, B., & Sarmiento, T. (2011). The future for older workers: Good news or bad? *Public Policy & Aging Report, 21*(1), 3–10.

Harris, D. (2007). *The sociology of aging* (3rd ed.). Lanham, MD: Rowman and Littlefield.

Harris, L. (1990). *Sociology of aging* (2nd ed.). New York, NY: Harper and Row.

Harris-Perry, M. (2011, March 3). The war on women's futures. *The Nation,* p. 12.

Harrop, F. (2009, March). No reason for the rich to get overwrought. *Sarasota-Manatee Herald Tribune,* p. 20A.

Havighurst, R. J., Neugarten, B. L., & Tobin, S. S. (1968). Disengagements and patterns of aging. In B. L. Neugarten (Ed.), *Middle age and aging: A reader in social psychology* (pp. 161–172). Chicago, IL: University of Chicago Press.

Hawes, C., & Phillips, C. D. (2007). Defining quality in assisted living: Comparing apples, oranges, and broccoli. *The Gerontologist, 47*(Special Issue III), 40–50.

Hawthorne, F. (2009, March & April). How safe is your pension? *AARP Magazine,* p. 62.

Hazell, T., Kenno, K., & Jakobi, J. M. (2007). Functional benefit of power training for older adults. *Journal of Aging and Physical Activity, 15*(3), 349–359.

Healthy Sex: His and Hers. (2006, December). *Consumer Reports on Health,* pp. 1–5.

Heron, M. (2011). *Deaths: Leading causes for 2007.* (National Vital Statistics Reports, vol. 59, issue 8). Hyattsville, MD: National Center for Health Statistics.

Hewlett, S. A., & Luce, C. B. (2005, March). Off-ramps and on-ramps. Keeping talented women on the road to success. *Harvard Business Review,* pp. 43–54.

High Blood Pressure: New Definitions, New Priorities. (2003, December). *Harvard Men's Health Watch,* pp. 1–5.

Hoffman, R., & Wood, E. F. (1991). *Meditation: New path to problem solving for older Americans.* Washington, DC: AARP.

Howell, S. C. (1980). Environments and aging. In C. Eisdorfer (Ed.), *Annual review of gerontology and geriatrics* (pp. 237–260). New York, NY: Springer.

HSBC. (2006). *The future of retirement. What the world wants.* London, UK: Author.

Hudson, R. (2008). Do unto others...*Nursing Standard, 23*(8), 20–21.

Hudson, R. B. (2005). Getting ready and getting credit: Populations of color and retirement security. *Public Policy & Aging Report, 12*(3), 1–7.

Hunter, W. W. (1968). *Preparation for retirement.* Ann Arbor, MI: Institute of Gerontology, The University of Michigan-Wayne State University.

Institute of Medicine. (IOM, 2008). *Retooling for an aging America: Building the health care workforce.* Washington, DC: National Academies Press. Retrieved from www.iom.edu/agingamerica

Institute of Medicine. (IOM, 2011). *The health of lesbian, gay, bisexual, and transgender people: Building a foundation for better understanding.* Washington, DC: National Academies Press.

Internet Crime Complaint Center. (2012, May). *2011 Internet crime report.* Retrieved from www.ic3.gov/media/default.aspx

Investor Protection Trust. (2010, June 15). *Elder investment fraud and financial exploitation.* Retrieved from www.investorprotectiontrust.org

Jacoby, S. (2005, July & August). Sex in America. *AARP Magazine,* pp. 55–58, 82.

Jerant, A. F., Fenton, J. J., & Franks, P. (2008). Determinants of racial/ethnic colorectal cancer screening disparities. *Archives of Internal Medicine, 168*(2), 1317–1324.

Juarez, D. T., Davis, J. W., Brady, S. K., & Chung, R. S. (2012). Prevalence of heart disease and its risk factors related to age in Asians, Pacific Islanders, and Whites in Hawaii. *Journal of Health Care for the Poor and Underserved, 23*(3), 1000–1010.

Kalish, R. A. (1987). Death and dying. In P. Silverman (Ed.), *The elderly as modern pioneers* (pp. 360–385). Bloomington, IN: Indiana University Press.

Kaye, H. S., Harrington, C., & LaPlante, M. P. (2010). Long-term care: Who gets it, who provides it, who pays, and how much? *Health Affairs, 29*(1), 11–21.

Keating, N. L., Norredam, M., Landrum, M. B., Huskamp, H. A., & Meara, E. (2005). Physical and mental status of older long-term cancer survivors. *Journal of the American Geriatrics Society, 53,* 2145–2152.

Kellogg, S. (1993, September 26). Generational gulf: Economic spat rocks the ages. *The Grand Rapids Press,* p. A8.

Kelly, P. A., Dyer, C. B., Pavlik, V., Doody, R., & Jogerst, G. (2009). Exploring self-neglect in older adults: Preliminary findings of the self-neglect severity scale and next steps. *Journal of the American Geriatrics Society, 56*(S2), S253–S260.

Kempermann, G. (2009). The neurogenic reserve hypothesis: What is adult hippocampal neurogenesis good for? *Trends in Neurosciences, 31*(4), 163–169.

Kent, M., & Li, R. (2013). *The arts and aging. Building the science.* Washington, DC: National Endowment for the Arts. Retrieved from www.arts.gov

Kim, G., Bryant, A. N., Goins, R. T., Worley, C. B., & Chiriboga, D. A. (2012). Disparities in health status and health care access and use among older American Indians and Alaska Native and non-Hispanic Whites in California. *Journal of Aging and Health, 24*(5), 799–811.

Kirchheimer, S. (2009, June). Speaking out. *AARP Bulletin,* pp. 14–15.

Klein, J. M. (2004, December). The love patch. *AARP Bulletin,* p. 18.

Kline, D. W., & Wenchen, L. (2005). Cataracts and the aging driver. *Ageing International, 30*(2), 105–121.

Kochanek, K. D., Xu, J., Murphy, S. L., Miniño, A. M., & Kung, H-C. (2011). *Deaths: Final data for 2009* (National vital statistics reports, volume 60, no. 3). Hyattsville, MD: National Center for Health Statistics. Retrieved from www.cdc.gov/nchs/products/nvsr.htm

Koff, T. H., & Park, R. W. (1993). *Aging public policy: Bonding the generations.* Amityville, NY: Baywood.

Komisar, H. L., & Thompson, L. S. (2007, February). *National spending for long-term care.* Fact sheet. Washington, DC: Georgetown University.

Koppen, J., & Anderson, G. (2008, November). *Retired spouses. A national survey of adults 55–75.* Washington, DC: AARP. Retrieved from www.aarp.org/relationships/love-sex/info-11–2008/retired_spouses.html

Kotkin, J. (2009, October 19). There's no place like home. *Newsweek,* pp. 42–43.

Krauss, I. (1987). Employment. In G. Maddox (Ed.), *The encyclopedia of aging* (pp. 206–208). New York, NY: Springer.

Kravitz, D. (2011, November 6). Many Baby Boomers staying put amid bad economy. *The Grand Rapids Press,* p. F3.

Kristiansen, H. W. (2003). Narrating past lives and present concerns: Older gay men in Norway. In G. Herdt & B. DeVries (Eds.), *Gay and lesbian aging: Research and future directions* (pp. 235–263). New York, NY: Springer.

Krout, J. A., Moen, P., Holmes, H. H., Oggins, J., & Bowen, N. (2002). Reasons for relocation to a continuing care retirement community. *Journal of Applied Gerontology, 21*(2), 236–256.

Krugman, P. (2012, February 19). The dependency paradox. *Sarasota Herald Tribune,* p. 17A.

Kubler-Ross, E. (1969). *On death and dying.* New York, NY: Macmillan.

Kubler-Ross, E. (1975). *Death: The final stage of growth.* Englewood Cliffs, NJ: Prentice-Hall.

Kubler-Ross, E. (1981). *Living with dying.* New York, NY: Macmillan.

Lacey, H. P., Smith, D. M., & Ubel, P. A. (2006). Hope I die before I get old: Mispredicting happiness across the adult lifespan. *Journal of Happiness Studies, 7*(2), 167–182.

Langa, K. M., Chernew, M. E., Kabeto, M. U., & Katz, S. J. (2001). The explosion in paid home health care in the 1990s: Who received the additional services? *Medical Care, 39*(2), 147–157.

Lapierre, S., Erlangsen, A., Waern, M., Diego, D. L., Oyama, H., Scocco, P., . . . the International Research Group for Suicide among the Elderly. (2011). A systematic review of elderly suicide prevention programs. *Crisis: The Journal of Crisis Intervention and Suicide Prevention, 32*(2), 88–98.

Larsen, D. (1990/1991, December & January). Grandparent: Redefining the role—unplanned parenthood. *Modern Maturity*, pp. 32–36.

LaViest, T. A., Gaskin, D. J., & Richard, P. (2009). *The economic burden of health inequalities in the United States*. Washington, DC: Joint Center for Political and Economic Studies.

Lawton, M. (1980). *Environment and aging*. Monterey, CA: Brooks/Cole.

Lawton, M. (1983). Environment and other determinants of well-being in older persons. *The Gerontologist, 23*(4), 349–357.

Lawton, M. P. (1985). Housing and living environments of older people. In R. H. Binstock & E. Shanas (Eds.), *Handbook of aging and the social sciences* (2nd ed., pp. 450–478). New York, NY: Van Nostrand Reinhold.

Leerhsen, C., Lewis, S. D., Pomper, S., Davenport, L., & Nelson, M. (1990, February 5). Unite and conquer. *Newsweek*, pp. 50–55.

Leming, M. R., & Dickinson, G. E. (2011). *Understanding dying, death, and bereavement* (7th ed.). Belmont, CA: Wadsworth.

Lester, H., Mead, N., Graham, C. C., Gask, L., & Reilly, S. (2012). An exploration of the value and mechanisms of befriending for older adults in England. *Aging and Society, 32*(2), 307–328.

Levine, C. (2004). *Always on call: When illness turns families into caregivers*. Nashville, TN: Vanderbilt University Press.

Levitz, J. (2009, May 19). Laws take on financial scams against seniors. *Wall Street Journal*.

Levy, F. (1987). *Dollars and dreams: The changing American income distribution*. New York, NY: Russell Sage Foundation.

Levy, B. R., Zonderman, A. B., Slade, M. D., & Ferrucci, L. (2012). Memory shaped by age stereotypes over time. *Journals of Gerontology, Series B: Psychological Sciences and Social Sciences, 67*(4), 432–436.

Lewis, R. (1992). Pensions: A mixed bag. *NRTA Bulletin, 33*(7), 1.

Liao, Y., Bang, D., Cosgrove, S., Dulin, R., Harris, Z., Stewart, A. . . . Giles, W. (2011). Surveillance of health status in minority communities—Racial and Ethnic Approaches to Community Health across the U.S. (REACH U.S.) Risk Factor Survey, United States, 2009. *Morbidity and Mortality Weekly Report, 60*(SS06), 1–41.

Lichtenstein, A. H., Rasmussen, H., Yu, W. W., Epstein, S. R., & Russell, R. M. (2008). Modified MyPyramid for Older Adults. *Journal of Nutrition, 138*(1), 5–11.

Lin, K., Croswell, J. M., Koenig, H., Lam, C., & Maltz, A. (2011). *Prostate-specific antigen-based screening for prostate cancer. An evidence update for the U.S. Preventive Services Task Force*. Evidence Syntheses, No. 90. Rockville, MD: Agency for Healthcare Research and Quality. Retrieved from www.ncbi.nlm.nih.gov/books/NBK82303/

Locke, M. (2011, July 10). In retirement, single women struggle. *The Grand Rapids Press*, p. F2.

Lohr, S. (2005, March 6). The late, great "golden years". *The New York Times*. Retrieved from www.agewave.com/media_files/nygolden.html

Longcore, K. (2006, May 23). New book discusses sex and the older woman. *The Grand Rapids Press*, p. E1.

Lopata, H. Z. (1979). *Widowhood in an American city*. Cambridge, MA: Schenkman.

Luria, A. R. (1968). *The mind of a mnemonist. A little book about a vast memory*. New York, NY: Basic Books.

Mackinlay, E., & Dundon, C. (2012). An exploration of health and religion in elderly people through the lens of scriptural reminiscence. *Journal of Religion, Spirituality, and Aging, 24*(1–2), 42–54.

Magnusson, P. (2006, July & August). Why many Americans may be working when they retire. *AARP Bulletin*, pp. 22–23.

Mahoney, S. (2006, May & June). The secret lives of single women. *AARP Magazine*, pp. 50–73.

Mahoney, S. (2007, July & August). The new housemates. *AARP Magazine*, pp. 50–53, 90–93.

Market turmoil slaps retirees. (2008, September 23). *The Grand Rapids Press*, p. A1.

Markides, K. S., & Eschbach, K. (2005). Aging, migration, and mortality: Current status of research on the Hispanic paradox. *Journals of Gerontology B: Psychological Sciences and Social Sciences, 60B* (Special Issue II), 68–75.

Masters, W. H., & Johnson, V. E. (1970a). *Human sexual inadequacy.* Boston, MA: Little, Brown.

Masters, W. H., & Johnson, V. E. (1970b). *The pleasure bond.* Boston, MA: Little, Brown.

Mather, M. (2012). The emotion paradox in the aging brain. *Annals of the New York Academy of Sciences, 1251,* 33–40.

Matthews, A. (2004, May). Staying up late with Sue. *AARP Bulletin,* pp. 34–35.

McClintock, J. (2006, November). Easy living. *AARP Bulletin,* pp. 26–27.

McCoy, K., & Hansen, B. (2004, May 24). Haven for the elderly may expose them to deadly risks. *USA Today,* pp. 1A–11A.

McFadden, S., & McFadden, J. (2011). *Dementia, friendship, and flourishing communities.* Baltimore, MD: Johns Hopkins University Press.

Medawar, P. B. (1952). *An unsolved problem in biology.* London, UK: H. K. Lewis.

Medicare Board of Trustees. (2012). *Annual report.* Washington, DC: The Boards of Trustees of the Federal Hospital Insurance and Federal Supplementary Medical Insurance Trust Funds. Retrieved from www.cms.gov/ReportsTrustFunds/

Mellor, M. J., & Rehr, H. (2005). *Baby boomers: Can my eighties be like my fifties?* New York, NY: Springer.

Merriam-Webster's Collegiate Dictionary. (2008). *Purpose.* Springfield, MA: Merriam-Webster.

Mickle, K. J., Munro, B. J., Lord, S. R., Menz, H. B., & Steele, J. R. (2010). Foot pain, plantar pressures, and falls in older people: A prospective study. *Journal of the American Geriatrics Society, 58*(10), 1936–1940.

Mitford, J. A. (1963). *The American way of death.* New York, NY: Simon and Schuster.

Mitford, J. A. (2000). *The American way of death revisited.* New York, NY: Vintage.

Monk, A. (1994). Retirement and aging: An introduction to the Columbia retirement handbook. In A. Monk (Ed.), *The Columbia retirement handbook* (pp. 3–11). New York, NY: Columbia University Press.

Monk, C., & Munnell, A. H. (2009). *The implications of declining retiree health insurance.* Working Paper 2009–15. Chestnut Hill, MA: Center for Retirement Research at Boston College.

Moody, H. (1990). The politics of entitlement and the politics of productivity. In S. Bass, E. Kutza, & F. Torres-Gil (Eds.), *Diversity in aging* (pp. 129–149). Glenview, IL: Scott, Foresman.

Moody, H. R. (1998). *Aging: Concepts & controversies* (2nd ed.). Thousand Oaks, CA: Pine Forge Press.

Moore, O. (2006, November 12). Wedded bliss? You bet, study shows. *The Grand Rapids Press,* p. A18.

Morse, D. (2010, July 7). In the D.C. area and across the U.S., scams against seniors are on the rise. *Washington Post,* p. A01.

Mosqueda, L., Brandl, B., Otto, J., Stiegel, L., Thomas, R., & Heisler, C. (2008). Consortium for research in elder self-neglect of Texas research: Advancing the field for practitioners. *Journal of the American Geriatrics Society, 56*(S2), S276–S280.

Mount, B. M. (1976). Use of the Brompton mixture in treating the chronic pain of malignant disease. *Canadian Medical Association Journal, 115,* 122–124.

Munnell, A. H. (2011). *What is the average retirement age?* Issue in Brief 11–11. Chestnut Hill, MA: Center for Retirement Research at Boston College. Retrieved from http://crr.bc.edu

Munnell, A. H., & Muldoon, D. (2008). *Are retirement savings too exposed to market risk?* Issue in Brief 8–16. Chestnut Hill, MA: Center for Retirement Research at Boston College. Retrieved from http://crr.bc.edu

Munnell, A. H., & Soto, M. (2008, September). *The housing bubble and retirement security.* Issue Brief, Number 8–12. Chestnut Hill, MA: Center for Retirement Research at Boston College.

Munnell, A. H., Soto, M., & Golub-Sass, A. (2008, October). *Are older men healthy enough to work?* Issue Brief Number 8–17. Boston, MA: Center for Retirement Research at Boston College.

Murphy, C. (2008). Chemical senses and nutrition in older adults. *Journal of Nutrition for the Elderly, 27*(3–4), 247–265.

Musil, C. M. (2010). Grandmothers and caregiving to grandchildren: Continuity, change, and outcomes over 24 months. *The Gerontologist, 51*(1), 86–100.

Naik, A. D., Teal, C. R., Pavlik, V. N., Cyer, C. B., & McCullough, L. B. (2008). Conceptual challenges and practical approaches to screening capacity for self-care and protection in vulnerable older adults. *Journal of the American Geriatrics Society, 56*(S2), S266–S270.

National Association of Area Agencies on Aging. (2006). *The maturing of America. Getting communities on track for an aging population.* Washington, DC: Author. Retrieved from www.n4a.org/pdf/MOAFinalReport.pdf

National Cancer Institute. (2012). *What is cancer?* Bethesda, MD: Author. Retrieved from www.cancer.gov

National Center for Health Statistics. (2012). *Health, United States, 2011: With special feature on socioeconomic status and health.* Hyattsville, MD: Author. Retrieved from www.cdc.gov/nchs/data/hus/hus11.pdf

National Center on Elder Abuse. (2012). *Statistics/data.* Retrieved from www.ncea.aoa.gov/Library/Data/index.aspx

National Council on Aging. (2012). *Senior centers. Fact sheet.* Retrieved from www.ncoa.org/pressroom/fact-sheets

National Council on Aging. (n.d.). *Top 8 ways to protect yourself from scams.* Retrieved from www.ncoa.org

National Health Care Quality Report. (2012, March). Agency for Healthcare Research and Quality (AHRQ) Publication No. 12–0005. Rockville, MD: AHRQ. Retrieved from www.ahrq.gov/qual/qrdr11.htm

National Health Policy Forum. (2012). *Older Americans Act of 1965: Programs and funding.* Washington, DC: The George Washington University. Retrieved from www.nhpf.org

National Institute of Neurological Disorders and Stroke. (2011, July). *Shingles: Hope through research.* NIH Publication No. 11–307. Bethesda, MD: Author. Retrieved from www.ninds.nih.gov/disorders/shingles/detail_shingles.htm

National Institute on Aging. (2009, September). *Hormones and menopause.* NIH Publication No. 09–7482. Retrieved from www.nia.nih.gov/health/publication/hormones-and-menopause

National Institute on Aging. (2010). *Hypothermia: A cold weather hazard.* Retrieved from www.nia.nih.gov/health/publication/hypothermia-cold-weather-hazard

National Kidney & Urologic Diseases Information Clearinghouse. (2011). *Awareness and prevention series.* Retrieved from www.kidney.niddk.nih.gov/index.aspx

Neale, R. E., Purdie, J. L., Hirst, L. W., & Green, A. C. (2003). Sun exposure as a risk factor for nuclear cataract. *Epidemiology, 14*(6), 707–712.

Neimeyer, R. A., & Van Brunt, D. (1995). Death anxiety. In H. Wass & R. A. Neimeyer (Eds.), *Dying: Facing the facts* (3rd ed., pp. 49–88). New York, NY: Taylor & Francis.

New Findings on Frailty and Diet: Higher Protein Consumption Linked to Lower Incidence of Frailty Among Women Aged 65 to 79. (n.d.). Retrieved March 19, 2012, from www.healthinaging.org/search/?q=New+findings+on+frailty

Nichols, J. E. (2004). Prevention of HIV disease in older adults. In C. A. Emlet (Ed.), *HIV/AIDS and older adults: Challenges for individuals, families, and communities* (pp. 21–36). New York, NY: Springer.

Noonan, D. (2003, September 29). High testosterone. *Newsweek*, p. 50.

Novelli, W. D. (2005, December). Reimagining America. *AARP Bulletin*, p. 30.

Novelli, W. D. (2007, December). Time to get mad—again. *AARP Bulletin*, p. 32.

O'Connell, M., & Lofquist, D. (2009). *Counting same-sex couples: Official estimates and unofficial guesses.* Washington, DC: U.S. Census Bureau. Retrieved from www.census.gov/population/www/socdemo/files/counting-paper.pdf

Oatley, A. (2011, April). Volunteering is her "spice of life." *Community That Cares*, p. 1. Retrieved from http://gulfportseniorfoundation.org/newsletters/

Older Americans 2008: Key indicators of well-being. (2008). Federal Interagency Forum on Aging-Related Statistics. Washington, DC: U.S. Government Printing Office.

Older Americans 2010: Key indicators of well-being. (2011). Federal Interagency Forum on Aging-Related Statistics. Washington, DC: U.S. Government Printing Office. Retrieved from www.agingstats.gov/agingstatsdotnet/main_site/default.aspx

Older Americans 2012: Key indicators of well-being. (2013). Federal Interagency Forum on Aging-Related Statistics. Washington, DC: U.S. Government Printing Office. Retrieved from www. agingstats.gov/agingstatsdotnet/main_site/default.aspx

Olubayo, J., & Brown, E. N. (2007, December). New houses built with changes for tomorrow. *AARP Bulletin,* p. 10.

Omnibus Budget Reconciliation Act of 1987. (1987). Public law 100–203. Subtitle C: Nursing home reform. Washington, DC: U.S. Government Printing Office.

O'Shaughnessy, C. V. (2012). *Older Americans Act of 1965: Programs and funding.* Washington, DC: National Health Policy Forum.

Palmore, E. (1977). The facts on aging: A short quiz. *The Gerontologist, 17*(4), 315–320.

Patterns of Medication Use in the United States. (2006). Boston, MA: Slone Epidemiology Center at Boston University. Retrieved from www.bu.edu/slone/SloneSurvey/Slone Survey.htm

Patterson, M. C., & Perlstein, S. (2011). Good for the heart, good for the soul: The creative arts and brain health in later life. *Generations, 35*(2), 27–36.

Payne, B. K. (2009). Elder abuse. In J. Miller (Ed.), *21st Century criminology: A reference handbook* (pp. 581–590). Thousand Oaks, CA: Sage.

Peck, R. C. (1968). Psychological development in the second half of life. In B. L. Neugarten, (Ed.), *Middle age and aging: A reader in social psychology* (pp. 88–92). Chicago, IL: University of Chicago Press.

Pension Benefit Guaranty Corporation. (2012). *Annual exposure report.* Retrieved from www.pbgc. gov

Pension Benefit Guaranty Corporation. (n.d.). *Fact sheet.* Retrieved from http://pbgc.gov/res/fact-sheets/page/pbgc-facts.html

Pension Rights Center. (n.d.). *Pension inequities targeting women. Fact sheet.* Retrieved from www. pensionrights.org

Perlin, L. I., Mullan, J. T., Stemple, S. J., & Skaff, M. M. (1990). Caregiving and the stress process: An overview of concepts and their measures. *The Gerontologist, 30,* 383–594.

Phelan, A. (2008). Elder abuse, ageism, human rights and citizenship: Implications for nursing discourse. *Nursing Inquiry, 15*(4), 320–329.

Piver, S. (2004). *Hard questions for adult children and their aging parents.* New York, NY: Penguin Group.

Pollitt, K. (2011, April 18). Women under the budget knife. *The Nation,* p. 9.

Pope, E. (2007, April). Labor pains. *AARP Bulletin,* pp. 16–18.

Povich, E. S. (2005, December). Winter of discontent. *AARP Bulletin,* pp. 8–20.

Powell, E. A. (2006, September 28). Study: Communities unready for elderly. *The Associated Press.* Retrieved from www.boston.com

President's Commission for the Study of Ethical Problems in Medicine and Biomedical and Behavioral Research. (1981). *A Report on the medical, legal, and ethical issues in the determination of death.* Washington, DC: U.S. Government Printing Office.

Quinn, J. B. (1992, June 5). What you'll need to retire early. *Detroit Free Press,* p. 10F.

Quinn, J. B. (2011, November). Getting its story straight. *AARP Bulletin Special Report,* pp. 21–28.

Reeves, W. C., Strine, T. W., Pratt, L. A., Thompson, W., Ahluwalia, I., Dhingra, S. S.,...Safran, M. A. (2011). Mental illness surveillance among adults in the United States. *Morbidity and Mortality Weekly Report, 60*(3), 1–32.

Reyes, K. W. (1992, June & July). You've just won...*Modern Maturity,* p. 10.

Reyes, K. W. (2007, May & June). Money and sex. *AARP Bulletin,* p. 80.

Rhyne, C. (1981). Bases of marital satisfaction among men and women. *Journal of Marriage and Family, 43*(4), 941–955.

Riekse, R., & Holstege, H. (1992). *The Christian guide to parent care.* Wheaton, IL: Tyndale.

Riekse, R., & Holstege, H. (1996). *Growing older in America.* New York, NY: McGraw-Hill.

Riley, M. W. (1983) *Aging and society: Notes on the development of new understandings* [Lecture]. Ann Arbor, MI: University of Michigan.

Roberts, K. R. (2010). The CLASS Act: A new paradigm for aging in America. *Public Policy & Aging Report, 20*(2), 36–38.

Roelofs, T. (2011, April 13). Age is the new political rift. *The Grand Rapids Press,* pp. A1, A8.

Roelofs, T. (2011, May 3). Women surpass men in number of college degrees. *The Grand Rapids Press,* pp. A1–A2.

Rogaeva, E. (2002). The solved and unsolved mysteries of the genetics of early-onset Alzheimer's disease. *Neuromolecular Medicine, 2*, 1–10.

Roger, V. L., Go, A. S., Lloyd-Jones, D. M., Benjamin, E. J., Berry, J. D., Borden, W. B., Bravata, D. M.,...Turner, M. B. (2012). Executive summary: Heart disease and stroke statistics—2012 update: A report from the American Heart Association. *Circulation, 125*(1), 188–197.

Roos, S. (2002). *Chronic sorrow: A living loss.* New York, NY: Brunner-Routledge.

Roosevelt, J., Jr. (2001, June). Social security's enduring truths. *AARP Bulletin,* p. 32.

Rose, M. R. (1991). *Evolutionary biology of aging.* Oxford, UK: Oxford University Press.

Rosen, R. (2007, March 12). The care crisis. *The Nation,* pp. 11–16.

Rosenbury, L. A. (2007). Friends with benefits? *Michigan Law Review, 106*(2), 189–242.

Rosenwaike, I. (1985). *The extreme aged in America.* Wesport, CT: Greenwood Press.

Russell, R. M., Rasmussen, H., & Lichtenstein, A. H. (1999). Modified Food Guide Pyramid for people over seventy years of age. *Journal of Nutrition, 129*(3), 751–753.

Rutten, T. (2009, January 15). The failure of the 401(k) gets scant attention. *The Grand Rapids Press,* p. A15.

Ryers, K. W. (2006, November & December). The movers and the stayers. *AARP Magazine.*

Salamon, M. J., & Rosenthal, G. (2004). *Home or nursing home: Making the right choices* (2nd ed.). New York, NY: Springer.

Salthouse, T. A. (2010). *Major issues in cognitive aging.* New York, NY: Oxford University Press.

Saltzman, M., & Walker, S. A. (2008, March & April). Staying connected to those who care. *AARP Bulletin,* pp. 26–28.

Saxon, S. V., Etten, M. J., & Perkins, E. A. (2010). *Physical change and aging: A guide for the helping professions* (5th ed.). New York, NY: Springer.

Schaie, K. W. (2011). Historical influences on aging and behavior. In K. W. Schaie & S. L. Willis (Eds.), *Handbook of the psychology of aging* (7th ed., pp. 41–55). New York, NY: Academic Press.

Schiller, J. S., Lucas, J. W., Ward, B. W., & Peregovy, J. A. (2012). *Summary health statistics for U.S. adults: National Health Interview Survey, 2010.* Hyattsville, MD: U.S. Department of Health and Human Services.

Schnittger, R. I., Walsh, C. D., Casey, A. M., Wherton, J. P., McHugh, J. E., & Lawlor, B. A. (2012). Psychological distress as a key component of psychosocial functioning in community-dwelling older people. *Aging and Mental Health, 16*(2), 199–237.

Schoenborn, C.A., & Adams, P. F. (2010). *Health behaviors of adults: United States, 2005–2007.* Vital Health Statistics, 10(245). Washington, DC: National Center for Health Statistics. Retrieved from www.cdc.gov/nchs/data/series/sr_10/sr10_245.pdf

Schulz, J. H. (1992). *The economics of aging* (5th ed.). New York, NY: Auburn House.

Schulz, J. H., & Binstock, R. H. (2006). *Aging nation: The economics and politics of growing older in America.* Baltimore, MD: The Johns Hopkins University Press.

Scientists Unveil MyPlate for Older Adults. (2011, November). Retrieved from www.nutrition.tufts.edu/research/myplate-older-adults

Scripps Gerontology Center. (2008, Winter). Scripps hosts national and long-term care business institute. *Age and Agency, 9,* 1–7. Oxford, OH: Miami University.

Seiberling, K. A., & Conley, D. B. (2004). Aging and olfactory and taste function. *Otolaryngologic Clinics of North America, 37*(6), 1209–1228.

Sharpe, C. C. (2004). *Frauds against the elderly.* Jefferson, NC: McFarland.

Sheehy, G. (2010a, June 28). The caregiving boomerang. *Newsweek,* pp. 70–72.

Sheehy, G. (2010b). *Passages in caregiving: Turning chaos into confidence.* New York, NY: Harper Collins.

Sheehy, P. (1981). *Dying with dignity.* New York, NY: Pinnacle Books.

Short, K. (2012, November). *The Research Supplemental Poverty Measure: 2011.* Current Population Reports, P60–244. Washington, DC: U.S. Census Bureau. Retrieved from www.census.gov/hhes/povmeas/

Shugarman, L. R. (2010). Health care reform and long-term care: The whole is greater than the sum of its parts. *Public Policy & Aging Report, 20*(2), 3–7.

Simmons, T., & Dye, J. L. (2003, October). Grandparents living with grandchildren: 2000. *Census 2000 Brief.* Retrieved from www.census.gov/prod/2003

Simonton, D. (1990). Creativity in the later years: Optimistic prospects for achievement. *The Gerontologist, 30*(5), 626–631.

Single Life in Vogue for 51% of women. (2007, January 16). *The Grand Rapids Press*, p. A3.

Sloan, R. P., Bagiella, E., & Powell, T. (1999). Religion, spirituality, and medicine. *Lancet, 359*(9153), 664–667.

Slon, S. (2007, May & June). A new way to retire? *AARP Magazine*, p. 4.

Social Security Administration. (2003). *Income of the aged chartbook 2001*. Retrieved from www.ssa.gov/policy/docs/chartbooks/income_aged/2001

Social Security Administration. (2011, August). *SSI annual statistical report, 2010* (SSA Publication No. 13–11827). Washington, DC: Author. Retrieved from www.ssa.gov/policy/docs/statcomps/ssi_asr/2010/index.html

Speakman, J. R., van Acker, A., & Harper, E. J. (2003). Age-related changes in the metabolism and body composition of three dog breeds and their relationship to life expectancy. *Aging Cell, 2*(5), 265–275.

Stanford Patient Education Research Center. (n.d.). *Chronic disease self-management program*. Retrieved from http://patienteducation.stanford.edu/programs/cdsmp.html

Steiner, R. (1989). *Don't get taken*. El Cerrito, CA: Wide Awake Books.

Stengle, J. (2011, December 25). More folks working into their 70s, 80s, 90s. *The Grand Rapids Press*, pp. F1, F3.

Stephens, M. A., Townsend, A. L., & White, T. M. (2000). Comparisons of African American and White women in their parents care role. *The Gerontologist, 40*, 718–728.

Stevey, T. E., & Associates. (1989). *Fulfilling retirement dreams*. Laguna Hills, CA: Leisure World Historical Society.

Stone, A. A., Schwartz, J. E., Broderick, J. E., & Deaton, A. (2010). A snapshot of the age distribution of psychological well-being in the United States. *Proceedings of the National Academy of Sciences, 107*(22), 9985–9990.

Stone, R. I., Bryant, N., & Barbarotta, L. (2009, October). *Supporting culture change: Working toward smarter state nursing home regulation*. New York, NY: The Commonwealth Fund.

Stories from the heart. (2012). Retrieved from the website of the Meals on Wheels Association of America www.mowaa.org/mrs-cosgrove

Sugar, J. A. (2007). Memory strategies. In J. E. Birren (Ed.), *Encyclopedia of gerontology. Age, aging, and the aged* (2nd ed., pp. 145–151). Oxford, UK: Elsevier.

Sugar, J. A. (2007). Work and retirement: Challenges and opportunities for women over 50. In J. C. Chrisler & V. Muhlbauer (Eds.), *Women over 50: Psychological perspectives* (pp. 164–181). New York, NY: Springer.

Sun, F., Park, N. S., Roff, L. L., Klemmack, D. L., Parker, M., Koenig, H. G.,…Allman, R. M. (2012). Predicting the trajectories of depressive symptoms among southern community- dwelling older adults: The role of religiosity. *Aging and Mental Health, 16*(2), 189–198.

Suzman, R. M., Manton, K. G. & Willis, D. P. (1992). Introducing the oldest old. In R. M. Suzman, D. P. Willis, & K. G. Manton (Eds.), *The oldest old* (pp. 3–14). New York, NY: Oxford University Press.

Taeuber, C. M. (1993). *Sixty-five plus in America*. Washington, DC: U.S. Bureau of the Census.

Taft, A. (1991, September 3). Thinking of retiring? Women find they have to think again. *Detroit Free Press*, p. 3E.

Tatara, T. (1994). *Elder abuse: Questions and answers*. Washington, DC: National Center on Elder Abuse.

Tergesen, A. (2012, April 9). Same room, different ailments. A program in which patients with varied problems help each other expands nationwide. *The Wall Street Journal*, R9. Retrieved from http://online.wsj.com

The Beacon. (2011, July). *Mystic Valley Elder Services by the numbers*. Retrieved from www.mves.org/newsandevents/beacon/2011july.htm

The MetLife Study of Caregiving Costs to Working Caregivers. (2011, June). Westport, CT: MetLife Mature Market Institute. Retrieved from www.metlife.com/mmi/index.html

The MetLife Study of Elder Financial Abuse: Crimes of Occasion, Desperation, and Predation Against America's Elders. (2011, June). Westport, CT: The Metlife Mature Market Institute.

The Week. (2011, December 23). Retrieved from http://theweek.com

Tibbitts, C. (1968). Some social aspects of gerontology. *The Gerontologist, 8*(2), 131–133.

Toedtman, J. (2009, May). Time for a new financial game plan. *AARP Bulletin,* p. 3.

Torres-Gil, F. M. (1992). *The new aging: Politics and change in America.* Westport, CT: Auburn House.

Trafford, A. (2005, November 6). When spouse retires, real work begins. *The Grand Rapids Press,* p. 13.

Truman, B. I., Smith, C. K., Roy, K., Chen, Z, Moonesinghe, R., Zhu, J.,...Zaza, S. (2011, January 14). CDC health disparities and inequalities report—United States, 2011. *Morbidity and Mortality Weekly Report, 60* (Supplement).

Truman, J. L., & Planty, M. (2012). *Criminal victimization, 2011.* Washington, DC: Bureau of Justice Statistics.

USA TODAY. (2007, October 17). p. D9.

USA TODAY. (2009, July 20). p. A10.

U.S. Bureau of Labor Statistics. (2011). *Women in the labor force: A databook.* Retrieved from www.bls.gov/cps/wlf-databook2011.htm

U.S. Bureau of Labor Statistics. (2012). *Volunteering in the United States—2011.* Retrieved from www.bls.gov

U.S. Census Bureau. (1993). *Sixty-five plus in America.* Current population reports. (P23–178 RV). Washington, DC: U.S. Government Printing Office.

U.S. Census Bureau. (1996). *Selected social characteristics of baby boomers 26 to 44 years old: 1990.* Washington, DC: U.S. Government Printing Office. Retrieved from www.census.gov

U.S. Census Bureau. (2007). *Current population survey. Annual social and economic supplement.* Washington, DC: U.S. Government Printing Office.

U.S. Census Bureau. (2010). *Decennial census 2010.* Washington, DC: U.S. Department of Commerce.

U.S. Census Bureau. (2011). *Age and sex composition: 2010* (2010 Census Summary File 1). Washington, DC: U.S. Department of Commerce.

U.S. Census Bureau. (2011). *Projections of the population by sex, race, and Hispanic origin for the United States: 2010–2050.* 2010 Census Summary File 1; U.S. Census Bureau, Table 4. (NP2008-t4).

U.S. Census Bureau. (2011). *Statistical abstract of the United States: 2011: Tables 549–550.* Retrieved from www.census.gov/compendia/statab

U.S. Census Bureau. (2012). *America's families and living arrangements. Table H2.* Retrieved from www.census.gov/hhes/families/data/cps2012.html

U.S. Census Bureau. (2012). *Current population survey. Annual social and economic supplement, 2011. Table 1.* Retrieved from www.census.gov

U.S. Department of Agriculture, Food and Nutrition Service, Office of Research and Analysis. (2011, September). *Characteristics of Supplemental Nutrition Assistance Program (SNAP) households: Fiscal year 2010* (E. Eslami, K. Filion, & M. Strayer. Project Officer, J. Genser). Alexandria, VA. Retrieved from www.fns.usda.gov/fns/research.htm

U.S. Department of Health and Human Services. (2012). *National plan to address Alzheimer's disease.* Retrieved from http://aspe.hhs.gov/daltcp/napa/NatlPlan.shtml

U.S. Department of Health, Education, and Welfare. (1972). *Public assistance programs: Standards or basic needs.* Washington, DC: Author.

U.S. Department of Labor, Women's Bureau. (1986). *Facts on U.S. working women: Caring for elderly family members.* (No. 86–4). Washington, DC: U.S. Government Printing Office.

U.S. Food and Drug Administration. (2010). *Indoor tanning: The risks of ultraviolet rays.* Retrieved from www.fda.gov/ForConsumers/ConsumerUpdates/ucm186687.htm

U.S. Government Accountability Office. (GAO). (2010, September). *Guardianships. Cases of financial exploitation, neglect, and abuse of seniors.* Washington, DC: Author. Retrieved from www.gao.gov/products/GAO-10-1046.

U.S. House of Representatives, Select Committee on Aging. (1992). *Age discrimination in the workplace: A continuing problem for older workers.* Washington, DC: U.S. Government Printing Office.

U.S. House of Representatives. (1963, February 21). *President Kennedy's message to aid elderly citizens.* Washington, DC: Author.

U.S. Senate Special Committee on Aging. (1993). *Consumer fraud and the elderly: Easy prey?* Washington, DC: U.S. Government Printing Office.

U.S. Senate Special Committee on Aging. (2005). *Old scams, new victims: Breaking the cycle of victimization.* Washington, DC: U.S. Government Printing Office.

U.S. Senate, Special Committee on Aging. (1991). *Aging America: Trends and projections.* (HHS Publication No. FCOA 91–28001). Washington, DC: U.S. Government Printing Office.

U.S. Social Security Administration. (2011). *Income of the aged chartbook, 2010.* Retrieved from www.ssa.gov/policy/docs/chartbooks/income_aged/2010/iac10.html

Valanis, B. G., Bowen, D. J., Bassford, T., Whitlock, E., Charney, P., & Carter, R. A. (2000). Sexual orientation and health: Comparisons in the women's health initiative sample. *Archives of Family Medicine, 9*(9), 843–853.

Van Horn, C. E., Corre, N., & Heidkamp, M. (2011). Older workers, the Great Recession, and the impact of long-term unemployment. *Public Policy & Aging Report, 21*(1), 29–33.

Vinick, B. (1978). Remarriage in old age. *The Family Coordinator, 27,* 359–365.

Vladeck, B. (1980). *Unloving care: The nursing home tragedy.* New York, NY: Basic Books.

Walljasper, J. (2009, January & February). A new deal for neighborhoods. *AARP Bulletin.*

Ward, B. W., Barnes, P. M., Freeman, G., & Schiller, J. S. (2011, June). *Early release of selected estimates based on data from the 2010 National Health Interview Survey.* National Center for Health Statistics: Atlanta, GA. Retrieved from www.cdc.gov/nchs/nhis/released201106.htm

Warren, J. R., & Hernandez, E. M. (2007). Did socioeconomic inequalities in morbidity and mortality change in the United States over the course of the twentieth century? *Journal of Health and Social Behavior, 48,* 335–351.

Weinstock, J. S. (2003). Lesbian friendships at and beyond midlife: Patterns and possibilities for the 21st century. In G. Herdt & B. DeVries (Eds.), *Gay and lesbian aging: Research and future directions* (pp. 177–210). New York, NY: Springer.

Weismann, A. (1882). *Über die Dauer des Lebens* [Over the duration of life]. Jena, Germany: G. Fischer.

Where Do ORS Retirees Live? (2009, October). *Connections,* pp. 1–2. Lansing, MI: Office of Retirement Services (State of Michigan).

Whoriskey, P. (2012, January 13). Older Americans trying to remain in the workforce. *Sarasota Herald Tribune,* p. 54.

Wilcox, S., Sharkey, J. R., Mathews, A. E., Laditka, J. N., Laditka, S. B., Logsdon, R. G.,…& Liu, R. (2009). Perceptions and beliefs about the role of physical activity and nutrition on brain health in older adults. *The Gerontologist, 49*(S1), S61–S71.

Williams, G. C. (1957). Pleiotropy, natural selection, and the evolution of senescence. *Evolution, 11,* 398–411.

Williams, R. H., & Wirths, C. G. (1965). *Lives through the years.* New York, NY: Atherton.

Wilper, A. P., Woolhandler, S., Lasser, K. E., McCormick, D., Bor, D. H., & Himmelstein, D. U. (2009). Health insurance and mortality in U.S. adults. *American Journal of Public Health, 99*(12), 2289–2295.

Wolf, R. S. (1988). The evolution of policy: A 10-year retrospective. *Public Welfare, 46*(2), 7–13.

World Health Organization. (2011, August). *Elder maltreatment.* Fact sheet no. 357. Retrieved from http://who.int/mediacentre/factsheets/fs357/en/index.html

Xiang, L., & He, G. (2011). Caloric restriction and antiaging effects. *Annals of Nutrition & Metabolism, 58*(1), 42–48.

Zelinski, E. M., Dalton, S. E., & Hindin, S. (2011). Cognitive changes in healthy older adults. *Generations, 35*(2), 13–20.

Zorn, E. (2011, May 5). Change of subject: Medicare is going bankrupt! Again. *Chicago Tribune.* Retrieved from http://blogs.chicagotribune.com/news_columnists_ezorn/2011/05/medicare-is-going-bankrupt-again.html

Index

CPSIA information can be obtained
at www.ICGtesting.com
Printed in the USA
LVHW09s0706050818
585985LV00011B/244/P